The truth is irrelevant; it only matters what people believe,
for that's what you'll be up against your entire life.

Belief systems are what wait for you in the dark.

HANDS
DOWN

a story of incarceration

by
Logan Crannell

'I was standing
You were there
Two worlds collided
And they could never tear us apart'

- Michael Hutchence, INXS

To those who made me aware,
incarcerated or otherwise

& for Jack, my good sir

INTRODUCTION

I don't identify as a victim. It's a choice. Nor am I the political type, but my disillusionment with this country is intolerable. I'm not using this space to vent about the Bible, the 2nd amendment, racial profiling, election meddling, school shootings, immigration, body shaming, or police brutality.

No, I'm saving my ammunition for one target – the MeToo Movement.

I'm a straight man that worked in a gay bar for years. I lost count of how many men grabbed my ass or flirted with me. Didn't phase me in the slightest. Hell, I was flattered by it. I didn't file lawsuits and voice outcry for their behavior. I *chose* to be in that environment; in a nightclub full of homosexuals drunk and high on cocaine. It came with the territory. I was not a victim.

When I got sexually harassed by a convicted murderer in cellblock, I had no intentions of reporting him to the deputies. If I got forced into an act of sodomy, I planned to rip his testicles from his body. If he *had* molested me, I wouldn't see myself as a victim. If I'd eviscerated the son of a bitch, he wouldn't be a victim either. Sexual urges and survival instincts couldn't care less for morality.

In my last relationship, detailed in this book, I experienced every possible form of domestic violence, and, like most men, did not press charges. I can't speak for other men's motivations; perhaps it's the gender roles beaten into them as kids, or the fact authorities don't take the claims seriously. Violent women generally get a slap on the wrist, if that. In a battle of he said-she said, men tend to lose. For me, I didn't involve the law, *because I put myself in that situation.* Therefore I didn't have the right to ask for sympathy and pity.

Sure, I hold her accountable for what she did, but I blame myself for letting it happen. I invested her with power she didn't have. I could have stopped it, but I was weak. Taking accountability can be painful.

I stood in a court of law, accused by that woman, of domestic violence, kidnapping, rape, assault, battery, strangulation and a litany of other crimes – *all because I hurt her feelings.*

Yes, women are out there with personality disorders, pathological fears, and severe emotional problems. They want revenge, and a safe place to harbor personal vendettas. The MeToo movement provides the support they need, like an umbrella protecting them from the rain.

They drag down the integrity of women who've actually experienced real trauma, thereby damaging the credibility of the movement as a whole. Cowards. Charlatans. Sympathy-seeking, self-proclaimed victims. And the court systems and media nurture and enable their actions.

It's a dangerous cultural climate. When a man suggests we take a closer look at the accuser, women say, *'How dare you imply these poor women are lying!'* Well, it turns out some of them *are* lying. That's what liars do, and they do it in front of juries or in front of cameras, depending how high-profile the case may be.

Am I meant to believe that throughout Hollywood, actresses have never used sex as a weapon to manipulate and take advantage of men in order to further their careers? If so, I'm laughing. Those mirrors show more than age lines.

The filmmaker Terry Gilliam said in an interview: "It's crazy how simplified things are becoming. There is no intelligence anymore and people seem to be frightened to say what they really think," adding that, "It is a world of victims. I think some people did very well out of meeting with Harvey (Weinstein) and others didn't. The ones who did knew what they were doing. These are adults. We are talking about adults with a lot of ambition."

Terry stated the absolute truth. And he got ostracized and shamed for it. Our society can't handle the cold maturity of a statement like that. It's not *sensitive* enough. A person's feelings have become paramount. It's simply unacceptable to hurt them. What a startling indication of an insecure society. Waves of self-entitlement are crashing into the hard realities of the world.

Everything falls on a spectrum. That includes abuse. However, 'due process' is a term that elicits rage. Harmless jokes on an elevator can put you up for review. Kind terms of endearment in the workplace can get you fired. The proposition that harassment 'has degrees' brings about rallying cries and petitions.

How gratifying it is for them to belittle a man, and how strange they can't see the obvious; that drive for empowerment is the same as their aggressors, albeit cloaked with moral indignation. As long as people have sex, predators will be among us. No amount of public whining and finger pointing can change the nature of humanity, dark as it is.

There are truthful women fighting the good fight, by bringing awareness to the sick behavior of powerful men. I hope they don't get swept away by the inevitable backlash. Job opportunities will disappear. Decent men won't take the risk of emotional investment. Have they successfully blacklisted themselves? How many perceive them as a liability?

The MeToo Movement is founded on the wounded ego of imagined self. Ironically, time remembers us all as equal, whether we were or not.

I'm not a victim. Neither are you.

-L.C
June, 2018

1.

OFF
THE
GRID

"Are you antsy to get back on the road?" Carrie spoke to my ear

We laid together, under the movement of a ceiling fan, in her home. The windows offered a morning view of the remote desert landscape. What I'd seen only in faint outlines, when we arrived after sunset, had now become clear. She, however, was holding my attention.

I'd found a kindred spirit, in Carrie. We met, over drinks in a bar, past the railroad tracks of downtown Flagstaff, Arizona. Sitting outside, on the patio, I told her my story. I'd chosen to travel, with my cattle dog Jack, living mostly out of my truck. My marriage had ended amicably. The town, though, was too small for opportunities - so, I packed what I could, and gave the rest away.

It got late, and Carrie lamented her long drive home. I invited her to my hotel room, which was a bold gesture for me. She stretched her arms and smiled, gladly accepting. It was the last night I could afford to sleep there.

"Logan, can I ask you something?" she inquired, on the bed

"Of course."

"Are you attracted to me?"

"Yes, I am."

"Then come sit next to me."

I was leaning against the dresser, with a beer in my hand. I confided that I wasn't ready for sex, and Carrie respected that. We crawled between the sheets, and I felt the warmth of her body on mine. I couldn't explain it then, but the connection I had with her was like that of a lifelong friend. If I cheapened it with casual sex, she might feel obligated to leave afterward.

Jack, my protector, sat at the foot of the bed, keeping a close eye on her.

"He's so leery of me," she said, chuckling

"It takes him a minute. He's nervous around strangers. His last owners abused him."

"Did you get him from a shelter?"

"Yeah, they found him eating out of a dumpster. He had a week before they were going to put him down. Nobody wanted him."

"He's handsome," she said, letting Jack smell her hand, "How long have you two been together?"

"Six years."

"It's sweet that you saved him."

In the morning, Carrie had to work. Knowing I was low on money, she offered to let me stay at her house and left her contact info on the nightstand. She kissed me goodbye. I had the afternoon to think about it. Jack settled in her warm spot on the bed, plaintively looking to me for his morning walk and breakfast.

He and I went down the three flights of stairs and through the parking lot. I inspected my truck, since I had no keys for the lock or ignition; I cranked it manually. Heading up to the room, Jack eagerly sniffed for the correct door on the row.

I checked out of the hotel and got coffee for my hangover. I drove without a destination, ascending into the foothills. The Lowell Observatory rested at the highest vantage point, calmly viewing the sky above. There was no one around, and I parked in a grove of pine trees. The air was crisp. I studied the architecture of the buildings and imagined seeing the night sky with the technology housed inside.

I meditated, taking in the palpable energy of that place until it started to rain. The sound of the drops falling against the metal were so relaxing that I drifted off to sleep. Jack curled up by my legs, awake and entranced by his surroundings. It was a peaceful moment for us. When I woke up, I decided to go towards Carrie's house.

.

Her directions led me to a grocery store off Route 66. The rest of the drive was an off-road trek through the desert – *though I didn't grasp how far.* Carrie met me at the store. We bought groceries for a home cooked meal; fresh veggies, chicken, and a bottle of whiskey.

I parked my truck in a secure spot, bringing anything of value with me, then we drove off in her van, with Jack. The pavement ended, and we hit the rugged terrain, as the sun began to set - the headlights cutting a path. Miles rolled by and landmarks were gone, to my untrained eyes. We told energetic stories, but sometimes the awesome power of the desert put us in silence. The miles continued to pass, and I lost all sense of time and distance. The horizon line stared us down unceasingly. Even as the last rays of light faded, I felt the sensation of being watched by an ominous force.

It was dark when we got to her property. I could make out three quiet houses (her relatives occupied the other two). Solar panels and water tanks were stationed about, vital as temples. I saw a chicken coop or housing for other animals. Two large dogs ran up to greet us as we approached Carrie's porch. Jack was unpredictable around other dogs, so I fielded him from getting too close.

Inside, a single wall divided the open floor plan. The space on the left was empty for remodeling. The warmth had migrated to the right, in the bedroom and kitchen. Carrie and I relaxed. That small, bright room the two of us were in supplied the only light in a limitless black expanse. We were safe.

.

A perfect night-in needs good music, and Carrie had one hell of a record collection. We took shots of whiskey as we thumbed through the stack, smelling the vinyl and admiring the artwork. We settled on the Tom Waits record *'Orphans.'* She blew off a little dust and placed it on the turntable. The rich sound from the speakers filled the air.

We made dinner; I marinated the chicken in basil lemongrass olive oil that I got from a shop downtown. Carrie prepped and seasoned the veggies. While it cooked, we enjoyed the company of one another. She put her arms around me. There wasn't a table, so when the food got plated, we sat on the bed and savored it. Thanks to Carrie, I felt restored.

We spent the rest of the evening cuddled in her bed, watching campy 80s horror films on VHS and drinking local beer. *How could I be so comfortable with her, yet so uncomfortable with myself?*

.

We woke up, hair disheveled and hungry. Carrie brought me outside to the chicken coop. A rooster followed behind me, clucking suspiciously. There were the rise and fall of the hens' cadence, as Carrie rifled through the straw, finding fresh warm eggs. We had them for breakfast, with hot coffee.

After eating, we decided to explore. We climbed a wooden fence along the property line, while the dogs trailed behind us. There was nothing in the distance - the desert stretched, to no end. As we walked, Carrie told me stories of her experiences living out there. Pointing to a watering hole, she mentioned a run-in with hunters waiting to shoot the wildlife. We visited the grave of a beloved pet. I snapped a few photos of Carrie, though she was shy.

She had wanted to paint her living room but confessed to a lack of motivation. I inspired her to pick up a brush with me. We taped along the trim and baseboards. Then, spent the afternoon painting the walls blue while listening to Mogwai records. It was the least I could do in exchange for her hospitality, and I think it helped her, in a way, to get out of a personal rut.

Carrie asked me to stay awhile, and I wondered if I should. It came so naturally, being with her. With every hour, it felt more like I belonged there, and that's what scared me. I was struggling with comfortable feelings. *I wanted to drive out of myself until nothing was familiar anymore.*

When she spoke softly in my ear, asking if I'd be leaving soon, she already knew the answer. I resolved not to lose her altogether. As she returned me through the desert, cattle blocked the road and were stubborn in clearing out of the way.

Standing beside my truck, I held Carrie in my arms, and she pressed herself to my chest.

"Call me when you get to where you're going," she said

"I will," I promised

.

I headed north for Boise, Idaho. My friend Hollace moved there and spoke well of it. Due to his recent divorce, he had a spare room. I didn't consciously choose to live in Idaho long-term. I drifted, taking it one day at a time. I knew I needed money, and Boise seemed my best option.

As I passed through Utah, I contacted another close friend, Tom, who'd started a record label. We scheduled some videography gigs. I shot two music videos, and a live concert during a five-day period. I'd made movies all my life - visual media was how I communicated with the world.

My proudest achievement, titled *'The Torment of Pablo Pastoral,'* got performed with marionette puppets, on sets built by hand. I figured I'd finish the editing and voice recording in Idaho.

For a series called *Life Chronicles,* I kept a camera rolling on my own life. I paused every few years to weave the recordings into a story, in the vein of subjective journalism. I stored fifteen years of footage on five external hard drives, in a cigar box, under the driver seat of my truck.

I had produced sixty-three video projects and burned out. But I still captured the stories unfolding around me out of habit. I continued shooting material for the fourth part of the *Life Chronicles* series. I traveled throughout the southern states, staying in haunted hotels, in an attempt to speak with the dead. I assure you, it's not my intention to convince you of the supernatural - *but I cannot tell this story without ghosts.*

Remember, this book is not about truth, but belief, and how people choose to act in accordance. This is my interpretation of the events.

2.

GASLIGHTING

Boise, Idaho - I took Exit 54 to Broadway Avenue. The first business I passed, a cut-rate bar named *Jim's Alibi,* looked too seedy, even by my standards. I made a note to avoid it. I turned left to the residential area where Hollace lived. The cross streets ran diagonal – Euclid – Chamberlin - Beacon – Manitou. My GPS failed, unable to pinpoint its location. I liked that I got lost and had to use my eyes to find the address.

Hollace's house was set back from the street, in the center of the block. Concealed by two large pines and a wire fence adorned with metalwork, it sat at the end of an extended driveway. I jumped the curb, and my V8 engine roared to a stop at the end of the concrete. Hollace stood outside - on the wooden porch that would become our mecca.

I joined him in a cigarette, not making it through the front door. He and I launched into an intense conversation. We hadn't seen each other in three years, but we picked up as if it were yesterday.

What we said that autumn evening was a manifesto. We were riding a crest that rarely comes in a person's life, and we didn't want to blow it. Hollace and I sought to earn our income with the artistic skills we'd honed for decades; he being the most skilled musician I knew. Hollace contributed scores to my movies, giving sound to my images without instruction.

We mainlined confidence into one another. We strove to take our lives into our own hands. We got disenchanted by broken relationships. Putting our energy in the wrong places. We worked hard for others with little to show for it. We got keyed into the possibilities of ourselves. *We were in our element when we had nothing left to lose.*

Hollace and I weren't just reading from the same book - we were on the same page - the same sentence - the same letter.

.

Our stomachs growled, and Hollace suggested Mongolian barbecue, which I'd been craving. Navigating the lanes went faster on a bicycle, he advised. My Schwinn Varsity lay dismantled in the truck, so I borrowed one of his.

Riding behind Hollace, I saw glimpses of the city and the fall colors streaking by. He knew the geography well, as any hustler should. It was dusk, with magic hour lighting. Adrenaline coursed through me – I felt liberated. Our spirits were soaring.

At the restaurant, chopsticks in hand, with a delicious meal in front of us, I observed my friend. Hollace, a gypsy through-and-through, had pieced together an incredible wardrobe over the years. If he had any new tattoos it got hard to tell; he was covered with ink from his shoulder line down. An old fedora hat rested on his golden curls.

On the way home, we stopped at a convenience store and grabbed some beer. I set up a mat with blankets and turned in early.

.

In the morning Jack nudged me, respectfully. He was the best alarm clock. I got up and quietly checked out the home. The room I had smelled faintly of cat piss. Crack pipe burns, from the previous tenant, littered the carpet. I didn't mind. An Indian tapestry hung loosely across the high window, blocking harsh rays of the sun.

The bathroom attached to my bedroom; privacy would be minimal. It had an accordion style door you'd imagine seeing on a 1970s airliner, dividing off first class. The bathroom itself was small and cramped with the clothes washer. The standing shower looked very French. A tiny window above the sink opened up to the alley.

Jack curiously smelled the fenced yard, potted garden and compost pile. In the afternoons, he'd lounge on the shaded porch and stare at angry squirrels. The side of a narrow wooden shed connected the fence line. It contained a clothes dryer, tools, and a workspace. Outside the perimeter was a storage shed, most likely a horse stable in a former light.

The living room reflected Hollace's personality. Filled with keepsakes coveted from around the world. He had a remarkable instrument collection. The favorite was a Greek Bouzouki, which he used for busking and stage performances. His banjos had elaborate engravings along their necks.

The kitchen ran the far wall of the living room. Cupboards, packed with a surplus of grains and beans, cut down our food costs considerably. A rack by the stove got crammed with an array of spices. A loft above the kitchen could be reached by ladder. That's where Hollace slept; his sacred space, and I kept out of it. A rickety electric furnace built into the floor between the kitchen and my room supplied the heat.

Hollace called the house *The Lonely Heart's Hotel.*

I should make special mention of the flies - holy shit. We hung flypaper from every corner, and within hours they got switched out. Hollace set out jars of poison on the porch. They crawled on you, day and night. Poor Jack lost sleep, snapping at them so often. Fortunately, the season was brief, lasting a few weeks.

I converted a mid-nineteenth century wooden door into a desk. I setup my Mac computer, Canon 7D camera, and speakers powered by a Marantz receiver. I stored my puppet collection and hung worn out clothes in the closet. I lined books against a wall. A 1979 Sequential Circuits Pro-One synthesizer got placed in the living room so guests could experiment with it.

Hollace and I went to a thrift store. Boise was big in second-hand shops, which I liked. As I looked at clothes, I got drawn to a leather jacket; smooth to the touch, and tight-fitting, with a white stripe. I hesitated over it for awhile, acutely aware I needed the money, but my intuition told me it was crucial that I get it. I don't recall ever having the sensation that an article of clothing *belonged* to me, the way that jacket did.

I wore it that night when we hit downtown.

Two Worlds Colliding

It was raining, so Hollace and I took my truck. I parked near 8th street, in the heart of the activity. We tucked into a nightclub called *Liquid* and immediately started networking. As the attendant at the door stamped my wrist, I saw a woman bent over a pool table getting whipped by a man in bondage. Fetish night. The DJ played Industrial music to an empty dance floor. I noticed that in many of the clubs we visited; the bar and patio would be full of people, with a few of them dancing. Boise was a drinking town.

Hollace had it dialed in. He knew who would be where on any given night; in the same seat with the same drink in their hand. He'd done his legwork, and his efforts had me reaping the benefits. Hollace kept a black booklet for notes and numbers, compiling leads for us. At home, we'd go through it, differentiating the socialites from potential collaborators.

"Dude, I have to take you to the Basque District!", Hollace exclaimed
For two city blocks, you cross a line into another culture. They had a market, a museum, a boarding house, and the Bar Gernika. Also, two restaurants, Bardenay and Leku Ona.
"They put on cultural events at the Basque center, and play live music in the streets," Hollace said, "and check out the symbolic designs they have imprinted on the sidewalk!"
Even the streetlights gave off a different feel from the rest of town. Most odd was a preserved log cabin that resided there, standing its ground. We sat on a bench, and Hollace rolled me a cigarette.

We carried on to the *Cactus Bar, Pengilly's Saloon, Tom Grainey's, The Whiskey Bar,* and *The Balcony.* The way Hollace introduced me, I realized he'd heralded my arrival for weeks. Several people were expecting me. We visited with sound engineers, musicians, photographers, painters, belly dancers, and other personalities.

We stopped at the *Piehole* for a slice of pizza and a beer. The rain had slowed to a drizzle, and we sat outside watching the locals pass by.
"Where to next?" I asked
"We've gotta go through Freak Alley. You're gonna love it!"
We walked down a dimly lit, aging alleyway and got engulfed by sprawling murals. Some fifteen feet high, flowing with psychedelic imagery. *'This is the most god damn seriously fucking cool place in Boise!'* Hollace said with exuberance. It was amazing. I stepped around slowly, recording footage for my video project. Hollace likened the experience to frying your balls off on acid.

We exited. I felt exhausted, and Hollace was drunk. I aimed for home, but he insisted we go to one more bar – *Neurolux.* I could see it up ahead. It was crowded. As we came up to it, I checked the time - 11:58 pm.

Hollace stayed outside, chatting people up on the front patio, sectioned off by a short rail fence. I went inside for a drink. As I waited for the bartender, I instinctively scanned the sea of faces around me. Across the busy room, I saw a woman with disarming beauty. She seemed out of place somehow. *'That's the one woman here that would never talk to me,'* I thought to myself.

I put her out of my mind, paid for my drink, and headed outside to sit with Hollace. He was conversing with a lesbian couple about music festivals. I sat in, only half listening, lost in my thoughts. When my drink was almost gone, I glanced to my left. The same attractive woman had taken a seat nearby. Our eyes did not meet.

I finished my drink and tried to pull Hollace from the scene. We were standing on the sidewalk by then, and he was leaning over the railing to engage people further. I got impatient. That's when I heard her voice from over my shoulder. My heart fell for that voice, right there. Her accent rounded every letter perfectly.
"You're a good looking man," she said
I turned to face her, that elegant woman, "That's very kind of you to say..."
I climbed over the fence and sat in front of her.

Our words meant nothing; we spoke with our bodies. The motion of our smiles made clear intentions. I had to take charge, *'Then maybe I can come to your house tomorrow night and make you dinner?'* I heard myself offer to her.
She paused, enjoying that I was so bold. 'Sure,' she said, giving me her phone number. I acted as though I had somewhere else to be, and we said goodbye. I grabbed Hollace by the arm, and we set off down a side street.
"I can't believe that just happened," I said
"What?" Hollace asked
"She gave me her number."
"Fuck yeah! That's rad!"
"I'm making her dinner tomorrow night at her house."
"Shutup! Seriously?!"
Now it was my turn to insist on one more bar. We descended a concrete stairwell to an underground bar named *10th Street Station* - where my life would change forever.

Hollace and I claimed a table in the corner and talked. I liked that place; it was quiet and unassuming. The bartender, K.C, was the frontman for the local band Velvet Hook. He would soon hire me to record their live show, giving me my first paying gig in Boise.

My mind kept drifting to that stunning woman. Her name was Elena. *Would our date tomorrow really occur?* I checked to verify I had her number programmed right. I rolled the phone in my hand, while Hollace slurred on about some event. Suddenly, the phone vibrated and rang, giving me a start. It was her.

"Hello?" I said, plugging my other ear

"Hey, Logan? It's Elena. What are you doing?"

"Hanging out. We're at a bar down the street. What's up?"

"Can I come over?"

"Yes, you can! Let me go up to the street to meet you. It's hard to find. Start walking to tenth street."

"Ok."

"I'll head up now," I said, hanging up the phone, "Hollace, she's here, man! I'll be back!"

"Huh?"

I jumped up from the table, leaving Hollace to soak in his beer. I ran up the concrete steps and began to follow the path we'd taken from *Neurolux.*

"Logan! I'm here!" I heard her call from the opposite direction

I turned to see her standing there, alone, and I walked over to her.

"Hey, we got a table. Come join us."

"Ok."

Elena sat across from me and ordered a glass of red wine. Hollace, to my right, rambled on to her about how great I was. She saw the humor in my embarrassment. Her laughter was genuine, coming from such a flowing voice. I wanted to keep that laugh in my heart.

I barely spoke, and neither did she. We held eye contact for long periods until it got too overwhelming. I reached over and put my hand in hers. We hadn't expected this night, both of us vulnerable and fascinated, as if we'd been taken from the world and put back into it with a new sense of purpose.

The three of us went up to the street for a smoke. Hollace struck up a conversation with two young panhandlers standing on the corner. Elena and I sat on the marble steps of the *Idanha Hotel,* sharing a cigarette. Again, we had small talk. As we stood up, she put her hand on the back of my neck and pulled me forward, kissing me deeply. Our fingers went wild on the texture of our clothing, wanting skin. She thrust her hand down my pants, and we nearly fucked in the street.

We regained our composure and headed downstairs. We didn't stay much longer. I paid the tab and walked Elena to her car. *'I'll follow you,'* she said, getting behind the wheel. I didn't have my bearings yet, so Hollace guided me home, being careful not to lose her.

When the door to my room shut, Elena and I started tearing our clothes off. She was menstruating, but that didn't stop us for a second; we were smeared with her blood. We *devoured* each other. Our bodies crashed, flesh against flesh, unable to get close enough.

Whatever we desired was granted permission. Better still, we didn't even have to ask. We may have wanted to die that night, at that incredible peak; every inch of us felt alive, pulsating like we were driving off a cliff. We owned that night. We owned our bodies. We dared tomorrow to come and challenge us, so we could beat it back with fists and screams, demanding life on our terms.

In the early hours, we collapsed from exhaustion. Elena left early, to where she did not say. I knew she'd return. *She had to.* I was laying in bed when I heard her coming up the walkway with a change of clothes from a friends house. Mascara stained her cheeks. She rested her face on my chest, giving me a frayed smile.
"Can we do that again?" she asked

.

What I didn't know is that Elena was supposed to move to New York that morning. There was a job position for her there. I learned that much later when she confided to me over a cigarette.
"Why?" I asked, "Why did you stay?"
"When I saw you I knew you were the man I wanted to be with. I told them I couldn't come."
What could I say to that?
"I've never been in love before," she said, "have you?"
"Not fully, no."

.

That first night melted into the second. We paused only to drink wine. Hollace, not to be outdone, had a threesome with two girls on the front porch. Elena and I took a hot shower, the water cascading down us. We licked it off each other, to the point of delirium. It was chilly when we got out, and we had sex wearing leather jackets. We bit, scratched and scarred, wanting others to see our territory.

Night after night, we were together; memorizing body with fingertips. We both became aware as the sex felt more and more like making love. With every secret we revealed, the more curious, open, and excited we grew.

We got lost in that room, and in that experience, emerged and rediscovered.

We were absolved of every bad memory,

Every moment of pain and betrayal,

Every act of injustice, every letdown,

Every night of loneliness, the loss of hope,

Every shameful feeling, every failure,

Every moment when our best wasn't good enough,

Everything that ever pulled us away from the happiness we deserved.

We were absolved of it all, starting over in each other's arms,

We'd found each other, just when we'd given up the search.

We bared our souls, everything. A shared cathartic release.

We gave one another the very best of ourselves, without hesitation

We knew there was no going back, and no longer a reason to try.

We found everything we needed in our arms, our kisses, our radiant eyes.

Every breath got shared, and we needed each of them to survive.

The warmth of every touch sang across our skin.

We followed the sound of our voices, to where we did not know,

As they rose and carried, each utterance bringing us somewhere new.

We were one body, in unison, finally completed, in ecstasy.

I rested on the porch, under the partial shade of the pines, my elbows on my knees, head lowered. A lit cigarette dwindled in my hand. Elena had gone to work; she was a successful businesswoman. Hollace sat in his usual chair. I struggled thinking about Carrie.

"I don't know what to do, man. I really don't," I said

"Carrie sounds like a rad chic."

"She's a wonderful person. I've talked to her on the phone, and she wants to fly out here to visit."

"Damn. That may lead to something."

"Even if we agree to be friends, we'll keep getting closer, and that'll cause problems with Elena."

"Yeah, Elena seems like the jealous type."

"I guess I just didn't expect her to stay. I didn't think she'd want to know me."

"Elena's a great gal, man. She knows what she wants, and she's crazy about you."

"Fuck, I wasn't looking for a relationship, but It's stupid not pursue happiness because the timing isn't convenient."

"Elena's pushing hard, huh?"

"Yes, she is. I think we could get somewhere, though. I just need space."

"So, it sounds like you may be staying in Boise longer than you planned?" he said, with his tattered grin and coy laugh.

"Yeah, well..."

Who was this woman? She came out of nowhere and completely blindsided me. We spent every possible second together. When she had a shift at work, seeing her leave behind a pair of shoes or an elegant dress, gave me a sense of relief; it was an assurance of her return.

Elena had two children. Eight-year-old Hetty was in the custody of her father in Los Angeles. Her son Aidan, seven, was a savant who spoke little, and was efficient with electronics. He lived with Elena, at her parent's house, in a neighboring city. I got the impression she had a brutal and costly divorce, and sought to pick up the pieces.

.

"What do you think, Sir? You like her too?" I asked Jack

I always ran my thoughts and concerns by him. He didn't pretend to have the answers. He loved and counted on me, and that kept me focused, with our best interests in mind.

When Elena first met Jack, I didn't think to warn her of his aggression towards strangers. He was curled up on our sleeping mat when she dropped to her knees, took his face in her hands and rubbed her nose to his. Jack had never accepted anyone in such a way, without hesitation. Elena scored big points with me for that.

I stopped speaking to Carrie, and I know it hurt her.

.

For our first official date, Elena and I went to a fine-dining Indian restaurant, the *Bombay Grill.* It was late, and we were the only cover. She bought gifts - a bottle of Givenchy cologne and an expensive pair of Ralph Lauren sunglasses. It was wholly unnecessary; her company being more than enough. I expressed gratitude for the gifts, and we ordered a bottle of wine. I noticed our hands were the same size. The length and circumference of our fingers were identical, like a mirror image. We marveled at that detail.

She ate vegan, having been raised that way since childhood. I admired that. I was vegetarian for ten years and vegan for two. I drifted from it when I became a sushi chef and married my former wife. I enjoyed picking dishes from the menu that we both could share. *'Spicier the better,'* we'd request, begging the chef not to treat us like Americans.

We talked a lot about her children. Then we discussed the implications of her last name - or rather her ex-husbands. The full weight of it hit me. His net worth was $650 million. You may not know the man personally, but you could be putting money in his pocket. You might even be in his debt.

When Elena left him, she stole his pride. Now he wanted it back - he wanted Elena back, and I was the guy standing in his way. For the sake of this book, I will call the man 'Scott Bunk.'

Three weeks ago I was living in my truck. Now I was going up against one of the wealthiest people in the country.

Directly underneath the *Bombay Grill* was the *10th Street Station.* After dinner, we went and claimed our table in the corner. We were forming our rituals, in familiar places. The house was empty when we arrived, and we had sex on top of the washing machine - not that someone else's presence would've distracted us.

.

Elena had money, or came from it, but she was the most generous person I knew. Elena arrived daily with groceries, alkaline water, organic produce, and wine. She insisted on not coming empty-handed. Hollace and I were grateful, though we didn't want to be reliant on her. We'd go to local food banks twice a month for supplies.

Hearing the distinct sound of the spring loaded gate banging shut, followed by the tap of Elena's heels on the walkway, the rustling of paper sacks and the clinking of bottles; that was the sound of happiness for me, knowing that within a minute, she'd be wrapping herself around me. *'What are you doing? Do you want a glass of wine?'* she'd ask.

When the kitchen sink clogged from no disposal, we couldn't get it clear, despite our tools and effort. I'd taken to washing the dishes in the yard with a garden hose. As I scrubbed the glassware, on my knees, I asked myself, *'Will I be able to keep this woman?'* I was resolute that the answer be 'Yes.'

Hollace traveled in strange circles; he was a swinger, and that's how he met Bridgette, who had a sex change. She was fantastic. Elena and I loved Bridgette. With her dry humor and wit, she fit right in and did a remarkable job of keeping Hollace sober and focused.

The four of us were a dysfunctional family. We'd sit on the porch, listen to music, drink and tell stories. On the weekends we'd double date and go downtown. On evenings in, we took turns preparing dinner. Elena had a passion for cooking and made excellent pasta dishes.

I'd help her by slicing the mushrooms, onions, tomatoes, butternut squash, and bell peppers. She'd prep the garlic, basil, and rosemary. She'd then saute it all in a white wine sauce. We had fun in the kitchen.

I made Japanese hot pot. I'd simmer vegetable broth with soy sauce, habanero hot sauces, sesame oil, sake. I'd add in onions, mushrooms, zucchini, daikon, bok choy, carrots, peppers, and noodles. Then, top it off with cilantro, sprouts, cucumber, and avocado. Elena accompanied it with saffron rice. Bridgette got ambitious and tackled a recipe she wanted to try - a flavorful Thai coconut curry. Hollace complemented it with Indian couscous and naan bread.

As bartender, I poured cocktails with a range of ingredients. Fresh mint, lemon, grapefruit, cucumber, lime, ginger, honey, lavender, or soymilk and coffee. A favorite was muddled apricots with turbinado cane sugar, vanilla simple-syrup, Lunazul tequila and a slice of lime.

Hollace and I continued to network. *The Lonely Heart's Hotel* became known to touring bands as a safe place to sleep. On weekends, musicians set up camp in the yard or found available space on the floor inside if it was too cold. Jam sessions passed in waves, styles meshing together to create something new.

In the morning dozens of empty beer cans, bottles of wine and liquor covered the lawn. Cans amassed in piles on the kitchen tile. We'd separate the aluminum from glass, and load the crates into my truck. I'd take a weekly drive to the recycling plant.

Boise was in a unique position, located between Salt Lake City and Portland. Most bands drove through Idaho without much thought to booking a gig. With the launch of the Treefort Music Festival, though, they were beginning to find an audience. Many of the musicians in Utah were searching Boise for venues, and Hollace and I were its ambassadors. I liked coming home to a house full of people. We kept the energy pumping, building momentum.

.

Elena showed me another side of Boise. The swank lounges like *La Mode* and *Red Feather.* The restaurants *Juniper* and *Matador.* I socialized with Boise's more elite and wealthy residents - business owners, stylists, and official-types. There was old money in Idaho.

We must've looked famous together; people stopped to stare at us we generated so much light. They wanted that shine to rub off on them, and they'd strike up conversations, inviting us to some occasion. Between Elena and Hollace, I saw the full spectrum of the city. With the two of them by my side, I felt I could accomplish anything.

Elena loved her car and had it customized for speed. It turned her on, to toss me the keys. The two of us could take a joyride, tearing through the side streets, late at night, pushing the car up to 80mph. We'd scream past houses, with minimal deceleration around turns. We'd blast music through the sound system, 'Sail' by Awolnation. I'd tell her to touch herself, and she would, not taking her eyes off me.

We were invincible - and even if we weren't - we'd found the person we wanted to go down in flames with. It was a win either way.

.

I secretly judge a woman on if she can expose me to fresh music. Elena turned me on to Lana Del Rey, and her songs became part of the tapestry of our lives. Songs like *'Born to Die,'* *'Videogames,'* *'Young and Beautiful,'* and *'Summertime Sadness,'* resonated with us.

Our favorite game was picking online music videos. We'd then explain why the song had impacted us, and what memories were attached to it. We loved discovering one another in that way. One song captured a special time and place for both of us, and we cried at the beauty of it, *'Never Tear Us Apart,'* by INXS. It became a source of strength.

.

We learned each other's insecurities. Elena confessed to being sexually molested as a child, and she feared that would repulse me. I felt nothing but empathy. She needed constant affirmation of my love, which I had no problem supplying. I knew earning her trust would be difficult. Elena struggled to give me that.

"Do you really think Logan likes me?" Elena pleaded to Hollace, in my absence
"Elena, I've told you, I've never seen him this happy."
"I love him so much, and I'm scared he doesn't feel the same way."
"He loves you, I promise. He's not going anywhere, ok? You've gotta give him some breathing room."

If Elena got exposed to the sun for too long, it would cause her skin to bruise. She kept it a secret, thinking I'd leave her if I knew. Ironically, I was born with a skin condition that caused it to be abnormally dry. It took ten years to find a medication and regiment that made the problem unnoticeable. It relieved her, knowing I wouldn't judge her for imperfections. I didn't suggest activities in broad daylight, and she recommended a skin cream called which proved to be far more effective than what I had.

It was endearing that the muscles in her cheeks were so tight from a lack of smiling, that she'd get perturbed when I made her laugh, *'Oh my gosh! Baby, stop making me laugh! It hurts!'*

I'd never felt attractive, and Elena gave me the confidence I'd lacked. *'You're such an amazing and beautiful man.'* She taught me the value of self-respect. Because of her, I saw the extent to which I'd surrounded myself with people who didn't value that quality. A light switch went on for me; it was the first step in that personal reinvention I was hungry for.

.

We had a party at *The Lonely Heart's Hotel*. Elena brought a friend, Bethany, whom she'd known most of her life. I hated her, outright. I thought she was a snake in the grass, though I honored their friendship and kept my opinion to myself. It was a memorable night, with creative energy all around. People eager to meet, share ideas, drink, play music and celebrate. I remember leaning up against the front doorway, observing the crowd. I started coughing uncontrollably. Elena came up to me.

"Baby, are you ok?"

"I can't...." I couldn't speak or finish a thought

I lost balance, and she put my arm on her shoulder for support.

"Let's get you to the room," she said, helping me walk as I failed to suppress the coughing

I collapsed on the floor. My blood pressure bottomed out, and Elena couldn't find a pulse. Everything got soft and distant. It was a calm way to die; fading out like it was a dream, in the arms of your lover.

"You're not allowed to die, you hear me?" she said, her voice nervous

"I want your eyes... to be the last thing I see," I said, trailing off

"That's very romantic, baby. You're such a romantic man, but you're not getting enough oxygen to your brain. I'm going to take care of you," she said, mixing up essential oils and rubbing them on points of my body for circulation. She sang in her original language. I don't know how long she laid there with me. My vision came into focus. My lungs expanded. She told me she loved me.

I'd worn myself thin, and it wouldn't be the last instance, by any means.

.

I'd quietly watch Elena get dressed in the mornings. No matter how much we drank, she woke up with no semblance of a hangover. I studied Elena as she put on her makeup, causing her to grin deviously upon seeing my reflection in the mirror. I wondered if I'd be a good makeup artist. Elena encouraged me to try and offered to introduce me to friends she knew in the industry. The idea of applying art to a person's face to help their self-image intrigued me, and it paid well. I had the time to try, and with Elena, as a tutor, I wouldn't lose interest. I kept the idea in mind.

It was our custom to leave short notes for the other to find, filling our days with a positive and hopeful tone.

.

Hollace and I got invited, plus one guest, to a social gathering at the *Boise Creative Center* - a multi-level warehouse, sectioned off into studio spaces, and rented out to a broad range of artists. They were hosting a fundraising party.

The impact of that night would set life-changing events in motion.

With Elena on my arm, we explored the complex, each grabbing a glass of red wine from the makeshift cocktail bar. The ground floor had been converted into a dance hall, with a lineup of DJ's prepared to spin for hours. White Christmas lights were strung wherever possible for ambiance. As usual, people crowded the outdoor space, with a small group of them dancing.

As we went from room to room we got introduced to many artists. A metal worker cutting a restaurant sign; a band in a jam session (we left Hollace there); a young photographer showed us his gallery; painters freestyled large canvases. Elena and I got lost and ended up on the roof, overlooking the city lights. We took that moment for ourselves. As we descended to the ground floor for more wine, Elena saw a friend and left my company for a bit.

I went to the food bar, and the man operating it spoke to me.
"I'm John," he said, giving me a firm handshake
"Logan."
"Having a good time?" he asked
"Yeah, I'm pretty new to the area."
"Welcome to Boise! Are you taking some pictures? That's a nice camera," he said, gesturing to the Canon draped on my arm, "You should make a documentary about this place."
"Do you have a budget?"
"Nope."
"Then I'll have to turn that offer down, my friend. I need a paying gig."
"You're looking for a job?"
"Yes, I am."
"Do you have any restaurant experience?"
"Seventeen years. I started at the front of the house and worked my way to the kitchen. Sushi was my main deal."
"No shit. Well, hey listen, there's a new vegan and vegetarian cafe opening up next month, and I'm the head chef. Do you have any knowledge of vegan food?"
"Yeah, actually I do. Plus, my girlfriend is vegan, so that helps."
"That's great. Maybe I can get you in the door. I'm talking to the owner tomorrow, and I could put in a good word for you if you're serious about it."
"Absolutely. If you need any help getting the place set up, I'm available."
"I'm sure we will. Let me get your info. Hey, did you see that guy welding that metal sign out there?"
"Yes, I did. He might do some character voices for an animated video I'm doing."
"Nice, well that's the sign for the restaurant. We're hanging it at the site shortly."

I stood alone, people watching, with a drink in my hand. I thought about the job prospect. I didn't want to be in the food industry anymore. In fact, I made a personal vow not to, but his offer sounded like a unique opportunity. There weren't many vegan eateries in Boise, so we'd be forging ground. I like a gamble. Besides, I needed income, and it could keep me creatively engaged.

I headed towards the outdoor balcony to find Elena when she ran up to me and whispered in my ear.
"We need to go," she said urgently
"What's wrong?"
"Scott has one of his people here. He just confronted me."
"What? Where is he?"
"He was over there," she said, pointing at the area by the DJ booth
"Do you see him anywhere now?" I asked as we turned to scan the crowd
"No, baby we should go."
"Alright, let's grab Hollace."

The drive was tense, with a lot of unanswered questions, *'He said it's time for me to come home!'* she cried. When we were safely indoors, I made her a drink to calm her nerves. Hollace and I were talking on the porch when we saw a white SUV stop at the end of the long driveway. It paused there, its engine idling, making its presence known. It slowly drove off. That's when it all began.

Whoever it was, tracking us at the event, had evidently followed us home – but I had the distinct feeling they already knew where we lived. An hour later, the same vehicle circled the block, slowing to a crawl as it passed. Each night after sunset, for the next four nights, the SUV would appear once more.

We refused to be intimidated. Hollace and I kept vigil on the porch. As they drove past, we'd raise our middle fingers in the air and yell, beckoning them out. A line got drawn in the sand. The wolves wanted Elena – *and they could not have her.* Not while I was standing.

With me now involved, Elena didn't know what to expect. I knelt beside her, and put my hand on her knee.
"Listen to me, Elena. I'm not scared of him. He's a cowardly piece of shit, you hear me? I'd do anything to protect you. I'd take a bullet for you if it came down to it."
"You're not going to leave me?" she sobbed
"Not a chance. You're stuck with me."
I meant it. Every word.
We caught the license number. Elena ran the plates with her lawyers and confirmed that the vehicle was indeed registered to 'Scott Bunk.' The identity of the driver was unknown.

You might ask why we didn't call the authorities. You don't 'call the cops' on a man wealthy enough to buy the police department – not on a vague harassment charge. Elena was in the middle of a year-long custody battle that had cost a fortune. We had to build a case. I had to trust that her lawyers, who were becoming increasingly aware of my role, would take what Elena and I documented to the highest officials.

.

Dreams bring another layer to this story.

Elena fell into somnambulistic trances that I could not wake her from. I learned to let her be, as any disturbance on my part seemed to shape her dream for the worse. In the beginning, the dreams were innocent; she'd shoot her arms upward, and her fingers danced as if she were playing the piano. We'd converse, and I'd ask her questions, trying to fill in her experience.

Elena wholeheartedly believed they were messages from God. The dreams brought her happiness; her and I, walking with the children on the beach, dressed in white. Images of us as a family.

It did concern me that Elena rarely went home to her son, Aidan. She often spoke to her parents on the phone, who lavished the boy with attention. I didn't want them to resent me for taking Elena away. So, I pushed for the chance to meet them, or at least suggest she go home to visit, but Elena would find a reason not to. I suspected she needed a break from being a mom, and time to figure herself out.

.

We massacred that white bedroom carpet. Not a day went by without us up-ending a glass of wine, if not an entire bottle. It was a disaster. The carpet in the living room was in rough shape, as well. Hollace spoke to the landlord and scheduled a professional carpet cleaning, to which we promptly forgot the date.

Bridgette and Elena were quite a pair; they talked fashion, music, and politics. I remember the two of them in the kitchen while Bridgette taught her how to pack cigarettes on the palm of her hand. They were like kids laughing over a game of Paper–Rock–Scissors.

When Bridgette declared she needed work, Elena made it her mission to help her get a good paying government job and assisted her with a resume and references.

.

7 am - It had been an evening of heavy drinking. Elena slept on top of me. Jack was comatose. Hollace laid up in the loft, with Bridgette and a hippy girl.

My eyes shot open, "Elena... Elena, wake up..."

"Huh? What's wrong baby?" she mumbled, wiping her saliva off my chest

"What is today?"

"I don't know. Wednesday or Thursday?"

"Is it Thursday?"

"I think so. Yeah, it's Thursday."

I leapt out of bed and into the living room.

"Hollace!" I shouted, "Hollace! Wake up!"

"What's up dude?"

"Please tell me the carpet cleaners aren't supposed to be here in an hour!"

"Oh shit! Is today Thursday!?"

"Yes. You said eight-am right?"

He slid down the ladder.

"Everything has to be off the ground floor of this house. All the furniture. *Everything!*"

The hippy girl said her piece, "I'm pissed! I'm fucking pissed right the fuck off!"

Hollace stood there, head lowered in shame, biting his nails.

I tried to be rational, still partially drunk, "Well, we can be pissed about it or..."

"This is not reasonable," Bridgette said flatly

"It's so fucking far from reasonable! I can not even handle it!" the hippy girl said

I put my hand weakly on Hollace's shoulder, "You just... need to go over there. It's not going to happen."

I'm sorry, Y'all, but I'm gonna start moving stuff."

"Look," Bridgette pleaded, "you don't have to tell them you were drunk and shit. Just tell them you got the days mixed up. Get the next appointment that's good for them."

I added, "She may not give a shit. Just be like, 'look I'd love to have this guy's number so we can -"

"Are you guys going to make me reschedule?!" Hollace interrupted

"YES!" we all said unanimously

"Not rescheduling will be worse," Bridgette went on, "He's going to be here before we're ready and we'll hold him up."

"I can have this whole thing ready in an hour!" Hollace stated

"No. You can't dude," I said

"Alright! I hate you guys! Fuck!" Hollace said as he shut the front door behind him

"Thank you!" I said, slowly moving towards my room, "Sorry guys. Back to bed."

Hollace returned to inform us that the landlord refused to reschedule. We had less than forty-five minutes to move everything. Five miserable souls crammed what they could onto the linoleum tile of the kitchen. The rest got carried outside. We felt damned.

Jack didn't know what to think, and I failed in trying to explain it to him.

.

John contacted me at the vegan restaurant, and I lined up an interview with the owner. Unfortunately, the only position left was the dishwasher. I accepted. John understood that with my qualifications it was a slap in the face, so I knew he'd scheme to raise me in the ranks.

In the meantime, I helped by painting the walls, installing the speaker system, and hanging artwork. More importantly, though, I aided in setting up the kitchen. I observed John during that process. He was deliberate and thoughtful about how our workspace got arranged. We had amusing talks, and discussed the menu, over a beer.

.

Elena had to fly to Chicago for a job meeting and a series of seminars. She'd be gone four days. We'd yet to be apart, especially for that duration, and we hated it. I got anxious that some man would sweep her off her feet.
"There's no sense in you leaving your car at the airport and paying for parking," I said, "It's a mile and a half from here. You can leave it with me. I'll protect it."
"You promise?" she responded, her eyes squinted in a joking manner
She entrusted me with it, and I drove her to the airport terminal. We kissed goodbye, already missing each other. We texted often.

.

With Elena gone, I surrounded myself with friends. Tom happened to be in town looking for music venues while promoting his record label. He gave me a call, and I joined him downtown. I pointed out a few bars that might be receptive to his one-man band dirty blues style. He toured the country, crooning over a slide guitar and harmonica, with a suitcase fashioned into a kick drum.

Tom got excited by sound, and ideas in general. There was never a dull moment in his company. It says a lot that after being his roommate for five years, I still wasn't tired of him.

We stepped out of the sun and grabbed a cold beer inside a quiet bar off 7th street, and had a discussion about synchronicity. The topic of intrigued us both. Tom had a book on it, in his van, the title of which I can't recall. I had read Carl Jung's book *'Synchronicity: An Acausal connecting principle,'* and Roderick Main's *'Jung on Synchronicity and The Paranormal.'*

"I have to tell you about the significance of how Elena and I met," I said as we sat down at a table.

"What have you got?" he asked excitedly

"You're the only person I've told this to."

"Ok," he said, getting more attentive

"When I came to Boise, the first afternoon I was here, I went to a thrift store with Hollace. I didn't have much money, but I saw this black leather jacket, with a white stripe, and I had to buy it. My intuition demanded it. It felt like the choice wasn't even up to me, you know?"

"Right, so then what?"

"Here's the crazy part. The night before, Elena had a vivid dream that she was supposed to go to Neurolux, the bar we'd meet in and that at exactly midnight a man would come into the bar with his drunken friend. That man would be wearing a black leather jacket with a white stripe. In the dream, *she* was meant to approach *me*, as I would not approach her. Guess what time I showed up."

"Midnight! That's fucking crazy!"

"I checked the time on my phone right as we were going in. Two minutes to midnight. And get this, when I first saw Elena, I said to myself 'That's the one woman here that would never talk to me."

"That's fucking incredible, man! So you're happy with this girl! I can tell. I don't think I've ever seen you this happy!"

"She's the woman I want to spend the rest of my life with, man. I love her."

"Well, congratulations! Cheers to that!"

.

Later, we arrived at *The Lonely Heart's Hotel,* where Hollace greeted us with a local microbrew. We invited him into my bedroom to carry on the conversation. Tom dressed well; he sat before us wearing a pressed, white button-down shirt, and necktie. His haircut was sharp and clean. He enthusiastically told us of a dream-vision he recently had.

"When I was a boy, my mom had one of those tri-fold vanity mirrors, you know the kind I mean, with the two side mirrors that fold in and out?" Tom explained as we acknowledged, "Well, I used to put my head in there, and I would move those mirrors."

"Hell yeah!" Hollace clapped

"But, here's the thing that used to scare me, and I'd forgotten all about it," he snaps his fingers and grins, "Until I had this vision. I used to close those mirrors around me and go 'RAAAAAAAAA!" he gave an expression of psychotic rage in slow motion, his fist raised in the air.

Tom continued, "In the vision, I was once again looking in that mirror, only at the age I am now, *and then I stepped into the mirror.* On the other side, I was naked. I saw a beautiful river, and on my side of the river, it was a lush, green environment. On the opposite side was a dismal swamp, and a dark forest. I cupped my hands to my mouth and yelled into the forest, *'Come and drink water!'* Then I heard a low, demonic growl. Out of the forest came a child – me. It was me at the age of eight years old, naked, and from head to toe I'm painted blue. Now, when I was a child, I had a turtle shell that I would fill with berries. I'd mash them up, paint myself blue, put on a loincloth, and run through the hills with my dogs."

"Dude! Healing the inner child within!" Hollace interjected, "I've heard about this, like if something happens to you at a certain age, you freeze in that age, even though you grow up, you fracture."

"Yes! *You fracture,* and who is this child right?" tom noted, "Go back and rediscover it because there are two sides to the child too. There's the light and the dark. You know what it made me think of after I had the dream? Twin Peaks. Bob. Remember? I looked this up to see if there was something real to it. It turns out William Burroughs was the inspiration for that, and he got it from Native American culture. The White Lodge is the positive side, and the Black Lodge is negative. In the Black Lodge you meet yourself, and if you're not prepared – the other version of *YOU will annihilate your soul.* In the Bible, it says the kingdom of heaven is within, and that hell isn't a lake of fire, but a place of weeping, wailing and the gnashing of teeth. Gnashing."

Tom pretends to chew on his arm.

"You will eat yourself. You destroy yourself if you're not ready to meet yourself. So in the vision, the boy comes up to the river, naked and blue, with his wolf. Now, years ago, I was walking down the street, and a homeless guy asked me for money. When I pulled out some change, he reeled in fear and shouted, *'You have a wolf inside of you!',* and he took off running. That was weird, I thought. Then I met a girl that said I had an entity attached to my soul that's leeching my energy, and that it has convinced my soul that the real entity is me. She tried to pull the entity from me and failed, *'I can't do it,'* she said, *'I weakened it, but it's there. It's always been there.'*

Tom paused, then went on.

"Anyway, back to the vision. I'd called the boy to drink water, and he was standing across the river with his wolf. The boy yelled, *'YOU DON"T EVEN HAVE A CUP!',* meaning I didn't have the means to give him the water. The boy huffed angrily, and the wolf snarled. I said, 'We can drink straight from the river,' and I laid on my belly. I never took my eyes off the boy since I was scared he might attack me, and I drank water from the river. Then I sat up, and a shock snapped me out of the vision...

Ok, I thought, *that's when my ego fractured.* The light side is now starting to come to power, but I need to go back and address the dark side."

"See, in the vision," Tom finished, "the wolf is a manifestation of the ego. The wolf isn't real – it's a manifestation of the boy. The boy is the light side, and the wolf is the dark side. The wolf will do anything to protect the boy because the boy is the ego. But, ultimately, what needs to happen, is the boy needs to sit calmly on the wolf and *ride the wolf wherever he wants the wolf to go."

.

Hollace got frustrated, thinking his instrumental music was too difficult to market.

"If I give my weird ass music some vocals," Hollace lamented, "Maybe then it'll be personable enough to sell."

"Try it out," Tom began, trying to inspire him, "If you feel it adds an element that is missing, then that's up to you. But, there are tons of instrumental acts. Some of the biggest acts in the world right now are instrumental. It still sells. You just think it won't sell when it will. Anything will sell. You can sell people anything. Half of the time with music, as long as you're not god-awful, and they like you and your story, that's it."

Hollace pondered it, "I think Kim Gordon from Sonic Youth said, 'people don't pay for talent. They pay for confidence."

"Yeah, they want what that they're not experiencing."

"Which is normally confidence," Hollace chuckled

"Well that, and a different way of life and view of the world. They're hoping that by going to your show, that some of how *your* living is going to become part of how *they're* gonna live. It's like people who watch television all day long. It's not going to change anything for them. Most people aren't made for anything special to happen in their lives. They don't believe in the magic world. You know what I mean? But we do, so why the fuck shouldn't we be getting paid for it?!

Hollace laughed, nodding his head.

"We should be getting paid for it, so we can continue to do it, right? That's what I think," Tom said, "Just be like, 'You know what? I do this, and I'm going to share it with you. I'm going to tell you stories that are going to make you howl with laughter, or scare you, or make you cry, and then I'm going play some songs for you'. Half of my show is stories, anyway. I thought for awhile, 'eh, these stories get long-winded. They're not gonna want to hear this shit'. Fuck no! They fucking love it!"

In Portland the other night, this table was heckling me," Tom continued, "They were like *'Thanks for sharing!'* Then I launched into an awesome song, and those same hipster assholes got up and danced, and then they offered to let me stay at their house, you know what I mean? They just got sold something they weren't experiencing. Something real, and you've got that Hollace. Why the fuck shouldn't you be getting paid for it?"

Hollace sat quietly, at full attention.

Tom concluded, "It's easy. The first step is believing it's possible. Then we need to figure out when you want to go on tour, and put together a press kit. It's very easy. It'll take us ten minutes. Short bio. A picture or two. One of Logan's videos. Then we send it out. It's fishing. You send out a bunch, and then you wait. When they respond, you ask three questions. What time would you like me to load in? How long would you like me to perform? And, how does compensation work at your venue?

.

The next morning Tom had to get on the road. As we said our goodbyes, he approached to give me a brotherly hug, which Jack misinterpreted as a threat. He clamped his jaw down on Tom's heel, though he didn't maul him too badly.

"Jack! Leave it! Shit, sorry man," I said, calling off Jack

"Damn. Great guard dog."

"Yes, he is. You alright?"

"Yeah, I'm good. He didn't even tear my pants. Fuck you, Jack," he said, half-jokingly

"Where are you headed to?" I asked

"Denver. Then to southern Utah. Keep in touch," he said, walking to his van, "I'll be coming through this way in a couple of months."

"Sounds good," I said, raising my hand in lazy salute.

It would be the last time I saw my friend, Tom – except once more, in a dream.

.

In Chicago, Elena's colleagues urged her to come out to the clubs with them. Instead, she stayed in her hotel room and talked to me via Facetime. We couldn't resist persuading one another to do kinky sexual acts.

When our interaction calmed to simple texting, filled with loving words, I sent her a link to my website, saying *'In case you get bored, you can check out concert videos I shot when I was younger.'* I wanted to share with her. What she chose to watch were parts of the *Life Chronicles* series, which my ex-wife collaborated on.

Elena flew into a rage, demeaning me for nearly an hour, through a torrent of rushed text messages. She refused to call me directly or let me answer. Her words hit me like glass. She ended our relationship, disgusted that we'd ever met, and derided herself for having feelings for me.

Elena said a friend would be sent to the house to collect her things. I had to accept that it was over, and goodbye. I felt numb. Stunned.

The videos had no sexual content. They were spiritual art projects. What bothered her so intensely is that I looked *happy* with my ex-wife, in the footage. Elena suspected I still loved my ex, and that my love and affection for her was a lie. She couldn't accept my previous marriage – yet here I was, willing to deal with her ex-husband for the rest of my life. Elena's past *was* my present. I couldn't handle the hypocrisy. My former wife was a decent, respectful person - after the divorce papers got filed, we went our separate ways.

Elena would demand the videos not only be taken off my site but destroyed, to prove my love. It sickened me, her believing she had the rite to erase the contributions of dozens of people, merely because she felt threatened by them.

There's a ring that I wear on a chain around my neck. My mother kept it on from the day of my birth to my twenty-third birthday, when she gave it to me as a gift. I swore not to remove it. Elena believed it was secretly related to my ex-wife until I convinced her otherwise.

Why didn't I leave, rather than try to make amends? The fight was based solely on irrational fear. There had to be a constructive way to address it and strengthen our communication. I wasn't going to give up on our potential at the first sign of trouble. I obliged her and removed the videos from my site. I told her I erased them - though there was not a chance in hell of me doing so. I safely stored them on my external hard drives.

I'd been looking for a definitive sign to stop making movies – and here it was. Unfortunately, that's how I viewed the situation, rather than see it as a burning red flag. Did my relationship with Elena mean more to me than creating art? I searched myself hard for that answer.

Yes. She was more important.

But, what circumstance led Elena to contact me? That's the real story.

.

The cafe had its first mandatory employee meeting. I couldn't have felt less confident. Elena was in Chicago. No one collected her things. I didn't know if I had to pick her up at the airport. I drove to work in her car and tried to keep up appearances.

Roughly twenty people were there, socializing. I poured a glass of water and remained quiet. I couldn't stop thinking about her. A man in his late twenties approached me and shook my hand, *'I'm Orrin,'* he said. I put on a smile. His presence comforted me; he had a good energy. *Interesting fellow,* I thought. He had tiny ceramic animals woven into his beard. Evidently, he was John's Sous Chef, so we'd be working closely together. I didn't want him to think of me as an asshole; I knew I had a guard up, even though I tried to be open.

What I'm attempting to say, is that I was verging on a breakdown.

.

The meeting got underway, and we all pulled up a chair and formed a circle in the dining area. The owner asked us to stand up individually and tell the group about ourselves. I didn't know what to say. *Who was I, without Elena?* I didn't rightly know. I rehearsed a vague lie.

The person beside me spoke, and I was up next. Suddenly, my phone vibrated with a text message. I urgently pulled it from my pocket, and read it.
"Hi. my name is Aidan," it said
I froze. *Oh my god.* Elena's seven-year-old son was texting me. A tear fell down my cheek, and I quickly brushed it away.
"Hello?" Aidan texted
I was in a tailspin. My voice was shaking.
The owner looked at me, "Ok, your turn. Tell everyone your name and something about yourself."
I have no memory of what I said to the group, but I'm sure it was fast and stupid. I replied after sitting down, humbled beyond measure.
"Hi, Aidan. My name is Logan. It's so nice to hear from you,"

I didn't linger with the group – I left immediately. Aidan texted me the whole way home, getting impatient if I stalled, either because I was driving or left utterly speechless as to what I should say. There was no dodging the kid; he wanted answers, and I wasn't going to lie to him. I grabbed a cold beer from the fridge to calm my nerves and went to the porch. For two straight hours, Aidan conversed with me, in text.
"I like robots," said the boy who communicated through machines, "They're how I talk."
"Robots are neat. I like them, too." I said

"I get sad when they break."

"Yeah, but I bet you can fix them."

"I like to help robots they are my friends. Do you like my mom?" Aidan asked

"I care about your mom very very much."

"Do you love her."

I paused. "Yes, I do."

"I love my mom, but you don't want to make her mad."

I breathed a sigh, "I'm afraid I already did, buddy. She doesn't want to talk to me anymore."

"You need to hug it out."

"I'd love that if she wants to."

Aidan disappeared, and five minutes passed when I got an incoming call from Elena. I hesitated for a second and picked it up.

"Hello?" I said

"Are you talking to my son?" she asked, the anger in her voice subdued by the shock of what was going on

"Yes, I am."

"What's he saying?"

"He says we need to hug it out."

"... oh my gosh...," she gasped under her breath, "he said that?"

"Yeah. He's saying a lot of things. We've been talking for over an hour."

"What?"

"Yep. I'm being honest with him."

"... oh my gosh..." she sighed

"Am I picking you up at the airport?" I asked

"Yes... How are you?"

"Honestly? I'm a mess." I said, defeated

"So am I... I'm sorry."

"I love you."

"I love you, too."

"See you, soon."

Elena hung up, and the texts from Aidan continued. Then, another message came through in a new thread.

"Hi. I'm Hetty," said Elena's eight-year-old daughter

Aidan contacted Hetty in California and sent her my phone number so she could join in. For the next forty-five minutes, the two of them texted me nonstop. They were so bright and curious.

"Are you rich?" Hetty asked me, point blank

"No, I'm not."

"And my mommy still likes you? You must be really nice!"
(she had fun using emoticons)
"What do you do," Aidan asked
"I work in a restaurant. What kind of food do you like?"
"I like pizza."
"Pizza is awesome."
"Yeah."
"My brother drives me crazy sometimes." Hetty lamented
"You must miss him, though, living in California."
"I guess so."
"I heard you were going to be coming out soon to visit? Maybe I can meet you."

"Yes! You sound way nicer than my jerk daddy!" (more emoticons)
"He's a jerk, huh?"
"Yeah. He just likes money."

Hetty dropped off for a bit. When she returned, her texts had a different tone. The emoticons were absent.

"I bet you make my mommy happy!" she stated
We'd already established that.
"Well, she's a little mad at me right now sweetie, but I promise I'll do my best to make her happy."
"Good luck! She's really high maintenance!"
It was quite funny. *I'm showing Elena this*, I said to myself. For some reason, though, it struck me odd. Her brother was a savant, so I did not underestimate Hetty's intelligence. But she spelled 'maintenance' correctly. Most *adults* struggled with that word. Hetty had to leave, and I told her how honored I felt to have spoken to her, and that I was excited to see her in person.

Aidan actively texted until he got informed his dinner was ready.
"I'm having tater tots."
"Good deal."
"I have to go."
"It was great talking to you, Aidan. Thank you."

Aidan, however, would have the final word.
The text read – 'Checkmate.'

I sat there on the porch, dumbfounded, with a hapless grin on my face.

What the hell just happened?

I went to the airport and helped Elena retrieve her luggage. She stood next to me in the kitchen, as I cooked for food. Our words confirmed our love; we were terrified of losing each other. I remember she wore a soft white sweater. It made her look vulnerable. I saw her wear white only a handful of times, and perhaps that was the reason why.

We suffered the temporary pain of losing what we had, and it wrecked us both. We built our relationship stronger.

.

I kept hearing an accordion in the alley, behind the house, around mid-morning, when I was waking up. I wandered back there to see who was playing it. His name was Kelly, and he cut an imposing figure, yet he was a soft-spoken and well-read man.

"Does the sound bother you?" he asked, politely
"No, not at all."
"Right on. I'm practicing for a show I've got coming up with my band."
"What's your band?"
"New Iron Front. We do hardcore punk."
"Awesome."
"We have a new album coming out next month."
"Sweet. Need any video work done?"
"You make videos? No one around here does that."

I'd often sit in my room, with the window open, listening to the floating sound of his accordion. When it stopped, I'd walk out, and we'd chat about all sorts of topics. We committed to doing a music video for their upcoming single *'Dogs In The Fight.'* It started with complex ideas that gradually got stripped due to budget constraints. We decided to shoot a raw live recording of their show at a venue called *The Shredder.*

How Kelly described it, *The Shredder* didn't have much in the way of lighting and sound (he was correct on that). I also had logistical problems - they were a five-piece band. I had five cameras, but just two hands.

.

Things were ramping up at The Lonely Heart's Hotel. Hollace had secured a slot in The Hyde Park Street Fair, for his middle-eastern band Sadhiki. Hollace assembled a group of four percussionists and an entourage of belly dancers. He led with his Greek Bouzouki. The practice space was, of course, our house. I liked coming home to a group of gypsies beating out rhythms on the porch. Being Hollace's live videographer for ten years, it was a given I'd record the show.

Bridgette managed Hollace, ensuring he attended practice dates and urged his full sober effort. Without her, I don't think the show would've worked as well as it did.

We arrived at Hyde Park on a hot sunny afternoon. Not a cloud in the sky. Bridgette let Hollace drink one beer to loosen his fingers, and not a drop more. The stage sat under a ground level tent in the shade, but the dancers would be outside in the sun. The backgrounds were cluttered with noise. My apertures went crazy adjusting to the harsh contrasts of light and shadow. I could at least pull clean audio right off the mixing board, though.

I assigned cameras to the line of percussionists and aimed a stationary camera at Hollace. I roamed outside the tent with my Canon 7D, recording the dancers from lower angles and tight close-ups to limit distractions. It got so hot, my cameras were overheating and shutting down. That knocked holes in my editing plan. I worked around it, using split screen and overlapping techniques to bring up the energy.

.

Elena and I were in high spirits. I wrote a letter to her, wanting my feelings on paper, for her to read whenever she felt low. I should have simply handed it to her, rather than get it in my head to put it online.

I had a Facebook page that I hadn't posted a single thing upon. I wasn't a fan of social media. So, I figured if I did add a message for the public to see, it better be damn well worth it.

I asked Elena beforehand if she was willing to have me publish it to her account, *'I think you should do it,'* she said, *'We have nothing to hide or be ashamed of.'*
I agreed:

'I've been attempting to write you this letter for a few weeks now, during a moment alone. But missed flights, bad weather, car trouble, sickness, and passion have prevented that from happening. And I'm grateful for every second of it. It's my birthday tonight, and you're passed out on the bed behind me because you don't feel well. I made you dinner and drinks, as I try to do every night we're together. I hope that they made you feel better. You've made the act of making food exciting to me again. Now, picking up a knife turns me on more than holding a camera.
I've reached the point where I can't imagine waking up without you laying next to me, and since the last week of August, when we met, there's only been a few nights that has happened. And those few nights left me with a pain in my stomach. I connect with you on a physical, emotional, and spiritual level. I've never felt that before. And I'm willing to go to any lengths necessary to honor and celebrate that until my final time.

We've finally found the happiness we've both been fighting for. It's an untouchable happiness that belongs to us. We've fucking earned it. No one can interfere with it, and I will defend it with my life. We've stared into each other's eyes for hours on end, and not one second of that time refutes the fact that we are in love, and happy.

I'm so grateful that this is an evening that I can stop typing, turn around and cuddle up next to you, as you quietly voice the dream you're in out loud, and subconsciously wrap your arms and lips around me.

I love you, Elena. And that's the first time in my life I've meant that.'

Posting the letter would be a grave mistake, the extent of which I wouldn't comprehend for months to come.

.

Elena owned property in California, which she listed on the market. Her plan being to sell it and buy a house in the north end of Boise. That prompted a house hunting adventure. We'd take the local listings, usually fifty to sixty houses, and independently write our top five choices. Then, we'd compare them to see if any of our selections matched up.

"I picked one of my favorites without even paying attention to the address, and it's the one were scheduled to see tomorrow!" I said

"The one on Wagon Wheel Street?" Elena asked

"Yeah."

"That's a beautiful house. What's the asking price? $435,000?"

"$449,900."

"I was only $14,000 off. I like the look of the twelfth home. That built-in office is nice."

"Wow! That was my third choice!"

"Whoa, really baby? Do you like the house on Travertine Way? It has a nice view and a bath tub. Number twenty-three. It's $609,000. It reminds me of my old neighborhood."

"I'd tell you something, but you wouldn't believe it."

"What?"

"That was my fourth choice."

"That's so cool! You've got good taste, baby. I can see Aidan loving this place. The colors of the home are perfect, and it's not too bright for him."

"That's my favorite one. More than Wagon Wheel."

"I totally agree!"

Elena would then phone up the realtors and schedule showings. I didn't see us buying a house as reality – it was too much, too soon – yet that didn't stop me from having fun touring the properties. The homes were incredible; stylish and immaculate. I studied architecture in awe. When the realtors let us be, we'd wander around, giddy with possibilities. *'Do you like the layout?'* Elena would ask, *'or should we look for something else? I want you and the children to be happy. Do you think Jack would like it?'*

The real estate agents didn't know what to think of us. They assumed us as far younger than we were. When Elena mentioned the value of her property in California, they'd get an expression on their faces like, *'Oh, shit. These two are for real,'* and invite us to see other listings.

.

The holidays were near, and Elena spent more time at home; Aidan had missed his mom for long enough. It was agreed upon that I would be a guest for Thanksgiving dinner, finally getting the chance to meet her family.

It was dark when Elena and I drove to her parent's house. When we got close, Elena pulled into an empty church parking lot. *'I need a cigarette,'* she said. We got out of the car and lit one up. We tried to relax. The air was cold and crisp. We could see our breath. I remember how gorgeous she looked. I knew she felt nervous. It was a big step for her, bringing me over.

Our words were few. Elena kissed me, and our eyes gave each other confidence.

.

Her parents spoke rudimentary English, especially her stepfather. Her mom divorced Elena's biological father in her youth. The two of them prepared an ethnic feast; partially vegan. I put my morals aside so as not to appear rude, and tried a bit of each dish. They were hospitable people, and I seemingly got a thumbs up of approval.

Elena had previously warned me that if Aidan didn't like me, he might punch me in the stomach like he often did to Scott. That was not the case; he got curious, glancing at me on occasion, from his own little dining table. The boy loved his iPad.

Her stepfather was a boisterous and animated guy. His goofy stories, aided by Elena's translation, were hardly believable, and therein lay their charm. He threw his weight around, to show me he was the man of the house when it was blindingly clear that Elena's mother steered the ship. She sat across the table, letting him have his fun, with a pleasant grin on her face, as if to say, *'You foolish man. Just you wait until the children leave...'*

.

After dinner, I sat in Elena's bedroom, seeing her belongings for the first time. They weren't quite how I imagined. Elena was in her parent's bedroom, discussing a matter in their foreign language. Unexpectedly, Aidan entered the room and approached me. He said nothing, and took my hand in his with a firm grip, gesturing for me to follow. He pulled me in the direction of the living room. The kitchen light was on, illuminating the otherwise darkened space. He paused at a small pile of toys in the corner. Aidan released my hand and picked up a specific toy that he wanted to share with me.

I hadn't noticed, but Elena came into the room and saw what had just occurred. I turned to see her standing there; her hands over her mouth, and her eyes wide.
"He guided me in here," I whispered
"He's never done that with anyone but family," she said

.

Eight days later, Elena and I were sitting up in bed...

"I'm pregnant," Elena said gently
The words lifted in the air, and could almost be touched. Speechless, I pulled Elena on to me and kissed her warmly.
"Are you happy?" she asked
"Yes, love. I'm so happy."
"I pray that God blesses us with this child."
"How long have you known?"
"Not long. It's the same feeling I had when I conceived Aidan."
"Should we take a test, or is it too early?"
"Let's give it a few days."
"Can we lay here all day long and hold each other?"
"That sounds great!"

.

"I don't understand why the test is negative! I know I'm pregnant. *I know* I'm pregnant. I can feel the changes in my body!" Elena exclaimed

"Ok, hey, calm down, calm down. I trust a woman's intuition over a grocery store piss test any day of the week. We have to get you to a professional," I said, putting her hands in mine

"I have a doctor I can call," she said

"Ok, perfect. Get in touch with him. It's gonna be ok. I trust your body. I love you."

"Love you too."

"We're having a baby, love."

.

When the doctor's test returned positive, we were elated. We laid in bed, staring up at the ceiling, imagining our future life. We wondered if the baby would be a girl.

"She's going to be one insanely attractive girl," I pointed out

"I know. She's gonna be beautiful."

"Well, let's hope she has your looks and my disposition, or we're in trouble."

"You're such a jerk!" she laughed, then continued, "God gave me another dream of her, last night."

"Oh yeah?"

"She spoke to me and said her name was Issachar."

"That's pretty. I can get behind that."

"I have to research it."

"Hey, love, remember when I told you about this ring on my necklace?"

"Yes, the one your mom gave you. She kept it on when you were born?"

"I want to give it to our baby when she's old enough."

"That's very sweet of you, my lover."

.

"Baby, I'm craving a cheeseburger," Elena said, ashamedly

"What?!"

"It's terrible, but I want one so bad."

"Well, now I sure you're pregnant."

"It's awful! Meat sounds good, though..."

"Are you telling me you've seriously never had a cheeseburger?"

"No, I haven't."

"Wow. I'm so proud of you. May I have the honor of being the first, and the last person in the world to buy you a cheeseburger from a fast food drive-thru?"

"Yes, baby. Let's go."

"What, this minute?"

"Yes! I'm so hungry."

"Ok, we'll do it. Am I about to witness this?"

"You sure are!"

"I won't tell a soul. I don't want to blow your reputation."

.

"Elena, I know you're afraid that I'm going to abandon you and the baby, but I don't work that way."

"My parents don't want me raising this child alone."

"Yeah, I'm aware of the pressure. There's no way I'm going to make the kind of money we need unless I start working for myself. I've gone through every idea I have, and if we get support, we could launch a mobile kitchen."

"That's a great idea!"

"I've been at the library printing off the information we need. Check it out."

"Whoa, how many pages is that?"

"About a hundred. I have everything. Permits, health codes, regulations, licensing, zoning, festival applications, food costs, local distributors. Every business in the country that manufactures food trucks, modification costs, websites that sell used equipment, and menu ideas I've been thinking about for years."

"You need to show this to my mom. She'll love this."

"She will, and furthermore I can do this right. I can make this work. It's a project we can be part of as a family. We each have cooking skills."

.

"Elena, I want you to understand something."

"Ok," she said, her eyes on me

"Before you, I never considered having a child."

"Really?"

"I had no desire to, and there were a hundred reasons for it."

"What changed?"

"I believed I wouldn't find the woman I'd respect and care for enough to share that experience and responsibility with. Then you came and washed that doubt away."

"Baby, I don't know what to say. I have to get used to being with such a romantic and humble man. "

"Yeah, you'd better."

.

"Logan, I got a call from the assholes at the doctor's office!"

"What's up?"

"They said there was a mistake at the office!" Elena said, crying

"What did they do?"

"They said they mixed the results up with another patient! I said what are you saying?! She said *I'm sorry, but your test is negative!*"

We were crushed. We felt robbed and violated. It didn't make sense. We tried calming ourselves and left the house. Our minds were in a fog. We ended up in a booth at Neurolux, in the afternoon. The place was empty. I recall the sensation of the cold glass of beer in my hand.

"I told that girl I wanted to speak to the doctor NOW! She said she's busy! I said I don't care! Your office has made a mistake! I will make sure my lawyers deal with this issue! *How dare you!*"

"It's so unprofessional. They can't do that to people."

"There's a poor girl out there that wants a baby and doesn't know she's pregnant."

"It goes both ways. She could've had a one night stand with a guy in a bar, and can't take care of a kid."

"Shit, that's true. I can't process this. It's too much."

"We'll get each other through it like we always do..."

.

Two days later, things weren't adding up.

"I'm still feeling changes in my body, Logan! I have to be pregnant!"

"I agree. You're burning up," I said, placing the backs of my knuckles to her forehead.

"I promise I'm not crazy. My body is reacting."

"I believe you. Listen, let's do one more test, from the store, and we'll see what it says."

The result showed positive. The roller coaster ascended once again.

"We're going to be parents, Elena. This is happening!"

"I knew it," she said, hugging me

"We need to stop the drinking."

"You're right. We do."

"We have to get you healthy."

"Ok."

"I'm going to be by your side, ok?"

"I'm so happy you're in my life, and God is giving us this child."

We did our best. We wanted Issachar more than anything. She was part of us.

.

In late December, while I worked alone at the cafe, prepping for the night crew, my phone rang; Elena said she'd had a miscarriage.

"We lost it?" I confirmed

"Yes."

"I'm leaving. Are you at your mother's?"

"Yes. Just go home. I'll meet you there," she said, then hung up

I braced myself against the counter. I broke down and cried uncontrollably, clenching my teeth. Minutes passed, and I had to pull it together. I knew Elena was counting on me, and that she would be inconsolable. I couldn't fail her.

I arrived at the house before her and cleaned myself up. I heard Elena's car in the driveway, and I stepped out onto the porch, into the winter night. As she came through the gate, I saw her strength dissipate.

Elena buried her face in my chest. I felt her shudder with tears. Her mauve leather jacket was cool on my hands. We wrapped our arms tighter until we were one body; one heart, generating heat. The snow fell softly around us. There was no wind. The tears grew cold against our cheeks.

I think a part of me will always be standing right there, holding her.

Leaving Broken Heart's Behind

Without Elena's company, I felt miserable. The second I clocked out, I'd go straight to her. We thrived on one another; nothing was valid until we shared it. I tried to be everything to Elena. I feared the second I broke contact, physically or emotionally, the spell would somehow shatter. The idea of that propelled me forward, to impress her further and deepen our connection.

Four months had passed. It was March. Orrin and I ran the kitchen. John resigned for personal reasons, prompting Orrin to take the lead. My position as dishwasher shifted in minutes to Orrin's Sous Chef. He knew I could handle the pressure, and his friendship was the reason I carried on there as long as I did.

We were in the middle of a lunch rush.

"Do you know what the future of humanity is, Logan?" Orrin asked, working the grill

Orrin brimmed with epigrams and black humor.

"I have a general idea, but I'm sure you're gonna clarify it," I said, as I managed incoming tickets and plated finished orders

"It's desolate. Very desolate."

"You gotta be kidding me."

"Unless we acknowledge that animals be afforded certain rights, our future is bleak. Climate change, resource depletion, epidemics, ocean acidity, species extinction. These are all major concerns that have serious implications to the wellness of our species, and they can all be connected to our attitude towards animals. From what we can tell -"

"Order in!" I called out, "One vegetarian Hindi wrap!"

"Right away!"

"Second order in! One Veg Medley! One Taco Special! One vegan Hindi wrap!"

"How are we looking on the Hindi mix?"

"Uh, we got enough for six orders."

"Is it on the prep list?"

"You know it."

"Good man. So here we are, you and I, two people working in the same place based on the needs of our circumstance. Take you, for instance, a well-meaning, well-dressed hipster with refined tastes and a penchant for class."

"I'm not a hipster, asshole."

"And then there's me, a grungy metalhead with a predilection for cynicism. Yet here we both are, struggling to meet one common goal. *Money.* The bills have to get paid, our stomachs must be filled, and our desires placated. I've got the two Hindi wraps coming over now, they need plating and garnish."

"Ready to go. How far out are we on the Veg Medley and Taco Special?"

"Just over a minute."

"Perfect. Hey, Catherine!" I shouted out the window to the girl working the coffee bar.

"Yeah?" she called

"I need a Latte, stat!"

"No problem! How many shots of espresso?"

"Four, and make it sexy!"

"Ok!"

"And don't forget like last time or your fired!" I said, smiling to myself

"I won't forget, I swear!"

"Atta girl!"

"Money is such a tedious concept," Orrin continued, "The incessant need to trade away our time and labor for an increasingly devalued digital currency. However, we as a society agree that it keeps everything in check, so we find ourselves doing things we'd rather not be doing so we can pay for things *that we shouldn't have to pay for.* Superior species indeed!"

"Wait, you're getting paid?! Since when did management start paying us?"

"Well, we're certainly not getting the raises we got promised!"

"Order in! We got two Hindi wraps!"

"Damn the Hindi!"

"And we got a Special Two, same ticket!"

"Do we have enough ingredients for it?"

"Hang on," I said, running to the fridge, "We have enough for this order and maybe a second. Is this a recipe from the boss lady?

"Yes, sir!"

"Do you know what's in it?"

"Not a clue!"

"Is she even in the building?"

"Who knows, probably fondling a cucumber in an alley somewhere."

"Alright then, fuck it! *Eighty-six Special Two, everyone!*" I shouted to the wait staff.

"Here's your Latte, Logan!" Catherine beamed

"Bless your heart. Thank you."

"And your girlie is here to see you," Catherine added, "She just showed up."

"Oh yeah? Do we have any new tables?"

"Nope."

"Tell her I'll be right there. Did she order a coffee?"

"Yes."

"Good, don't let her pay for it. I'll take care of it."

"Sure thing."

"Hey, Orrin, once this order is up I'm going to step out for a minute."

"Yes, Yes. Run. Go to your love, you sexy bastard!"

"Don't be jealous, Orrin. We've talked about this. Someday you'll meet a woman and fall madly in love."

(I had no idea he was dating the waitress, Danielle.)

I exited the kitchen and walked across the dining area. As I approached Elena, I studied her body language. She usually looked so poised, like a model in a still photograph. Why did she appear unsettled? She hadn't taken her sunglasses off, and her phone wasn't on the table.

"What's wrong, babe?" I asked, taking a seat

Her hands clasped around her coffee cup.

I rubbed her arm, "You ok?"

Elena shook her head, "I got in a high-speed chase," she said, "Scott's cousins tried to run me off the road."

We'd dealt with the cousins before. Elena had picked me up from the cafe, for an impromptu date. When we left the parking lot, merging onto State Street, Elena recognized the two men driving a blue truck, in the rearview mirror. She turned to identify them, out the window. *Were they waiting for me to leave in my own vehicle?* We decided to beat them at their own game.

'Turn here!' I said pointing to a side road, but Elena had already thought of it. She tore down the lane while their truck got locked in traffic. Elena re-emerged onto State Street, maneuvered to get behind them and sounded her horn. We flipped them off out the window. I saw the humiliation on their faces as we streaked past.

"I was on my way to see you," Elena said, still clinging to her cup, "and they came up on my bumper and started gunning their engine, so I sped up. They pulled up alongside me and swerved into my lane. That's when a sheriff saw what was going on."

"The sheriff?" I replied

"Yes, baby. He pulled those bastards over! I put my car in turbo and left."

We'd learn that the cousins got arrested. The driver swung on the sheriff and missed. Cocaine was found in the vehicle, and they both were drunk.

As we sat there, in the cafe, a smile crept on our faces; *We got 'em. We got those fuckers.* We celebrated with top shelf Tequila that night, raising a glass to the victory.

Scott Bunk was not thrilled. He posted his nephews' bail, and they got extradited to California. Beyond that, I have no information. Situations like that were relegated to Elena's lawyers, after which I was no longer involved.

.

That winter, the living situation became painful in *The Lonely Heart's Hotel*. A lot of snow fell that year, and the influx of visitors to the house dwindled. However, one man slept on the living room floor more often than not.

"Does he live here?" I asked Hollace

"I think so. He's getting divorced. His wife kicked him out. Is that ok?"

"Does he have any money?"

"Yeah, he has a job."

"Alright. We can find a use for him then. What's his name?"

"Will."

.

Hollace went on a downward spiral. It hurt, to watch my friend fall apart. When he and Bridgette broke up, he started hanging out with junkies, seeking to bring him to their level. I worried for him; his internal organs weren't holding up.

I didn't know how to piece him together. Maybe I failed him as a friend. Perhaps I was too selfish, wrapped up in my affairs. Maybe I didn't give enough attention to his struggle. Hollace didn't have a desire to help *himself*, but did that justify the distance I put between us? Our goal of living independently, through art, was finished. The networking stopped. When I had to fall on menial, dead-end jobs, it hurt my pride. I carried on, though, using the marketable skills I had, while Hollace believed he didn't have any.

I vouched for him at the cafe, and he got a job working with Orrin and I, as our dishwasher. Without fail, he'd show up late and so drunk he could barely walk. He spoke aggressively, and his rude jokes offended the sensitive employees. Orrin and I could handle the crass humor, but we couldn't tolerate his inefficiency and lack of ethics; he'd slink off to the restroom for extended periods, leaving us without clean kitchenware.

The lowest point came when Hollace retreated to the restroom after less than an hour of work. Forty-five minutes passed, and he remained locked inside. The owner approached me.

"Logan, I want you to kick the door in," the owner instructed

She got prepared to call the police, or an ambulance, based on what we saw

'Goddamn you, Hollace,' I said bitterly, as I raised my foot, kicking the door with force. I didn't want to break it – I tried to wake him up if he'd passed out. I heard movement. *'Hollace, get the fuck out here!'* I shouted with my mouth to the door – it unlocked and slowly opened. Hollace stumbled to the dishwashing station, where he got surrounded by management and escorted out of the building. Orrin and I hung our heads.

The staff felt relieved, but I didn't – I had to go home to the consequences.

.

The trauma of losing our child bonded Elena and I, for better or worse. Jack had sensed the pregnancy as well and got extra protective of Elena. The two of them got close, and I'd often catch her singing to him. He consoled us in our grief.

I had snowball fights with Jack in the yard. Elena recorded a video of us, through the window. Jack gave a master class in jumping, launching himself to catch snowballs in mid-air. In retaliation, he'd joyfully slam me backward into snow drifts.

Aside from Elena and Jack, I confided in Orrin the most. The synchronicity that led to the two of us meeting was remarkable: while I drifted in Arizona, Orrin lived and worked thirty-four hundred miles north-west, in a small town in Alaska. He had a chef position in a restaurant there. Interesting how he disliked the female bartender - *who was none other than Scott Bunk's sister.*

Orrin quit his job in disgust, and headed to the states, living in his camper trailer. There was no particular reason for him to choose Boise. Like me, he wasn't familiar with the area. Being vegan, he got word of the cafe opening, and inquired about a job, thus meeting John. Then I showed up, having fallen in love with Scott's ex-wife.

.

Elena and I got to know Will, the new resident. He integrated himself into our club of divorcees. He was a tall man, aged, with a stubbled gray beard and shaven head. He didn't spare peoples feelings, and I respected him for that. I detected a current of anger under his hardened surface, coupled with a bit too much practical knowledge.

He was a man who *did* have compassion, albeit selective. If he committed to a person or goal, it got carved in stone. If Will had second thoughts about shacking up with us, he didn't mention it. I think he chose to stay because he'd grown to care about us. Whatever his shortcomings, he treated us genuinely.

Without the procession of visitors, *The Lonely Heart's Hotel* felt isolated, like an outpost cutoff until spring. Will changed it's title, deeming it *The Lighthouse*. Elena, on the other hand, referred to it as *The Devil's House.*

.

When I was twenty-one-years-old, a dark entity attached itself to me during a paranormal investigation, in the mouth of Big Cottonwood Canyon, Utah. An abandoned paper mill rested there, mostly in ruins from the weather. I was an atheist then, and I went to the location with impunity and disrespect.

The rumors of hauntings stemmed from stories of people dying in fires, and a caretaker said to have killed himself on the grounds. Public records were scarce, and I wrote it off as folklore. I *did* note the one common thread of the accounts - that a malevolent presence resided there.

I did the investigation with five friends. We jumped the chain link fence ignoring the risk of fines for breaking into a historic site. Every entryway was heavily barricaded. A plank of wood covering a second-floor window seemed our best bet. We pummeled it with rocks and used a pipe as a pry bar until it hung by a nail. We scaled the wall, boosting each other up one at a time.

As if the barricade weren't enough, a heap of furniture – wooden tables and dozens of chairs - were piled up against the window frame. We shoved them aside, clearing a path, and wormed our way into the cavernous space, clicking on our flashlights. I held a cheap camcorder, searching for anything out of the ordinary. The air was suffocating.

We explored the boiler room, and the tower overlooking the valley. We kicked up dust on the sprawling main floor, which used to be a dance hall in the early 40s. The acoustics were damp. The roof had collapsed in several areas. Rays of light from the setting sun peeked through the cracks and holes. I read that a river flowed underneath the structure, in a network of catacombs. We weren't equipped to traverse it, and we saw no entrance, regardless.

On the upper floor, of the west facing wing, we investigated our final room. It was there we noticed something wasn't right. We crossed the threshold of a doorway, and the temperature dropped roughly twenty degrees. The sweat on our skin from the previous heat and humidity became chilled. Our banter ceased, and we grew quiet, lost in thought, feeling disconnected from one another.

The focal point of the room was a decrepit fireplace, and I got drawn to it. I lowered to my knees and aimed my camera at its interior. In an attempt to communicate, I muttered, *'Show yourself to me,'* under my breath. My eyes were closed when I spoke, letting the camera see for me.

The negative energy got overwhelming. We decided to wrap it up the and leave the building. My friend Kevin and I were foolish enough to take a memento - I grabbed an antique book, and he lifted an old Humpty Dumpty doll. Kevin, first to descend out the window, realized he'd left the doll in the room. He shouted up to Daniel, who was last in line.

"Hey, bro! Go back and get my doll!"

"Uh, what doll?" he asked nervously

"The Humpty Dumpty doll. I left it by the fireplace."

"What does it look like?" Daniel said, grabbing at straws, not wanting to reenter.

"The one that fuckin' looks like Humpty Dumpty, dude!"

Daniel begrudgingly went to find it.

I don't know why I stole that damn book; the content wasn't intriguing. It smelled of mold. I threw it on my porch and forgot it. I reviewed the video footage on my editing system, intentionally saving the fireplace clip for last. I was leery of it. When I had nothing else to review, I cued it up.

I heard myself mumbling on the recording, asking the entity to show itself when an image materialized on the screen. I rewound the tape and hit pause. I stared into the eyes of a fully formed face - almost human, with the snout of an animal.

The lights in my apartment surged, and the bulb nearest me burnt out. I felt an oppressive force, and my pet ferret began choking in the corner. For whatever reason, my initial reaction was to pick up a vinyl Led Zeppelin record and play 'Whole Lotta Love,' as loudly as my speakers would go. I packed a few items, grabbed my ferret and left the apartment. I returned, with caution. I spent hours analyzing the image, trying to debunk it, to no avail.

A darkness lingered in the house. I had disturbing nightmares. I'd wake up, sensing a presence watching me through the window. Daniel alerted me that Kevin got paralyzed in a car crash. I couldn't shake it. That's when I made the connection - *the fucking book.*

Was it a coincidence that only Kevin and I were singled out? It was hardly worth the chance. I drove to the old mill and placed the stolen book by the ruins of the eastern wing. I apologized for what I had done. Fortunately, the energy in my apartment returned to normal. I printed off the image of that face and stored the twenty-nine frames of video in safe keeping.

The foundation of my belief system got forever changed. That event triggered an intense period of study and spiritual discovery that carries to this day.

I disclosed that event because unexplained activity had us on edge, at *The Lighthouse.*

My first encounter happened on a quiet afternoon, while Jack and I were alone. Hollace had gone out for a pack of smokes and a beer. Elena went to work. I sat in my room, editing, with Jack laying beside me. A sound startled him to attention. In the reflection of my computer screen, I saw the closet door open quickly and fluidly. I spun around to face it. There was a pause - then it slammed shut forcefully. Jack growled, and my arm hair raised on end. I got up slowly, ushering Jack to the yard.

Will slept in the living room, surrounded by Hollace's banjos and guitars. He was increasingly anxious, stirred by the sound of plucking strings. He recorded the noises on his phone.

Elena had it the worst. We consistently heard a disembodied female voice in my bedroom, giving Elena stern warnings like, *'He's mine!'*, while other times the voice offered terms of endearment, *'Love you.'* Once, as Elena dried off from a shower, she briefly witnessed the apparition of a woman, standing by a painting on the wall.

The disturbance we observed *as a group* manifested as music - jazz or big band. While indoors, we'd perceive it, silence each other and try to pinpoint the direction of the ethereal sound. We'd run outside where it'd obviously be louder if it were playing from a nearby street – *nothing.* Indoors, it would still be pervasive.

These external experiences led me to wonder when, and if, they'd affect us *internally* as well. Unfortunately, danger rose from Hollace.

In the depth of winter, Hollace would sit in his chair on the porch, for hours on end, oblivious to the freezing wind. He'd drink, smoke, and write meticulously in his journal. It contained the outpouring of his soul. Whether or not it was legible to others didn't matter. He wrote obsessively small as if each letter held a secret.

When I woke at 9 am for my job, I'd go to the porch for a cigarette. Hollace would already be in his chair, intoxicated with a beer in his hand, wrapped in his thick trench coat. That coat unsettled me. Hollace had been a cemetery gravedigger for years. He buried bodies wearing that same trench coat; it smelled like earth. Hollace had a courtship with death; it was his old companion, and he relished taunting it.

The four of us used to have lively discussions on the porch, debating topics from the metaphysical, to religion and politics. I joined in the beginning, though I grew tired of fallen angels, the Illuminati, and popes eating babies. Besides, the cold bothered my arthritis. Elena invested herself fully in the debates, and Hollace goaded her with issues sure to get an emotional rise.

Afterward, Elena came looking for a fight. I'd get accused of not caring about important issues, and she'd say, *'Well, maybe we shouldn't be together anymore.'* It became a vial pattern, with her threatening to leave me, over the smallest of slights.

I had enough and yelled at Hollace.
"I'm fuckin' sick of this. You wind Elena up with shit you *know* will upset her, then you send her to me like a fucking ticking time-bomb, and all I have to do is gaze at her wrong and BOOM! You know how she is, so please stop doing it. It's causing real problems for us."

It didn't deter him much. The routine continued, though Elena finally wised up as the conversations got morbid. She began feeling uncomfortable and pulled back.

Hollace studied intense literature; *The Book of Enoch* and other Biblical Apocrypha. He traveled fearsome roads in his mind. I didn't think he felt satisfied to read about those forces – he wanted to summon them and challenge their power head-on. Hollace sought a god-mind awareness, and for the wrong reasons.

Hollace and Jack were not friends, and rightly so. I hated leaving Jack at the house. Hollace had taken to nailing dead squirrels to trees to watch them decompose. On one occasion, Hollace moved toward me, and Jack sunk his teeth into his right calf muscle. It wasn't his customary 'grab the ankle' warning bite – he straight fucked Hollace up, leaving a permanent scar.

.

Had a spirit attached itself to Hollace, leeching his energy? Or was his behavior solely the late stages of alcoholism? I couldn't entirely accept that. To blame it on the booze, I felt I negated the risk of a potentially more harmful force. Alcohol doesn't slam doors with invisible hands and whisper in our ears at night. A bottle of rum paled to the voicing of incantations, a*nd what if the spirit attachment is what encouraged Hollace's drinking to begin with?*

Radical as that theory might be, Elena attacked me one evening without provocation. She charged, clawing at my face. I yanked her hands away, then she bit my neck, drawing blood. I shoved her backward onto the bed and firmly planted my knee in her chest while pinning her wrists.

Elena bit at my face like a feral animal. When that didn't produce results, she drove her knees into my kidneys and kicked me in the back of the head with her shoes. That episode went on for roughly three minutes. When she relaxed, I let her go. Her confusion upset me. *'Why are you mad, baby?'* she asked, concerned.
Whatever the cause for the activity at *The Lighthouse,* the smartest solution was to vacate.

I warned Hollace, at the end, but I doubt he listened.

"My friend, if you think you can go up against the darkest forces in this universe when you can't even hold a job as a fuckin' dishwasher... Brother, you're gonna lose."

.

Elena and I were in my bedroom.

"God gave me a dream about you last night," Elena said, her voice strained

"And?"

"You've got to get out of this house. I think Hollace is going to try and hurt you. It was a horrible dream. Jack was barking and snarling, and Hollace went after you."

"I don't know what's wrong with him. Do you think he'd really *attack* me?"

"That's not all. In another dream, my children and I are searching for you. We can't find you anywhere, and we're scared. We keep searching, and we finally find you," Elena says, gesturing to the corner, "You're in that closet, hanging upside-down and you're not moving. Baby, I've talked to my parents, and they want you to move into their house. We're concerned for you. Please move out of here and stay with us."

"They seriously want me to live there?"

"Yes."

"If I leave, what's Hollace going to do? What do I even say?"

"We'll think of something. I don't feel safe here."

.

The following night, I arrived home late. Elena wasn't there. As I entered, I saw Will coiled on the couch, subtly on guard, *'Go easy,'* he said. I frowned and looked up at the loft; Hollace laid there, brandishing a samurai sword, and muttering unintelligible phrases.

"How long's this been going on?" I asked, not taking my sight off Hollace.

"For a bit," he said

"What's he saying?"

"It's just.... babble."

Hollace sat up and stared at me. He raised the samurai sword up like a rifle, aiming the tip of it at my face. He glared down the length of the blade, with a sick grin. He held it there, pointed at me.

"Will, let's go outside and have a talk," I said, motioning to the door

We both took a deep breath and lit a cigarette. *Hollace had to go,* despite any plans Elena and I made. While he and I talked, Hollace was inside, thrusting the sword into a wall. He slipped and cut his hand.

.

The next day, I found the words to tell Hollace of my departure, when he surprisingly beat me to it, stating he was moving to Utah to be with his family. He felt awful for abandoning me, unaware that I plotted to vanish, myself.

It struck me how lucid and sober Hollace acted. I recognized the man I'd known for a decade; his personality restored. We had a heartfelt conversation in the kitchen, about the history of our friendship. *Was this a goodbye?* He wanted to read a passage from his journal and asked me to record it. We set up a camera on the porch, with Will shining a light out of frame.

Before he read it, Hollace stated, "It all has a purpose, well timed. All like lining up in these weird cycles, in such coincidences. Everything just pops up, it lines up, to certain sequences of other past situations in life and it just continues to roll on and on. The only reason I stopped doubting is that that the coincidences and the synchronicities are just like..." he trailed off, lost in memory, then said, "I hope this place made a difference. That was my intent with this whole fucking thing. I wanted a gypsy landing pad."

"What did you want to read?" I asked
He picked up his journal and began,

Slipping through cracks is especially on the regular menu - switching headspace is a breath of fresh air - one must not forget - hands - once spoken – twice – thrice - entwined words we say - caught in a paradox – duality – confined in a confined space - pair of beautiful doves - in site of the same line - two birds with one stone - if not four - one or the other - in the same choice - drastic difference in the fork of the road - heart paralyzed in absolute beauty of indecision - left or rights - none refundable

.

Later, I tossed my keys to Will.
"You're the caretaker now, my friend."
"What's the landlord going to say?"
"She'll be fine."

Will once asked if he could sleep on our floor – and we gave him the whole house.

In mid-January, I unceremoniously packed my things into the cabin of my truck, leaving my sleeping mat behind, *'We've got a real bed now, buddy,'* I said to Jack.

.

Neckties.

I hadn't had a job that required neckties, nor a person I sought to impress by wearing them. Now the necktie I chose from my collection readied me for the day.

It was my third week at a department store I'll refer to as *'Gerald's.'* I had no experience in the retail industry or with the rules of a corporate company. The job brought me out of my comfort zone, which I liked. Management guaranteed me six hours a week – for the rest, I had to hustle. An online listing showed the understaffed areas for each shift, so I had to have initiative. I racked up hours storewide, learning my strengths; I had good sales at the wristwatch counter.

The one department closed to the scheduling system was the Fine Jewelry bay. It stood as an island with its own politics. I got intimidated walking by it; the stern women who ran it got locked in there, day in and day out.

Elena persisted in making me the best-dressed person on staff. She bought me a sharp modern suit and helped me select a new wardrobe. I developed an affinity for neckties and other accessories. I had my eye on a silver and white Bulova watch; it was pricey enough to be on display behind the fine jewelry counter, out of my reach and budget. My philosophy is that every man should have a well-crafted watch.

.

I still had the notion of becoming a makeup artist. With Elena as my teacher, I got shown the basics of application, and the proper use of brushes. She put complex makeup on half of her face, and then I would duplicate it on the other. It felt natural to me. I loved the intimacy of it; maybe a bit *too* much. It was so sensual, with her as my model, that we couldn't resist jumping each other's bones. To further my education, I needed a mentor that I wasn't compelled to have sex with. I sat in on sessions with various artists, each with their own style and technique, and compiled methods.

For a weekend escape, and much-needed privacy, I rented out a bed-and-breakfast in the small town of Star. It had a French design to it, with a cozy wine bar on the ground floor. The room was spacious and decorated with antique furniture. Elena had a makeup artist stop by to give me a tutorial. I put a camera on a tripod, to record her lesson for reference.

Elena had considered thrift stores as beneath her standards, though she had a second opinion when she saw the clothes I scored for pennies on the dollar - old Isaac Mizrahi blazers and classic Oscar de la Renta cardigans. In a town called Emmett, while we were on an escape, I discovered a vintage Prada handbag for a mere $25, when it was well worth $500.

.

I came to Boise craving independence, and now I was more *de*-pendent than ever. I relied on the kindness of a family I barely knew, with a cultural divide, in an economically poor town, on the western edge of Idaho. The saving grace was that I had Elena and Jack. *Maybe a break from the city was needed,* I thought and resolved to keep a positive outlook.

Vegan eateries were limited, save for a tiny Mexican spot called *Rey del Taco*. The young girl that ran the kitchen fawned over Elena and me as a couple and cooked us food with love.

Orrin and I quit the cafe amid growing discontent, in March and April, respectively. The business permanently closed its doors within a year. Orrin landed a ground level job at the post office and started earning real money. I was hungry for a new skill set, and although I didn't view *Gerald's* as a career path, there were chances for education and advancement.

.

I had a fondness for old, run-down, dive bars. Elena was surprised at how much she enjoyed them. Cheap booze, humble people, and you could smoke indoors since the laws in Caldwell were different than Boise. When the two of us walked in, we turned heads.
"You may be the classiest thing this joint has ever seen," I'd say to her, out of the corner of my mouth.
"They probably think we're European."
"If they ask, tell them we're touring America with our band."
We'd go to our favorite bar, *The Tavern*, order two whiskey cokes with lime, and unwind. We found solace in that ritual. Jack sat in with us once and ordered water on the rocks.

Elena got betrayed by her lifelong friend, Bethany, whom I did not like to begin with. We discovered she'd been receiving money from Scott, in exchange for information on Elena, and our relationship. When Elena confronted Bethany, she flew into a rage, eventually admitting to the charge.
"Why? Why would you do that to me?" Elena pleaded
"Because I deserve nice things too, Elena!" was her response

Bethany then sent me a private message on Facebook, stating that she'd have my head cut off and my body burned. She accused me of being extremely abusive and controlling of Elena, who was shocked when I showed her the text.

We tried to find humor, at our customary table in *The Tavern*.

"Does she not realize," I said, "that if I told you *what shoes to wear,* that you'd scream at me for three days?"

"I know right!" Elena laughed

"Am I abusive to you?"

"No. Not at all! You're a kind and gentle man. Where does she get this shit?"

"I don't know. I guess she's projecting her own failed relationships onto us."

"Probably. She thinks all men are evil."

"We know some quality people, love."

.

Then, we got a package in the mail containing documents from Scott's lawyers. He filed charges against Elena, claiming we'd caused him distress, and he demanded custody of Aidan, along with child support. As Elena had an emotional talk with her parents, I thumbed through the stack of papers, absorbing what I could.

Halfway through, I saw a photocopy of the letter I'd written to Elena, and posted online. The lawyers had seized on it and were using my words to hurt us. They took words written out of love and distorted them to present Elena as an uncaring mother, and me a destructive influence in the lives of the children.

It sickened me. *What had I done?*

Their legal battle was a war of attrition - Scott had broken Elena's bank. Her lawyers were working pro bono, all her savings gone. She couldn't fight any longer.

I was personally involved in a dangerous game.

How high were the stakes?

Ultimately, we lost Aidan. He went to California to live with Scott. Elena forced one stipulation: that Scott employ a doctor to help Aidan overcome his troubles. Elena wanted the move at least to be beneficial for her son. It was a binding contract that Scott would not fulfill.

.

Scott became obsessed. His lawyers raided the social media accounts of my family and friends, pulling any photos that gave the impression of me as unstable or of low moral character. He'd call Elena's cell phone while she worked, and if she turned her phone off, he'd call her on the company line, *'Why do you like Logan?'* he'd demand, *'What does he have that I don't?! Does he fuck you better than me?! Is that it?'* The calls would rain in, putting Elena in bad standing with her employers.

Elena and I erased our Facebook accounts. We agreed to tighten our circles, and not speak candidly or carelessly to anyone. We no longer went to Boise, except for our jobs. I seldom texted Orrin and Will. Elena texted her friend Mandy, whom I viewed as a trustworthy and caring person. Beyond that, we went into hiding.

"I think I'm justified in pressing charges, Elena!" I said, losing my cool
"Logan, we have to keep building a case. My lawyers document everything this asshole does. "
"Can I go on the record with your lawyers and tell them my side? I'm part of this now."
"Yes, I talked to my lawyers, and they think it's about time to bring you in. Soon, baby. We have to be patient and trust in God."

.

We lived for four-and-a-half-months under the roof of her parent's house. They were colorful folks, like watching a religious soap opera. Concussively loud. They'd admonish me for remaining quiet as if it were a personality defect.

Her parents were overly generous to me. I was not to miss a meal, and if I were running late to work, they'd send me out the door with an awkward plate of food in my hand. They cosigned for a new iMac computer, to help me further my art. I had no credit card, as I don't believe in spending borrowed money. I *did* understand that if Elena and I conceived a child, it would be critical for me to have an established line of credit. Thus I had to start somewhere.

I knew I'd fall out of favor with her parents if the drinking didn't stop. Elena and I didn't dare to face that problem. We were high functioning alcoholics, with addictive personalities.

We worked hard, and drank hard, with no healthy means to alleviate our stress. My failure is that I saw our alcoholism as a physical addiction, and our quitting as a physical process. I convinced myself that we could overcome it with willpower and discipline.

.

'Do you want to have a cigarette with me?' Elena would ask when her folks went to bed. They didn't approve of her smoking, so we'd sneak out like school kids and sit in the grass, cuddled up against the side of the house, and whisper to each other. In those moments, I learned the most about her.
"Did you have a dream about Issachar?" I asked
"Yes, how did you know?

"You said her name. You were giggling, and caressing the air."
Elena smiled, "We were playing around and laughing. She was so beautiful."
"She was happy?"
"Yes, she was."
"Good."
We'd pass the cigarette back and forth. She'd often get distracted and forget to share, apologizing for her manners. Elena would tell me how much she needed me, and how lost she'd be without my love.

Guilt weighed heavily on Elena. With Aidan's birth, she sank into postpartum depression, which led to a breakdown, and her threatening to kill herself and drown the children. She believed Scott and his family manipulated and pushed her to desperate acts. Scott had her committed to an institution.

Would I ever hear the full story? I doubted it. Instead, I focused on Elena's regret and pain; that was real. She loved her children dearly and wasn't capable of hurting them.
"You're an incredible mom, Elena," I said
"You give me so much strength."
"My brother had a wild dream about me,"
"What is it about?"
"He dreamt that I died and left a 'monument' that baffled and inspired all who saw it."

.

A bar in the old downtown district shared a hallway with a hair salon; the smell of acetone was horrible. Hairspray was lingering in that hall from 1980. You held your breath entering from the street and tried not to vomit from the acrid air. As you hurried down the hall, taking a left into the sealed off bar. The aroma of smoke and liquor brought welcome relief. *Do you want to go somewhere nice, or a dive bar?'* I'd ask Elena, gauging her mood. *'A dive bar!'* she'd usually reply.

The bar itself had dim lighting, with a lot of red coloring. A darkened staircase ascended to a locked iron gate - presumably an office. A retired boxer owned the place; photos of him in his fighting days hung on the walls. He may have been handsome at one point.

We got regularly served by the same waitress. She'd ask us to forgive her beforehand for her mistakes, saying, *'It's my first day, guys.'* (She told us that for months.)

If they had a good stout beer on tap, Elena ordered that, and I stuck to a pilsner.

"Baby, are you alright?" she asked

"Yeah. Worn out," I said, withdrawn

"Me too. What are you thinking about?"

"That I'm tired of drinking every night. We're better than this."

She quietly reflected, "You're right."

"I'm not saying we need to quit, I know I can't, but we have to slow it down."

"What did you have in mind?"

"Maybe if we drank on the weekends? I don't know."

"We can try. The kids are coming to visit in three weeks, and I don't want to be drinking when they're around, anyway."

"Neither do I, but what happens when they leave? We're gonna get depressed, and drink more to compensate. We need another outlet."

I paused, taking a drag off my cigarette.

"I know you want the kids back," I continued, "but that's obviously not going to happen right now. So, we can either drink ourselves to death or get our shit together. We're not in a position to take care of them if they *did* live with us."

Elena nodded in agreement.

"I've been thinking of going back to school, to get my degree," Elena said

"So have I."

"For what?"

"Floral design. It's the one passion that's stuck with me through my life, so maybe that's a sign I should do it professionally."

"That would be great, baby. I'll talk to my parents. They can help us with tuition."

.

On the way home, we parked on an old country road and had sex in the car. We stripped in the back seat. '*We need to have lots of fun before the kids get here,*' she said licking my neck. We were insatiable.

As we finished together, oncoming headlights washed the interior of the car.

"Shoot, this is private property!" she said

"We can't get dressed that fast!"

"Put your shirt on!" she said, reaching for hers.

We climbed over the seats, and she got behind the wheel. The truck passed.

"I think the windows were foggy enough, they didn't see anything!" she said

"Let's get outta here, shall we?"

.

It's easy, amidst the drama, to forget the lighthearted days Elena and I shared. It was *'life,'* plain and simple, and that's what made them so great.

We'd coast, riding those times, marking special memories on a calendar as our holidays, so in hindsight, we'd remember that it wasn't *all* difficult. Those underappreciated days served to bind us.

"I love you more than yesterday,"
we'd tell each other.

"Do you still love me?"
"More than yesterday."
"How much more?"
"Ten times more."

Our periods of happiness tended to end with someone trying to put a wedge between us. Elena's mother had a vision appear before her, in the middle of the afternoon, while cleaning the house. She claimed it as a vision from God, and described an image of Elena against a black cross; her face deathly pale. In one hand, Elena held me – and in the other hand, the children. Her mother interpreted it as a dire warning and told Elena she might have to make a choice.

The vision disturbed Elena. It planted a seed in her mind, despite my research showing opposing interpretations.

.

Elena and I carried on, each day feeling like a test, undeterred by the words of others.
"I'm starting to look rather British," I remarked, surveying my wardrobe, as I got dressed.
Elena laughed, "You're my handsome British lover!"
"Right, but I'm not British."
"You are now! No one can tell the difference!"
"Ridiculous."
"What department are you working in today?"
"I am a shoe salesman. A bunch of assholes are in that area, so I fit in."
"You know what I love about you, baby?"
"You finally found something?"
"You're such a chameleon. No matter what environment you're in, you adapt," Elena said, snapping her fingers, "It's amazing. I just walk into places with my big mouth and piss everybody off."

We texted each other incessantly; words of love, encouragement and sexual innuendo. It kept our blood pumping. Our coworkers imagined we led glamorous lives when our routine was to lock ourselves in a room, with a few bottles of cheap wine, and binge-watch Gordon Ramsay's *Hell's Kitchen.*

My job at *Gerald's* was going well. I'd proven myself to be reliable and hardworking. I didn't have to dig for hours – department heads were calling my number.

"How's your day?" Elena texted

"Well, I coordinated a funeral, then I helped a gentleman get a suit fitted for his wedding. Then I taught a group of grown men how to tie a tie. The cycle of life, and all that shit."

"Oh my gosh."

"That's nothing compared to what I'm doing now."

"What are you doing?"

"I'm helping a woman find a bow-tie for her dog."

"Where is she?"

"In the dressing room with the dog."

.

At home, an incident occurred known historically as *'Jack Dog Vs. Jose The Handyman.'* – In that legendary bout, street-fightin' Jack walked with the title. It occurred early, at 8 am. I wasn't notified by Elena's parents that a maintenance man would be repairing a sprinkler system in the fenced backyard since they forgot the date themselves. I woke up hungover and opened the sliding glass door for Jack so he could do his business. I headed to the bathroom.

I heard a man scream in abject terror, and I ran out to the yard. There stood a Mexican man with the right pant leg of his Levi jeans ripped clean off. He brandished a dinky PVC pipe, his face contorted in fear. I looked at Jack - the piece of clothing was on the lawn in front of him.

"Go easy, Jack," I said, thinking the man might be robbing us, since he hopped the fence illegally, *"Who are you?"* I shouted.

"Como?"

"Jack, GET HIM!"

"YES!" thought Jack

It was *ON.*

"AIIEEEE!!" The man screamed

He dropped the pipe, turned, and ran towards the fence. He knew it was futile to try and climb it – there was no time - Jack would tear his ass down. The man opted to bank left, and ran the length of the yard, yelling in vain for Jack to heel. The man's desperate bid to get distance wasn't happening for him. They did circles around the yard.

At this point, Elena's father came out demanding answers.

"Jack, leave it!" I commanded

He ran over to me with a grin of absolute pride.

"Who are you?" her father asked, "What are you doing in my yard?"

The man coughed and gagged, trying to get the breath to speak, "I'm..... Jose.... *The Handyman.*"

I brought Jack in the house while her father and Jose had words. Jack, however, just needed a quick break. When her father partially reopened the sliding glass door, Jack *launched* out. It was *ON.*

"Oh no!" screamed Jose, turning once again to flee to the fence. Jack darted after him. Jose banked right, opting for the marginal security of a tree. Jack chased him around the tree before I could get out the door to call him off.

The man threatened to sue us until Elena's mother got involved. She verbally tore the man to shreds, exclaiming that *'Jack was a good dog protecting his family, and what do you think you're doing climbing over our fence?'* She picked up the man's pant leg off the grass and handed it to Jose, then instructed him to leave.

Jose the Handyman left the property a broken man. Debased. Humiliated. Traumatized. Jack, the victor, spent the rest of the afternoon laying in the sun, keeping a close watch for Jose's return. That, of course, wasn't a concern.

.

We needed a vacation. For Elena's birthday, I told her to pack her things; we were going on a road trip, with Jack. I rented a private cabin, in the town of Mccall, on the southern shore of Payette Lake.

It was gorgeous. The air crisp and clean. The lake shimmered a bright, pale blue; a gentle ripple of waves covered its surface, moving from the east with a steady breeze. A forest of green pines rushed up the face of the mountains; the peaks streaked with snow.

Sounds were vibrant. I remember the rough crackling of the gravel road leading to the cabin. The sharpness of the key in the door. The smile on our faces as we settled in, *'This is so nice, thank you, lover.'*

Our energy; warm and illuminated. Nothing could touch our happiness. We relaxed in each other's arms, on our bed for the night, while Jack found his spot on the couch.

.

We walked the main street, alongside the coastline, her hand in mine. It was the offseason, and the solitude made it seem like the town got placed there for us. I reached into my coat pocket, checking to see if the engagement ring was secure. Would it fit? *Yes, it would. Our hands were the same size.*

We stepped into a bar for a drink and asked the bartender for a nearby restaurant that served vegan dishes. He suggested Chinese food at *The Red Pavilion.* It had lower level had dockside seating. We were the only patrons and ordered spicy meals to share. I did my best to teach Elena proper chopsticks techniques, that being a comical routine of ours. She refused to read her fortune cookie. We picked up ice, fruit, and liquor from a market, for cocktails at the cabin.

.

That night it rained lightly, as we sat on the porch, looking out to the lake. We felt at peace.
"Give me your hand," I said
She reached out. I took her hand, turning her palm upwards. I slipped her the ring and closed her fingers around it.
"Elena, I love you. I want to spend the rest of my life with you. I want to help you raise your children and be apart of their lives. I promise to love and protect all of you, as a family."
I released her hand, and she opened it to see the ring.
"Will you marry me, Elena?"
Tears filled her eyes, as she nodded.
"Yes!" she said, kissing me, pulling me close.

We were going to prevail.

.

In the morning, we walked on clouds, seeing the sights. We had a vegan breakfast with coffee, went to a bookstore, and admired the historical architecture of the buildings, savoring each moment of our company.

During the drive home, we stopped at a roadhouse for a cold beer. I asked the woman if they had a drink menu, and she, along with a few other people laughed at me, *'It's a beer bar, honey. What you see is what we got,'* she said gesturing to the taps. Elena got upset they spoke to me so rudely. We took our beer to a table in the corner, and I excused myself to use the restroom.

When I returned, her beer was untouched.
"Let's leave," she said, curtly

"What's wrong, love? Did they say something to you while I was gone?" I asked, in the car

"I want to honor what God has blessed me with," she said, "I don't want to drink anymore."

I'd hoped to hear her say that. Would it last? I didn't know - But, her heart was in its place.

.

We eagerly awaited the visit from the children. Admittedly, I got nervous to meet Hetty. I prepared myself for a headstrong and spoiled little girl. Would she accept me? Elena feared Scott would play his games and switch the pickup dates at the last minute. Elena's father had poor health and was in no condition to drive to California to get the kids, yet Scott forced him anyway. Elena stayed home for legal reasons.

When the car pulled into the driveway, Elena and I went out to greet them. Hetty was half asleep, and Elena carried her into the house.

"Hi, Hetty. I'm Logan," I said introducing myself

She gazed at me, rubbing her tired eyes, "Hello, sir. I'm happy to meet you."

Hetty endeared herself to me instantly.

.

The kids lived with us for a brief three days, when a violent fight broke out. The initial arguing was in a foreign language. I won't tolerate fighting in front of children. Hetty and Aidan were in the room, confused over the yelling.

"Hetty, sweetheart," I said, kneeling to her eye level, "I need you to take your brother and go to our bedroom, ok?" I said, ushering them down the hall. I went back to the argument between Elena and her parents.

"I have no idea what you people are saying, but you're scaring the kids," I said

Her father moved past me, to the bedroom. Then Elena's mother went off on me.

"And *YOU!*" she exclaimed, pointing her finger, "*YOU* work for Scott, *too!*"

"*What?!*" Elena said in shock, "Mom, that's too *much!* What are you *talking about?!*"

"What did you say to me?" I said, rage seething inside of me

"You work for Scott! *I know it!* Always so quiet, watching us always!" she snarled, nearly hyperventilating

"Are you out of your *fucking mind*, lady?" I said, my eyes hunting her relentlessly

She got in my face, despite Elena's effort to stop her, *"Don't* you speak to me like that, *boy!* You show me *respect!"*

"Lady, I've shown you all the respect you deserve. How *dare you* accuse me of working for Scott!"

"You do!"

"Mom, please stop this!" Elena pleaded

"I may be quiet, but you don't know when to shut your mouth."

her father strong-armed me from behind and dragged me out the front door.

"You work for Scott!?" he bellowed, "You work for Scott!? Get out of my house! Get out!" I could feel his labored breathing. His left eye had popped a blood vessel, and his socket was bleeding.

Elena came to my aid, and her father grabbed her upper arms and started shaking her violently, yelling at her. She begged him to stop. I went into the house, and saw Hetty in the room, crying miserably. *Goddamit.* I yanked him off Elena and slammed him against the wall.

"If you touch her again, I WILL FUCKING KILL YOU!"

I knew in those seconds that a single sharp jab to his stomach could rupture his distended internal organs. In that moment, I held his life in my hands.

Why was I thinking like this? Who the fuck was I becoming?

Those Small Hours

For two months we drifted. They were slightly more gracious to Elena, who had seven days to vacate.

Scott got word of our eviction and wanted Hetty and Aidan returned to California immediately. I could not accept that. *I wasn't going to let that sonofabitch win.* I *had* to save the visit for Elena and the kids. I encouraged her to spend those seven days with them and to put out the fire with Scott, while I found a solution. I left Jack in her care.

Orrin set me up for a night, in his city apartment. He lived with his girlfriend, Danielle, and I didn't like to intrude. I couldn't count on any of my contacts; it seemed inevitable I end up at *The Lighthouse*.

.

Will didn't have roommates, preferring solitude. He and I knew the house wouldn't be safe for the children, though he felt indebted to me for sheltering him in the winter.

It was strange, walking around that property; memories came to me like half-remembered dreams. I couldn't escape that place. I didn't dwell on my feelings, or they might have consumed me. I felt uncertainty creeping in at the edges.

"Alright, hear me out," Will said, handing me a cigarette
I lit it up and waited.
"You can move in with my ex-wife," he said
"That's the woman I heard you calling a psycho?"
"Yes it is," he said flatly
"I'm not sold yet."
"Look, there's a lot of bad blood between Karen and me. But, she's a good woman. That's why I married her and had two kids with her. We've talked, and she wants to help you guys. I can only introduce you, though, so you've gotta take it from there. She's going to have questions."
"What's the house like?"
"It's a good size. Plenty of room and Elena's kids will have playmates with my two daughters. My youngest is the same age as Hetty. And there's a fenced backyard for Jack. He should get along with my dog, Leah.
I thought for a minute.
"Call her up."

Karen agreed to take us in, and provide safe housing for the children. I hadn't delivered the news to Elena yet. In my truck, I took a moment for myself, resting my forehead on the steering wheel. I would've cried if I weren't too exhausted. I missed the freedom of the open road. My truck gave me grief while I lived in Utah. I wasn't sure she'd get Jack and I out of town, never mind thousands of miles across the country. She didn't fail me, though. I admired her for that.

The past winter took its toll on my truck, with the drive from Boise to her parents home. Now we faced the commute from Garden City. I knew she couldn't hold up much longer, and gas costs were high.

When Elena and I arrived at Karen's house, she offered us her large master bedroom, relegating herself to the couch. We felt guilty, but she was adamant.

.

Scott fucked off, and the children reentered the picture. We treated the whole experience as an adventure or a sleep-over with friends. They had fun playing with Karen's daughters, in spite of the confusing transition. Hetty wondered if she'd done something wrong to cause the fight, and Elena explained it wasn't her fault.

I'm sure Hetty, accustomed to living in mansions, got disappointed with Karen's house, though she kept her manners. Hetty realized her upbringing was privileged. We earned our money, unlike her trust-fund father, and Hetty learned the value in that. Aidan felt content wherever, on the condition he had his iPad, though he discovered playing in a sandbox could be equally fascinating.

The children adjusted fast, and opened up to us, in their brilliance. Hetty, curious as can be, never tired of drilling me with questions, especially when she noticed the engagement ring on her mother's finger. I'd be honest with her, even while blushing.

Hetty spontaneously started calling me 'Loulou.' We weren't sure why, but I adored it. I said to Elena, *'Someday, she'll stop calling me that, and it's going to devastate me.'*

Elena radiated happiness; Hetty and Aidan were her life. In their company, I saw the woman I had fallen in love with and wanted to marry.

"I think you gave my mom magic tea!" Hetty exclaimed when Elena wasn't nearby

"Oh yeah? How's that?" I asked

"I've never seen her in such a good mood!" she said, "She didn't used to smile like that!"

"Well, I *did* give your mom magic tea, but I've got a problem."

"What?"

"I drank some of it myself," I said, wincing

"OH NO!" she said, shocked, "How much did you drink?!"

"*A LOT.*"

"Oh my gosh!" she said, slapping her hands on her cheeks, "You're in *so* much trouble!"

"I know. You've gotta help me. I don't know what to do!"

"Ok, Loulou! I'll help you!"

The kids brought out the best in us. Life was light; like a soft outline. Through them, we saw everything fresh and new. I would've gone to any lengths, without question, for Hetty and Aidan

Elena's fight for custody became my fight.

.

Aidan's thinking made us all a bit envious; he viewed the world in a pure form. He enjoyed the soundtrack of Terrence Malick's film, *'Tree of Life.'* We had it on constant rotation, with the compositions arranged on a playlist.

When we managed to pry Aidan from his robots, he loved going to the park to chase the ducks. When the four us walked together, he would silently take my hand. I imagined him older, going to the park to think his best ideas, with some bread in his pocket. We did an impromptu photo shoot with Elena's phone, capturing the day's events.

Aidan got scared in department stores. So did I, for that matter, so we stuck to outdoor activities, making sure to put sunscreen on his mom so she wouldn't burn in the summer sun.

We had a great afternoon at the zoo; Aidan held my hand until the crowds overwhelmed him, then he'd want his mom. Hetty dragged me around and we laughed at the monkeys. The reptiles grossed her out, of course, even though she was intrigued. Aidan liked feeding the goats and giggled at the sounds they made. Elena and I gave each other loving glances.

.

There's a country club in Boise where Elena used to bring Aidan. I had no intentions of going there, yet Scott saw fit to have me barred from it for life. He spoke to the owners, and they wouldn't allow me on the premises. Perhaps Scott didn't want his golfing buddies seeing me with his ex-wife, buying his son ice cream.

Jack adored Hetty. He got completely enamored with her. I'd never been so proud of Jack, who behaved like a proper gentleman. He followed that little girl wherever she'd go, protecting her. He'd sleep beside her at night. The two of them watched videos, while Hetty petted and talked to him. It took a lot to win Jack's heart – and Hetty won it in spades.

Aidan moved rapidly compared to the other kids, which gave Jack anxiety. However, the boy was prone to dropping vegan pizza, so Jack remained on standby, from a distance.

The children slept, bundled on the bed between me and Elena, who'd crawl over next to me, and kiss my neck..

My hard work at *Gerald's* paid off when the manager of the fine jewelry department approached me, as I sized a watch. She was an older woman who had no time for bullshit.
"Logan, me and the gals in jewelry have been talking about you. I'm impressed by your numbers. You have a good sales record, and you open a lot of new accounts."
"Thanks."
"You come in looking sharp. I like that," she said with a wink, "We were wondering if you'd be interested in a position behind the counter in fine jewelry."
I didn't know what to say - I at least got out an affirmative *'yes.'*
In her office, I got a summation of what the job entailed. She wanted to be confident I knew the full extent of what I'd signed up for. The company did a background check, which didn't bother me; I had no criminal record. I gained security clearance, then did protocol training.

I met the Loss Prevention team, who monitored us with surveillance cameras. An undercover agent, Marco, patrolled the counter and retail floor. He did a commendable job. I enjoyed seeing him get the drop on shoplifters. I received combinations to the safes, containing roughly $750,000 worth of jewelry. Also, a set of keys, strictly assigned to me, to be secured around my wrist while on duty.

Three months ago, I was a departmental errand boy with six scheduled hours a week. Now, I had the key to the master safe.

I had an anxious first day - getting thrown into the cage with those stern women. I didn't want them to see me as a young blood trying to steal their commissions. I'd remain a decade behind them in experience, and expected one hell of a learning curve up ahead. I vowed to be useful, and retain whatever lessons they were willing to teach.

They called the counter *The Shark Tank.* As I stepped in, a loud buzzer signaled my entrance. I closed the gate behind me and introduced myself to the women, who, as it turned out, were not stern at all; they were four of the most wonderful people I have ever known.

They lavished me with information - and homemade cookies. Also, fresh vegetables from their gardens, knitted hats, and Baklava from family recipes. They shared their stories, with as much acerbic wit and jaded humor that I could carry with both hands. In short, they adopted me and treated me like a son. It honored me.

They taught me customer psychology, tricks of the trade, and crash courses in gemology, and diamond quality. Hell, they knew every woman within a hundred miles that had too much of their husband's money - *and how some of them thrilled in buying jewelry from men.*

Hetty and Aidan's visitation ended, and Elena's father drove them to California. Elena sank into depression. I anticipated that and did my best to keep her spirits up, though I failed. I desperately tried to find us an apartment. I thought if we could establish a home, a space that belonged to *us*, it would mitigate the stress in our relationship.

Karen asked us to divide our time between her home and *The Lighthouse,* and we obliged, expressing our gratitude for her hospitality. Every two or three days, Elena and I packed up our cars, and either moved to Boise, or Garden City. We endured that process for weeks, and by the tenth rotation from city to city, Elena and I felt utterly defeated.

The four of us adults did have memorable evenings. Elena taught Karen's eleven-year-old daughter the basics of cooking and knife skills. She was a bright girl, and curious about the two enigmatic lovers, who usurped her mother's bedroom.

One night, I converted their kitchen into a sushi bar and treated them to my favorite specialties. I loved catering parties. Moments like that lifted morale. Karen's children were hesitant to taste the sushi, and she advised them, *'Someday you'll appreciate what he's doing.'* I was known for my vegan futomaki roll when I rolled sushi professionally, which delighted Elena.

Jack had an ideal companion in Leah, Will's shaggy dog. The two of them had mock battles in the yard. Jack crashed to the ground submissively, while Leah pounced on him, causing them both to roll in the dirt, hollering like puppies, until they collapsed in the shade.

Will and Karen's attempts at reconciliation couldn't move past the old wounds and cycles of abuse. It pained Elena and I to listen to them argue. We'd sneak out, and go to a nearby Irish pub.

During our rotations at *The Lighthouse*, Elena and I stayed active. The energy of that house had such sadness to it; like it heard your whispers. It was eerily quiet, which we counteracted with conversation, music, and sex. We resumed going on romantic dates in a growing downtown.

Will related a disturbing story of Hollace.
"So, when I cleaned out the loft," Will said, "I found remains of animals."
"Jesus, Will."
"Yeah. I don't know what he was doing up there, but it sheds light on the fly problem you guys were having, doesn't it?"

Will officially gave up on his relationship with Karen, and began seeing a younger girl. I knew nothing about her, other than she was apparently on heavy medication. Elena had a couple of talks with her on the porch.

I didn't care about Will's sex life or marital problems; they weren't my business. Will and Karen sent each other brutal text messages with regularity and, unlike me, Elena chose sides. She and Karen drank, and Elena instigated matters further, priming Karen for emotional decisions.

I stumbled upon a third-floor apartment within our budget, and minutes from our jobs. It shared a fence with Ann Morrison Park, with an area to walk Jack. The property management dragged its feet on the remodeling and they refused to let me see inside, or show a demo, expecting me to rent the unit sight unseen.

I signed a year lease and put down a heavy deposit, based on a black and white photograph printed on paper.

At the last minute, they pushed our move-in date by three weeks. Those twenty-one days of constant shuffling passed like an eternity. The drinking escalated, and Karen was Elena's new partner. They commiserated for hours, winding themselves up into a hyper-emotional frenzy, which I'd suffer the brunt of.

She'd say cruel things, like *'Do you even think of the baby we lost?!'* Elena was sure I still harbored love for my ex, and that she and I were secretly married. She had her lawyers do a background check on me.

"Elena, have I *ever* said I'd leave you?"
"No."
"Have I *ever* said that I was going to give up on you?"
"... No."
"Then why is *my* commitment being called into question, when you accuse me of shit like this and break up with me *every other fucking night?*"

Sometimes, Elena couldn't have the final word.

.

Karen inherited the wardrobe of a deceased relative, keen on fashion. She had her daughter bring out a box of the woman's vintage clothing for Elena to model. They fit as if tailored to her form. The three of them played dress-up. I passively watched the fun.

Will came through the front door, and approached me.
"Come outside," he said

We stood in the dark driveway.
"Scott's SUV is back," Will said gravely
"What?" I said in frustration
"It's been circling the house for the last two hours."
I rubbed my eyes. "You're certain of it?"
"Yes, I am. It had the same plates."
"The plates I warned you of?"
"Yes. Listen, these people have harassed you and Elena for over a year," Will continued, "and now they're threatening my family. It needs to stop. I'm not going to tolerate it."
"Understood."
Nothing more got said - I turned and walked into the house.

"Baby, look at this!" Elena, beamed

She wore a gorgeous floral print dress that seemed designed for her. Elena appeared beautifully, standing there. Her smile, so genuine. I couldn't ruin that moment. I didn't have the heart to tell her it had all started over. I commented how pretty she was, hoping to hide my pained expression.

I could write more on those sleepless nights. The anger and forgiveness. The dreams, and wishes for tomorrow.

But, I'm sure you'd like to know how it finally came crashing down.

How the momentum spiraled out of control.

I'm sure you want to know why I began writing this book,
with a pen hidden in my sock, from the isolation chamber of Ada County Jail,
while facing fifty years in prison.

All Perfect Light and Promises

To wake up naturally, in our warm bed, stretching our toes, in our quiet apartment. To kiss Elena's soft shoulder, waking her gently, so she'd roll onto my side of the bed. To have her drape her arm on me, and say she loved me. It made the hardships we'd endured worthwhile.

To start our day with love guiding us. To see her walk naked, and smiling, telling me her fantasies. To take a hot shower together, cleaning each other's bodies.

Elena would cook us breakfast, in our tiny kitchen. We'd sit at the dining table, or eat it in bed. She'd remark how it could've tasted better, even though it was perfect to me.

"What do you want to do tonight?" I'd ask

"Hang out. Drink wine. I just want to be with you, in our apartment."

"Sounds good, love."

I'd see her get dressed, and put her makeup on, grinning at me in the mirror. We'd drive to the same grocery store every day, and have a beer upstairs in their restaurant. Then pick up groceries and wine for the evening. She'd curse under her breath at people driving too poorly, and I'd laugh. We'd listen to the radio.

I'd uncork a bottle of wine, and pour each of us a glass before cuddling up on the luxurious couch her mother bought as a belated housewarming gift. We'd binge-watch Elena's favorite shows since she got offended by the dark programs that entertained me. Besides, I liked dramatic cooking competitions and lousy crime stories. We had fun cracking jokes.

"Wouldn't it be hilarious if they made one of these shows about us?" I mused, "Like ten years after the fact, with their information completely wrong!"

"Oh my gosh! What if they read our text messages in court?!" she gasped

"Oh dude, we'd be finished. Can you imagine?

We mocked the ominous narrator's voice;

"Logan was a pious man, with a strict temperament," I said, *"That was a stark contrast to Elena and her hippy roots. She was a soft-spoken girl and a lover of animals. His love for fast cars and his wild lifestyle went against her modest values."*

"His sexual deviance lead to many affairs," she added, giggling, *"She liked to stay home and read books, but Logan wanted to hit the clubs! She was timid and lived in fear of the monster in her bed!"*

Our small back porch became our new mecca. We lived on the third floor, and from our vantage point, we looked upon a ravine of trees. Jack was quite fond of it, sticking his nose between the wooden panels to breath in the smells.

Still, during those moments, that I learned the most about Elena.
"I love you," she'd say, with that flowing voice
"I love you, too."
"*I love you so much*... I'm so grateful to be with you."
She and I were forever connected, "You're my life, Elena."

"Are you all mine?"
"You have me. I'm all yours."

"You still love me?"
"More than yesterday, love."
"Sorry I'm such a bitch."
"Me too."
"You're a jerk," she'd laugh
"Hey, at least I got a smile."

"...You're such an amazing man."
Her words gave me butterflies, "And you're the woman I've always wanted."
She'd stare into my soul, with those gorgeous eyes.
"I can't wait until we're married, and we're living in our home, with the children," she'd say
"Things are going to get easier, Elena, We've been through so much, and we still love each other."

She often spoke of that house we would someday own; I used to see it as our future.

We'd go indoors, and perhaps make love on the stairs, leading up to our loft that we converted into a lounge.

I couldn't face that Elena and I were in a holding pattern.

.

Then, Elena lost her job, with few openings in town. With rent due, I also searched, to be safe; I wasn't about to let us get evicted. Elena felt like a failure, and I swore to take care of her, as she had done for me.

Stress dissolved our happiness – and we could not regain it.

October 5th - 7:00 am. Elena and I went to bed, following an uneventful evening.

She sat up, with a start, woken by a dream. A confused expression spread over her face as if she didn't know who I was. The corners of her mouth were pulled back in fear, and she breathed shallowly.

"Elena, what's wrong?"

"I'm leaving," she said, throwing on her clothes

She picked up only two things to take with her – her Bible, and a large framed drawing of Aidan's. I plaintively asked her why. She panicked, and backed against the wall, awkwardly clutching at the picture frame.

"I'm not coming back," she said and rushed out the door

I let her go.

What should I have done? I was hurt and pissed off. I had to open the jewelry counter at *Gerald's*. As my shift progressed, anger gave way to indifference. I felt like a ghost, not wanting to be seen. Fortunately, there weren't any customers, and the gals weren't scheduled.

Then, my phone chimed with a text message from Will.

"Do you know where Elena is?" he asked

"I have no clue. She had another psychotic breakdown and left me," I replied

"Well, she's with Karen, causing serious fucking problems, telling her lies about my girlfriend. Now my girl wants to beat the shit out of Elena."

"I'm leaving work early and heading to your place."

I rested on the porch of *The Lighthouse*, talking to Will and his girlfriend. I studied the girl; her words were merely trash talk. She wasn't a viable threat. Will, on the other hand, talked of legal action, for complicating his custody battle with Karen. They had a right to be upset. So did I.

The emotions fleeted, however, and we discussed the matter rationally. I explained how incidents like this were becoming more frequent, and severe. I couldn't fight this battle on my own. I needed help.

"A month ago, Elena woke up and ran through the apartment screaming and laughing like a child, knocking shit off tables," I said, "I got afraid the neighbors might call the cops. In the morning, she had no memory of it."

"It sounds to me like she has a dissociative disorder, Logan, and I'm not saying that from a place of ignorance. I grew up around that," Will advised

It lessened my burden to share information, and tempers cooled off when they understood Elena's psychology.

"Well, shit. What's done is done," Will stated, "Do you want to walk with us to get some pizza and beer?"

"Sure. I'll chip in."

We brought the food to *The Lighthouse,* and relaxed, watching a movie. Things returned to normalcy, at least in that house.

"Y'all be safe," I said, as I closed the front door

I stood on that porch for a minute. Again, I had the sensation of memories swelling up like resurfaced dreams. It would be my last visit to *The Lighthouse.*

.

I hadn't heard from Elena. I called her mother, and she did not answer. I decided not to leave a message, thinking it may worsen the situation.

That night, I sat at the bottom of the stairwell, in the parking lot, breathing the autumn air. An elderly man approached me as if his sole purpose was to deliver me a message; it seemed unreal.

For a full hour, the man spoke, and I said nothing for the entirety of it. His negative words dismantled me. He didn't merely attack religion. He tore apart any belief in a higher power and scrutinized humanity's path, the church, birthrights, and lies perpetuated for centuries. As if to ask me for the acquiescence my very soul. He wouldn't be satisfied until I gave up. In him, there was no hope or the root of love and understanding. He had the bleakest worldview I'd encountered – or perhaps not – *as he sounded like me* when I was an over-educated teenage atheist.

Between his words, in the syntax, I could hear him say, 'Where'd you go wrong, kid? You had it figured out, and then you got weak and stupid. *You fell for it.'*

He finally walked off, and his suffocating presence lifted.

I went upstairs, snorted a painkiller, and opened a bottle of whiskey. I stood ashamed, in front of Jack. I'd never felt that empty. I realized that I had *nothing* to look forward to. *All* of my plans were based on Elena. I had no personal goals. Without her love, I was a shell of a human being.

I caught up on TV shows that Elena wouldn't let me watch, drinking shot after shot, wishing the pain to go for good.

I woke up on the floor, with Jack licking my face. My head lay pressed against the wall, and my neck stiff. I must've slumped off my chair and knocked myself out. I crawled to the bedroom and slid onto the bed. I desperately needed sleep. *'I'm sorry, Jack. Come and lay with me, buddy.'*

6:52 am – my phone lit up with a text message from Elena.

"Nice to know you think I'm once again having a psychotic breakdown!?"
(Will had forwarded my text to Karen, who in turn showed it to Elena.)

"I'm staying out of this, Elena. Please stop."
"So what exactly have you said to your friend Will about me? All I've ever done is care about you and love you, but clearly, you've decided to take sides against me, with your friend!"
"You upset people yesterday. They wanted to hurt you. I don't know why you went to that house and stirred them up. I don't want to hear their negative conversations, and I don't want them involved in ours. Please keep me out of it. I'm depressed as it is."
"Who wants to hurt me?"
"Nobody anymore. I've calmed them down. I'm begging you to please stop getting involved in their lives."
"When you say those people, who are you talking about?"
"I refuse to fuel this fire. I'm done. If you want to have a civilized conversation with me, I'll be here. I need to get some sleep."
"You're a big-time coward! My life has been threatened, and I will send this text to my lawyers. If anything happens to me, my lawyers will know who to question! And I will send this text to my ex-husband. He has a right to know that his ex-wife is getting threatened!"
"Elena, their lives are not our business. And your life isn't threatened. Quit being ridiculous. Just let it lay. I'm no longer texting you."
"It upsets me that you never stand up for me! I stand up for you! My ex was right about you all along! I hate to admit it, but he was right! You've just been milking me this whole time ... *'I love you, Elena, I will do anything for you!'* You never meant any of it! Well, hopefully, your friends will pay your bills and buy you nice clothes and sunglasses and a nice car and good food! I see that you're the type of person who feels he's entitled to these things. You are picking those people over me! That is how you stand up for me?! Asshole!"
"How you'd even think that is staggering to me. I've never *not* stood up for you, nor am I picking anyone over you. You've been the center of my life since I met you. I've fought beside you through everything. I'd never let anything happen to you. You know that in your heart. Please talk to me without anger. You're my best friend, and we are better than this. "

"I hope it was worth it, for you to stand by your friend and turn against your ex fianceé! So funny how you go against that hand that feeds you! And why did you call my mom and be a coward and not leave a message?"

"Elena, you can't storm out of the house at 7 am saying you're not coming back and expect me not to be upset. You can't. People say hurtful things in a space like that. I'm sorry I said that, but I felt angry at that moment. I think I had a right to be upset. I wanted to talk to your mom but didn't want to cause any further problems. I'm suffering from a lot of depression as well, and I need help. Life has not been easy for us at all, but I've never backed down. I do apologize for saying *one* hurtful text about you. It was out of place, and I was very frustrated and trying to do my job when Will texted me."

"My lawyers said if anything happens to me and you know who threatened me, they will seek out information. I sent them the text you stated about me having a psychotic breakdown, and I sent it to my ex-husband too!! I hope your decisions bring you a better life! You never loved me or cared about me! Obviously, your loyalty is somewhere else."

"That's so wrong, Elena. I left work immediately and went to assess the situation and calm things down - because I LOVE YOU, and how you've managed to twist that so severely, I can't understand. That's so unfair."

"You left work early to cater to Will and his girlfriend! Why didn't you leave work early to try to work things out with me? Shame on you. Now I am obliged to send these texts to my lawyers because you admit they were the people who were planning to hurt me! You fool! Thanks for giving me the information! Fuck you! Your as big a loser as him!"

"You're not even making sense, Elena. You've been avoiding Karen ever since we left, and going to her house is no different than me talking to Will. Why on earth did you have to get us involved with their problems again? Why couldn't you just come home and talk to me?"

"I've been avoiding Karen because you told me too!"

"No, Elena. We BOTH, as a couple, agreed to avoid both of them if they were going to bring negativity into our lives. And look. They're doing it again. If you'd just come home, things would be fine between us, and we'd be working things out. Doesn't all of this make you sick? I don't want to fight with you anymore."

"Too late! We are done! I hate to admit this, but Scott is so right about you! He warned me this would happen! You're friends with someone who is threatening my life ?! My lawyers said I shouldn't come to you because you are a threat too!"

"That wasn't the situation at all. They said nothing bad about you. They were just upset."

"Fuck you asshole! A man stands up for his woman! I feel sorry for your ex-wife having to deal with this shit! *If she even is your ex-wife!* I have action now to take this to the police and make a report!"

"What on earth are you talking? Why?"

"You left work early and drove there! A real man would've looked for his fiancée and been worried about her!"

"This is too much Elena. I gave you space because I thought you were at your parent's home. You said you were never coming back. Can you honestly tell me you would have wanted to see me if I went to Karen's?"

"It would've been nice, but you fucked up bad!"

"So did you."

"Oh, pity me! It's all about you! You always manipulate the situation! Stand up and be a man! Text Will and say I will no longer be friends with you! You disrespected my fiancé, soon to be ex. I would love to see that text, but of course, you don't have the balls! At least I know my ex-husband did! He was willing to stand up for me, you asshole!"

"You can't speak to me like this. Your behavior is out of control."

"Now it's my fault?! Yeah right, you're going send that text! Are you butt-hurt having to say goodbye to your best friend? You'd rather lose him than me!"

"Elena stop! It's unforgivable what all three of you have been saying for the last 24 hours! I've never fucking picked anybody over you! But, for a year you've accused over and over again of doing so!"

"Now your God???"

"What? Wow. You are unreachable."

"I've never met such a foolish man, willing to lose all that's good in his life over a fucking guy! What are you guys, gay fucking lovers?! I'm sending this to my lawyers! Violence?!"

"All of this is violent, Elena."

"When are you going to be at the apartment? I'm picking up my stuff."

"Can we have a real conversation?"

"I need to let my lawyers and Scott know what time I'm going there. This is serious stuff, and they are very concerned something could happen to me."

"You're going to be perfectly fine. You can come after I get home from work."

Elena opened the door and slammed her purse on the kitchen counter.
"So you wanna talk?!" she shouted

I did, though she obviously didn't want to listen. We argued for hours, and I got hit with an ultimatum - I had to apologize for *my* behavior, for her to consider staying with me. I had to write an email to Will, ending our friendship, and apologizing to *him* for what I said about *her*, and how wrong I was to do so.

Elena made no apologies. She felt that wasn't required – she'd done no wrong. It would be five months until she expressed a slight remorse for her actions. By then, however, I had changed.

The fight ended strangely, when I said to Elena, *'After all we've been through, and overcome, don't we owe it to ourselves to at least try to fix this?'* Then I made an intentionally stupid remark, and she laughed. That was that. The ice cracked. We watched a television show. The next day she was pleasant, singing me love songs in her first language.

We changed our phone numbers.

.

I didn't trust Elena anymore. My respect for her deteriorated and got replaced with resentment. I maintained our relationship from a guarded distance.

I knew for certain that I would not allow myself to revisit that sense of profound emptiness. I wanted my life back. I started forming my own goals, striving to exist independently of her.

There was a second fundamental change - I stopped blaming myself for her transgressions.

.

Job interviews weren't panning out for either of us, and I made a sacrifice in auctioning my Canon camera. I dearly valued that machine; for a decade it had spoken on my behalf. I didn't anticipate using in the future and thus justified my selling it, covering the rent for a month. Elena, in turn, sold a high-end baby stroller that Aidan had outgrown. With the bills paid, I explored the job market.

Throughout my adult life, I've stopped and asked myself, *'What's the ballsiest thing I can do today?'* I applied for jobs I wasn't remotely qualified for, and more often than not, I got hired. Thus, my mindset when I sought employment at *United Bank*, as a customer service representative in their call center. The salary position offered health insurance, monthly incentives, and paid vacations – yet every aspect of the job filled me with apprehension. That's why I applied for it.

I thought the interview went good, but I did not get the job. That irritated me, so I reapplied in the debt collecting department, which got me *exceedingly* further out of my comfort zone than the other position – *and they hired me.* Three hundred people got interviewed, and twenty of us made the cut.

It involved eight weeks of intensive training, at forty hours per week. They did a background check and took my photo for my security badge. The retina of my eye got scanned into the database, as it would each morning, granting me access to the building. I switched exclusively to nights, at *Gerald's.*

I hated that couch Elena's mother lavished upon us. Don't get me wrong; its mauve coloring and golden highlights were appealing to look at. It was undoubtedly the most comfortable couch I'd sat or slept on. But that didn't change the fact it symbolized what I'd spent my life trying to avoid: vanity and the careless waste of resources. The couch cost $4000. I ruminated on how we could've furthered ourselves, and our education, with that amount of money.

She and I spent most nights on that couch - that cushioned object of idiocy - watching television and drinking wine. It was expansively rich enough that we both could sleep on it if the mood struck us. It welcomed you into luxury and denial. The couch got hailed as the centerpiece of the living room. All other furniture and accessories had to abide by it.

Jack, of course, let the issue slide; he figured it big enough to fit all three of us, and to him, that's what mattered. Perhaps he had a healthier method of thinking.

.

I started my job at *United Bank* in nine days. I went downstairs to check the mail, slapping the hood of my truck as I walked by, on a chilly afternoon.

A few hours later, Jack and I took a lap around the apartment complex. When we came full circle, standing in the stairwell, I shot a glance and noticed my parking spot was empty. For a second, I thought we had the wrong building. *'My truck is gone,'* I said out loud. Jack looked at me, sheepishly. *'Jack, the truck is gone. It isn't there'*.
In the apartment, Elena dabbed on her makeup.
"Babe?" I said
"Yeah?"
"My truck is gone," I said, numbly
"What do you mean?"

I searched the property, confirming the truck to in fact be missing. A cop arrived to file the report.
"You're most likely not going to see the vehicle again. At least not in one piece," he said
I ran my fingers through my hair, locking them behind my head.
"I start my new job soon, and I can't get there," I sighed
"I understand. We'll do our best."

It posed a serious problem - having two jobs, in two cities, with no transportation. Using Elena's car on a daily basis wasn't feasible. I had no savings, or I would've bought a cheap vehicle from the want ads.

Unexpectedly, Elena's parents came to my aid. They agreed to cosign with me for a brand new car. Five months ago they kicked me to the street, and now this. *Had I proven my worth? Was the vehicle a peace offering?* They apologized to me for their actions, saying they couldn't understand what they'd done, and that, possibly, the devil had influenced them.

I got tired of being put in difficult positions; each choice preceded by hesitation. If I accepted, the feud would end, and for Elena's sake, she wouldn't have to choose sides. *United Bank* expected me in three days.

I decided to be the better person, and forgive them.

When I met them at the dealership, a car had been pre-selected, for specific reasons I figured. I wasn't in a position to be choosy, regardless. I took the car for a test drive, adjusting to how low the seat was in comparison to my truck. My foot felt heavy on the sensitive brakes . Aside from that, it handled smoothly. I had no experience with smart cars and got spoiled by the interface and functioning gauges. It got excellent gas mileage, and the sound system appealed to me.

I signed for it. The monthly payments were high; I had no choice but to keep both jobs, and hope Elena found employment.

.

On the first day of training, I got acquainted with the security system and located the training room. I showed up early, and had my choice of seats; the desks were arranged in a 'U' shape so we could face each other. I came prepared, with a folder, notebook, and pens. I may have dressed the part, but I was an odd man out. Some of my teammates had previous call center experience, albeit not on this level.

I studied them as they got situated, seeing with whom I could connect. One man, in particular, didn't give a shit about fitting in. His worn-out sneakers, faded jeans, and flannel shirts were in contrast to the rest of us. His scraggly beard reached to his mid-chest, and he pulled his long hair back. At roll call, he stated his name as Tony, with a deep crackly voice, like he smoked a pack a day – which he did.

Inevitably the two of us would end up talking. *He probably thinks I'm in a band,* I thought. I got that a lot, for some reason. Must've been the hair.

Our instructor eased us in, so we got comfortable with the three-hundred-and-twenty hours of education ahead. Not a minute of it got wasted. We didn't use scripts, like other call centers. The methods learned were far more complex. We focused on speech patterns, and tapping into the client's unspoken needs. That helped us govern and redirect the call. They were reteaching us how to speak, using certain words at key times. As the class progressed, we received information on Miranda Rights, and state by state legislation, which we'd have to internalize.

To manage call volume, we had to keep them at an ideal length of four minutes or less. In that window, we had to gain the clients trust, determine their financial situation, resolve any conflicts and take the payment. I wondered if any amount of planning could prepare us for the reality.

We got a tour of the site and shown the floor where we would someday work. I panicked a bit. The cubicles, the phones, the noise, the fluorescent lights, the environment as a whole fed my social anxiety. *Can I navigate this?*

During a fifteen minute break, I relaxed in a fenced off employees-only area. Tony walked up to me.
"Hey, man. Do you play any instruments?" he asked
I smiled, "No, I don't. I used to make movies, though."
"Right on. I play guitar. Mostly metal."

We hit it off, and he mentioned his interest in buying a Mac computer.
"'I have an older model I might be willing to sell," I replied
"Really?" he said, perking up, "How much were you thinking?"
"I'm not sure. Want to make me an offer?"
"Four-hundred?"
"Deal."

Tony had two kids, and money was tight, so I let him pay in installments. He and I became friends.

.

I got a phone call from the Boise Police Department.

"Hello, Mr. Crannell?"
"Yes?"
"This is Officer Peterson."
"Hello."
"We found your vehicle, the 1996 Chevy Blazer."
"What? The whole thing?"

"Yessir. It was located in the Walmart parking lot, in Nampa. It appears as though someone had been living in it. Paraphernalia was also retrieved from the vehicle."

"Ok, I'm at work, but I can be there in less than an hour to pick it up. Is that ok?"

"Well, the truck got towed to the impound yard."

"Wait, I'm not getting charged to get it out of impound am I?"

"Yessir. There is a charge. I do believe the fee increases by the day, so I suggest resolving it shortly."

"Damn. Alright, thanks for finding it."

Orrin picked me up, and we drove to the tow yard. I could count on Orrin, and together we laughed at the irony of my predicament. I paid the costly fee, with the little money I had. We verified the truck started up fine. *'What's with all the junk food wrappers?'* he quipped. After we said our farewells, I sat in the driver seat, inspecting the random objects scattered about the cabin - an old jacket, a pocket knife, and flashlight. The interior got trashed and smelled foul, which made me sad.

As I drove her home, I had a moment of sentimentality. The truck had returned to my life - but there was a new car in her parking spot. I remembered a time when it was just me, Jack and my truck; the three of us, against the odds – and we prevailed. Jack taught me the meaning of loyalty. My truck, endurance. I couldn't have gotten this far without them. Now I had to say goodbye.

What had I replaced her with? A high-end modern thing that would likely malfunction in a few years.

I listed the truck and sold her to a young cowboy that wanted to take it off-roading and out to rodeos; giving her a new life. She deserved it.

.

For the last two weeks of training, our instructor brought us to the floor and we took live calls, under strict supervision. They let us test the waters prior to throwing us in head-first. I got partnered with a guy named Ken, whom I considered one of the brightest people on our team. We connected our headsets using a Y chord so we could listen to each other's mistakes.

Ken's had an inbound call, from a client seeking to do a payment. Ken handled it smoothly and professionally. *'Maybe this isn't so hard,'* he and I commented. I had an outbound call to Louisiana, and a woman answered the phone.

"I thought I told Y'all motherfuckers to stop callin' me on this gawddamn motherfuckin' phone!"

(click)

"Ouch. Sorry, man," Ken said
"That didn't go very well."
We laughed nervously.

.

I hit my stride at *Gerald's,* when I persuaded a woman shopping for $30 fashion earrings, to buy a $500 pair of diamond studs. Women desire that one piece of jewelry they believe will capture their beauty; an object they can covet. They rarely find it among the stores inventory, meaning considerable time is spent on the phones, combing the network of departments nationwide.

For Christmas, *Gerald's* gives its employees a credit card with an unspecified limit. I bought myself a bottle of Dior *Sauvage* cologne and a pair of Burberry sunglasses. I had misfortune with sunglasses - I set a limited edition pair of Chanel's on the furnace and melted them. The Ralph Lauren's Elena gave me got scratched when I tripped in a ditch picking flowers. The replacements got stolen. I guarded my Burberry's and made monthly payments.

I purchased, with cash, that silver and white Bulova watch I daydreamed about, and sized it myself.

In the jewelry bay, when I heard the alarm of the security gate closing, I reached safety. I could forget the outside world and do my job. I'd engage in studying gemstones and diamonds with our magnification lenses, like a meditative practice. The jewelry counter put a physical barrier between people and me, save for the gals I worked with. They had no idea, the extent to which their kindness helped me.

.

Hetty and Aidan visited us for the holidays, bouncing from our place and Elena's parent's house. They loved our apartment, especially the loft we'd converted into a movie theater for them. I had my old Mac computer up there, so the kids could lounge on a bed of pillows and blankets, to watch cartoons.

Jack was delighted to see Hetty; they palled around like old times. The kids provided a welcome breath of fresh air, helping us to rediscover the goals we fought for.

Hetty and Aidan were excited to see an animated film yet to be released in theaters. I managed to find an online torrent file for a screener copy of the entire movie, with crystal clear image quality. I downloaded it and surprised them; I was pretty much their hero, for that. Elena and I set up the loft, and they had a blast.

"It's amazing what you did for them. They're so excited," Elena said, "Hetty's bragging to her friends she gets to see the movie. Not even their rich asshole father could've done that."

I got gratification listening to them, giggle at the show.

.

"What's one of your favorite songs?" I asked Hetty
"I don't know. I like a lot of songs," she replied
"Pick one."
"Pompeii!"
"Pompeii? By Bastille?"
"Yes, I think so!"
"Crazy! That's one of my favorite songs too!"
"No way!"
"It's true!"
"That is crazy!"
"What's another song you like?" I inquired
"Love Me Like You Do!" she announced
"Ellie Goulding, huh?"
"Do you like that song?"
"That's a total girl's song!"
"Yep!"
"Alright, me and you can listen to Bastille, and you can drive your mom wacky with Ellie Goulding. Deal?"
"Deal!"

.

Behind the home of Elena's parents, there lay a massive, sprawling field, yet to be developed. At its center, in the far distance, stood two gnarled, towering trees. After Elena got the kids dressed in their winter clothes, the four of us would trek through the snow to reach those trees, while Jack ran wild.
"Hetty, do you want to help my collect sticks? We can play fetch with Jack," I'd say
"Sure!"
Jack knew she couldn't throw too far, so he'd move in closer to accommodate her. I think Aidan liked the sensory experience of snow, though he got grouchy when his nose turned red and frigid.

.

I spoke with Hetty on another occasion.

"Loulou," Hetty began, with disappointment in her voice," My dad says you've known my mom for a long time and she moved to Idaho to be with you. He says you're not letting us be a family."

I masked the rage in me, keeping my voice level.

"Your dad said that? That I knew your mom before she moved to Idaho?"

"Yes," she answered

"He said I'm trying to take your mom away from you guys?"

"Yes."

"Honey, listen to me," I said

"Ok."

"Are you listening?"

"Yes."

"That's a lie. We want *more than anything* to have you and your brother live with us. But, your mom is *not* going back to your dad? Do you understand?"

"Yes, but why would my dad lie?"

"Because he's jealous your mom is so happy with me. Sometimes, anyway," I shrugged

"Ok," she said, smiling

.

I helped Hetty with her homework. We were alone. The assignment was to pick ten labeled items out of the fridge, so Hetty could write a grocery list and practice her spelling and penmanship.

"Alright, so we need ten things, eh?" I said opening the fridge.

"Yep!"

"Let's start with lemonade!" I set the jug on the table and supervised, while she began writing

"Let's get some veggies in there, like tomatoes!"

"Neat! And lettuce?"

"Sure."

She had a few errors that I guided her on, but she was a quick study.

"We should do some Asian food, yeah?" I suggested

"Yeah!"

"How about soy sauce and wasabi?"

"What's wasabi?"

"Do you like spicy food?"

"I love spicy food."

"Then you're gonna like wasabi. Maybe we'll try it. We should totally have you spell popsicles, though, then we can each have one after your homework."

"Awesome,"

"Do you want to mess with your teacher?" I laughed

"Yeah!"
"Perhaps we should have you write Worcestershire sauce."
"What is that?!"

That's when the memory hit me – the memory of my first text conversation with Hetty.

I grabbed a scrap piece of paper and placed it in front of her.
"Sweetie, can you do me a favor?"
"Sure, Loulou."
"I want you to try and spell a word for me."
"Ok."
"The word is 'maintenance.'"
"Whoa! That's a tough one!"
"I know it is. Do your best, honey. *Main-te-nance.* Sound it out."
"I'll try!"

She gave it a sincere effort yet didn't come close. That meant the phone had switched hands. The only person with Hetty when I initially texted her was Scott's mother. *She had pretended to be Hetty.* It made me sick. Nothing was sacred to these people.

.

The drinking escalated when the children left for California. I busily attended both jobs.

Two photographs caused conflicts.

Elena sent Scott a photo of me and her at the park, with the kids. I don't know why she did it, other than to get a reaction, by presenting us as a family. He didn't like Aidan holding my hand, though the real catalyst was Elena's visible engagement ring.
"What, are you fucking pregnant? Is that why you're marrying him?!" Scott said snidely

He demanded to know the date of our wedding and swore to ruin the ceremony. Elena and I hadn't chosen a time or place; we waited for our lives to be less complicated. I wondered if our marriage would happen, though Elena gave me assurances. She called me her husband, and referred to me as such, in the company of others.

Scott sent us pictures depicting the children as happy in his mansion. In one photo, a detail caught our eye - taken on the ground floor of his house. In the background, it unintentionally showed a hospital bed. We knew Scott had poor health and walked with a cane, but how sick was he, exactly? *Were his attacks the last throes of a desperate man?*

Scott employed five nannies to care for the children. One of which Elena knew, and they'd trade private information on Scott's activities - like the fact that he continually flew to Oregon for unknown treatment.

Death, it seemed, was the only way for this war to end.

.

Then, Elena got notified through legal channels, that Scott forged her signature on a life insurance policy. There weren't too many ways for me to interpret that act. Her parents and I decided it wasn't safe for Elena to be alone. We carpooled, and when I worked, she stayed with her mother. I kept vigil in parking lots, whenever we drove somewhere.

I recall a single day, when Scott texted or phoned Elena three-hundred-and-thirty-four times, switching from aggressive insults to self-pitying bullshit, *'Do you even have a heart?'* he'd plead. In the midst of so much potential violence, Elena couldn't resist instigating him further, speaking to him in a fashion she knew would get a rise. I repeatedly warned her of emotional outbursts.

Elena bragged to me that the United States would not grant her citizenship because she'd mouthed off to the wrong people. There was brief turmoil when it appeared the government wouldn't renew her Visa. Being ignorant of immigration laws, I didn't question when her parents paid $1500 to extend Elena's residence.

.

Scott's psychological abuse shifted from obsessive to poisonous when he offered Elena a $1.8 million home – on the condition she left me. He sent photos of the property to make the option real. She told him, no, and that made me proud. *Was it a testament to our love? How valuable could my companionship be?* He then offered a relative of Elena's $150,000 to talk her out of marriage. Scott attempted to buy Elena like an object, and decrease my worth in the process, by instilling doubt in her mind.

In the company of his lawyers, Scott watched my *Life Chronicles* videos. He complimented me, in a text to Elena, saying that I should've been in Hollywood. I thought that was cute - it's nice to hear from my fans.

In California, Aidan rebelled. He'd grab flower vases and send them shattering through windows and glass doors. He'd routinely change the passwords on Scott's computers, locking him out, or frying them altogether. *Good job, kid.*

Most dire, Scott convinced himself that my marriage to Elena was a plot to get access to the children's inheritance money. I wanted no part of it, and neither did Elena. We were willing to sign legal documents, stating we could not utilize their finances in any way, shape or form. Elena simply asked for custody. Nevertheless, I got viewed as a threat.

.

From January 1st thru March 12th I worked seventy-two days in a row, without a day off. The majority were double shifts scheduled at both jobs.

How did I justify that? I had obvious reasons - car payments, and the burden of rent and utilities. I had the moral obligation of supporting Elena, as she did for me when I moved to Boise. Though my unemployment spanned thirty days, not ten months as Elena's did.

Her parents brought us groceries and assisted Elena with her car payments. They talked of sending her to school. When Elena graduated, I planned to get a degree in floral design. Her parents offered to fund it, but I did not intend to use their money.

In hindsight, those justifications now read like excuses. I believe I didn't want the opportunity to think about my life. I immersed myself in tasks and duties, locked in a constant state of reaction – doing what needed to be done – to get results. I knew my body would collapse, quite literally, at some point – *and collapse it would.*

Ten years ago, I had an accident; I broke my right arm completely in half, fractured my spine and damaged a disc in my neck. After six months of physical therapy, I was able to move my arm, though I had severe nerve damage. Arthritis and calcification of my spine caused painful inflammation.

That incident is relevant to this story, because those months of non-stop activity made my injuries hurt like yesterday.

I'd been on painkillers for three years; I couldn't function without them. I sat at my desk popping pills throughout the day. They calmed my nerves enough to let me field the hundreds of angry phone calls. I'd clock out and head to *Gerald's*, then take more medication to cope with the physical demands of the job. I knew the narcotics would linger in my system long enough to get me home, where Elena would give me massages and wine. That's the cycle I buried myself in.

My doctor's hands got tied when government restrictions barred clinics from prescribing real medication. Instead, he put me on anti-inflammatories and sent me to a specialist. To abate the withdrawals, I rationed out my private stash. Working at *United Bank,* I finally had insurance, so I decided to address the problem.

The specialist succeeded where her contemporaries did not. She correctly diagnosed me, noting I had multiple unrelated elements. She detected a bone spur in my neck, whereas other physicians blamed arthritis for the pain. She also concluded the numbness in my arm was due to a cluster of pinched nerves in my elbow, which could get remedied with an operation.

.

On Sundays Elena attended church, a different one each week, struggling to find a service she approved of. She'd get upset, saying, *'The pastor barely spoke of the scriptures,'* or *'The congregation was so insincere.'* She wasn't able to find people that worshiped the way she did; they're faith didn't seem as strong. I don't think Elena believed in a forgiving God – she sought Old Testament.

I went to a church with Elena, for support, knowing she valued the experience. I wish she would've shown my own beliefs the same regard. Buddhism, and middle eastern philosophy, *massively* influenced my life, saved me in fact, from a bitter viewpoint of the world. Elena regarded those teachings as satanic in nature. I tried to integrate her beliefs that coincided with mine, for us to reach common ground.

What I *couldn't* reconcile was the hypocrisy of her system. She'd text me scriptures, begging me to read the Bible. *'We need to make God the center of our lives. We don't do things for man. We do them for God. We follow God's laws, not man's laws,'* Elena commanded daily.

Furthermore, Elena thrived on vanity. She *celebrated* man's creations; the luxury cars, the fashion, the liquor, the money, the status – yet when it came to *man's laws* – then, suddenly, God entered the picture, to supply a higher order and purpose. I found that contradictory, having witnessed her years spent in court battles. I saw that Elena was quite fond of man's laws. When she had no money left to fight, she'd say *'We need patience. It's in God's hands. I will sit back and watch my enemies fall.'*

If God *did* create this world, in its splendor and natural beauty, Elena vehemently disliked it. Elena had no communion with nature. She followed her strict vegan diet for health reasons, having no objection to animals being killed. Elena upheld man's vanity to God's grace in ways *that I* couldn't even forgive.

.

According to Elena, God continued to give her dreams. One of them, in particular, plagued her. In the dream, she and I are sleeping in bed. The walls were made of glass, and the room is slowly sinking underwater. The bed is shifting, and the headboard is dipping downwards. Elena tries to wake me, but I do not stir. The water pressure will soon shatter the glass, and we will drown.

She'd implore me, saying that, *'We need to make a pact and covenant with God.'* I'd explain to her that God had been the center of my life for the last seventeen years – though she would not listen. *Her* God wasn't the center of my life. I had to get on my knees and repeat a prayer with her, word for word. She cried throughout it. It meant nothing to me. I did it solely to appease her.

.

When Elena couldn't sleep she'd sit on the couch, watching the videos of televangelist preachers until dawn.

Our sex life turned into a disconcerting job. The spontaneity and passion we had, that flowed so naturally, had gone. I got pressured for sex from the moment I came home, and through the evening, just to wake in the morning to further sexual demands. My attraction to Elena had crumbled. I couldn't open myself to someone I didn't trust. It killed me to see Elena with such a lack of confidence. What happened to the vivacious woman to whom I fell in love?

"You know you can do things to me while I'm asleep, right?" Elena said, for the fourth time, "I'm all yours."
In each instance, I shunned her. I likened it to date rape, and I believe she got hurt by my rejection.

That didn't stop Elena from initiating sex with *me* while I slept. I'd wake up with her on top of me, and I'd tell her to stop. She'd get angry and move aggressively on me. I complied, not wanting her to get mad. Other mornings, I yelled at her to leave me be and dealt with the consequences.

.

Elena told me of a disturbing experience that occurred while she drove on the interstate; she claimed to have seen a demon walking along the asphalt.
"It was tall, and as I passed, it turned and looked at me," she said, "Its face was gnarled and twisted. The cars in front of me swerved to avoid it."

I believe that *she* believed a creature had been on the road that day. I had no explanation that *didn't* grieve me. Had her mind constructed a hallucination upon a real figure? What caught my ear was the remark that *other* cars had driven clear of it.

In the mornings, if I saw a quarter bottle of wine on the kitchen counter, I'd pound it straight from the container. I knew if Elena woke up and got that first taste, she'd buy more with the money I left for her. Or, she'd go to Mandy's house. The two of them brought out the worst in each other.

.

To beat rush hour, I cut work early one afternoon, at *United Bank.* The interstate was crowded, yet streaming fast. I glimpsed a girl in an older car, weaving through traffic at high speeds. She drove right past me, and I kept my eye on her, as she entered another lane, ducking out of sight.

Do you want to know the song was peaking on the radio?
'The Power of Love' by Huey Lewis and The News.

I nearly died listening to Huey Lewis and The News.

Suddenly, a cloud of smoke rose up in front of the cars ahead. The girl's car reappeared, driving backward, perpendicular to the street. She'd spun out of control, and four lanes of traffic were coming directly at her. She panicked and gunned it across the lanes - crashing head first into the concrete guardrail in an attempt to get clear. The van next to me, in the farthest right lane, slammed into the side of her car with such force it lifted it off the ground – *it landed on its side on top of the guardrail* – and began sliding the length of it, with sounds of metal getting destroyed.

In seconds, the vehicle in front of me slammed its breaks, and I swerved into the far right lane – *I was now driving parallel to the car shredding across the guardrail* – a few feet above me. Parts of the girl's car rained down onto my hood and windshield. For that brief moment, she and I were traveling at the same speed – until I floored it as her car flew off the rail – spinning in midair – and crashed to the street – *rolling back* into a new wave of oncoming traffic. Fortunately, they had the opportunity to brake.

I screeched to a halt and ran to her car. Liquid and fuel were spraying everywhere. Blood trickled on her forehead. I got her out of the car, and she ably stood on her own. No one got seriously injured.

I had gotten too good at dodging bullets – surely one had my name on it.

.

I had a mild allergic reaction to the anti-inflammatory my doctor prescribed. The second medication put me in the hospital. Fortunately, I swallowed it in Elena's company.

"Babe, there's something wrong," I said

"Sweetie, look at me. Your pupils are dilated," she said, concerned

"I can't understand my thoughts. I'm, it' so... I'm hallucinating."

"Oh, my gosh, Logan. Your skin is breaking out in hives. We need to get you to the hospital."

"My jaw keeps locking."

My hand-eye coordination faltered as I got my shoes on. Oxygen didn't seem to reach my lungs. My pulse rate got sporadic.

I don't remember Elena getting me to the car or the drive to the emergency room. In the lobby, I shouted to be seen. Soon, I laid on a gurney getting injections, while the doctors did a battery of tests. It's a blur, except for Elena holding my hand.

I went to work the next day, albeit reserved in my approach.

.

I had nightmares.

Jack and I were traversing a country road, in the middle of the night, with a thickly wooded forest on either side. We got nervous and walked faster than normal, sensing we might be in danger. Then, we heard a sinister cackle in the trees. That single voice grew to a multitude.

They taunted and harassed Jack, calling his name. He trembled and shrank in fear, at my feet. I screamed into the trees, full of rage, *'YOU FUCKING COWARDS! Come after ME! LEAVE MY DOG ALONE!'*

The heckling continued. I picked Jack up into my arms, and I ran. I ran as fast and as hard as I could. My lungs burned.

I woke up shaking and pulled Jack onto the bed with me. I told him I loved him. He licked my hand, and we both drifted to sleep. He and I entered another dream, where we encountered pure evil, in a large enclosed space, that resembled the dance floor of a cheap nightclub. The walls, ceiling, and floor were painted black. Rotating stage lights, shaped like globes partially embedded in the floor, projected thousands of tiny white letters onto the room's surfaces.

Every three seconds, the stage lights spun and locked in a different position, changing the arrangement of the letters. *Were the lights automated to be random, or did they have a pattern?* I didn't know. It was a puzzle gone berserk. I pressed against one wall, with Jack beside me.

On the opposite side of the room, half concealed in shadows, a demon stalked us. It appeared wraith-like; its shape undefined. It carried itself as if weakened or in pain. Perhaps it was starving. It voiced the gurgling sounds of sickness or disease. It paced back and forth, like a caged animal, yet it did not move nearer to us, even though it craved to. I rushed to discern the rules of the game. *Was there a way out of the room? Why wasn't the demon charging us?*

Jack growled and snarled, ready to fight, though holding his ground. Every three seconds, the thousands of white letters shifted with the movement of the lights. When they temporarily locked, the demon would stop pacing to study them. *It was connecting the letters into words.*

Suddenly, the demon found one within the puzzle, and an alarming sound echoed off the walls. The demon contorted and took a step forward, groaning and leering. It then resumed pacing.

Is this even a game – or are we trapped in here waiting to die? I searched around in the darkness. There had to be a more profound rule - something I missed. The alarm signaled; the demon having discovered another word. It drew closer to us. Jack started barking. *If I found a word, would it force the demon backward?*

I woke up and felt ill.

.

Then, Elena and I sustained the worst news.

A woman, in Scott's employ, had followed us for a period of five months. We were shocked. *Five months?* Who was she? How could we not notice her for that duration? We racked our brains trying to visualize *just one* face we'd seen in several locations.

Elena's lawyers stated that *she was willing to come forward and testify against Scott, for what he'd paid her to do.* Elena promised to keep me updated.

Roughly a month elapsed, and Elena hadn't mentioned anything of the woman. I brought it up, over a glass of wine. Elena became distant, then emotional.
"It's not going to happen," she said morosely
"Why?"
She shook her head and shut down.
"Why?" I asserted
"Logan, she's dead."
"...What?"

"The police found her body," Elena said, in tears
"Elena... What are you saying?"
"She's dead! Ok, she's dead! It's over."
Elena covered her face with her hands.

Silence. I did not comfort her.
We never spoke of it again.

Why didn't I push for information? I couldn't handle the confirmation that a woman may have died because of us.

It burned in my mind. Scott thought I aimed for the children's inheritance. If he *was* a dying man, trying to secure his family legacy, who knew what he was capable of? I'm talking about *millions* of dollars. In this world, people get shot over twenty bucks.

I prepared myself for the worst. I refused to get caught with my guard down. I had a navy green messenger bag that I filled with weapons. I carried it with me wherever I went. I kept a pair of brass knuckles in one pocket, and a switchblade in the other.

.

At 5:30 am, I left the house, driving to work in the pitch black.
There were no other cars on that long stretch of highway.

I played a song, turning it up loudly.
I took the car to 130mph.
I turned the headlights and interior light off.

I closed my eyes and kept them shut – for a full minute.
In that sixty seconds, I had to trust that I would not crash.

I kept them closed, accepting that if the car *did* crash, I would die.
I had to be willing to receive my death, with open arms.

I felt that I had an out of body experience, tearing through that void.

I opened my eyes to the surrounding darkness and paused for a moment.
I was still alive.

I fired the headlights on, their light taking my course, with determination.

At 6:00 am, only a handful of employees were inside the *United Bank* building. I locked my messenger bag in the trunk and walked through the parking lot. I held my face to the retina scanner. No matter how hungover or dilated your pupils, the machine managed to recognize you. I entered through the revolving door and nodded to the security guard. I held my security badge, embedded with holograms, up to a sensor, signaling the elevator. I checked my watch.

I exited onto the third floor and through a row of empty cubicles. The overhead lights were dim that early. As I approached my desk, I could see my teammates grasping at their coffee mugs.

"There he is!" Ken said, upon seeing me, "With forty-five seconds to spare!"

"That's how I roll, yo."

Tony shot me a look of exhaustion.

We logged in precisely at 6 am and then had five minutes to get our computer programs booted and running with a series of passwords that changed monthly. Then, we'd connect our headsets, check our signals and wait.

"How many days in a row is this for you, bud?" Tony asked me, as we listened to the static

"I'm not sure," I said, glancing at my calendar, "Sixty-three I think."

"Jesus, man," he sighed, shaking his head

"I don't know how you manage," he said, "The only way I'd do that to myself is if one of my kids died."

I didn't say anything, but his statement got me thinking. *How much pain was I not facing?*

I had typed notes, tacked to my cubicle walls, as visual reminders. A black and white photocopy of an Alex Grey painting hung to my right. Gemstones and mementos gathered on my desk, at the base of my monitor. My floral design books got stacked to my left; I studied them in-between calls.

Our team had diminished; only six of us remained, of the original twenty. The rest either quit, got fired, or transferred to larger portfolios having twenty-five to thirty people on board. The six of us held out, a tight-knit group, like renegades in the corner. In one month, we saved $1.5 million in accounts. That's legit. We were proud of ourselves, as we should've been.

Based on time zones, at that hour, our job consisted of waking up New Yorkers to push for money. That shift gave us the most resistance, but we were too seasoned to take no for an answer. We'd power through it, until the sun rose, filling the space with light, and waves of co-workers. We'd begin to receive calls spreading westward across the country, as the world came to attention.

I got the first call, at 6:09 am - that familiar beep in my left ear, as I signaled the others to get ready. Here they come.

"Thank you for calling Citibank, and my name is Logan. Can I start by getting the name on the account, please."

I pushed the mute button, "Fuck. I already failed this call, Tony."

"Why?"

"They're in Massachusetts."

"Ah, shit. Did you forget to tell 'em your personal ID number?"

"Yep. Hope they don't review," I laughed

Wake up, Logan.

The audio of every phone conversation got recorded, along with the video capture from our dual monitors. On a monthly basis, eight calls, amongst thousands, were randomly pulled by our team leader and reviewed (they consulted us individually). He'd bring me into his office, and we'd listen to the call, discussing what I could improve. It unsettled me to hear my voice like that. Six of my eight calls had to pass, for me to receive a financial incentive, and even then it wasn't a guarantee, as many factors went into the final decision.

When I received my first, and only, incentive check, I put it towards a paid vacation for Elena, Jack and I.

.

I bought a wedding ring. Why? I made a promise, to be there for Elena and the children, for better or worse. In spite of our problems, I still loved her, ignoring my resentment. I thought that by showing my commitment, she'd trust me and that an affirmation of love would somehow negate the chaos around us. I was a fool.

My mother got a plane ticket, for June, and Elena was excited to meet her. I think my hopes for her flying out were to harness as much positive energy and support as I could.

In finding the ring, I scoured the country for the ideal piece. The gals at the jewelry counter had plenty of advice, and I put the word out. Fortunately, Elena disliked diamonds, and most gemstones, except for black onyx. I declined roughly thirty rings, then I met a woman online, operating an estate sale in upper New York.

An elderly woman had passed, leaving an impressive collection of jewelry. Among the pieces was a black onyx eternity band, made in England in the early 1920's. It had a channel setting, with gorgeous engravings in the silver shank. Remarkably, the deceased woman had the same size hands as Elena. It wouldn't have been possible to resize.

When I clocked out for vacation on March 12th, with the realization that the seventy-two days had ended, I ran in the parking lot like an idiot. I didn't know what to do with myself. I rushed home, threw Jack and Elena in the car, and we left. I had reservations at a lodge up in Sun Valley, one of the wealthiest cities in Idaho. At that elevation, there was still snow on the ground, and the nights got chilly. Elena was keenly aware I had the wedding ring; there would be no surprise in that regard. But its design and history remained a mystery until I placed it in her hand. She loved it and felt honored to be its bearer.

Would our vacation put the wind back in our sails, and rediscover the love we shared for one another? After our stay in Sun Valley, we took a road trip, driving through Hailey, and spending a night in Twin Falls. We then drove East, to Pocatello, stopping at interesting shops, antique stores, and restaurants along the route. We did what we pleased, and relished it.

Upon our return to Boise, Elena got a job, which meant I could quit *Gerald's*. I cried, as I said goodbye to the gals. They gave me their best wishes. I'd miss them.

.

Elena and I had a romantic date downtown, in a German pub named *Prost*. It got cold, though spring was near. We drank our Germanic beer and stepped outside to share a cigarette. We huddled close to one another; absorbing each other's body heat.

I noticed Elena glaring at someone over my shoulder, and I turned my head. Three jocks were walking in our direction. The one in the center gave me an arrogant glance and cocked his head. I laced my fingers through the brass knuckles in my pocket. I repeated his gesture, nodding my head as if to say, *'You sure are tough, with three of you.'*

They scoffed at me as they entered the bar. Elena and I went home.

Later, Elena received a text from Scott.
It read, *"Did you have fun on your date at the German bar?"*

I reached my breaking point.

How did Scott anticipate where we'd be? I asked myself that, hate coiling inside me. We'd arrive at a location, and within minutes, *they'd be there. How does that sonofabitch know where we are?* That's when it struck me – I held the answer in my hand the whole time. *Was he was tracking Elena through the SIM card in her phone?*

.

Elena laid in bed; the sheets pulled up to her face. Tears stained her cheeks.

"I'm so disgusted with myself," she cried

"Why, love?" I asked, sitting beside her

"I want to burn all of my clothes. I'm so sick of the vanity."

I hadn't expected her to say that.

"Ok. Could donate or sell them? I'm sure they -"

"No. I don't want anyone else to absorb their negative energy," she said, cutting me off, "I want them destroyed. I want to burn them."

"Alright. If that's what you want, I'll help you."

I felt the woman I loved coming back to me. Could I reach her again? I knelt down and kissed her forehead.

"Do you want to have a cigarette?" I asked

"Sure."

We rested on the porch, our defenses lowered.

"Elena, can I ask you something?"

"Yes."

"Why have you told me so many times that you don't love me?"

She paused.

"Guilt," she said, with sadness in her voice

"For what?"

"...The children..."

Those words may have been the most important she ever said to me.

.

She and I were driving on Front street, with Elena was behind the wheel. A white truck came up on our bumper. Elena fixated on the rearview mirror.

"What do you see?" I asked

"Oh fuck!" she exclaimed

"What? Who is it?"

"It's Scott's sister! What the fuck is she doing here?"

I jerked around, as the truck cut into the next lane, edging alongside us.

"Motherfuckers!" I shouted, rolling my window down, "Who's the man driving?" I asked

Elena looked across my lap, "I don't know! I don't recognize him!"

She sounded the horn and flipped them off, as I reached out the window, *'Pull over!'* I screamed, pointing at the side lane. I felt for the knife in my pocket. The driver had a cap on, and Scott's sister cowered nervously.

I envisioned how it would unfold. When they parked and got out of the truck, I'd coax the driver to get within reach – then I'd stab him in the face repeatedly, with the blade concealed in my hand.

I *wanted* Scott's sister to run for it. I wanted to chase her down and open that bitches throat on the sidewalk. I wanted to spit on her dying body, as she bled out.

I *wanted* to wait for the police - so I could lay claim to the justice I had wrought.

They did not stop. As they sped off, I took a quick photo of their license plate instead.

.

I strolled by the chain link fence that divided the apartment complex from Ann Morrison Park. I was creating a flower arrangement for Elena, searching for a third primary color.

On the opposite side of the fence, I saw a patch of beautiful yellow flowers. I pushed my shears under the chain links, freeing my hands to get a better grip. My shoes had poor traction. I climbed up and jumped to the ground. I examined the flowers, wanting to pick the finest three. I loved how they smelled. I cut the flowers at a good length, and held them in my teeth, as I got ready to scale the fence. At the top, my foot slipped, and I fell – piercing my right forearm on the sharp points of the fencing, and tearing my skin.

I had four lacerations and a gouged vein. The nerve damage in that arm was so severe; I could barely feel it. I picked up my flowers, and shears, and headed to the apartment, bleeding badly.
"Logan, What did you do?!" Elena gasped
Her maternal side kicked in, and she cleaned the wound. I *did* feel the rubbing alcohol.
"Ouch. Ouchy. I got your birthday flowers, love."

.

For Elena's birthday, we invited Mandy for cocktails. Aside from the children and Elena's parents, Mandy was our only guest in the ten months we'd rented the apartment.

I made my specialty; whiskey, with muddled apricots, turbinado sugar, and vanilla syrup. I checked my Bulova watch as I started pouring the cocktails - 7:05 pm. *(In that minute, less than a mile from our home, a skirmish broke out on Myrtle street, amongst a group of transients. One of the men, nicknamed Zeek, ran from the police, and later arrested in the lobby of a hotel.)*

I'd learned to put distance between Elena's drinks, as it lessened the chance of her getting confrontational. She and Mandy did what I assumed – sit on the porch and debate upsetting affairs.

When Mandy had to go, Elena promised to drop her off, and head straight home. I should've driven her myself. Hours passed. Without Elena, I thought about my life, and events I allowed to happen. Actions that I allowed to happen. Consequences. Mandy didn't care if Elena drove intoxicated, nor did she care about the resulting drama. I, of course, enabled it myself, and just because we'd avoided consequences, didn't mean they weren't real. If Elena got a DUI, her custody battle and visitation rights would get lost. With a felony, she may even get deported. What would a crime to for her Visa?

I got sick of the irresponsibility, convincing myself that *'If only I do this'* or *'If only I do that,'* then things may get easier, or at least be sensical. We'd win, and get the life we craved.

I finally understood that the behavior wasn't going to change. The problems wouldn't stop, and I felt ashamed of myself for ever thinking they would.

.

June 3rd - I came home with two bottles of wine. Elena's car wasn't in her assigned parking; she had to be with Mandy. I walked Jack, then uncorked one of the bottles and poured myself a glass.

Elena opened the front door, tears streaming off her face, and leaned against the refrigerator for support.
"Elena, what's wrong?" I asked
"Scott," she cried, holding on to me
"What did he do?"
She was hyperventilating, *"He's going to take my children away unless I leave you."*
I listened carefully.
She continued, "He says I can never talk to my parents again! I have to come back to him, or he'll take my children away!" she sobbed, "And that I have to get rid of you forever."
"Those were his exact words? *That you have to get rid of me forever?"*
"Yes."

I placed my hands on either side of Elena's head, forcing her to make eye contact, instead of averting her eyes.

"Do you not understand how great this is?" I replied

"What are you talking about?" she said in confusion

"He's playing his last card, Elena. He's desperate."

"He's going to take my children!"

"No, he isn't. He can't. You're both missing the point."

"What?"

"The kids are almost old enough to decide for themselves who they live with, *and they'll choose you.*"

"No. I have to leave. I have to go to him."

"It's smoke, Elena."

"I have to go to him."

I could not reach her and got frustrated, "So, you're going to sell your parents and me up the river, out of fear. The people who love you and take care of you?"

"I have to go! He's going to take my children!"

"It's a fucking trap, Elena! He knows how you'll react."

"I'm leaving."

"Have you told your parents this yet?"

"No."

"Of course not. So fuck the rest of us, and how your choices affect us?"

Elena entered the walk-in closet and started grabbing clothes. I knew this routine. I went to my side of the closet and grabbed a shirt and shoes.

"Running off again?" I asked dryly, "Am I supposed to chase you this time? I wouldn't want you to be offended."

"Leave me alone!"

"Make sure you pick the right pair of $500 shoes."

"If you have such a problem with me, we shouldn't be together, then!"

"There's the catchphrase! *My god,* I could time your statements on a watch. This is boring."

"Fuck you! Stay away from me."

I went into the kitchen and saw her car keys on the counter – she'd had far too much alcohol. *No,* I thought. *This stops now.* I shifted gears. I rested my elbows on the counter, the keys in front of me, while she gathered her things. The front door was behind me, to my left.

"I'm fucking done with you!" she muttered, storming towards the door

"You're not going anywhere," I said flatly

"Yes, I am!" she screamed, snatching the keys

I reached out and harshly grabbed her upper arm. I ripped the keys out of her hand and shoved them in my pocket, *'Now what?'*

"I'm leaving anyway!"

Once again, Elena went for the door, with my hand still gripping her arm. I jerked her from it. She flailed, and I didn't feel like getting hit, so I sent her backward – *right onto that big fluffy fancy fucking couch.*

"If you want to act like a fucking child I'm going to treat you like one, Elena. You're fuckin' drunk, and you ARE staying. You *will* deal with this problem. *Who the fuck raised you?"*

She shot up off the couch and retreated to the bedroom.

"Keep on writing those checks, Elena."

She rifled through her purse and grabbed her phone - I yanked that from her, too.

"Yeah?" I continued, "Gonna call your lawyers? Gonna call Scott? Who are you going to hide behind, Elena? Who are you gonna pay to clean up your fuckin' mess this time?"

"You're a fucking asshole! Give me my phone!"

"No. I refuse. People's lives are not toys for you to play with! You think you can say and do whatever you want whenever you want to do it. You're a spoiled little bitch!"

"Then why do you stay with me?!"

"I have NEVER, said that I'd leave you, or give up on you, despite your accusations! I've *never* said I was going to leave you, *but I'm saying it now.* I give up on you, Elena. You're a fuckin' joke. Scott can have your sorry ass. I'm fucking done. I'm not going to live like this. You two fucks are made for each other. You're both a couple of bitches that like to hide!"

Physical rage swelled in me, "I'm going upstairs. Leave me the fuck alone."

"Why?" she demanded

"Because I'm *this fucking close* to hitting you," I said, holding my fist to her face

"You asshole! I know Scott's verbally abusive, but he'd never hit me!"

"No, he'd just have you killed, you stupid bitch."

I stormed up the staircase to the loft. Elena barged up.

"You're pathetic," she said in a guttural tone, "You're a cowardly piece of shit! I can't believe I ever loved you! You think you can talk to me like this? Do you know how many men would want to be with me? Give me my keys!"

"No. you get your keys when you sober up, and how dare you call me a coward when our entire fucking relationship is structured on *your* fears!"

She berated me, and I went downstairs. I poured another glass of wine. Elena picked up the bottle and emptied it into her own. The profanity continued. The same vicious words and recycled arguments.

There comes the point in a fight, when the participants either remove themselves from the company of one another, or they give up, worn out by repeated information. Our resolve had gone. In the living room, Elena gave up. So did I. We both cried. I sat on the floor. So did she. There was no reason to push it further – the raw damage laid us bare.

"I can't live like this anymore," I said, "I'm done."

I threw her keys on the kitchen counter.

"Fuck it. You're sober enough. If you want to leave, leave," I said defeated, "I'm tired of looking at you."

Elena did not go.

She and I had no desire to be awake, and solemnly went to bed, facing the pain of tomorrow with exhaustion.

My alarm chimed at 5:00 am, for an early shift, though I didn't need it; I couldn't sleep. Elena watched me as I got dressed.

"Can I have my phone back, please?" she asked

"I gave it to you."

"I don't have it."

"I put it on the counter by your keys last night. I'll get it."

I handed it to her while she lay under the covers.

"When I get home we'll talk, alright?"

"Ok."

"I'm sorry, Elena."

"Me too."

I kissed her forehead and left with a heavy heart.

.

When I returned, Elena had gone; presumably to Mandy's. I stretched on that fucking couch with Jack. I thought of the words I'd said, and maybe I'm a cold person because it felt empowering to stand up for myself. I rarely did in our relationship. That, however, didn't make it acceptable.

Elena opened the door calmly. She straddled me and placed her hands on my chest. We stared into each other's eyes.

"I don't want to be scared to come home to you," she said

"I've been scared of you for over a year, Elena."

"What do you mean?"

"I never know when you're going to end our relationship. I can't build anything with you."

Elena said nothing

"Are you sorry for last night?" I asked

"Yes."

"Well, I'm sorry for the things I said to you. We're both wrong. How did we get that vicious? We have to make sure that never happens again."

"You're right."

Based on her subsequent actions, Elena intended to remain in Idaho. The lease on the apartment expired in a month, and we toured rentals together and talked of the future. In my mind, though, I wondered if I could afford an apartment on my own.

In the week following our cruel argument, Elena often encouraged me, as if she had a newfound commitment. Oddly, she became supportive of my animated movie and strove to help me complete it, as did her parents.

I got sick and rested in bed. Elena nestled up next to me; her breath warmed my neck.
She spoke to me.
"I used to believe in you," she said, peacefully, as if saying goodnight
"What?" I asked, "You mean you *still* believe in me, right?"
"No..." she whispered, "...Past tense..." and fell asleep

I can't tell you how much that hurt.

Imagine my hesitation, picking my mother up at the airport, two days later.

She welcomed Elena with open arms, *'Let's have fun!'* she said. I sincerely hoped that bringing our families together would prove beneficial.

Elena cooked a homemade meal; pasta with shelled clams on the side, in a white wine sauce. I said grace, thanking God for being able to share a meal with the two most important women in my life.

We picked music videos and shared stories. Elena had solid job leads, on top of her ambition to attend college. The way she spoke, it seemed as though she intended to work two jobs *and* go to school. My mother and I inferred that was logistically impossible. Elena didn't like that.

I joined Elena on the porch, without my mother. When the door closed, Elena immediately said how rude our comment had been.
"Elena, there are not that many hours in a day. It wasn't an insult. Grow up."
"I want to be a yuppie again," she said
"I'm sorry?"
"I miss being a yuppie."
"Elena, where I come from that's not a goal you aspire to."

"Why? What does it mean?"

"Assholes who get everything handed to them, and don't appreciate any of it. People who flaunt their financial status. I have no interest in that."

She grimaced.

.

The three of us enjoyed a nice afternoon at a vineyard, far out in the country, chatting over a wine tasting. I hadn't seen my mother in four years, and it was good to catch up. We coordinated a visit with Elena's parents. During the drive, I asked Elena to stop, and cut flowers on the side of the road, for her mother.

When we arrived, Elena acted strangely. Her parent's welcomed us, and her father prepared a brunch. Our mothers engaged in an enjoyable conversation that I had high hopes for, yet Elena dodged in and out of the room, texting a woman whom she'd bad-mouthed for years. It became paramount that we attend her cookout. *How could that be more vital than our parents forming a bond?*

"We need to go. They're waiting for us," Elena said, pacing the floor

In that very moment, I knew my fate had been sealed. I knew it in my heart, and in my bones. Elena sought to get me out in the open, in a crowd, for a reason. Did I refuse to go, and prolong it until my mother got on a plane to Florida? Or, did I let it unfold, while she still could help me?

We left with Elena.

.

She ditched us at the cookout, leaving my mother and me to socialize with strangers. I poured us cocktails. The woman who owned the house, Rachel, had an upbeat personality and showed us her art projects. Why did Elena speak so negatively of her?

My mother got restless, and a few people she befriended asked her to join them at a bar around the corner. I told her I'd catch up. I overheard Elena outside, say, *'And then they told me I couldn't work and go to school. Can you believe that? Who does that?!'*

Elena flirted with a youth group teacher, wanting Aidan to spend time with him. When she left for another drink, I sat next to the man.

He smiled at me, and said to my face, *"Kid's are shit."*

"You know that woman you were talking to?" I asked

"Yeah, she's hot."

"That's my fiancee."

A pallor spread on his face.

"Listen to me," I said, "You *will never* go anywhere *near* that woman's children, do you understand me, you fuck?"

He nodded his head.

I found Elena, in the garage.

"Elena, let's go."

"Where's your mom?"

"At the bar."

"What, she left us?"

"Yes. She can go where she pleases."

"Let me get Mandy, and we'll go pick her up."

"Fine."

The bar was unfamiliar to me. *Where am I?* I looked at the sign - *Jim's Alibi.* My mother sat at a large outdoor table, with the people from the cookout. Elena ordered drinks with Mandy and gave me the cold shoulder.

"You can finish your vacation without me," Elena said, "I don't like your mother. She's a bitch."

I ripped the drink out of her hand and threw it on the ground.

"You've had enough, Elena. For this life and the next."

Mandy glared at me with disgust, and I gave her the most insincere of smiles as if to say, *'Thank you for the joy you bring to us. Fuck off.'*

They exited, cursing me – or so I thought.

I joined the table with my mother and told her what had transpired, and I cried a bit. A woman got up and hugged me.

"I think that bitches high heels are on a bit too tight," she said, "You're better than that, sweetie."

I laughed, feeling somewhat gratified, "Thanks. Yes, I am."

The kind woman took her seat.

"I'm still here you asshole!" I suddenly heard Elena in my right ear. She'd eavesdropped on us, from an obscured table. I shot up, as she retreated. I shouted at her, aware of the bouncer to my right.

"We are DONE! We are DONE!" Elena screamed

Her words echoed inside my head.

Mandy got in my mother's face and called her a bitch. I wasn't going to accept that. I pulled Mandy away, saying *'Please stop.'* In seconds, the bouncer shoved me so hard from behind I got whiplash. I spun, confused, and he shoved me again, yelling *'Get the fuck out!'* I stumbled, and he lifted me off the ground and slammed me against a brick wall, marking my leg with a permanent scar. He dragged me to the parking lot.

"Yeah, you're a real big man!" I said, "Go protect your little piece of shit bar. Scumbag."

I spat at his feet.

Elena tried to steal my cell phone, snatching it off the table until my mother forced her to give it up *(The relevance of that act I didn't initially catch)*.

I walked to a gas station with my mother, and fell apart inside the store, in shock of the monumental disaster. She called a cab to the apartment. We wondered if Elena might storm in. My mother slept on the couch.

The next morning I drank beer rapidly; my nerves shot. I laid on the couch, while my mother fixed lunch. Jack, I believe, saw clearly. He placed himself on top of me, in a way he hadn't previously done. He buried his face in my neck. The warmth of his love radiated through me. I hugged him tightly; *so tightly*. He tried to bring me comfort, *'I love you, Jack. With all my heart.'*

When my phone rang, I knew that moment had to end. Jack seemed aware he might not see me again.

"Yes?" I said answering the phone

The number was coded. A woman's voice responded.

"Hello, I'm with the Boise Police Department. We're in the parking lot. Could we talk for a minute? We have a few questions."

"Yes. I'll be there."

"I'm coming with you," my mother said

"No... Stay here."

I left them and walked barefoot down the stairs, and into the parking lot. I squinted my eyes in the sunlight. The pavement got hot on my feet, and I stepped lightly. The lot was empty. I circled the building, realizing I was drunk. *It had to be questions about the bar,* I thought. *What else could it be?* I still saw no one. When I got to the stairwell, I anxiously looked down the street at three empty cop cars. *They must've had a hard time parking.*

I felt a presence behind me, or did I hear a radio or footsteps? I turned to see four police approaching me. I may have shaken their hands. The female officer, barely five-foot-one, spoke to me, and the three male officers casually leaned on trees or cars.

"We wanted to ask you a few questions about what happened at Jim's Alibi, last night," she said

"Ok. That's fine."

"What's your side of the story?"

"Story? My fiancee has a serious drinking problem, and she's getting self-destructive. Her and her friend Mandy we're insulting my mom, and I got afraid they were going to fight, so I separated them."

I glanced at the other officers, who focused on her rather than me. *Were they spectating?*

"Did you grab Mandy?" she asked

"I guess. Not really."

Goddamn me for stammering.

"Did you or didn't you?"

"Yeah, I mean I put my arm around her, but I didn't grab her."

"Can you show me where?"

I made a gesture to my waist. *Wait, Mandy's shorter than that.*

"Did you and Elena get in a fight in your home week ago?" she asked

"Uh, yeah we got in an argument. Like nine or ten days ago."

"What about?"

"Her ex-husband. He's following us and threatening to take her kids away. I got tired of being disrespected."

"Explain how she's disrespecting you."

My thoughts scattered. Were they questioning me in a crime?

"She talks of having kids one minute, and then gets drunk and acts like she doesn't care. Look, I don't understand, I thought we were talking about me breaking up a fight in a bar."

"We watched the video footage from the bar, and several witnesses said you attacked Mandy and put your arm around her neck."

Wait that doesn't make sense.

"I mean... I may have touched her shoulder. I didn't attack anybody."

"Have you ever gotten physical with Elena?"

"What? No. She tried to drive drunk, so I grabbed her and took her keys. I'd never hurt her. I've never hit anybody in my life. What was I supposed to do?"

"About what?"

"Taking her keys. What was I supposed to do? I'm asking you, from one person to another, what was I supposed to do? Let her leave?"

"You're supposed to call us."

"Why, so my fiancee can get a DUI? I let her leave when she was disturbed before, and she went around town causing problems."

"Has Elena ever been arrested?"

"No."

Why did I say that? She got arrested for a DUI in another state.

"Has Elena ever gotten physically aggressive with you?"

"No."

Wait, yes she has. Why am I defending her?

"Have you ever locked Elena in the closet?"

"I'm sorry? Of course not."

This has nothing to do with the bar.

"You two weren't in the closet during your fight last week?" she asked

"What? I mean, I went in there to grab a shirt I think..."

You're failing this, Logan.

"Did you push her or shove her?"

"I pulled her onto the couch."

"Is it possible she got injured? Did she hurt her head?"

Stop talking, Logan.

"I don't think so, no."

"Alright, I believe I've heard enough, Mr. Crannell. I'd like to thank you for being cool with me. At this time I am placing you under arrest for domestic battery."

I laughed, "Uh, ok."

I held my wrists out, willingly.

"Please put them behind your back."

"Sure."

I got led down the street, to their car. As we walked, she asked how I rated my relationship to Elena, on a scale of one-to-ten.

"When things are going well, I'd say an eight."

"How about the last few days?" she asked

"Fine. Look, Elena *has* gotten aggressive with me. You asked earlier, and I said no."

I could hear myself backtracking.

"Well, Mr. Crannell, you're not allowed to lock Elena in a closet, or throw her around the house, drag her by her hair, and you're definitely not allowed to strangle her."

"I have never done that."

"Well, Mandy testified to seeing several marks on her neck."

She lowered me into the vehicle, and I sat on the hard plastic bucket seat. They locked me in there for roughly fifteen minutes with the windows rolled up on a hot summer day, while the four of them had a conversation. I was already dehydrated prior to my arrest. I must've sweated out the alcohol, as I sobered up and recollected that she hadn't given my Miranda Rights.

I heard one of the males officers say to her, *'Don't you forget to read him his rights.'* She opened the door and pulled a booklet from her uniform; she didn't have them memorized. I read Miranda Rights three hundred times a day, at my job. There's a precise time for it, and yes, I hold the Boise Police Department to that same standard.

The female officer continued to ask me questions.

"Mr. Crannell, have you ever forced Elena to have sex with you?"

"What did you just say? Absolutely not."

"You've never done things to her in her sleep, or forced yourself on her?"

"I'm done answering questions. This is over. What happens next?"

"So you're no longer willing to cooperate, Mr. Crannell?"

"No, I'm not."

"You understand that what you're doing is wrong, don't you?" she said, "You can't perform violence upon women."

"That hurts. I grew up seeing violence like that, and I promised myself *never* do that to another person."

"But you *are* doing it," she said

Those were her exact words – 'You *are* doing it.'

3.

A D A
COUNTY

The police cruiser pulled into the empty parking garage of Ada County Jail. I could not hear my bare feet on the pavement, as I walked with the officer; just the echo of her boots and the shaking of keys. She opened the door to booking for me. My handcuffs were removed, and I got asked to take a seat.

There was a man to my left, standing behind a computer on a metal table. My arresting officer paused in the doorway, before exiting. She turned her face, and looked at me, as I looked up at her. *'Good luck, Logan,'* she said. There was an uncertainty in her voice that stuck with me.

The male officer began the intake process, asking me standard questions.
"Weight?"
"One hundred and twenty-three."
"Height?"
"five foot eleven."
"Hair color?"
"Brown."
"Eye color?"
"Brown."
"Do you have any tattoos or distinguishing marks?
"Um, I have a surgery scar on my right arm, and tattoos on my chest of boots becoming feet, and death riding a horse."
He gave me a tough stare, "So, no gang tattoos?"
"No, sir."
He handed me a small plastic receptacle.
"I'm going to have you put your personal effects in this container. Please remove any jewelry, rings, or piercings."
All I had was my mother's ring on a chain around my neck.
"I get this back, right?"
"Yes, sir."
I carefully refastened the chain to prevent the ring from getting lost and handed it to him, bitterly.

I remember being irritated by the booking procedures, thinking I'd be there so briefly. Whatever lies Elena told them, there was no evidence to support it. I figured someone of authority would ask for my version and conclude they had nothing to hold me on. If they did decide to charge me, my family would post the bail. I assumed it would be a small amount.

I prepared myself to be locked up for two days - at the most four. I thought that was reasonable, as no crime had taken place, other than the outburst at the bar, which was nothing but a public disturbance. I told myself to sit tight and be patient.

I got fingerprinted and photographed. The image of my face, along with a barcode and inmate number, was transposed onto a thick plastic bracelet secured to my wrist. They did not do a cavity search. I stripped in a private stall, as instructed, and put on a solid orange uniform with black Velcro shoes. I hated the way it fit me. I neatly folded my tailored jeans and button down Calvin Klein shirt and gave them to the officer, who put me in a holding cell and gave me a pamphlet on rape (stating what I should do if sexually assaulted).

Then, I got transferred to the Close Custody Unit. I did not know it was a holding tank strictly for violent inmates. I thought I'd be in that room for the duration, while the situation resolved itself. There were four, two-level, iron bunk beds. Three were empty, and I took the top corner bunk. The thin steel frame popped as I laid down, waking the man below me. It was a jolting sound; one we'd hear all day and night as we shifted our weight. The vinyl sleeping mats were uncomfortable, and it stuck to my skin when the sheets slipped.

I was in shock and disbelief, not consciously able to grasp the passing of time. Far more concerned for Jack's safety than my own, the first call to my mother focused on his rescue. She had put some money on my account, enabling me to make phone calls.

My mother attempted to get Jack and my belongings, but Elena barred her entrance into the apartment. So, she got a signed court order permitting her access, to which Elena also disobeyed. Mandy's mother, Caroline, became Elena's messenger, in a profound example of bad parenting. Caroline texted my mother saying they were taking Jack to the pound, where he'd be put to sleep.

My mother was staying at a cheap motel on State Street. She contacted Caroline saying, *'If you take that dog to the pound I will have you arrested!'* She ordered Elena and Caroline to bring Jack to her motel room immediately.

That night, at 10:30 pm, they drove to the motel and dumped Jack out of the car like a piece of trash. My mother wasn't notified and found Jack cowering in the parking lot. *When I heard this - I could taste the acid in the back of my throat.*

.

I spent the rest of the day on my bunk. There was a large pane of glass that looked out to the busy hallway. An officer had written each of our last names on the window with a black marker. From our perspectives, the names ran backward.

That got to me, psychologically. I was getting filed. Marked.

There was a metal dining table bolted to the floor. I often peered down upon it. It got painted a grayish-blue. Thousands of anxious hands had picked and scraped away at its finish. The areas of paint that remained on its surface looked like islands and continents on a world map of the insane.

.

In the morning, the staff gave us a bowl of oatmeal and an apple. I wasn't hungry and gave my meal away. I kept my apple, though, holding it in my hand for awhile. I liked it's bright red color; it was the only thing that seemed real. Later, I placed it at the center of the table.

I paid little attention to the other inmates. They were noise, except for the man in the bunk next to mine, named Mendoza. I appreciated how easy he made it look. He was cool as ice, but it wasn't for show; he had self-assurance.

I kept my eye on the window. When an officer transferred one of us, he'd erase the inmate's name from the pane. I did a double-take when I saw Elena walk by as if getting a guided tour; she was radiant, her hair cut short, like the night we met - as if she'd already dropped the last two years from memory. *It couldn't be*, I told myself. *Some woman had her image.*

.

That afternoon, I got scheduled in Video Court for my bail hearing. I wasn't sure of my actual charges and didn't know what the appointment entailed. I assumed I'd be brought to the courthouse downtown, though they merely walked me down the hall and put in a cage with a group of inmates. They called us alphabetically, and one by one, we were led through a narrow, unmarked door. From the sound of it, each inmate was shown leniency and received a bail reduction. I felt confident for my turn.

The room had no point of focus and bad lighting. I didn't know what to do, and the staff was irritable. A woman pointed at a chair, next to a shrewd man with glasses - he would be arguing for my bail. A microphone sat on the desk in front of me. There were two video monitors. One showed a live feed from the courtroom, aimed at the judge and a woman seated lower than him. In the other, I could see myself and the man next to me. I looked awful, and it got broadcast in the court, for the public to see.

After the formalities, the seated woman started the proceedings.

"The State of Idaho versus Logan James Crannell. The District Court of the County of Ada states that Logan James Crannell is accused by this information of the crimes of Count One, Attempted Strangulation, Felony. Count Two, Domestic Violence, Felony. Count Three, Kidnapping In The Second Degree, Felony. Count Four, Battery, Misdemeanor."

She went into detail.

"The crimes were committed as follows. Count One, that the defendant, Logan James Crannell, on or about the third day of June, in the County of Ada, State of Idaho, did willfully and unlawfully choke or attempt to strangle the person of Elena, by placing his hands on her neck and throat and applying pressure, and where Elena and the Defendant are household members or had a dating relationship."

Seeing my expression on the monitor for others to observe was disconcerting. I tried to compose myself, but I'm sure I failed.

"Count Two that Logan James Crannell used force and violence upon the person of Elena by grabbing her, throwing her around, and pushing her, and by committing said battery did inflict a traumatic injury upon the person of Elena, with a bump on her head and bruising on her body.

Count Three that Logan James Crannell did seize and confine Elena with the intent to cause her to be kept and detained against her will.

Count Four that Logan James Crannell used force and violence upon the person of Mandy by grabbing her and placing her in a chokehold. All of which is contrary to the form, force, and effect of the statute in such case and against the peace and dignity of the State of Idaho."

I was in a daze when the man initiated the argument for bail. The Judge asked for a recommendation. The man next to me snapped me out of it with a question,

"How much can you pay?" he asked abruptly

"$15,000," I said

I don't know why I chose that amount. I was fishing. I didn't have it, but I had to counter with something. *Cash?'* he asked sharply, covering the microphone as if that amount was unheard of. He put it to the Judge, who refused it and showed no remorse.

"Bail is set at $500,000," the Judge stated

As I rose from my chair, I felt punched in the stomach. Those were the court's words, and I had yet to read Elena's testimony. Little did I know it to be far worse.

.

The next thing I recall was speaking to my mother on the phone.

"I, uh... Had my bail hearing," I said numbly

"I know. I was there," she said, her voice pained

"What? How were you there?"

"I was at the courthouse downtown. I watched everything on the monitor. My god, Logan, she tore you to pieces. You were the only one that didn't get a reduction! What are they trying to do to you?"

"They're trying to bury me."

"Your dad and I are trying to find you the best attorney we can. Your aunt came up from Utah. She's staying with me at the motel with Jack. We have a consultation with an attorney tomorrow, and then I'm driving to Utah. I have to take a flight back to Florida from there."

"What about Jack?"

"I don't know. Your dad and aunt can't keep him. I don't know what to do."

.

When I hung up the phone, my hand shook like a leaf. The two names remaining on the window were Mendoza and Crannell. They'd be coming for us soon.

"Yo, I got bailed out while you had Video Court," Mendoza said

"Why are you still here?"

"They hit me with another charge as I walked out the door."

"Are you kidding? Did they keep your money?"

"You know it. That's how the cops do it in here. They wait 'til you're at the gate," Mendoza said, with a sly grin

"Fuck. I'm sorry to hear that. I don't think I'll have that problem, though."

"Why? What's up?"

"My bail is $500,000."

"Half a mil?" he asked quizzically, *"The fuck you do?"*

Mendoza and I got put in an iron cage and told to strip. Our new uniforms were orange with white stripes. Emblazoned on the back, in bold black letters, read 'ADA COUNTY JAIL'. They issued us a plastic crate, and a change of clothes including an orange sweater with lettering, a pair of rubber sandals, underwear, one pair of socks, and black Velcro sneakers. It got cold and wore my long sleeves.

The two of us were taken down a corridor, reaching a security gate that opened up to a small chamber. A medical office lay to our immediate left, along with a massive steel door to Cell Block 7. To my right, the entrance to Cell Block 8. That's where Mendoza and I were going.

"Gentlemen!" the officer belted out, "You are about to enter Cell Block 8! What separates this from the Maximum Security wing, is that even though you'll be living under the same security regulations, you'll be housed with medium security inmates! The officers on duty will direct you to your new cells! You will see a yellow line painted clearly on the floor. Do not cross it! You will pick up your mattress and linens at the control desk! Do you have any questions?"

We did not. I looked to Mendoza, trying to find some consolation in his body language and calm demeanor – but his eyes were darting back and forth. There was panic there. We heard a thundering mechanical sound in the walls, as the steel door rumbled open to the general population. The air changed instantly. Dozens of inmates walked the main floor. Immediately came the jeers and cat-calls, most directed at me. It's incredible how fast my problems from the outside world disappeared - at the flick of a switch, Cell Block 8 became my reality.

"Crannell! You're in cell 821, Bunk 1! Drop off your crate and come get your mattress!" said an officer at the desk

I saw a light on in the open cell - second to last, on the left side of the block. I kept my head down and moved forward. When I reached it, a man was standing inside - a Mexican, stout, and marked with gang tattoos. He stirred a cup of coffee with a plastic spoon and wore a rosary. He commanded an authority altogether different from the guards. He got right in my face and pointed his finger at my forehead.

"You better not be in here on some domestic or kid shit, motherfucker!"

I clenched my jaw. He didn't give me a chance to respond before he brushed past me to the main floor. My eyes followed him.

I dropped my plastic crate and knelt on my knees. I put the palms of my hands on the concrete floor. It grounded me, to touch something real and familiar. A man stuck his head in the cell and yelled, *'Hey new guy, you've got you're sweater on backwards. The letters face back!'* I stared up at him as he laughed and walked off. *'Goddammit, Logan, get your shit together. Get it together. Do not fuck this up!'* I cursed at myself, my palms still firmly planted on the cold concrete. I tried to regulate my breathing.

If they believe these bullshit charges, I'm done in here. Be smart, Logan. Be smart. I collected myself, fixed my sweater, and stepped out to the floor. I went to the control desk and picked up my mattress and bedroll. I dropped them off in my cell, as I sized people up. I sat by inmates playing a game of cards, and a thin man with glasses and an underbite glared at me.

"What are you in for?"

"I don't want to talk about it," I said, evasively, wishing I hadn't

"You better speak up, man. We need to know who the fuck we're living with, you know?"

"Domestic," I said, not elaborating. "You?"

I don't recall what he said, but I watched him go up to the Mexican man and say, *'Yo, you got a domestic.'* Fuck. I looked for someone who didn't appear interested in why I was here. I scanned the room and focused on the only black guy. He had kindness in his eyes. He was having a conversation, though I didn't need to hear his words - his composure and reserve said enough. I introduced myself during a pause. His name was Benjamin, and he invited me to have a seat at his table.

Benjamin read the other man's Discovery file (the papers sent by the prosecution containing police reports, witness testimonies, and photos. I didn't have mine yet). He gave the man advice, and explained general legalities to him, to which the man was grateful. He left, and Benjamin focused on me, not prying into my situation.

He asked me, "Would you like a cup of tea?"

"I don't have a cup," I said

"Sure you do. They wrap it up in your bedroll."

"Oh, ok. I didn't check it."

We walked to my cell. Benjamin was a large man, six-foot-three and two-hundred-fifty pounds. His eyes were big and saucer-shaped, complimented by a young smile. He had a tonal quality in his voice that relaxed me. The cell had two bunk beds. Mine was on the top left. I unrolled the linen bundle; two blankets, two sheets, two towels, one pillowcase (no pillow), one small plastic cup, and one plastic spork.

I turned to see Benjamin getting two tea bags from the plastic crate assigned to Bunk 3, on the top right. He was my cellmate, and I hadn't even known it. Maybe he paid closer attention to me than I thought.

"Make sure you get your hygiene supplies from the desk before lockdown. You're gonna be in here awhile," Benjamin advised

As we left the cell, I glanced back over my shoulder. I'd met two of them. Who had the fourth bunk?

I kept Benjamin talking, which wasn't hard. If he stayed engaged, no one would approach me. Above the control desk, the clock centered on the wall read 10:15 pm.

"Gentlemen, get your hot water and head to your cells, please! Be sure to close the door behind you!" an officer announced

.

The man occupying the bunk below mine came in last and shut the door. I saw him for a couple of minutes, then the lights went out. His name was Kyle Rory.

The cell had two fluorescent light strips, running parallel to our bunks. One hung roughly two and a half feet above the upper beds. At night, that one shut off entirely. The strip nearer the cell door dimmed drastically, serving as a sort of nightlight.

When my eyes adjusted, the three men were nothing more than silhouettes. Benjamin continued talking. The Mexican man, whose name was Alex, conversed with Kyle and ignored me. I coasted through that first night, without having to address questions that I, myself, didn't have the answers to.

I felt at odds with everything. From my top bunk, I saw the room and these people from a strange perspective, as if I were floating – my conscience escaping from my body. Or was that my pathetic attempt at a coping mechanism?

.

I prayed that night, with my face turned to the wall, blankets pulled over me. I don't know why I did, other than the sense of complete helplessness. Perhaps I was more familiar with Elena's beliefs than my own.

Please God, change her heart

Lord, her parent's know me to be a gentle person. They know this can't be right. God, guide them to help their daughter

Please God, give my parents clarity. I'm not the best son, but they know I haven't committed these acts. Please fight for me. Please help me

God, I'm lost in here. Please give me the strength to get through this. You've put me here for a reason, and I need you to help me see. The love inside of me is yours

Please God, change her heart

.

I fell asleep and had a symbolic dream.

Elena appeared before me, in a bright place. There were pillars in the background, like old Roman architecture. Elena wore a flowing dress. She danced, as if intoxicated by the gentle wind encircling her, aloof as if the gravity of what she'd done meant nothing. She tilted her head to one side and giggled, then leaned over and kissed me, 'I forgive you,' she said softly. Her anger had gone, and it was a kiss goodbye. In the dream, my body and mind understood that I would be released and that I was going home.

Suddenly, the overhead fluorescent strips blasted on in the cell. I had believed the dream, wholeheartedly. I laid there, glaring up at that light, so close to my face, alerting me to this cold death. Its loud hum burrowed itself into my mind. *Was it really going to end like this?*

The lights came on at 4 am, as they would every morning. I waited for something to happen. Nothing did. I drifted back to sleep. At 5:45 am, the cell door opened with a loud, jarring bang – like a gun popping off. The sound ricocheted off every surface. My three cellmates jumped to their feet, and within fifteen seconds, were out the door.

Breakfast got served. I heard the inmates forming a line, and one by one they stated their last name and cell number. I had a hard time waking up. *'Last call!'* shouted the officer. I wondered if it was mandatory to attend. I put my shoes on and walked out to the main floor.
"Where were you when I said the last call, Crannell?" the officer questioned
"Sorry, I just woke up."
"You have to be quicker than that. The food trolley is gone. You'll have to wait for lunch."

I went to my bunk, to get warm. They had us on a strict schedule, though I wasn't paying much attention to it, yet. I sat there and studied the cell.

The sink and toilet combined into one appliance. The water from the sink went down a pipe that drained into the toilet, which, I learned, could only be flushed every five minutes. A piece of polished metal drilled to the wall worked as a mirror.

The floors were smooth, stained concrete. The walls stood twelve cinder blocks high covered with thick white paint. The cell number was stenciled on the back wall, in a forest green, along with the bunk numbers - either ½ or ¾. A thick sheet of metal protruding from the wall, near the toilet, served as a writing desk, with a stool bolted to the floor in front of it. There were four fixtures on the wall that we could hang clothes or towels on. The smooth metal knob moved like a joystick in all directions. I couldn't figure why they designed it that way.

The cell door was solid steel, except for a window, a bit wider than my hand. Below that, a slot used for food trays, exchanging of paperwork, linens, and if it came down to it, the firing of tear gas or projectiles. On the wall beside the door was a red emergency button that deployed officers to the cell.

I walked, one foot in front of the other, measuring the length of the space. Roughly eighteen feet long, by ten feet wide, with a four-foot distance separating the bunks, which took up a lot of the floor.

The jail supplied us with a small bottle of citrus hand soap that doubled as shampoo. Also, a short tube of clear gel toothpaste, a stick of deodorant, and a two-inch toothbrush. If we wanted more than that, it could be ordered off the commissary list.

.

Thirty minutes for breakfast passed, and we were put on lockdown. My cellmates went to sleep, and I figured we might be in for a while, though an hour later two officers loudly entered the cell.
"Morning gentlemen! Please stand for headcount!" one of them shouted
My cellmates hopped up to attention and stood at the foot of their bunks. I awkwardly followed suit. I was incoherent, until the hard impact of jumping barefoot off the bed jolted me. The sharp pain shot up my ankles.
"Name and bunk number, please!" they ordered
"Uh, Crannell. Bunk 1."
"Rory! 2!"
"Douglas! 3!"
"Ramirez! 4!"

The officers required us to stand, verifying we weren't injured.
"Thank you, gentlemen! Is everything working ok?" he asked, referring to the plumbing and fixtures
When they left, my cellmates returned to sleep. I tried to rest.

.

When the cell door opened for our thirty-minute lunch break, I was punctual, yet last in line. I said my last name and cell number, and the officer gave me four pieces of bread, two squeeze packets of peanut butter, two packets of jelly, two cookies and a packet of flavored vitamin C powder to mix with the tap water. I messily prepared a sandwich since we weren't allowed utensils to spread the PB&J.
I talked to Benjamin.
"When do they let us out again?" I asked

"We get our extended out time here in about three hours. That gets us outta lockdown for about two hours and fifteen minutes. That's our social time. That's when you wanna make your phone calls, or go out to the rec yard. Most of these fools just sit around and watch TV, though."

During that extended time, I studied the layout of Cell Block 8, the way I had done my cell.

Two officers manned the control desk, overseeing the activity on the main floor. Every fifteen minutes a buzzer sounded, and one of them walked the perimeter, briefly peering through the window slat of each door, performing a cell check. Two tiers of cells ran parallel to each other. Grated iron staircases on either side lead to the upper level. I counted the doors. *Twenty-two cells, four men to a cell. That's eighty-eight of us.*

The communal shower, located to the immediate left of the control desk, got concealed by a thick semi-transparent tarp. When it was unoccupied, I looked inside; a concrete bench stretched along the left wall. There were three thick pillars, with four shower heads spouting from each. Next to the shower entrance were private lockers, for prescribed medication, if we had any.

The television suspended from the 2nd tier landing. Closed captioning stayed on because the volume couldn't exceed a certain level. Below the TV they had a 'library' consisting of two shelves of books, beaten to hell. To the right of the bookcase was the hot water dispenser; essential, I'd find, for coffee and cooking.

To the left, a security door that led to what inmates referred to as *The Side Shoot*. It contained eight single-man cells, reserved for men in protective custody. *That makes ninety-six of us, then* (One cell, on the upper tier, actually held six bunks instead of four, bringing the total to ninety-eight inmates at full capacity).

Seven round steel tables checkered the main floor. A strip of seven payphones and two video chat terminals got stationed near one of the staircases. Twenty feet above the floor, three barred skylights were spaced evenly in the ceiling. The cell block itself was roughly one-hundred-twenty feet long, by fifty feet wide - though that may have been an over-estimate.

A schedule got taped to the wall, beside the hot water dispenser. I had no pen or paper, so I tried to memorize it. They released us in groups, called 'Walks,' one quarter at a time - meaning four Walks in total. I was on Walk 2. The jail implemented a repeating four-day schedule that determined your Walk's out time.

They had us in maximum security lockdown *for twenty-hours-and-fifteen-minutes a day.* We had thirty minutes for breakfast, lunch, and dinner, and then our two-hour-and-fifteen-minute social time.

.

Communication with the outside was done electronically, through a service called Telmate. It was a piece of shit system. We got issued a personal six-digit passcode, required to make phone calls or to log on to the terminal for commissary orders and video chats. We had two separate accounts for people to put money on - the phone account and the trust fund for ordering supplies.

I called my mother.

'To continue in English – please press 1,' said the electronic female voice
'Please enter your six digit passcode followed by the # sign.'
'After the beep, please state your full name and facility – followed by the # sign.'
'If you'd like to make a call please press one. To report a problem, please press 2.'
'Please enter the ten digit phone number you'd like to call, followed by the # sign.'
'If this is a prepaid call – press 1. If this is a collect call – please press 2."
'You have (7 dollars and 34 cents) left to make this call.'
'Please wait while we connect your call.'
(45sec of bad music)

She answered.

'This is a call from 'Logan Crannell' *an inmate at Ada County Jail. This call may be recorded or monitored. If you do not wish to accept this call – please- hang up now.'*
'Thank you for using Telmate.'
(after a 10sec delay)

"They put me in general population," I said
"What? They told me they weren't going to do that! This is such bullshit!"
"You've got to get me out of here. What's going on? Can anyone bail me out?"
I shouldn't have put that kind of pressure on her. Even at the 10% required to bond me out - $50,000 - she didn't have that kind of money. No one did. I knew it was selfish of me to have asked it, and I stopped pushing for the issue.
"Is Jack ok?" I asked
"Yes. He's right here next to me. I had a meeting with an attorney this morning, and it went well. He thinks he can help. He's going to go there and visit with you."

"Good. Ok."
"Please call me after you speak with him."
"I'll try. My phone time is limited."

An officer at the desk called out, "Gentlemen! Five minutes until lockdown! Please wrap up your phone calls and get your hot water!"

"I have to go," I said
"Ok, I wanted to tell you a went to a restaurant for food, and Elena was there drinking with a friend. She ran when she saw me!"
We said our goodbyes. It consoled me, talking to her. I'd be counting on her every move, and time grew short. Her flight would be leaving in four days.

The second I hung up that phone, I was sealed off from the world. I'd be locked up, until the morning.

Mendoza, in the cell next to mine, checked on me, as we headed in.
"Yo, you doing alright in there?" he asked
"I think so. How about you?"
"It's all good, you know? Take care, bro. Catch ya tomorrow."

.

Kyle Rory, my bunkmate, was a dangerous man. In my life, I've met very few with an energy as dominating as his. A seven-time convicted felon, a self-proclaimed Odinist, and ranking member of the *Severely Violent Criminals* (SVC). His body got built in prison yards. He had a laugh borne from the pain of others, and he reveled in telling stories of the pain he'd caused.

Kyle had a close-cropped auburn red beard and shaven head. Six-foot-one and two hundred and fifteen pounds. His green cat-like eyes and long lashes were the only details that betrayed his masculinity. They'd get a hold of you, and search you out coldly. Kyle wanted to know what he could take from you.

I had the distinct feeling that Benjamin's presence in the cell somehow mitigated Kyle's actions - like there'd been an incident resulting in them coming to terms with one other, however superficial it may be. I got a similar vibe from Alex, who usually ignored us and spoke with Kyle.

The air vent in the wall blew straight outward at my bunk. I couldn't avoid it; cold air blew on me night and day.

"How does it feel to breathe in that disgusting recycled air?" Alex asked, "All of those farts and bacteria from diseased convicts. I guarantee you in five days your throat will swell up and you'll get a fucked up sinus infection. It happens to all of us. Your body gets used to it, though, and it goes away after about a week."

(Alex called it correctly - my throat swelled, and I felt awful. The jail nurse denied me antibiotics.)

Using the toilet in front of three men was humiliating; you don't fully adjust to it. We respected privacy in that regard, giving a heads up, so we had the chance to shift our gaze.

We cocooned ourselves in blankets at night. It blotted out the overbearing fluorescent lights, the cold drafts, and smells. The sound of restless cellmates. Many fashioned their pillowcases into headbands and used them as blindfolds to sleep. I didn't get a pillow; they were hard to come by, so I wrapped my second uniform in a towel.

I had no technique for making my bed. The sheets slid annoyingly off the vinyl mat, which was a foot shorter than the bunk itself, giving us a little room to put our things. I cluttered mine with paperwork, utensils and hygiene products.

.

I frantically searched my mind for *anyone* who'd be willing to take care of Jack - it's not easy without a contact list. *Who could I count on for that unknown duration?* I ruled out Idaho - Orrin had cats, and Tony's apartment didn't allow pets. I thought of Utah, and people I used to know. Then it hit me – three years ago, my ex-wife and I went on vacation and left Jack in the care of a vet tech named Matt. He mentioned that if I ever found myself unable to care for Jack, he'd love to have him. I hoped that offer still stood.

In lockdown, I impatiently waited for the next out time. When the door fired open, I rushed to the phone, and alerted my mother to find Matt's number in my old phone. Thankfully, she delayed her flight.

.

Later that afternoon, I conversed with Ben. We stood in front of the bookshelf; I rummaged for a good book, and he was making a cup of coffee at the hot water dispenser.

"How old are you?" he inquired

"Thirty-six."

"Okay good. See, you gotta look at it like this. You're about halfway through your life, now. You can still *afford* to make mistakes. You're gonna get out of here, and keep on learning and living. You have a window of opportunity, you see? But me? *My window of opportunity is closing.* I'm fifty years old. I don't have another half to my life, 'cuz I don't see myself living to be a hundred, you know what I mean?"

"Yes, I do."

"I can't afford to keep making mistakes like this. Look around you," Ben gestured to the inmates on the floor, "Look at these kids. I can't be thinking like these jokers anymore. These knuckleheads. I can't do another ten years in a place like this. *I've got a newborn daughter I need to be raising out there.* If I mess up again, *that window is going to close on me,* you understand?

.

I sat at a table watching TV.

"Hey bro, mind if I sit here?" asked a tall, lumbering man with a clean-shaven head

"Not at all."

"They call me Wolf," he said, shaking my hand

He had a voice like a boxer, and he opened up to me. Wolf mentioned he was a satanist and I saw an elaborate tattoo of a pentagram on his chest. He confided that he was in a relationship with a Jehovah's Witness. He lamented over it and asked me if I'd be willing to read the letters she'd mailed to him. *'Uh, sure,'* I said. He went to his cell to retrieve them and handed me a thick envelope of folded papers. *How could I resist?*

The way she wrote and decorated the pages reminded me inexperienced love letters I got in high school. I had the impression she sought to convert him. Frankly, I think Wolf liked the attention, his level of self-awareness being broader than hers. She required a congregation to provide her with self-worth. I gave him my honest opinion, which he admired.

"Is anybody in here giving you a hard time?" he asked

"No, things are ok."

"You let me know. *I'll beat the living fuck out of 'em.* I always stand up for the little guy. You're my friend," he said, patting my shoulder coarsely

He seemed genuine, and I appreciated that.

Wolf had a scheduled video visit with the girl that night. He wanted me to see her, and I agreed. I thought it was great that two people of such wildly divergent beliefs were trying to co-exist.

.

"Crannell! You've got an attorney visit!" an officer announced

I got nervous, as I walked alone down a long, winding hallway. I reached the main control hub of the jail. Every automatic door in the building routed through that terminal.

"Last name?" the attendant asked

"Crannell. Attorney visit."

"Go through the metal detector to your left and approach the second door."

I'd failed to get a description of the man sent to represent me. I didn't know his age or nationality. I entered an area of private booths, with thick protective glass, and phones wired to the wall. The place was empty. I paced back and forth, worried I had the wrong location when an older man arrived through the visitor entrance.

He had strong features and chin length hair, slicked back. He dressed classy and understated. He motioned to a stall and picked up the phone with urgency. He had no case information at that point, meaning he came to get a read on me, and I to get a sense of him.

He clutched the phone and spoke into it with a seasoned voice as if he were telling me a secret. I had no idea where to put my energy. I was concerned about practical things, like my bills set up on autopay. If Elena still lived in the apartment, I vindictively wanted the power turned off.

"Absolutely not," he said, "Don't even think like that. You can't do anything to instigate her further. Besides, we need to know where she is. Right now, Elena wants to play the victim. She wants sympathy and attention. Well, I think it's bullshit. I don't believe in victims. You could punch me in the fucking nose, and I'm not going to call myself a victim. What I need to hear from you, *is how far do you think she'll go with this?"*

I thought earnestly and could not answer his question. We resolved to wait for my Discovery file. I wrote a list of personal belongings that I demanded Elena bring to his office, such as my external hard drives. He'd email her a subpoena.

Towards the end of our conversation, he said, '*You're not going to prison."*

He looked me in the eye when he said it. I held that comment with me, even if they were words of comfort.

My attorney brought me a few books and my skin medication. The jail wouldn't allow me to have them and put the items in my property.

One of my biggest fears was being cut off from my skin medication – and now I lived it. I couldn't wash my face without it. Soon, my skin would start badly peeling and cracking. I petitioned to see a doctor, by filling out a blue piece of paper called a medical 'Kite,' and put it in a mailbox by the control desk. Within twenty-four hours I'd get a response. Either an appointment got scheduled, or if they deemed my issue unworthy, a rejection letter would be sent to my cell.

They kept denying to see me.

.

I went out to the rec yard. I wanted to see the sky. They released us from cell block in groups of four and we walked that same winding hallway I'd traversed to see my attorney.

Outside, in the sunlight, I stood at the center of that empty concrete yard. The walls were twenty-five feet high, capped with three ascending rows of coiled razor wire. A chain-link fence divided the yard in half; the other side designated for Cell Block 7. There was a steel door at the far side, wide enough for large vehicles to pass through. It seemed forgotten.

I looked up at the sky; a storm was coming. Gray clouds concealed the sun, and light raindrops began to fall. A light breeze cut through and curled in the massive enclosed space. I felt in awe, witnessing so much power; I couldn't scale those walls, and I could not stop that storm. I let go of all control. I let it in.

I subtly joined the small group, walking laps around the perimeter. I spoke to no one. I saw Wolf at the far end of the yard, standing there like Frankenstein. He held a tiny insect in his hand, petting it. He didn't want someone to step on it, so he walked to the large steel door, and carefully placed the bug at the gap under the gate, pushing it to safety.

.

Benjamin told involved stories that lost me in their complexity. He was trying to work things out in his mind and used me as his sounding board. I'd occasionally nod in acknowledgment.

"Now Becky and Andre couldn't get the car to Virginia, because of what had happened the previous winter in Detroit, you hear?" Benjamin explained

"Sure."

"But by this time, I was in Los Angeles. I launched the record label with Markus, who I got introduced to by Andre's cousin David. But, David hadn't taken out the second mortgage on his house yet, you understand?"

"Right."

"So he got involved as a third party to the deals that Markus and I were forming along the west coast. I had come up from Miami in the car that I later gave to Becky after her son got arrested in Chicago. But none of that mattered, you see because the deal that I was solidifying with Dennis in LA would've taken care of the costs, *and helped Tabitha and me with the house we'd moved into in Sacramento, to raise our daughter.*"

Benjamin's thoughts kept circling to his newborn daughter as if she were the inevitable end of any path presented to him.

"I only held her once before I got arrested," he said, growing quiet

He trailed off, and I didn't know what to say. I gave him space. After a period of silence, he climbed off his bunk, walked across the cell, and hit the restricted panic button. Kyle, Alex and I exchanged looks with each other. We were to push that in the event of violence, and guards arrived prepared. When they saw no fight through the window, the door fired open.

"What's wrong with you?" the officer asked, annoyed

"I'm missin' my baby girl. My head ain't right. I need to be on my own."

"You know I can't just move you because you're having a hard time. Are you being threatened?"

"No, sir."

"Are you saying you're a danger to these guys or yourself? What are we talking about here?"

"I ain't saying anything like that! I don't want to have to hurt somebody!" Ben said angrily, "I'm missing my daughter, and I don't need to be bothering these guys with that. They don't need to be hearing it! They've got their own problems they're dealing with, and I want to be alone with mine."

The officer didn't want an escalation. He offered no promises to Benjamin, in regards to where he'd end up or for how long, but he obliged him. It was a sudden change, and I wished him well. Then, Ben rolled up his bunk and departed.

"Are you sad your boyfriends gone?" Alex inquired, with a smirk

"You like black dick, huh?" Kyle said, "Well, now you're stuck in here with us..."

Cookies on Cleveland

I told myself I was in an elevator, going up. When you're in an elevator with strangers, you don't feel the need to speak. You're waiting to reach your floor. With seemingly each minute that passed, Kyle pressured me to suck his cock, or at least touch it.

Kyle obsessed over his cock. In the shower, he'd take the position by the window, so everyone walking by would see it, as they got their bearings. His cock was his pride and joy. I hadn't taken a shower yet, and waited for my opportunity, wanting it to be empty. I needed my skin medication, regardless.

For now, Kyle tried to break me with his sick game.

I hate the smell of nervous sweat. It stunk up my uniform. The cheap deodorant we had didn't work, and I washed my clothes in the sink. To mess with me, Alex said it was our responsibility to keep our uniforms clean, and that we weren't issued new ones. I foolishly believed him, not knowing that every Saturday we were given a fresh pair, along with a clean bedroll (extra socks and underwear you had to buy off commissary for a high price).

Alex and Kyle passed a copy, back and forth, of Stephen Hunter's 'Dirty White Boys.' They got the idea to start calling me Richard, after the novel's character Richard Peed, a scrawny artistic type.

"I'll get it nice and juicy for you. *C'mon*, suck it, Richard! You know you want to. *Yes!* Can I fuck your tight little ass, Richard?" Kyle urged

"Do you like anal sex, Richard?" Alex asked

"I can come up there if you want, and fuck your mouth," Kyle said, "Or maybe I'll just yank you off that bunk by your ankles, while you're sleeping, and fuck you on the floor."

"When did you lose your virginity, Richard? We've been taking bets. Was it with a guy?" Alex inquired, "Are you going to hit the panic button, Richard?"

"If you do, you're gonna jerk me off first!" Kyle demanded, "Look down here, Richard! See how hard it is? Get on it!"

It never stopped. Kyle said each morning, *'I need you to suck my cock today. Are you ready right now?'* If Kyle took a nap during the day, which he frequently did, each time he woke, he'd pressure me further.

If I got emotional or retorted in some way, it fueled them to a higher level. I buried myself in cheap novels, trying to block their voices out of my head. I knew they'd get tired of not getting a reaction, *but where would it go from there?*

.

When the cell door opened and I could escape the confines of the cell, I felt free, even if I was in jail. An older man from our Walk approached me and asked how I got on in that cell.
"I'm struggling, man," I said
"I was a bit worried. That cell has the highest turnover rate on the block. Before you came in, Kyle and Alex were throwing people out left and right!"

I thought about that, as I ate my lunch.

I overheard Kyle bragging to a few inmates, over a card game.
"We've thrown seven people out of our cell, and the smallest guy has lasted the longest! He won't let me fuck him, though."
"Good for him," one of the men said

.

In lockdown, it didn't take long for the abuse to resume.
"When the lights go down tonight, you're getting fucked, Richard. I'm tired of playing games with you," Kyle stated
There was a pause, then I spoke, "You know what, Kyle? You're such a charming guy. Surely there's someone on this block willing to suck you off."
"Well, yeah, but it's only fun if they resist."
"Then fuck Alex. He's got some fight to him," I said, pointing in his direction
"I already have," Kyle said
"Fuck you, dude! Don't get near me!" Alex interjected. He didn't like that.

I'm going to pit these two shitheads against each other.

"I'm kidding," Kyle said, "I don't fuck Mexicans."
"I'm Mexican-Aztec, you motherfucker."
"Oh, ok. I'd hit that."

With each sexual remark aimed at me, I deflected it to Alex, "Tell you what, Kyle. Go ahead and fuck Alex now, and I'll see how I'm feeling after dinner. Maybe I'll help you rub one out."

"Why do you keep facing your ass to the wall, Alex?" Kyle joked

.

The water in our sink got lukewarm at best, no matter how often we primed the hot water button. Kyle forgot to get boiling water from the dispenser before final lockdown. I saw him take an empty potato chip bag and fill it with Ramen noodles and warm water, wrapping it tightly. The inside of the bag had a thin layer of aluminum that worked as a heat conductor to help cook the noodles. He put it under a blanket for fifteen minutes. *That was clever,* I thought.

I missed the Tuesday night cutoff time for my commissary order, so I went without supplies for a week. Kyle prepped a simple meal of beans, noodles, and tortillas. He shared it with us, and that showed me I had been marginally accepted.

The Cleveland Indians were playing The Chicago White Sox, in their first of three matches. During a game, the inmates in lockdown got updates from the Walk that currently had the floor and television access.

"I bet my cookies at tomorrow's lunch Cleveland wins!" Kyle shouted, through the crack in the cell door
 We had to be loud for our voices to carry. Kyle placed his bet with a man pulling for Chicago.

"You're on!" they hollered

"Check it out!" Kyle continued, holding the man's attention, "If Cleveland wins all three games, that means my charges are gonna get dropped!"

The man laughed, "Good fucking luck, bro!"

As Kyle stood at the door with his shirt off, I studied the 'SVC' tattoo across his back. The bold letters were as long as my forearm. Alex also had gang affiliations with *The Surenos*, who had allied with the *SVC*, to increase their numbers and influence.

Kyle had a sick gesture he'd do at the window. As people walked by, especially female officers, he'd curl his tongue like a serpent and snort like a hog as if he smelled them through the glass. It was evil as fuck, and he knew it, laughing defiantly afterward. Kyle worked like a shark. If he didn't smell blood, he moved on.

What *were* these two men charged with?

I decided to clear the air and talk about my case, what little I knew, without having Elena's testimony.

"So, honestly, what do you think the judge is going to do to me? I asked

"They're probably gonna give you a Rider. I can almost guarantee it," Kyle said

"What's that exactly?"

"You go to prison for six months, in a low-security section. They give you a bunch of classes and assess your behavior."

"It's the court's newest program to stop repeat offenders," Alex clarified, "But something like forty percent of 'em come back to prison, anyway. They set you up for failure. They want to keep you in the system to make money off you."

"They charged you with kidnapping?" Kyle said, beginning to question

"Yeah, for taking her car keys so she wouldn't drive drunk."

Alex and Kyle shot each other a glance of suspicion, though not regarding me.

"And she's saying you strangled her?" Alex asked, wanting to be sure he heard me right

"Yeah. Attempted, I guess. Whatever that means."

Kyle paced the cell as we discussed that, then extended his chest and bellowed, "FUCK THAT BITCH! *WHOOOOOOO!*" as if it were a release for him. His voice echoed and rang. He brushed off her power like it was nothing.

"What do *you* think they're going to do to you, Richard?" Alex asked

"I have to keep telling myself I'm going to walk out the front door, man."

My answer gave made him curious, "You really believe they're gonna let you walk on three felonies?"

As the night progressed, I inquired about the jail. The two of them weren't feeding me the usual misinformation to throw me off.

"What's up with the red shirts?" I said, standing at the window, "I see four inmates on the floor wearing a different colored uniform."

"They're workers. They serve food and keep the place clean. Whatever the deputies need 'em to do. It's a pretty sweet deal. They get extra food and get to sit around all day watching TV," Alex answered

"How do you get that position?"

"You put your name on a list. You should do it. Just talk to Whisper first. He runs the show out there. Oh, and they do haircuts once a week."

"I think I'll pass on these guys touching my hair."

"Probably for the best."

"If you want a razor to shave," Kyle mentioned, "You tell the deputy at headcount tonight, and they bring you one at 4 am."

"4 am? Damn. So, that's what these guards are? Deputies?"

"Yep."

I thought of signing up to be a Redshirt, but the idea of having to be cooperative with so many people didn't appeal to me. I liked giving my body a rest.

That's when it dawned on me – *I was still on my paid vacation.* I found great humor in that.

"What's so funny?" Alex asked

"I'm getting paid to be here," I said

"What?" he laughed

"I got arrested during a paid vacation."

They both laughed.

"So since you're getting paid, now will you suck my dick?" Kyle propositioned

"I'm not getting paid *that* much."

The conversation continued.

Alex had lost his seven-year-old daughter to an incurable illness. He carried that weight with him, in this place. The plastic rosary he wore could be purchased off commissary. A few inmates on other Walks wore them, and I wondered if they did so as a fashion statement. For Alex, I believe it held meaning.

His sentencing date was fourteen days out. He'd already done an inordinate amount of time for his offense, a misdemeanor drug possession and probation violation, and had hopes of going home.

"Methadone is the biggest fucking scam I've ever seen in my life," Alex stated, "This shit is way more addictive than heroin, and it takes months to withdraw from.

He detoxed through the worst period of it before my arrival. His feet ached, causing him to hobble when he walked. I imagine it hurt more than he let on. The jail administered methadone for the first two weeks of his incarceration, then weaned him off.

"What's fucked up, on the streets, is that if your prescribed dosage exceeds a certain amount, the detox facilities on the outside won't even treat you. It's one giant money machine."

Kyle got charged with armed robbery, to which he claimed innocence. I read his police report and had the inclination to believe him. Logistically, the cops were trying to put him in too many places at once, and for no good reason. Kyle spoke at length of his crimes; the things he'd done that suffered him no consequences. If anything, he felt insulted that the police accused him of such a poorly executed crime.

"I'd never pull off a robbery that sloppy," he said, "I don't own a gun like that."

Kyle's arrest was due to the testimony of a woman, who presumably pointed at him, to save herself from prison.

The previous night, I watched Kyle spread a towel on the ground, under the dim light shining through the window slat. He laid on it, chest down, and placed a notepad in front of him. He began writing. I drifted to sleep.

On this night, he read it aloud, and it was good lyrical prose, about the mountains up in Coeur d'Alene. He told us how he managed to get married, in the four months between his current lockup and his last stint in prison. He shared photographs of her; a pretty young girl, naively posing as sexy as she could.

.

We got on the subject of bad trips on psychedelics.
"I was in my house, partying with friends one night, and we were all tripping," Alex related to us, "They were all listening to music, having a good time and shit, but I kept getting this feeling like there was something outside my window. I got scared. So, I grabbed my gun and went out into the yard. I had this feeling like I was being watched. That's when I saw this tall figure by some trees..."
He paused, not wanting to continue. *"Have you ever seen the devil?* I did that night. I watched it spread its wings. I was fuckin' scared, bro. I brought my gun up and started shooting – BOOM! BOOM! BOOM! My friends came running outside and saw me freaking out in the yard. They grabbed me and pulled me back inside."

Kyle then told us his trip; the experience had reduced him to a writhing mass on his kitchen floor.
"I laid there, screaming at the top of my lungs and crying. It felt like days. My girl was there, taking care of me. She said I kept begging for forgiveness, but I didn't say from who. She put cold compresses on my head and forced me to drink water.

From what I heard, I suspected Alex had the ability to love himself and those nearest him. The demon he saw that night, like a terrifying outside force, came to take pieces of his life away.

Kyle, on the other hand, had the awareness that maybe *he was* the demon.

Without warning, the cell door flew open, catching us off guard. A deputy entered - a huge man, dwarfing Kyle in sheer girth. He had a bright blue flashlight attached to his shoulder.
"Rory! I've got an inmate coming in that needs a bottom bunk for health reasons. I'm moving you to Bunk 3," the deputy commanded
"Fuck that! I'm not taking a top bunk," Kyle responded
"Rory, stand up!"

Kyle complied, and the deputy stepped closer, backing him up against the wall to intimidate him. I lay on my bunk, propped up on my elbow, putting me at eye level with the two men, their faces right next to mine.

"I've told the doctors I can't do a top bunk because of a shoulder injury," Kyle said defiantly, "When I try to climb up there it dislocates my shoulder."

"It's not a request Rory, it's an order!" the deputy bore down on him

The light from the officer's torch lit Kyle's face from the bridge of his nose to his forehead, leaving the rest in shadow. Kyle instinctively turned his head and cast his eyes downward, as if bracing to get hit, and winced.

"I'll speak to the doctor about your medical records, Rory. I'll see what I can do. But for now, I need this bunk."

"Why does he have to be in *this* cell? Why can't you put him in a bottom bunk somewhere else?" Kyle argued

"It's the only bunk I have available."

"This is bullshit."

"Rory... Listen to me. If you want, I'll *find* you a bottom bunk. But, I can tell you right now it won't be on this Walk. Is that what you want? Do you want me to put you on a different Walk?"

"I don't want to go on a different Walk. I'm doing good for myself here."

I'll never forget the way Kyle said that. He had a vulnerability in his voice. *He wanted acceptance like the rest of us.*

"What you can't look me in the eye?" the deputy antagonized, *"Look me in the eye when I'm talking to you!"* Kyle shifted his eyes upward, his green eyes catching the light,

"So are you going to take the top bunk, Rory?"

"Yes."

Our new cellmate came; in his late fifties, arrested for performing a hate crime on a young Iraqi girl. In booking, he admitted to being drunk but didn't disclose his early stages of methadone withdrawal.

"Why didn't you tell 'em you were on methadone?" Alex implored

Having cleared the worst phase of his detox, Alex knew what this man, twice his age, was about to experience. He called the oncoming symptoms by the hour, predicting their intensity.

"I didn't want to tell 'em," the man gasped, short of breath, "I was afraid they'd give me another charge."

"Dude hit the button and tell them you need to go to medical. I'm fucking serious. You have no clue the *hell* you're going to go through. In the condition you're in, you could die. You need to leave. We don't want you in here."

The man was terrified, yet hesitant to hit the panic button. Kyle boiled; he didn't care to endure the man's plight and wanted his bottom bunk.

Hours dragged, and I could *feel* the man's misery below me. He convulsed and twisted in agony, making feeble, whimpering moans, *'Ooooh. God. It's bad,'* his breathing got labored. I couldn't block the sounds out of my head. None of us could. We each started in on him, putting so much fear in his heart he finally got up and pushed the button. When the officer arrived with backup, the man spoke of his condition. Within thirty minutes he went to medical.

.

I had a second vivid dream that night.

I was standing in the cell. Alex and Kyle were asleep; Kyle still on the top bunk and Alex below him. I heard a piece of music, floating over that image, which sounded vaguely like Preisner's *'Lacrimosa,'* dropped to half speed. That song came from a soundtrack that Aidan loved; as if my subconscious was trying to reconcile my being, by playing music that reminded me of happiness.

The whole dream moved in achingly slow motion. Alex and Kyle were awakened by a presence in the room, though it wasn't mine. It came from the direction of the cell door; a soft orange light that expanded as subtly as the sunrise.

Alex laid with his feet to the door. Above, Kyle faced the light head-first, his arms wrapped around his pillow. As they stirred, they looked into that radiating light, and a sense of genuine wonder filled their eyes. I watched the color drain from their tattoos, their meanings now lost. All of their inhibitions and grievances, defenses and failures, they all fell away, liberating their souls. The walls no longer held them.

.

I washed up in the empty communal shower, being careful not to get my face wet. The nozzle sprayed a fine mist, making the gelatinous soap difficult to rinse off – *but, the water was hot.* It felt amazing. I hurried to dry off when the deputy issued a five-minute warning for us to get in our housing. I put on a change of uniform and wore my dry sandals.

In the cell, Alex and Kyle were drinking coffee.
"Please tell me you kept your sandals on while you took a shower," Alex said
They both snickered.
"No. Why?" I said, then stopped myself
I'm an idiot.

"Do you have any idea how much cum and bacteria and disease is on that floor, man?" Alex mentioned, "That's why they *give you* the sandals in the first place."

"We call 'em sperm surfers," Kyle chimed

"Sorry guys, I'm gonna wash my feet in the sink," I said, as they continued laughing

I got desperate, sending three medical slips a day. I added ailments, like my rejection of the food costing me twelve pounds. That I was detoxing from alcohol and painkillers and had a lack of sleep from anxiety and depression.

They finally scheduled an appointment, and prescribed 25mg of Zoloft (which raised to 100mg). I got a generic petrolatum skin cream used for rashes. They were concerned with my weight loss and billed me for a milk supplement called *Boost*.

Aside from the standard 2400 calorie diet, the jail offered a vegan, kosher, or vegetarian menu. Also, a liquid diet for the sick. They insisted I stay on the regular meal, as it had the most calories. Ironically, it was basically vegan anyway, except the cake and bread. They didn't serve real meat, opting for textured vegetable protein.

In the chamber outside the medical office, I waited for the gate to open for Cell Block 8. The deputy who had custody of me spoke.

"Listen, are those boys in your cell giving you grief? Is that the reason you need the medication? I know those boys are trouble."

"No, sir. They're no problem. This is my first time in jail."

What a dickhead. He seriously thought I'd throw affiliated gang members under the bus? Or any inmate for that matter? There was a real possibility that I'd be going to prison with these men – a place with little protection.

I peered through the window to the massive Cell Block 7 - twice the size of Block 8. I got intimidated, seeing that much space. The jail sectioned off an area for sex offenders, separating them from the population. We'd only see them in the rec yard, through the chain-link fence lined with razor wire.

The Dorms were low-security housing for workers and inmates that had proven themselves not to be a threat. In that wing, they had privileges, like access to computer tablets, movies, music and a better commissary menu. In cell block, after a sixty-day probationary period, we'd be eligible to get reclassified and transferred.

.

Elena showed up unexpectedly at my attorney's office, catching us all off guard. She brought a few garbage bags of clothes, which my attorney politely helped her carry from the car. *'She was a complete wreck, Logan, sobbing uncontrollably,'* he told me on the phone.

"Is Logan going to be able to get out?" Elena asked

"No," he said, observing her, "He isn't, Elena. The bail is too high. These are serious charges."

He carefully pressed for more information, but she shut down and left in tears. The valuable items on the subpoena, such as my hard drives, were not included in the bags.

Did she seek to quit the fight? Did she feel powerless to stop what she'd set in motion? Her next move was in the air.

.

On nights when we had our extended out time from 8pm-10:15 pm, my Walk picked a movie on a cable network. I'd watched Stanley Kubrick's *'The Shining'* frequently in my life, and to a degree, the film had lost its impact. I imagined I understood what the story entailed - then I viewed it in a dimly lit room surrounded by convicts. *They got into it.* I also detected small details in the picture that I'd written off as continuity errors, when in fact they suggested another layer, based on dreams. I saw the movie in a new light.

Then an inmate brushed past me and whispered *'fuckboy'* in my ear.

Who threatened me? Our new cellmate - Chris, twenty-three-years old. A young member of the SVC, and friends with Kyle on the street. As soon as the door sealed behind him, Chris pulled a bag of drugs from his rectum.

Alex, in a panic, ran to block the window slat with his body, in case the deputies did their quarterly cell check. If drugs were found in the cell, we'd all receive charges. Alex planned to be released in less than two weeks, and I was pretty fucking keen on the idea myself.

Chris soaked the Oxycontin in water to dissolve the coating, then crushed it on top of the writing desk. He was so strung out he couldn't focus on the task, getting distracted by his conversation with Kyle. Agonizing minutes ticked by, while Alex kept vigil, *'The guards are starting the rounds, guys. Hurry the fuck up.'* Alex and I exchanged glances with each other. *This is insane.* When the deputies were two doors away on the row, Chris covered the pills with a sheet of paper, while they passed.

The two of them wouldn't stop talking, so I interrupted. Kyle, leaning on the wall, looked at me.

"Hey, Kyle. Why don't you help your buddy out, man? He seems to be struggling."

Kyle immediately snapped to attention, feeling embarrassed for not aiding Chris sooner.

"Yeah, you need a hand with that?"

"Uh, sure man, thanks," Chris said, monotone

Alex and I were glad to have Kyle in charge. He prepped the powder, and the two of them got high. The evidence was gone.

.

Whatever progress I'd achieved with Kyle disappeared, thanks to gang mentality. He and Chris threw their power around to impress each other, and they got malicious. Kyle punched the bottom of my bunk hard enough to pop the steel, jarring me awake to fuck with my nerves. He and Chris proceeded to mock me, in the style of the novel *Dirty White Boys*.

"Reeee—chard.....   RICH-urd...." Kyle leered

Chris joining in, "Riiichard. Fuckboy – Richarrrrd...."

They didn't let up.

Was I supposed to endure this abuse? To what end? To gain the respect of some twenty-three-year-old junkie who rented *American History* X too many times? Fuck that. Prison ethics allowed them to survive in their reality – not mine.

.

During out time, I approached Alex.

"Don't take this personally, but I need to get out of that cell," I said

"I figured."

"I talked to a deputy about moving to *The Side Shoot*, and he said only if I got physically threatened. I don't want to get anyone in trouble, but I want to be on my own. What should I do?"

Alex thought for a minute. "You're gonna have to tell them you're a danger to *yourself*. Tell 'em your suicidal, and they'll take you to medical. Dude, you'd love medical. It's quiet, and you get a private shower. It's awesome. I used to be in there. Listen, though, you have to be careful."

"Of what?"

"If you take it to far, they're gonna put you in The Turtle Suit."

"Is that a joke? Do they put you in a room with padded walls or what?

"No, I'm not kidding. Watch what you say. It's not a straight jacket, but they strip you nude and keep you in it, so you can't hurt yourself."

"Riiiichard.... huhuhuh..... REE-churd
"Fuckboy Richard....   Riiiichard.
"Hey, Fuckboy!
"HUHUH! RREEEE-churd!"
Any retaliation on my part caused them to get increasingly vicious. I'd try to sleep or read, but Kyle continued to punch the bunk. Then, he started grabbing me; he'd reach up from below and snag my arm or leg. I sat at the desk, beside Alex's bunk. Chris and Kyle carried on with themselves, and Alex spoke to me in a hushed tone.
"So, when do you think you're leaving?" he whispered
"At this rate, as soon as that door opens."
I wouldn't blame you..... In the slightest," he said, from the corner of his mouth

I got up and stood at the window, staring at the main floor.
"What are you doing, Richard?" Chris taunted
"I'm thinking, Chris. You should fucking try it sometime."
"What did you say?"
I turned to face him, "I said you should fucking try it sometime. Its called *thinking for yourself."*
"Oh, so you're singling me out because I'm the smallest guy in here?" Chris challenged
"I'm sorry? Are you fucking kidding me? And you're not singling me out to impress your fucking boy here?!" I shouted, pointing at Kyle
"You want to go? We can go!" Chris stated
"Chris, I'm facing *four* violent charges. Explain to me how fighting you would help my case? I'm asking you both to back the fuck off."

I'd tried my best to avoid that – drawing a line. I had to take action.

I didn't allow myself to think before I told the deputy I planned to commit suicide. I didn't want to weigh the risk of worsening my situation. I couldn't go on, though, in that cell. I needed to be alone if only for a few days, to get it together, and find a reserve of willpower I wasn't sure I had.

Maybe claiming to be suicidal wasn't even a lie; if so, it was not a hard one to deliver. I'm sure I left no doubt in the minds of the staff that night. Of course, the mere ideation of killing oneself wasn't enough for an official transfer to medical – they needed to know if I'd chosen my intended method. So, when I declared that I'd throw myself head-first off the second tier landing, I gave them what they asked for.

At 7:30 pm, a nurse and deputy pushed the medication trolley from cell to cell, administering pills. That's when Alex and I got our prescriptions. I heard the door next to ours pop open, and I got ready. Kyle and Chris were asleep. I slipped off of my bunk and cut in front of Alex, as he hobbled towards the door. It was a rude gesture, though I suspected he knew my agenda. When it opened, I took a deep breath, ignoring the male nurse, and instead locked eyes with the deputy. I pushed past the cart, and dashed out the cell, heading for the staircase to the left, and he quickly cut me off. That's when I voiced my intentions, with as much conviction as possible.

A female officer stood with me while I got processed and cleared for the medical ward. I couldn't place her nationality. She had beautiful black hair and kindness to her. We heard Chris in the background scream through the cell door, 'KILL YOURSELF!' The woman glared at him. *I've told these people you're not a threat, Chris. Quit your gangland bullshit for five seconds.*

It was lights out when they finished their procedural questions and escorted me from Cell Block 8, down the hallway to medical. We passed no one else. *I only heard versions of what could happen next.*

.

I stood in a dark chamber - a gurney to my left, and to my right, a glass-walled observation cell. A young male deputy approached me, holding the thick plastic uniform known as *The Turtle Suit*. He set it on the gurney and looked at me, trying to understand my mindset.
I pointed at the suit, shaking my finger, *"Is that Gucci?"* I asked
He stared blankly at me, in disbelief. *Shit, this guy is crazy.*
He stepped close. "Can I ask you a serious question?"
"Yes," I replied
"Do I have to worry about you hanging yourself tonight?"

It hit me, powerfully, to have another human being ask me that, with sincerity. Had it come to this, my life? I paused.
"No. You don't," I answered
"Oh, thank god," he sighed, as a wave of relief washed over him, "In that case..."
He left the smock on the gurney and told me to strip, as he issued a solid purple uniform, designating me as an inmate of the medical ward. When that cell door locked, I finally had solitary. *How long would I be in here?*

The cell had no bunk or chair; just a mattress on the floor, in the corner. Cameras were embedded in the ceiling. I put my sandals on and took a hot shower. I was pissed at myself for not tucking the skin medication into the lining of my pants as I exited cell block. The deputy said he'd have my crate delivered.

I had an avalanche of thoughts I wanted to put on paper, with no means to do so. I paced the floor, and talked out loud to myself, repeating ideas until they were committed to memory.

I started to experience an auditory hallucination from the acoustics of the cell. In one spot, I tapped my sandal on the concrete, creating an echo. I moved clockwise, as if my foot were a minute hand, tapping as I turned in a circle. Each position produced a unique echo. I picked a tone and did a subtle tap dance to a beat.

I noticed if I angled my ear at the upper left corner of the room, I could hear a piece of music; it grew louder as I approached. Was I detecting a song playing from somewhere in the building? No. It sounded like a collection of echoes, cascading over the top of one another, in an unending rhythm. Perhaps it was matrixing, but my mind filled the tones in with human voices; singers that I admired throughout my life. Whatever the cause, it offered me peace and comfort, when I needed it the most.

.

"Crannell, pack it up! We're moving you."
"Pack up what? You never brought my things."
"We're working on it. Grab your mattress and towel."

In the middle of the night, around 2 am, the same deputy came for me. I got transferred to a cell known as *The Suicide Room;* a darkened, narrowly shaped space. Along the floor, on either side, were three slabs of raised concrete, like above-ground tombs. On the far wall, I had a shower with no curtain. Again, I had no company. I chose to set my mattress near the door, on my right. There were no dimmed overhead fluorescents - just light from the control desk roughly twenty-five feet away. I got monitored through the thick glass of the facing wall, and with cameras fixed in each corner.

It felt ice cold in there. I wrapped myself in blankets. I desperately needed to get my thoughts on paper, as a form of therapy. I angrily beat on the glass and waved down the deputy at the desk. He studied me on the camera for a minute, then warily approached the door, cautiously putting his ear to the crack.
"What do you need?"
"Officer, can I PLEASE get a piece of paper and a pen?"
"You know I'm not allowed to do that!"

"*Please*, man! I need to be constructive, or I'm gonna go fucking crazy in here! Please! I'm begging you!" I cried out

"Dammit! Alright, look, if I give you a pen you have to promise me you're not gonna do anything stupid with it!"

"I won't! I promise! You have my word!"

He headed to the control desk. I pressed my face to the door, feeling the coldness of it. I looked down at my feet, to see a blank piece of paper and a small pen slip through the crack. I thanked him.

I began writing, and those writings became this book.

.

Early in the morning, I awoke to a man shouting my last name. I saw, with swollen eyes, a fat man with glasses, wearing a tacky Hawaiian shirt.

"Are you still thinking about killing yourself?" he asked

I laughed, "I've been awake for five seconds. Do you wanna give me a chance to think?"

He apparently wanted an answer.

"No," I said

He informed me I'd be housed in the cell next door, after breakfast; three fingers of french toast and watery maple syrup, which I poured on the ground.

Cell 921 - I entered a large room, with eight single-level bunks lining the walls, in a 'U' shape. The foot of each bed faced a steel and concrete table at the center of the room. On the wall to my right, hung an all-hours payphone. Past that, the sink and a private shower and toilet concealed by a thick curtain.

A few of the bunks, the first and third, were occupied. The occupants slept as if medicated; the clatter of the door didn't stir them.

"These guys won't give you any trouble. They're harmless," the deputy said, "Take whatever bunk you want."

I chose one on the opposite side of the room, Bunk 7, and fell asleep.

.

I had an unexpected visit from my attorney. As I walked to the visiting area, my stomach hurt, and my hands shook. He and I met in an actual room with no barriers between us. He was writing in his ledger when I came in, and he motioned for me to have a seat. It was a tense moment, and then he spoke.

"I talked to Elena," he said, "She asked me to give you a message."

Time stopped.

"She said, *'Tell Logan he blew it. He had a family that loved him and believed in him. The children loved him, and my parents wanted to pay for his schooling. He had a woman that loved him, but he blew it.'*"

That's the moment my spirit died.

Within seconds, everything inside of me slipped away.
I accepted every word of it – I felt gutted.
She was right.
I blew it.

It was my fault. I'd lost my love.
I'd failed Aidan and Hetty, those beautiful children. I wouldn't see them again.

I'd allowed Scott to win. I let my enemy win.
I let her parents confirm their doubts of me.
The wolves were at the door. I dropped my guard and let them in.

The bright future I'd seen for myself had gone.
All my hard work. All I had built.

I'd failed everyone, and betrayed all that was good in myself.
Everything I had been blessed with – reduced to ash in front of me.

And now my freedom and dignity were being taken away.
Now I was lost within these walls. She was right.
I blew it.

My attorney continued to talk, but I became distant. He said her parents were taking my car and computer system, *'They belonged to the family now.'* There were things I wanted to say, though I would have choked on the words. I didn't want to listen to my voice like that.

As I got escorted out, I looked over my shoulder to my attorney, standing dignified; jacket draped on his arm, briefcase in hand. He tried to give me a comforting smile, to show me some level of solidarity. I think he watched me until I was out of sight.

.

In Cell 921, I observed the layout of the medical ward. Nine cells formed a square, with the control desk representing one of its sides. The main floor was devoid of furniture. They didn't merely house medical patients here – it was a ward for the criminally insane. I had no contact with the more dangerous inmates, yet we'd lock eyes with each other while staring out our respective windows. Their eyes echoed like residual hauntings. I listened to those men scream, day and night. Sometimes they'd sing.

My two cellmates were eating lunch. I introduced myself. Mike, in his mid-twenties, got arrested for public intoxication. Muhoza, a refugee, apparently for marijuana. He spoke little English and had a mental handicap I couldn't identify, exemplified by a lazy right eye.

Both were quiet as church mice. Mike was teaching Muhoza how to read, explaining words while Muhoza read aloud from cheap novels. The deputy on duty would push in a book trolley upon request.

This environment is the closest I'm getting to solitude, I thought. Two days later, I finally got my crate. I thoroughly washed my face and applied the skin medication. It worked – not well – but, well enough. It gave me a sense of security, to have that problem solved.

.

We got one hour of outdoor recreation each day, and unlike cell block, we chose as a group when that break would be. We flagged the officer, and he directed us to a door that opened onto a thirty-by-fifteen-foot concrete pad, mostly enclosed with a riveted, metal awning covering eighty-five-percent of our view. *The remaining open space gave us real blue sky. Sunlight. Fresh air. A breeze.*

We requested those breaks during certain times, knowing there'd be a sunspot hitting the exposed wall. We basked in it like cats or lizards, moving with it until it crept too far into the corner. I ran laps, wearing myself out, music playing in my head. I'd lean on the wall in exhaustion. Mike and Muhoza were more relaxed and walked casually.

Muhoza, quiet in his ways, understood I was troubled. He came up to me and paused.

"Too much think, you die," he stated, simply

He remained motionless, with a haphazard grin, the sun in his face, his lazy eye staring off into the sky. It was a picture as still as a photograph, save for the small tufts of pollen floating in the air around him. I'll never forget that image.

The silly bastard may be right, I thought.

.

Mike and I explained to Muhoza what the term *'jacking off'* meant. He understood the act itself, but struggled to get the phonetics of it, and kept repeating it loudly, in different variations. Our sides ached with laughter. He started asking the deputies about it whenever they checked in, *'What is? How say?'*

I eagerly anticipated my first commissary delivery, thanks to my mother, who made sure I had money on my books. I ordered twenty-two items, and when my shipment arrived, it contained five of them; a tiny pen, notepad, Ivory soap, vitamins, and chapstick. The other items weren't permitted in the medical ward. I'd receive the rest upon my discharge. I was upset not to have my coffee, though the notepad made up for it. I wrote nonstop.

A female caseworker visited me, to evaluate my depression. She wanted to pull me out of medical, and I persuaded her to let me stay through Saturday. I had my initial court hearing that Friday and explained that a transition to an unknown cell wouldn't be the best for me. She agreed.

The prosecutor had failed to send my attorney the Discovery file, so my day in court would be nothing more than him asking for a continuance, which meant pushing the preliminary hearing out by two weeks. The process was mundane, and I'm going to bypass writing of it. I promise there will be plenty of dramatic courtroom events to come.

I rifled through my crate and found a lone teabag Benjamin had fronted me. I pumped the hot water button in the sink, getting it moderately hot. I let the tea brew and enjoyed it.

.

I had a third dream that night.

I was standing in front of my desk at *United Bank*. It appeared untouched. Judging from the light, it was late afternoon. My teammates were at their regular desks, busy with phone calls. Then, the energy in the room shifted. From behind me, a long dark shadow emerged, of a man, looming over my desk. My co-workers became aware of it unconsciously. They sensed a presence, and turned towards it, with hesitation.

Tony slowly rose from his desk, opposite mine. He appeared guarded, and his body language seemed foreboding. Tony glared at the figure casting the ominous shadow, trying not to show fear.

An unfamiliar female voice whispered in my ear, 'The man from Los Angeles is coming.'

The dream cut to a room, with Elena seated at a table, wearing her sunglasses. She was stuffing bills of money into the pages of a book and laughing.

I woke up with a sick unease. Had my subconscious warned me of danger I failed to see? *Why hadn't it occurred to me that Scott would get involved?* Was I supposed to believe that he'd miss his one golden chance to get rid of me for good? I became a sitting target in this place. What if he testified against me? He'd already paid Elena's friend for information. Why not pay them to lie? *Of course*, he'd manipulate the situation to his benefit.

.

I spoke to Tony on the phone, regarding my job.

He'd gone into my bosses office, explaining my arrest. They went online together, bringing up my arrest report. They were shocked to see the charges, to that I have no doubt.

"Listen, man. No one here believes this shit. Not at all," Tony assured me, "The whole team has your back. We're gonna do whatever we can for ya, bud. Our boss is talking to the higher-ups, trying to get permission to have us write letters to the court for you."

I knew I'd ultimately lose my job, but it felt gratifying to know my team was on my side. Management would work with me for as long as they could. *'They haven't touched your desk, man. It's exactly the way you left it,'* Tony said

I tried contacting my boss, though his answering machine triggered the automated system of the jail, disconnecting the call.

.

The deputies tossed a twenty-year-old refugee from Bombay into the cell, named Sandeep, a mere wisp of a boy. A quarter of an hour in, he buckled over sobbing into his hands. I'm sure it was a rough culture shock.

His family, I'd learn, ran a well-reviewed Indian restaurant downtown. Sandeep worked in the kitchen with his father and uncle and boasted about the greatness of the food. Sandeep, already married, had a newborn daughter. He got arrested for slapping and kicking his wife. I guess in Mumbai that behavior is so commonplace, that young people think it's socially acceptable. Based on the way Sandeep talked, it seemed funny to him, *'She hit me first,'* he'd say.

Mike and I read his papers and did our best to explain his charges, yet within an hour he'd pester us to go over it once more. The hardest thing for him to understand was the No-Contact Order like I had with Elena. Sandeep wasn't familiar with the term 'custody battle' was, nor could he grasp that he'd be unable to return home. I told him straight that his marriage was most likely finished.

.

Dinner got served through the slat in the door.
"They do not bring us rice?" Sandeep asked, puzzled
I laughed, "No, we don't get rice. Actually, no, on Saturdays we get overcooked brown rice with pineapples."
"I only eat rice," he rebuked, pushing his tray aside
"You're gonna have to adapt."
"Oh, I see. I will tell the guard to bring me rice."
"Sandeep, this isn't a fucking restaurant. There is no rice."
"I will not eat, then."
"Keep that attitude up, and they'll tie you to a chair and put it in your veins."
"You joke with me."
"Look, it took me two weeks to stomach the food here. I get it."
"Where is the salt?"
"There is no salt."
"I will ask the guard for salt."
"You *buy* salt here. On Wednesdays."

Sandeep's bail was $15,000 – meaning he needed $1500 to get out. He confirmed that fact with every bondsman in the city, never fully content with the answer.
"Will the judge lower my bail?" he inquired, repeatedly
"I have no idea. I don't know."
"I will ask the Judge to lower it."
"That's fine."

.

"You keep asking us questions like we've been here for years, man. Talk to your public defender. We're not lawyers!" Mike said, irritated
"I will tell the Judge she hit me first," Sandeep stated
"You're not going to say damn thing," I snapped, "You're going to let your public defender do their job and speak for you. Keep your mouth shut."
"Oh? Why do I need a public defender? Why can't I say for myself? She hit me and slap me!"
"Cry me a fucking river, Sandeep."

"Will I be able to go to my soccer game on Saturday?" Sandeep pleaded
"No, you won't."
"I will ask them."
"Sandeep..."
And yes, he did ask the deputy. And the next deputy. And the nurse.

In our small rec yard, we got Sandeep to laugh and joke with us; he and
Muhoza got on like school kids. They bizarrely treated the whole affair like a sleepover.
They played games, tearing up bed sheets to fashion a soccer ball.

I didn't know about the geography where Muhoza and Sandeep were born.
They understood each other's dialects, though, and I'm sure that was comforting to
them. Beforehand, Muhoza sang to himself as he wandered the cell, but having
Sandeep around made him less shy.

They urged Mike and I to sing songs with them. We compromised and agreed
to keep the beat. Mike flipped his crate and hit it like a drum, while I slapped the
bottom of an empty bunk for bass. They sang in their native tongue, in unison, and it
sounded beautiful. *Damn,* they could sing. I'm sure those were the happiest notes the
walls of that cell had ever heard.

The dynamic changed after that. Mike got transferred and replaced by a
harmless kid named Paul. He'd stolen money from his job to pay for drugs, plead
guilty across the board and awaited sentencing.

A man in his early thirties, dying from liver failure, took the bunk next to
mine. His skin was bright yellow, almost neon, and his ankles and feet were so swollen
that it pained him to wear socks and shoes. I figured he had three months to live. He'd
been arrested for public intoxication twice in a three week period, and his family bailed
him out. When the deputies for his release, I helped him put his foot ware on, while
they waited impatiently.

With rapidity, the remaining bunks got filled, in less than eight hours. They
were tough customers - most detoxing from bath salts or heroin. One man, a Russian,
took upwards of seventeen showers a day to calm his itching skin. Soap bottles littered
the floor. Another man, Conor, was in for attempted strangulation. He'd scheme
incessantly, trying to raise money for his bond.

In the bed to my left, a truck driver named Hill believed he had classified information on a secret government faction who proceeded to terrorize him. To my right, a barbaric looking guy with medieval-style religious tattoos. He slept all day, detoxing from bath salt.

.

I rested on my bunk reading a book. I could feel Sandeep staring at me from across the room. I ignored it to my best ability, though it became unbearable. I glanced in his direction, and sure enough, he'd locked on me; knees pulled up to his chin, his eyes glassed with tears. He got up and sat at the foot of my bunk, and resumed his stare.

"Mr. Logan," he said, feebly

"Yes, Sandeep?"

"Can you teach me how not to cry?" he asked

It was like Compassion, in the form of a kitten, pawing at my door. I knew some of the men in that cell would have no hesitations in kicking that kitten.

I went a bit rubbery.

"Sandeep," I began, searching for what to say, "There's nothing wrong with crying. *You just need to be careful who sees you doing it.*"

I had my doubts the advice would stick, but *his* response certainly stuck with me.

"Mr. Logan, I can tell you're a rich man. Even dressed like that," he said

This kid.

Last Night In Medical

Monday morning. The weekend passed, and I hadn't been transferred to cell block.

"Dimitri! Roll up your bunk. You're moving to seven!" the deputy announced

"Whatever," he groaned, getting dressed

"Hey man," I said, "This is going to ruin your day, but there are no private showers over there. You're in lockdown. I know you're detoxing, so you might want to take one more before you leave."

"Fuck! Are you fucking kidding me?" He shouted, throwing his shoe

Later, I stood in the rec yard, getting fresh air, on a hot and humid summer day. The far wall basked in the sunshine, and I pressed myself to it. I closed my eyes and looked in the direction of the sun. The inside of my eyelids flowered into colors of fiery red to sunflower yellow. I missed colors. I opened one eye, crossing it slightly, to study the side of my nose. It glowed orange and perspired. I could feel the sweat on my skin. I flared my nostrils. That act stopped my mind from racing and got me in touch with my body. I realized how separated the two had become.

Muhoza withdrew from being social. His singing irritated the other inmates. They'd scream at him, telling him to *'Shut the fuck up!'* yet he brazenly ignored them and carried on. I detected a common thread among the new arrivals - a dislike for refugees.

Conor, in particular, took his frustrations out upon them. His scheming phone calls got disrupted by Sandeep, who clung to the receiver like life support. He'd call the same bondsmen, asking the same questions, and beg them to call his uncle. He had his thirteenth breakdown, sobbing in his hands. He then went bunk to bunk, asking for the same tired answers. I caught him peeking over shoulders, trying to memorize phone passcodes.

The barbaric guy finally woke up and started laughing.
"Welcome," I said
"Fucking bath salts. Shit, I shouldn't have told those people I was gonna kill 'em."
"What people?"
"My family."
"Ah."
"They'll probably let me out tomorrow," he sighed
"Yeah, you keep telling yourself that."

We'd trashed the cell. I asked a deputy for a push broom. He feared I'd unscrew the handle and beat someone. The subsequent officer on duty handed it to me without question. My cleaning motivated others, and we agreed it was nice to get the cell straightened up.

The deputies gave us a crazed drunk, to fill Dimitri's bed. He berated the officers about legalities and consequences. Junkies shut their mouths, not wanting to bring attention to themselves. Drunks want to brawl, sue everybody, and brag how connected they are.
"My names Wild Bill, dammit!" he declared to the lot of us
He got charged with threatening to cut a man's fingers off with gardening shears. As the day progressed, he was jovial with us. I learned he had terminal cancer.

Wild Bill took a shine to Sandeep, and let the boy lament his domestic situation. Hill overheard it and stood up, his face red.
"Then you shouldn't kick your wife around you little fuck!"
Sandeep shrunk, and stuttered out, "Oh. It's... not good?"

I posed a question to the group.
"By a show of hands, how many are in here for attempted strangulation?"
I raised my hand, and five others followed suit.
"Wow. Isn't that interesting? It must be in fashion this season."
We compared bonds, and I had to convince them I wasn't joking in regards to mine being half a million dollars.
Conor laid on his bunk, curiously staring at me.
"What's up, Conor?" I asked
"You're taking this well," he said, "With charges like yours, I'd expect you to be losing your shit. You're really holding up."
I thanked him. Sandeep chimed in and told us Muhoza's bond, with a smile. It was $50.
"What?" I asked sharply
"His bail is fifty dollar," Sandeep said cutely
"Muhoza, how long have you been here. In jail?"
"Six month," he replied
I looked at Conor. *'Sticking it to the refugees, huh?'* he whispered

10:30 pm - Lights out. Sandeep and Muhoza prayed according to their Islamic faith; on their knees, forehead touching the ground. They hadn't done that previously. As the two concentrated, their prayers grew louder. The men on my side of the room woke up and seethed with anger. They started shouting, *'Terrorists!'*

A palpable negative energy coursed in the cell – a dissonance that affected me on a physical level. Hill started in. Then Conor. I could feel their tension mounting. They wrapped sheets around their heads and made aggressive insults.

The two refugees did not stop praying.

The man detoxing on bath salts started punching the wall and broadcasting racial slurs. Their hatred was unifying, feeding off one another, and gaining power.

The two continued praying.

It was going to end badly.
Unless I struck first, I thought.

"HEY!" I yelled, shooting up from my bunk, *"WE TOLD YOU TO SHUT THE FUCK UP!"*

I stormed across the room, grabbing the back of Sandeep's neck, with apparent anger. I knelt and whispered in his ear, *'Wrap it up, kid. Now.'* I knew he wouldn't. I walked to the window and started beating it with the palm of my hand until the night deputies rushed to open the door.

"Officer, get me out of here! I want to go back to the suicide room."

"We can't put you over there for no reason. What's going on?"

"Well, I fucking *will* be suicidal if I have to keep listening to this shit! Can you do something about these two?" I demanded, gesturing to the corner

The deputies stalked over, shining their flashlights at the two in prayer. One officer prodded Muhoza in the side. The energy in the room shifted, and the refugees ceased their activity. An officer approached me and said, *'Let me know if they get any weirder.'*

After that, the deputies doubled up their rounds, coming every eight minutes instead of fifteen, pausing for an extra moment, to survey the cell. *That was my aim.*

.

The next morning, an officer instructed me to roll up my bunk.

Paul had rods in his spine, due to an accident. His thin mattress provided little relief. The mat I had, from my first night in the isolation chamber, was high-quality fabric, double thick, with a built-in pillow. I wanted to keep it for my own ailments, but Paul appeared to be in rougher shape. To avoid a written violation for exchanging mattresses, I told him to get up quick and yank his sheets off. I threw my mat on his bunk, and he tucked he his blanket on it.

"Sandeep," I said, "When I get out of here, I'm going to that Indian restaurant of yours, to check in on you, so you'd better be there. You can give me some rice."

"Ok, Mr. Logan!" he smiled

"Watch these two whelps for me," I said to Paul

"Alright. Good luck, man." Paul said

"Same to you. Take care, everybody."

I felt anxious, leaving medical. I regained my orange striped uniform. I'd be heading to Cell Block 8, that much was certain. *What if they put me in my old cell? Would I be on the same Walk?* Getting assigned to a different Walk altogether had its problems. I'd be starting fresh, and things can always get worse.

"Any clue which Walk they're putting me on, deputy?" I asked

"Not sure what they worked out on that."

I stood in the chamber, dividing Block 7 from 8. There were the crack and bang of the gate opening and the change in the air.

With that, my introduction to Ada County Jail had ended.

Now, it was time to fight for my life,
and make unexpected friends along the way.

Cell 846

I nervously ascended the staircase to my new housing in the 2nd tier, on the right side of the block. A cell door opened, second to last in the row, numbered 846. I entered, and two of the three inmates were standing in anticipation; they looked as anxious as me.

"I'm Zach. Good to meet you," said the taller man, shaking my hand

"Call me Zeek," said the other

"I'm Logan."

I got assigned Bunk 3, top right, with Zach below me. The third man, laying on the other top bunk, greeted me.

"They call me The Reaper," he said, with a toothless grin

"I'm sorry?"

"They call me The Reaper."

"Oh, ok. I thought you said The Ripper for a second."

He laughed and pulled his blanket up to his face, like a kid.

The cell had a positive energy. I perceived no threat. These were three passive individuals, with no affiliations, waiting for their day in court. *Claiming to be suicidal, in order to leave Cell 821, proved to be one of my smartest decisions.*

These men didn't push for information. If one spoke, the others listened constructively. They had their routines down pat, and the cell had an odd harmony to it. They kept it clean. The air vent, in the ceiling, aimed at the floor, rather than in our faces. We had a clear view of the television and an aerial vantage of the main floor.

"What Walk is this?" I asked

"You're on Walk 3," Zach said, "Did you come from another area?"

"Yeah, Walk 2, and then I went to medical."

"Are you ok?" Zeek inquired

"I'm getting better."

I glanced at the walls, checking for a schedule.

"What's our out time today?"

"Um, I think it's at two-thirty, right Zeek?" Zach questioned

"Yes. Yes, it is. Out time is at two-thirty," Zeek said, officially, "It's a good schedule, today."

"Huh! Two-thirty is a good schedule," Zach confirmed, "It breaks things up."

Zach had an organized bunk, with personal books from the outside, and a modest supply of groceries in his crate. His piercing blue eyes, sandy blond hair, and sideburns brought to mind a young Paul Newman. He had one of those smiles that were both clean and dirty in equal measure. His voice carried a Midwest twang, with a hint of East Coast white boy gangsta.

"Hey Zach, I have no technique for these sheets," I said, "They slip all over the place. Can you show me how you make your bed?"

"For sure, bro. So, um. Ok. Put your mattress on the ground. I'll show you."

I tossed the vinyl mat on the ground, and it made a much louder smacking sound than I thought it would.

"Ok," he began, "pick up your sheet. First, you have to poke a hole at the top center and bottom center of it," he instructed, handing me a pen

I jabbed it through, then tore a hole at each end.

"Ok," Zach continued, "Bend the bottom of your mat up, and wrap the tips of the sheet underneath and put 'em through the hole. Tie the tips in a knot, and do the same for the other end."

"Ah, I see."

The sheets were tight, and the mat buckled under the tension.

"Once you lay on it, it'll flatten out, bro."

"Thank you. I appreciate that," I said, setting it on my bunk
I then draped my blanket and tucked the excess under the mat so it wouldn't hang in Zach's face.

"Can you do me a favor?" Zach asked

"Of course."

"Is it cool if I hang my towels from your bunk? I like having a canopy, so it blocks out the fluorescent lights."

"Yeah, no problem."

I tucked the towels partially under my mat, giving him the right amount of overhang.

"Tight! Thanks, bro!"

"You're welcome."

I still had no pillow, despite my requests. I stuffed my pillowcase with clothes and towels. I settled in. It got to me, how barren my bunk appeared; I had no visual reminders of anything. Nothing to meditate on, or pull strength from, and I sought to change that.

.

Had my mother reached Matt? The Telmate prompts finished, and her voice came through the line.

"How's Jack? Did you get a hold of Matt?"

"*Yes!* I drove to his house this morning. He promised to take care of Jack and treat him like family until you get out!"

"Oh my god! Yes!"

"I'm so glad I found him. My flight leaves in the morning. I'll do everything I can on my end. I love you so much."

"I love you too. Thank you."

We said our goodbyes.

I hung up the phone and raised my fists, pumping the air, *"YES! YES!"* I cheered, peaking the curiosity of the other inmates. I heard the voice of Mendoza from behind his cell door, *"Hey, yo! Concentration Camp!"* (His nickname for me, said in good humor). I jogged to his cell, unintentionally crossing the yellow line. The two-foot distance, between the row of cells and the line, was designed to prevent inmates from slipping contraband to one other.

"Crannell!" the deputy shouted, "Behind the yellow line!"

"Sorry!"

"You're back!" Mendoza said, "Hey, what's up? Why are you so happy? Did they drop your charges or something?"

"Nah, I found a home for my dog! My mom got him to safety! He's in good hands!"

"Your dog?" he replied, with a confused grin.

.

The inmates of Walk 3 formed a line for dinner. *'Special diets!'* the deputy announced. Since I had the *Boost* supplemental drink, I technically got on the list. The only other man on our Walk with a specific diet was Zach, so he and I cut in line for each meal. He had the kosher menu; not that he was Jewish, he just preferred the food.

"You can sit at our table if you want," Zach offered, "Me and a dude from the cell next door sit together. He's chill."

"Ok. Thanks."

I met Allen - a reserved and unassuming type that would've been at home on any couch, with a beer, watching football.

"What's in the kosher meal?" I asked Zach

"It's good, bro. They give you extra fruit in the mornings, with soy butter, and nine-grain bread.

"And for dinner?"

"Tonight it's beef stew, with real meat. None of the food is made in the jail. It gets flown in and blessed by a Rabbi or some shit. I'm not sure how that works. The only thing that sucks is the portions are smaller."

"And you don't get cake. That's the best part of my meal."

"Right! Allen usually hooks me up with his, though."

"Yeah, you can have it, dude," Allen motioned

"In that case, bring it up to the cell. I got a surprise for ya," I said

"Huh!" Zach grinned

I realized that my *Boost* drink, with its sweetened vanilla flavor, gave me one hell of an advantage. I was the one guy on the Walk who could supply it – and I suspected the rest of the crew didn't know what they were missing.

In lockdown, I poured the boost on top of Zach's bowl of chocolate cake.

"Try that, man."

He took a bite, and his face lit up, "Whoa! That Boost ain't no punk! Good-night!"

I dripped it on my cake, and we savored it.

"Hey, Logan, do you want a cup of coffee?" Zach offered

"I'd love a coffee!" I answered, "I'll return the favor when commissary gets here."

"I'm not worried about it, bro," he said, dumping a generous spoonful of instant granules into my cup

Those empty plastic coffee bags were essential. They were our only means of getting boiling water from the dispenser to our cells. Otherwise, we couldn't cook any food or have coffee or tea. They kept the stored water hot for a couple of hours.

"Let me pour some Boost in your coffee, Zach."

"Damn, bro!" he exclaimed, tasting it, "That's a whole new experience, right there!"

"Sweet."

"How did you get those books?" I asked, gesturing to the foot of his bunk, where he stacked them

"Amazon. You can't order them, though. Someone on the outside has to, and they have to ship from Amazon, or they get confiscated. I guess people were slipping drugs in the pages."

"I'll have to think of what to order."

It's challenging, with no back covers or reviews to read. *What literature would benefit me the most in this place?*

"Hey Logan," Zach said, "I have schizoaffective disorder, but I'm on medication now. If you ever see me doing weird hand signs, just ignore it. It doesn't mean anything. When I first got here, people thought I was throwing up gang signs, and it pissed some dudes off."

I laughed, "Ok, so it's like a nervous tic?"

"Yeah, and sometimes I get stuck on the texture of things."

"No problem."

"It's dumb stuff, I know. I don't want you worrying about it."

"It's all good. I'm pretty weird myself."

7:30pm

"Gentlemen! Please stand for headcount!" the deputy instructed, as he and his partner entered the cell

"Evenin', deputies," Zach said, cordially

"Evening, Morris. Please say your names as I call bunk numbers! Bunk 1!"

"Woodbury," said The Reaper

"Bunk 2!"

"Hadley," said Zeek

"Bunk 3!"

"Crannell."

"Welcome back, Crannell!" the deputy remarked

"Always a pleasure, officer," I said

"Are you feeling better?"

"I'm tip-top."

"Good. Bunk 4!"

"Morris."

"Thank you, gentlemen! Do we need anything in here?"

"Yes, officer, I was wondering if you could help me answer a question?" Zeek asked

Zeek was a bit of a runt; short and scrawny, with a showboating personality. He had a cackle, like an excited Dennis Hopper. I wasn't sure if his shaky hands were the result of a nervous condition or lack of alcohol. Probably both.

"You see," Zeek began, "I've been reading this book and it keeps referring to cops as 'pigs.' I don't get it. It's confusing me, and I was hoping you could clarify *why* they call cops 'pigs'? When did they start doing that?"

Dead silence.

The deputy cleared his throat, choosing to take it in stride, "Well, I believe they began calling cops 'pigs' around the 1950's, but I can't be sure."

His partner chipped in, "It also may have been because they were fat."

"Oh. Well, thank you. Thank you, officers. That helps a lot," Zeek said graciously

The deputies exited, and we stopped suppressing our laughter.

.

The Reaper didn't talk much. He had these over-sized, wayward eyes, reminiscent of the actor Marty Feldman. I could tell he and Zeek were transients from their empty crates, and constant panhandling of Zach's groceries. They seemed pieced together, and I imagined, slightly grateful for hot meals.

.

During lunch, on my second day on the Walk, and I hadn't paid attention yet to who lived with whom. Zach and Allen finished eating and left to use the phones. A man, in his early forties, sat in Zach's seat, across the table, and stared calmly at me. Two inmates stood nearby, like bodyguards. I studied the man, waiting for him to speak. He had a round and handsome face; a profile of a classic gangster, like the type you'd see in mugshots from Alcatraz.

"I see the nurses are giving you that Boost drink," he said, composed, noting the container in my hand

"They are," I acknowledged

"I want it," he said, flatly

His tone was serious, yet at the corners of his mouth, I faintly saw an impish grin he tried hard to conceal. *He had to be bluffing.*

"What's in it for me?" I asked

He paused, not expecting that response. "What do you want?"

"I'll tell you what," I began, "They give me one drink for breakfast and one for dinner. I don't wake up for breakfast really, but when I do, I'll hand you that one. Deal?"

"Deal," he said, grinning fully, "What do you want in exchange?"

"I'm good. If I think of something, I'll let you know. I'm Logan, by the way."

"Call me Trav."

Trav was my neighbor, in Cell 845. I started getting up earlier, so I could make good on my word. To avoid a write-up for sharing the *Boost*, Trav headed up the stairs after breakfast. I'd follow, walking by his cell, and remove the container from under my shirt, tossing it to him. It was a good investment.

Trav ran a clean cell – I mean it looked *immaculate.* The floor shined, and bed sheets got tucked to almost military standards. The bunks were free of clutter. Above the writing desk hung photographs and drawings.

To Trav's knowledge, I never asked for anything in exchange – but he gave me plenty. I admired Trav for his solidarity. Whenever I struggled, being in his company eased my mind. He'd give me that subtle impish grin and say *'Don't sweat it. You're gonna be alright,'* and I'd instantly believe him.

.

Early one morning, the crack and bang of the cell door did not wake me, nor did the fluorescent lights blaring on, or the call for breakfast. None of the aggressive noises of the jail coming alive had disturbed me.

I was awoken by something else - a song. A song that resonated with me, as one that Elena and I listened to often, together. An inmate, down on the main floor, had turned the television to a music station. I heard the gentle opening strains of U2's *'With or Without You.'*

My love came flooding back to me. *All of it, all at once.* Every warm memory. I held myself in a fetal position. All other sounds grew distant, as I listened. I felt a tear leave my right eye, and slide across the bridge of my nose, joining with a tear from my left, as they both moved off my cheek. Then, my eyes opened up, and I cried. I cried for the longest time. My heartache radiated through my body, as my tears continued to fall. I could feel the warmth of Elena beside me.

Later, I headed up the staircase to get paper from my cell when an inmate ran up to me.
"Hey, Logan!"
His name was Nichols, in his early twenties, short and tenacious as a bulldog.
"What's up?" I asked
"Hey, Zach says you're an alright dude, and that's enough for us!"
"Thanks."
"If you need anything, you let us know. Do you want some coffee?"
"Uh, sure. That would be great. I'm out until Wednesday."
"Come on up, bro! I'll hook you up!"
Nichols, also housed in 845, with Trav and Allen, loaded me up with three heaping spoonfuls of coffee. I again admired the cell's cleanliness.
"Thanks, Nichols."
"No problem! Like I said, let us know if we can help out."
"I will."

Billy had the fourth bunk in Trav's cell; as Irish as a pint of Guinness, the man loved playing cards. Billy had the physical stature of a roadie for the *Dropkick Murphy's.* Aside from nods and gestures, as I walked past his cell while he took a shit, I never had the chance to talk with him, for reasons I'll explain in a bit.

Whisper, the Redshirt worker Alex mentioned, was a full-bore member of the *Aryan Knights,* with tattoos heralding his allegiance. The simplest one, an *'88'* tatted above his left eyebrow, held the most power for me - it represented the *'88 precepts of The Order'.* Whisper's rules were right there for everyone to see – his skin read like a manual. He indeed pulled strings on the block, and his deep, gruff voice boomed off the walls.

Once a week, the Redshirts shaved our hair, upon request. It was first-come, first-serve, and the line formed fast. You staked your position by setting down a plastic chair and putting a book on the seat. The five cell doors on our Walk opened in loud succession – BANG! - BANG! - BANG! - BANG! - BANG! - And the race commenced. Our cell was fourth to be released, which put us at a disadvantage.

Even when I expected it, the concussive sound of the doors firing open caused me to jerk, followed by the recoiling of the steel sliding on its track. Then, we had to lock it in position, with a crash. That allowed the deputy who operated the control desk to send it a signal, releasing it with another loud pop so we could close it again.

.

Commissary Day. During lunch, a small envoy of carts came through the gate of Cell Block 8. I extended my wristband for verification and got handed a gray plastic crate filled with my order. It was a rush, finally getting my first real delivery. I hurried to the cell and dumped the contents onto my bed. I picked up each item and felt it in my hand. I smelled them and listened to the crinkle of the packaging.

A 20oz. bag of instant coffee. Hot chocolate mix. 10 count packets of salt and pepper. Peanuts. Fruit snacks. 100 count box of teabags. Potato chips. Hot sauce, and a strawberry shortcake pastry amongst the array. To have bathroom products gave me relief - I could bypass the garbage issued by the jail. Genuine deodorant, mouthwash, toothpaste, bar soap and a washcloth. I couldn't afford shampoo and wrote it on my list for next week. I got excited to build a small surplus.

To people on the outside, that may all be junk they can buy at a gas station. For us, it was like having pieces of our memory returned. It was home.

.

My Mother got concerned if I went too long without checking in. She continued working on my behalf, keeping me updated. If I needed a message relayed to someone, she made sure they received it. I tried not to vent my frustration on her. I knew she was just as upset by the circumstances. When the speed of the legal system wore me down, she kept me thinking positive.
"I thought about you a lot tonight," she said to me, "I'm so proud of you. You have such an amazing constitution. After everything you've lost, you still have your sense of humor, when most people would've snapped."

I'd call my father with any developments in the case. We had conflicting schedules, though when I did get a hold of him, his support seemed genuine. He offered me his old '96 Nissan Sentra when I got out, whenever that might be. Owning a car outright sounded great to me. I admitted, with embarrassment, I couldn't drive a stick, and he said he'd teach me.

.

"You're doing a lot better than I would be in your situation," my brother said, dryly, on the phone

"Well, you don't know until you've tried it. See if you can beat three felonies in a weekend."

"Is there anything I can do for you?" he asked

"Actually, yeah. Could you order a few books for me?"

"Sure. Anything in particular?"

"A book by Salman Rushdie. I'll let you decide which one."

"What else?"

"A photography book of Buddhist temples?"

"Ok. How do I send them to you?"

It unsettled me, to give him the mailing address of the jail, and my cell number; I *lived* here now. My brother stocked me with literature, becoming my private book dealer. It helped my spirit immensely, having books to look forward to each week.

.

With Jack in safety, I focused on retrieving my external hard drives. Life moves on, in your absence. It's frustrating to be obsessed with a goal, yet dependent on people who have a dozen goals of their own. Each phone call is a cliffhanger, filled with unanswered questions.

Tony had a meeting at my attorney's office, and I signed legal documents, providing him with the power to act on my behalf. The landlords agreed to give Tony the spare keys to my home, though my attorney advised him not to enter if Elena was present. We didn't know what she was capable of.

June 29th - Tony sat parked in front of my apartment, *'I don't like this at all,'* he must've said to himself. He checked my parking space, noting my car to be gone. Elena's vehicle sat in its designated spot, the engine crackling and hood warm. Tony got out and headed up the three flights of stairs to our door. Elena didn't know his face, which protected his identity.

The windows were open, lights on, and music playing. There weren't any voices. Tony didn't knock, as instructed, and headed back to the lot, checking the dumpsters by the building. He found nothing of mine.

I had a sick unease in the pit of my stomach. We had a month remaining on the lease. *Would Elena pay it or vacate? Would she destroy my drives out of spite, or send copies to her lawyers in an attempt to bring new charges?* Throwing them in the trash would be too boring for Elena. I wouldn't be able to rest until I knew what lay behind that door.

J U L Y

3:00 pm. I sat at a table, under one of the skylights. Tony readied to enter my apartment, and expected a phone call from me, in thirty minutes.

Where were my thoughts in that span of time? *I thought about Issachar.* I remembered holding Elena at night, feeling the warmth of that life growing inside her. *I knew, from a thousand fleeting moments, how different our lives would've been.*

3:30pm. Make the call.
"I'm here," Tony said, "I went to the loft and searched where you told me."
"Ok."
"The drives are gone, man. The cigar box you had them in was broken, in the middle of the floor.
"Was it empty?"
"Yeah. I've torn this place apart. There's not much here. I'm fucking sorry, man. I'm so pissed off."

Tony fit what he could into his car, and planned to return for the rest, soon. I thanked him, numbly, and hung up the phone. The wind exited my body. I sat in a seat and lowered my head to my knees.

'My god, Elena... What have you done?'

I rested there, despondent. Zach, walking laps along the yellow line, stopped and approached. He took a seat and put his elbows on the table.
"You're not overthinking, are you?" he asked, leaning in

"Yes, I am. I can't help it."

"Listen, bro," he said, "You can't think about the past and the future in here *because they're not ours. They don't belong to us, anymore.* All we get is today. You have to focus on the things you *can* control. It's the little things that save you."

It was wisdom, what he told me.

.

"Why are you in here, Zach?"

"It's stupid, bro," he said ashamedly, "It's embarrassing to talk about it."

"I won't judge you."

"I was out of my head, you know? My schizoaffective disorder got outta control, and I was doing a lot of hard drugs. I decided I wanted to die. Simple as that. I wanted to go out 'death by cop.' So, I went to that Winco grocery store downtown with a gun on me. I stole shit I didn't even need, some chapstick and batteries. That's how out of it I was. When security rushed me, I was gonna take out my gun and have them shoot me. I didn't want to hurt nobody. I just wanted to die."

"What happened?"

"It didn't go down like that. Four dudes chased me out into the parking lot, and when I drew my gun, they beat the fuck out of me. One of 'em grabbed my arm and wrestled the gun out of my hand. They took their boots to me, bro. Stupid shit. I deserve to go to prison for what I did. Somebody could've gotten killed, you know?"

Zach showed me the intake photo on his wristband. His face had scrapes like road rash. His eyes were soulless, cheeks gaunt from addiction. The man before me, a healthy, determined human being, had no resemblance to the person in that dim photograph.

.

That night in lockdown, as my cellmates conversed, I stood by the window slat.

"I suppose I owe you boys a story," I said, interrupting

"Huh!" Zach grinned, "We're about to hear some shit, aren't we!"

"Yes, you are."

I spoke candidly, for hours, telling them what you've read thus far in these pages. They gave me their undivided attention and feedback. It exalted me.

"That's a cold piece," Zach concluded, "That's some real dirt-bag shit, what she did to you."

"I think you might be overlooking something, Logan," Zeek pointed out

"What's that?"

"You said her ex-husband threatened to take her kids away unless she got rid of you, right?"

"Yep."

"And ten days later you're getting arrested. It sounds to me like her and Daddy Warbucks worked out a deal."

"It is possible, bro," Zach added, "It doesn't add up."

It got me thinking, as I paced the cell.

"So, the question I have, now that you guys are up to speed, is, do I file a police report against her for stealing my hard drives?"

"Hell yeah, you do!" Zach stated, "Let the gals in cell block show her what's up."

"I think you should," Zeek said

"What say you, Reaper?" I asked

He peered down from his bunk, "Go for it, little buddy!"

Earlier, I informed my attorney I wanted to press charges. He advised me not to, comparing it to jabbing a coiled snake with a stick. I decided to fire back. I got tired of my rights disregarded - tired of letting myself get kicked in the teeth.

The cell door opened for final headcount, after which I spoke.

"Deputy, I got word from my Power of Attorney, that the woman I lived with, stole valuable personal property from me. I'd like to file a report."

He explained the next steps, and that *'If she is found to be in possession of the property, she would then be put in handcuffs and charged.'*

I wrote as much useful info that I could and handed it to the officer. He said a detective would contact me soon, and then a warrant would be issued for her arrest. My cellmates and I applauded that.

.

Dinnertime.

I felt a fist rush past my left ear - the wind grazed my neck — though not directed at me.

Billy had swung on Whisper and failed to connect. I spun in my chair to see Whisper hit Billy with a right hook – then the two wailed on each other. The deputies charged, screaming *'Everyone get down on the floor, now!'* None of us complied, except the two fighting - they didn't want 50,000 volts in their chest. Whisper had laid on the ground, fingers locked behind his head before the deputies even got within range. Billy got tackled.

The rest of us got ordered to enter our cells, losing our out time. *What compelled Billy to fight Whisper?* We heard it regarded the size of the chicken patty Whisper served him ten minutes prior, in the dinner line. Whisper was stripped of his job duties and sent to *The Hole,* presumably with Billy, who I didn't see again.

Walk 3 had five cells, housing twenty men, at capacity. Each cell seemed to have one transitional bunk, with the other three reserved for more permanent residents. The last cell on the row housed Charles, Reggie, and a guy named Perry.

Charles, a soft-spoken man, in his early fifties, had done many years in prison. The system considered him to be 'institutionalized.' He'd seen the worst of people and had his fill. The tattoo work on his arms had no affiliations, from what I saw. He was kind and respectful and often checked in on me.

Reggie, a spirited kid from the Islands, was nineteen years old and tiny in stature. Because of his size, he got picked on, but he held his own. From a standing position, Reggie could do a front flip, roll in the air, and land on his feet in the same spot. When he got wind that I made movies, he enjoyed telling me his ideas.

Perry and I didn't have interaction in those opening weeks, though he'd eventually play a role in this story.

Then, we had Jimmy, further along in the row, in Cell 844. He was a live wire. He had a strong likeliness to the actor Michael Biehn in *The Abyss.* I remember evading him in the beginning because he had good looks; it *annoyed* me he had such perfect hair. I later told him that, and he thought it hysterical.

He propositioned me with a question, "What's the best film ever made?"
Before I could respond he cut me off, *"Young Guns!"* he said, excitedly, "Do you know what the second best film is?"
"Young Guns 2?"
His eyes got wide, *"Yes!"*
We debated it might be better than the original.

Jimmy had a cellmate - a full-blooded Navajo Indian. Jimmy called him 'Chavez,' so we ran with that. At night, Chavez did a ceremonial chant, the meaning of which I wouldn't presume to know. It resonated throughout the cell block, filling it with a strange peace. It was a powerful thing to hear - a freedom of spirit - in that place of imprisonment. I think it made the deputies uneasy as if their control were an illusion.

As the chanting faded out, Jimmy and his other cellmates continued the ritual and began howling like a pack of wolves. Our cell joined them, and clusters of inmates in the block followed, echoing a wild energy. That too would dwindle to a lone wolf's cry, Jimmy's; then cold silence.

.

My ballsy transfer to medical had garnered a little respect from Kyle Rory. He called me to his cell.

"What's up, dude? How are you feeling?" he asked, with a gnarled smile
"I'm alright. What's up?"
"Hey, I need a good lawyer, or I'm smoked!" he said, "Is yours any good?"
"I'll see if he takes referrals, Kyle. Hey, did Alex get sentenced? Is he in there?"

"Yeah, he's here!"
Alex got up from his bunk and walked to the window, defeated.
"What happened?" I asked
"They gave me a fucking year," he said flatly
"Wait, what? *For a misdemeanor?*"
He nodded.
"Are you staying here or going to prison?"
"Here."
I could see the resignation in his eyes. I didn't want my eyes to be like that.

.

The Reaper was a master card player. He spent his out times winning on the floor and then disgracing Zeek during lockdown. He only played for cake. His diet consisted entirely of it. He'd amass piles of the pastery, storing it in little Styrofoam bowls on our writing desk.

I didn't care for cards, and neither did Zach, but The Reaper talked us into a game of *Spades* and explained the rules to us. I felt privileged to learn from the guy. We flipped a plastic crate over and set it down between the bunks, covering it with a towel. Zeek, my teammate, sat diagonal to me.

The Reaper, seated at the foot of Zeek's bunk, farted unceasingly.
"Cake farts!" The Reaper quipped
"Dude, stop farting on my bed! What the fuck? Why would you do that?" Zeek protested, "Do I go up to your bed and fart? Why can't you go fart by the door like everybody else?"
"Don't be a bitch, Bud!" said The Reaper

"Grandpa," Zach advised, "You're gonna get used to calling Zeek a bitch in our cell, and one day you'll be on the floor, playing cards with some dude, and it's gonna slip. You're gonna call him a bitch, and he's gonna smack you. I'm just saying."

By this point, it didn't matter where The Reaper expelled. The accumulation of gas had formed like a low hanging fog. The only safe place to stand was under the air vent, but that paused the game. Instead, we wrapped pillowcases around our faces like bandits, covering our nose and mouth, and resumed playing. It helped, though our eyes still burned.

"Reaper, if you keep eating that much cake, you're going to fall into a diabetic Coma," I pointed out

"For real," agreed Zach, "That's what's up."

.

Zach read the Bible, though not an ardent Christian. He had curiosity towards all spiritual practices. He'd take a passage, clarify it, then think how one would integrate that teaching into one's life. Sometimes Zach got discouraged, and I was glad to see him questioning what he read.

He and Zeek did a nightly Bible study, and the two of them discussed at length their interpretations of each verse as they read it aloud. They'd invite me to join them, though I'd politely decline. Zeek closed the evening with a heartfelt prayer, albeit a long-winded one, thanking God for everything, from the dolphins to blades of grass.

"Goodnight, you guys! God bless," Zach would say, before pulling his makeshift headband over his eyes and sticking his earplugs in. He cared if we slept well.

.

I had scattered dreams- almost cheap, like a clearing of useless material. My subconscious purged itself of refuse; tired images and symbols that held no meaning, in here. Rooms and cities fluctuated. Suitcases got packed and unpacked with useless items. I remember running down a dark country road, my brother ahead of me, the sunset to our left. I walked European streets in the rain, hundreds of shuttling by, and not one familiar face. Bottles of alcohol were everywhere, yet I had no time or interest in drinking them.

Then, the chaotic dreams abruptly stopped, and I found myself in a small 1920s, Art Deco, studio apartment, on the second floor. The walls were painted red, and the north facing wall lined with windows overlooked a downtown street. I felt I could've walked straight to it, in reality, as if I knew the exact address. For the next week, my dreams occurred in that room, and no other. A series of women visited, freeing me of my physical attachment to Elena. I realized, however, that the north facing windows didn't receive sunlight. *Was this room another cell - an illusion of freedom?* Those dreams also quit spontaneously.

.

Zach's morning routine involved a forty-five-minute yoga session. He was quite accomplished; the series of positions he executed were not for a novice. I envied his discipline. My body ached badly and imagined I wasn't capable of his stances.

Zach walked laps from one end of the cell to the other, for roughly two hours, breaking to read a book for an hour, and then walked some more. Occasionally, he'd do another yoga session at night.

I tended to lay motionless and get consumed by my thoughts. Zach got aware when I went too long without speaking, and he'd snap me out of it.
"Don't do it, Logan. It's no good, bro! Get down here and walk with me."
I'd climb off my bunk and slip my sandals on, disliking the cold floor.
"Where are we walking to, Zach?" I asked as we paced the cell
"Right, ok. Let's see. We're in Virginia, on the beach."
"Nice. I haven't been. Are you from there?"
"Nope. I spent a lot of summers there when I was younger. I was born in Missoula, Montana."
"That's beautiful country. That explains the twang in your voice."

I'd overhear Zach say things to inmates out on the floor, that cracked me up.
"What are you doing there?" he'd ask
"Writing a letter."
"That's good. I write letters too. I'm glad to see you writing letters. You should keep doing that."

.

I taped a hand-drawn calendar to the wall, with an adhesive label. My cellmates appreciated it.
"Alright, Y'all. Circle your court dates. It'll help break things up. If you look at each day on the calendar, you'll see a smaller number next to it, either a one, two, three or four. That's our out time for the day I have *those* times written on this paper here," I said, taping the second sheet to the wall:

Day 1   Day 2
5:15 am – 5:45 am Breakfast   5:45 am – 6:15 am Breakfast
11:15 am – 11:45 am Lunch   10:45 am – 11:15 am Lunch
6:15 pm – 6:45 pm Dinner   2:30 pm – 4:45 pm Out Time
8:00 pm – 10:15 pm Out Time   4:45 pm – 5:15 pm Dinner

Day3   Day 4
6:15 am – 6:45 am Breakfast   4:45 am – 5:15 am Breakfast
8 am – 10:15 am Out Time   11:45 am – 12:15 pm Lunch
10:15 am – 10:45 am Lunch   12:15 pm – 2:30 pm Out Time
5:15 pm – 5:45 pm Dinner   *5:45 pm – 6:15 pm Dinner*

I circled the date of my Preliminary Hearing - three days out.

.

The writing pens issued by the jail were three-and-a-half inches long. The ink channel got inserted into a rubber tube that conformed to our hands. It prevented stabbings, but it made writing a labor, giving us cramps in our fingers.

The Reaper saw my frustration, and in secret he reinforced his own pen using a jailhouse method; wrapping the pen repeatedly with wet strips of paper, and then, when dry, using the adhesive label from our soap bottles to fasten it.

He gave me the pen as a gift and warned me to keep it hidden in my sock during out times since the jail considered it to be paraphernalia. Cell inspection occurred a few times a week. Deputies would come in and toss the place, searching for contraband, or a surplus of jail property like sheets or pillows. We had to keep receipts for commissary orders, as they'd check them for unlisted supplies.

.

The Reaper managed to harbor grasshoppers from the rec yard. He brought them into cell block and released them in our cell, and on the main floor. Inmates gathered to feed them pieces of steamed vegetables. They took care not to crush the wandering insects and cautiously stepped over them.

"Hey Grandpa," Zach asked The Reaper, "Where were you living on the streets?"
"In a tent by the Boise River."
"Aren't you afraid someone is going to steal your stuff while you're in jail?"
"I have kids watching it. I adopt street kids."

"How many have you adopted, Grandpa?"
"Ninety-four."

The Reaper got angry talking about his arrest, saying the cops searched him illegally. They found a gram of meth in a little vial on his keychain.
"I was holding it for a kid. It wasn't even mine," The Reaper said
"You don't do drugs, Grandpa?"
"Nope."
"You just eat cake, huh?"
"Yep."

The Reaper mentioned he panhandled from the same location each night - a gutted telephone booth in front of a nightclub on 7th street. I knew the spot he referred to. Elena and I breezed past it on many times of our drunken nights. I tried to recall seeing a figure seated there.

.

Zeek claimed he auditioned for the role of 'Bud Bundy' in the TV sitcom *Married With Children*. He said he didn't get the part because of his crooked teeth. It was hard not to believe him. He got upset about it even now, like *that was the day* things started to go wrong for him.

Zeek played The Reaper in countless card games, and he rarely won. That said, The Reaper still accused Zeek of cheating and doctoring the scorecard.
"You win every fucking game! How am I cheating?" Zeek pleaded, "Even if I were cheating you still win! Why do you even care?"
Zeek would get frustrated and stand by the window, pretending to watch TV.
"Hey! Bud Bundy! Acorn Head!" The Reaper antagonized
"Don't *call me* that *you... Fucking old man!"* Zeek would say, gritting his teeth, like an angry squirrel
"Come on, Bud!"
"No! I don't want to play anymore. Leave me alone!"
"Acorn Head! Come get your ass whooped at cards!"
"You dirty... *Fucking old bastard!"*
"ODG! Old Dirty Grandpa! C'mon, BUD!"
After a while, they'd make amends and resume their game. It was great entertainment for Zach and me.

.

The Reaper loved taking a shit prior to final headcount, thus defeating the guard's instructions to stand. He'd be sitting merrily on the toilet, reading a sci-fi novel, when the door opened.

"Would ya like me to stand, officer?"

"No, Woodbury. I'd rather you didn't."

The Reaper did his best to drive them crazy. He'd often plant himself flat against the cell door, out of sight, as the deputies did their quarterly cell check. When the officer glanced in, The Reaper would jump in front of the window and shout, 'NANU NANU!' causing the man to leap backward.

.

Zeek dreamt of being a moviemaker.

"What are you writing, Zeek?" Zach asked

"Movie ideas. I'm at number thirty-eight. Eleven more to go. I need to have fifty ideas before I get released."

"What's this one about?"

"It's a remake of Hitchcock's 'Room with a View,' *and* it's also a remake of 'Diehard."

"At the same time?" Zach inquired

"Yes, at the same time."

Zeek gave us the grand scope of his story, with zeal and drama, in far more detail than we could bear. He'd often stop, and second-guess himself, *'Or maybe it would go like this.'*

"I don't know, Zeek. I don't find that idea to be very creative," Zach said, bluntly

Zach had a dime-store science fiction novel under his bunk, called *Dark World*.

"Hey, that's a great name for a title," Zeek suggested, "That can be movie idea number forty-three. There's a world that's - "

"Isn't that copyright infringement, to steal their title?" Zach interrupted

"Yeah, you're right. I know! I'll call it Dark *Worlds*, and there'll be *two* of them."

Zeek was a panhandler at heart, intent on mooching supplies from us, acting as if he were entitled to our coffee. Earning an item through diligent work did not qualify as one of his principles. He'd bargain with Zach and me, yet all he had in trade was shit the jail gave us for free, anyway. The best deal for us was to exchange our goods for his morning fruit.

Zach let him borrow his pen so he could scribble his movie plots. Zeek returned it, chewed up.

"You have no respect for other people's property, Zeek. I don't want the pen."

"Take it. It's fine," Zeek urged

"No, it's not fine. Look how chewed up it is."

"I'll get you another one."

"That's not the point. What makes you think it's ok to do this? When I loan you something, I want it back in good condition."

"Dude quit busting my balls about the pen."

"All you do is take, Zeek. You're greedy. You don't care for anybody but yourself."

"You're right. I look after myself. No one else does."

"And why do you think that is, Zeek?"

.

Zach had a favorite saying, and it caused me to smile, without fail.

"We're in the thick of it now, guys," he'd say, usually at inopportune moments

It revealed the absurdity of our situations. In a nutshell, we were completely fucked, and very little could remedy it.

.

The prosecution finally turned in my Discovery file. Upon receiving it, my attorney drove to the jail at once. I read it with trepidation, and we both were blown away by its contents.

"The prosecutor say's he's waiting for results from the medical tests," my attorney said, through the glass of the visitor's booth, "He says they have photographs of Elena's neck, clearly showing bruises from you strangling her."

I felt numb. "I didn't touch her neck."

"I think he's bluffing. I don't think they're doing any tests. It's bullshit. They're trying to scare you into a confession."

"Fuckin' assholes."

"The level of trauma she's describing is so significant she'd have bruises and marks everywhere. Even her friend Mandy stated *on record* that she saw no marks on Elena's neck, the following day. Mandy did see bruises on her legs, though. What's that about?"

"She's allergic to the sun. Her legs and arms constantly have bruises. I don't know if we want to go down this road, but I'm concerned about something."

"What's that?"

"Elena asked me to do things to her, during sex. She liked being whipped and choked. I'm afraid there may be a mark on her neck from that."

"Jesus. How long ago was this?"

"At least two weeks before the fight, so I doubt there's anything. I'm working myself up."

"Stop doing that. We're fine."

"What if she bruised her neck to validate her story?"

"How crazy is this woman? Look, I'm convinced they're using scare tactics to get a confession from you. Stand your ground. I agree that if we use the sex angle, it may blow up in our faces. Is she so extreme that she'd injure herself? You knew the woman. What do you think?"

"I honestly don't know, and that's killing me."

"Let's discuss the kidnapping charge. What's this shit with you locking her in the closet?"

"The closet doesn't have a lock. Besides, it opens inwards."

"She says you left for 'some time' after you locked her in there."

"In a closet that can't lock? Where would I go? It's lies on top of lies."

"Exactly, and that's how we get her. She has to keep track of each lie she tells. She says you took her car keys?"

"Yes, I did."

"Technically, Idaho considers that kidnapping."

"Then I guess I've worked in too many bars. I thought it was against the law *not* to take the keys from a drunk. I reacted. I thought I'd get commended for it."

"Alright. The prosecution will have a difficult time pushing that charge when the court hears your motivations. They're using the closet incident as a means to support it. Why were you in the closet in the first place?"

"I went in there to grab a shirt and a pair of shoes."

"I'm not buying that for a second."

"Well, I'm sorry, but that was the case. We argued in their maybe fifteen seconds. Elena was grabbing shit and threatening to leave."

"Did you slap her in the face on that night or any other night?"

"I've never hit anyone in my life. Why would I stop her from driving just to turn around and hurt her myself?"

"There were no marks on her face. None."

"And there never were."

"Did you threaten to kill her if she left you?"

"The total opposite. I told Elena I couldn't stand to look at her, and that I didn't want to be in a relationship."

"She says you tried to cut her off from her family."

"The people that helped me get a car, and brought us weekly groceries, and offered to pay for my college? Why would I alienate them? We counted on their support."

"Your eyes changed when she mentioned Jesus, huh?"

"I promise I'm not possessed. The *entire* argument was over Elena going to her ex-husband. You need to understand that. He threatened to take her children away unless she got rid of me and stopped talking to her family. *That's the whole fucking fight.*

"That certainly sounds more plausible. What's with you telling the arresting officer her ex-husband followed you?"

"What of it?"

"You need to stop talking like that. People are going to think you're crazy."

"What's this shit at the bar with Mandy?"

"A huge disaster."

"Well, they're using it to show a pattern of behavior. That was a big mistake on your part. If you want my advice, don't ever drink alcohol with your mom and fiancee."

"Now you tell me."

"So, let's talk about what you *did do,* then. What happened?"

"When she rushed to the door, I grabbed her arm and took her keys. She went for the door again, and I whipped towards the couch."

"That's where the traumatic head injury comes in. That's why the domestic charge is a felony."

"Well, I *did* do that. I stated that from day one."

"I wish you hadn't. But even if Elena did get a bump on her head, it's a misdemeanor at best. There's no serious injury."

"She fell onto a pile of pillows."

"She's saying she hit her head on the arm of the couch."

"I didn't see that, and she didn't say anything. If she had, I would've helped her."

"She gave you no indication of an injury?"

"None."

"What else did you do?"

"I said plenty of terrible things."

"So you did call her *'a fucking bitch,'* and *'a spoiled little brat'?*"

"I sure did."

"It really bothers me she's accusing you of raping her," my attorney said, in finality, changing the tone of the conversation

"... Me too."

"Why would she say that?"

"I don't have an answer."

"I'm going to stay on top of this, Logan. You know you can call me at any time, right?"

"Yes. Thank you."

"I'll see you in court tomorrow. I'll talk with the prosecutor and get a feel for him. I'll see you beforehand."

"Ok."

I could tell from his face the hearing would be ugly. *They're gonna come at you hard.* We talked about bypassing it altogether. It was a dangerous move - waiving me over to felony district court – however, her testimony being read aloud, along with the statements from police, couldn't help our defense.

He requested I contact my friends and family, and have them write character references. It wasn't practical for me to handle the task, so it fell on the shoulders of my mother and Tony.

As I walked alone, down the hallway to Cell Block 8, I thought of what my attorney had said, *'Her anger comes from fear.'*

.

Dinner had already been served. I asked the deputy at the control desk to please get me a tray of food, when Zach jogged up.

"Yo, we lost a cellie," he said, bouncing off with no further details

I scanned the main floor. I saw Zeek, wearing his customary sweater, two sizes too big. *I had failed to witness the implosion of The Reaper.* During cell inspection, the deputies removed his stockpile of cake and threw it in the garbage. He'd *won* that cake. The Reaper screamed at the officers from the upper tier - admonishing them to hell, calling them thieving little bitches. They took him down. The Reaper was dragged off in cuffs. I did not see him again.

.

In the Discovery file, the police had a series of photographs of our apartment. Thirty-one photocopied black and white images of my former home, including a photo of that fucking couch, and my stolen computer system. A Gucci bag on the kitchen counter, my books, an Ikebana arrangement that needed water. Jack's bed. I shouldn't have looked at them.

There were two screen captures of Elena's phone; a text from my attorney, ordering her to bring specific items to his office, and a text from my mother saying, *'I can't believe you're doing this to my son and someone you said you loved.'*

I got withdrawn, and Zach understood why.

"Hey bro, if you want to talk, let me know," he said

Ada County Jail was a massive pressure cooker, and each event, no matter how small, would turn that dial up or down.

Something went wrong in my old cell, 821. Three deputies escorted Kyle to a private room for a solid twenty minutes. When he returned, I saw his face; he was *livid*, rubbing his beard in disgust. The next morning, Chris transferred to our Walk, where he had no friends. Kyle got sent to *The Hole.* Zach and a few others were already tracking Chris before I said anything.

"He's got a bad attitude," I warned
"That's what's up. I know. I can tell," Zach said

We were in lockdown, when the fire alarms rang, shutting off the air ventilation system. The three of us exchanged glances. Ninety-seven degrees outside, and we had no circulation. I admit I felt a bit claustrophobic. It got hard to breathe, and our uniforms stuck to our bodies. Without the static sound of the fan, I could pick up noises from around the block. It was an eerie sensation, realizing how much activity went on that we normally couldn't hear.

Zach laid on his bunk, quieter than usual, his face concealed by the towel canopy. Without the company of The Reaper, Zeek talked incessantly, and our tolerance ran thin, especially Zach's.

Zeek sat on his opposing bunk, and I paced the floor between them. He commented on my weight, saying that if I sweat off more pounds, I'd be an Ethiopian.
"Is that supposed to be creative, Zeek?" I asked dryly, "I got shit like that in high school, man."
"*Shut the fuck up, Zeek,*" Zach said sharply
I paused. That was an unfamiliar tone, for Zach.
Zeek tread lightly, "What, man? I was just-"
"I said shut the fuck up! Don't *ever* fuckin' talk to that man like that! You don't know what his body needs, or what his metabolism is like! You're not a fuckin' doctor, *so why are you talking shit motherfucker?*"
"Look, I was just saying"
Zach swung his legs off his bunk and planted his feet firmly on the ground, in a lunging position, his face blood red. Zeek crumbled.
"You wanna go for it, Zeek?" he dared
"No, man, I - "
"Then fucking apologize to that man!" he ordered, pointing at me
Zeek was speechless.
"FUCKIN' APOLOGIZE TO HIM!!" Zach screamed

"Logan, hey man, I'm sorry. I didn't mean anything by it. Ok? I'm sorry."
"Apology accepted, Zeek," I said
Zach laid down, locking his arms behind his head, face still red, as he breathed through his nose.
"Thanks, man," I said
He looked at me. We bumped fists, and he quickly locked his arms again.
"You got it, bro."

Zach Morris had my back. That was a good feeling.

It was my thirtieth day of incarceration.

My hearing, scheduled for tomorrow morning,
and I promised you an emotional day in court.

Preliminary Hearing

4 am - Razors.

An officer unlocked the tray slot, and cold air drifted in.
"Crannell! Wake up. Come get your razor," he called, setting it on the ledge
It had a single blade. No shaving cream. I edged my beard and shaved my neck, dabbing off the blood with a towel. I ran water through my hair. It was easier to get hot water in the mornings. I tried not to wake my cellmates, tapping my razor lightly on the metal sink. I put on my best fitting uniform. I meditated for thirty minutes until breakfast. I'd acquired a taste for the oatmeal. I tried tucking my pant legs into my socks, to protect my ankles against the shackles, but it didn't work. They came out with each step. After I ate, I waited for the deputy.

I got led through a winding corridor, to an area of holding cages. They kept us divided by classification. I being the only inmate from Cell Block 8.

I was then taken to an outdoor area, with a group. In my life, no other location has negatively affected me the way that site did. With no roof, four concrete walls, standing fifteen feet high, closed us in.

The elements, over the course of decades, had warped and stained the surface of the walls, giving them their own language. Those walls breathed. I did not want to place my hands upon them. It felt like a place of execution. It radiated death, cold and complete.

In the early stage of sunrise, the humidity clung to me, oppressively. The walls and ground smelled of wet stone and sediment. Inmates, since departed, had written on the walls with pens and markers, as high as human arms could reach - but the walls rose far above those marks. They'd be there, longer than any of us would live.
"Get up against the wall, Crannell! Hands against the wall, feet spread."
I faced that wall, smelling it, my hands absorbing its moisture, while the deputy ran a chain around my waist. He then locked the shackles on my ankles, having me raise my feet. My wrists were cuffed to my sides and secured to the chain at my waist. Even half-steps were too much.

.

The first time I got transported to the courthouse, to ask for a continuance, they put me in a van designed for nine inmates. On this trip, as we shuffled through the dark parking garage, we were directed towards a bus. As we boarded, single file, the only light came from an array of surveillance monitors positioned near the driver's seat.

Iron gates divided the bus into four sections, based on security level. The first area contained two seats, for maximum security. I was in section two. I took a position that allowed me to see through the windshield.

Suddenly, music blasted in the darkness as the engine started up. John Cougar Mellencamp's *Small Town.* It sounded incredible. The speaker system lined the upper rim of the cabin, and it kicked loudly.

The garage door opened and flooded us with light, as we drove off. My senses tried to adjust to the welcoming intensity.

.

As the empty freeway became downtown, buildings rose into my vision. The bus drove past the places of my old life; the restaurants and bars that Elena and I enjoyed, the sidewalks, and the familiar storefronts.

With each blink of my eye, memories streamed by.
Did I miss it? I knew I was supposed to, yet I felt so detached.

The next song on the radio happened to be one of Hetty's favorites,
that ridiculous one by Ellie Goulding, *'Love Me Like You Do.'*

The reality hit me in the gut.
I wasn't prepared for it and felt overwhelmed with emotion.

The seat beside me was empty, yet I could feel Hetty sitting next to me,
listening along, and smiling like we were driving to the store.
'What are you sad for, Loulou?'

You gave me strength, Hetty.

Simon and Garfunkel's *'The Sound of Silence,'* played. My mind wandered to
the sunlight, as it danced through the trees, and off the metal of cars. The song
continued as we approached the courthouse, driving down a ramp, underneath the city
itself, to our destination.

.

We hated the holding tank, there. The iron benches lining the walls made our
bones ache. Unable to relax, we took turns, using a roll of toilet paper to rest our head
on. The din and echo were so abrasive it required too much effort to understand what
was said. That underground complex served as the terminal where all inmates, male or
female, from jail or prison, came together. The facing wall of our cell, made of glass, let
us see the parade of convicts, in different colors of uniform, shuffle by.

.

8:30 am - I walked another extended hallway. The shackles tore at my ankles,
though the pain gave me something to focus on. The officer issued instructions.
"When you enter the elevator, go to the far wall and face forward."
Did it take us to the ground level or higher? I couldn't tell.
"Once inside the courtroom," the officer warned, "do not attempt to make eye
contact or communicate with *anyone* in the audience. Walk *directly* to your chair and be
seated. Do you understand?"
The elevator opened to a small waiting area and a walkway that led to the
court. I moved towards the door, in a single file line. I scanned the crowd subtly. Elena
wasn't there. I focused on my attorney's face, as he motioned me to a chair. The colors
were bright - greens, golds, reds, and browns. The noises got dampened, and whispers
defined. The prosecution's side of the room seemed in disarray. A female assistant
stood in for the prosecutor himself.

I received an amended list of charges, with the *'Traumatic head injury'* no longer attached to the domestic violence accusation. *Why did it remain a felony?* (That oversight got corrected, shortly)

"It's being postponed, until later this afternoon," my attorney said in a hushed tone, "They're stalling. They say they're still waiting for some bullshit medical records."

I rose for the Judge, and my charges got read aloud. Words were briefly exchanged, and the proceedings delayed until 1:00 pm. In seconds, I was removed, led to the elevator, and brought down to the empty holding tank.

.

I was alone in there.

I feared I'd reached the end of myself. I couldn't deal with it anymore.
Exhaustion wore at me, and I had four hours to wait for the officer.
My throat was dry, and I couldn't swallow. The water in the sink ran yellow with rust.

I paced for hours until I collapsed and fell to my knees.
I sobbed, but I was so dehydrated tears did not come to my eyes.

I chose to pray; my final time doing so.

I prayed for her absence.
I prayed for the harsh reality of this day to be too much for her.
I prayed for God to change her heart, that one last plea.
But, mostly I prayed for strength.

Again, I thought of Hetty, and I thought of Aidan.
I could not give up. Something swelled inside of me.

Maybe my spirit wasn't dead after all...

.

At 1:00 pm they announced my name on the speaker. In the elevator, the deputy issued the same warning, *'Once inside the courtroom, do not attempt to make eye contact or communicate with anyone in the audience.'* I would not comply. I stood in the small waiting room. My attorney came jogging down the walkway, visibly disturbed. He straightened his tie.

"It's a goddamn circus out there! She's here. Elena's here, and it looks like she's brought her whole family!"

The wind left me. I had to regain it.

"Waive it," I said, "Waive the preliminary."

He agreed it was the best decision. He went through the door, leaving me. I tried to regulate my breathing. *This is it. This is your moment of strength, Logan.*

I entered the courtroom, and looked immediately to the crowd. There was a family there, of her nationality, though not hers. Elena, seated in the row behind them, wore sunglasses and faced downward. Mandy sat beside her, with two children. My heart skipped a beat, thinking Elena had brought them, but they were Mandy's. *Who brings kids to this?*

The proceedings began. The Judge ordered me to rise and asked me a series of questions. He wanted to know that I understood the full extent, and risk, of what I had initiated, and that I did so of my own volition. *'Yes, Your Honor.'*

I took my seat, and my attorney whispered in my ear.

"I don't care *what* they told you, when you stand up, *you turn around and tell me who's in this courtroom. I want to know exactly who these fucking people are,*" he said

The Judge finished. I breathed deeply and exhaled. I rose, moving fluidly. Mandy and I locked eyes. She had a pained look on her face. I gazed at her coldly. Elena's gaze remained lowered. Then, a wave of people surrounded me - I was being ushered out by officers, my attorney trailing, hot with questions. I swept the crowd, confirming that no one else recognizable had attended.

I was a few feet from the doorway when I resisted the tide of hands and turned around. Elena was staring right at me, an expression of ambiguity on her face. I remained strong, my face showing little emotion. I raised my eyes to meet her own. For five slow seconds, we held eye contact. *In that moment, the world stopped for us; for the last time.*

.

On the transport to jail, that image of her burned in my mind. Elena couldn't hide from me, hard as she tried. The fingertips of her left hand were pressed against her temple and forehead, and spread apart, concealing herself from everyone but me, her body shaking. Elena's agonized smile, which conveyed so much shame, guilt, anger, and longing, left me with no closure.

We blew it, Elena. Not I. We.

A New Cellie

"How many mattresses are out there?"

"One."

It was our nightly ritual; the counting of the mats. At 10:30 pm, the deputies placed mattresses on the table by the control desk. The number of which signaled to us how many new inmates were on their way to cell block. On our Walk, we had the only cell with a vacancy. The lights went out. I waited for my eyes to adjust, then continued reading *The Screwtape Letters*, by C.S Lewis, a rare find from the jail library.

"Did anybody come in?" Zach asked

"Not yet," Zeek replied

"Well, I'm going to bed. God bless, you guys!" Zach said, pulling down his headband

I'd fallen asleep when Rick Kellner made his entrance, and he came in with a bang. Frankly, I wasn't sure if I'd like Rick. He bragged of his charges with such enthusiasm. I gave him the benefit of the doubt, thinking that underneath his thunder, there might be a man that grew up too damn fast.

.

Rick got pulled over, in what appeared to be a routine traffic stop, for failing to use his turn signal. Rick suspected otherwise. Across the road, he saw the girl he was supposed to meet, parked at a restaurant. He sent her a text; *bring me a cigarette.* Rick wanted to go in style; in a moment the officer would locate his warrant. Police started gathering and flanked his car. *Floor it, Rick.* He pushed it to 120mph, spraying them with gravel. *Maybe he'd get that smoke, after all.*

The cops tried to lay a spike strip on the road - Rick flew by while they busily unloaded it from the trunk. *Get your shit out of the car.* Rick rolled his window and opened the suitcase on the passenger seat. He tossed the pistol - and bags of drugs, as he crossed county lines.

He tore into a residential area, with no thoughts of stopping, losing police cars within the suburbs. He planned to weave onto the freeway. An intersection arrived fast – with another vehicle driving through it. He clipped its tail end. Rick's car spun out of control, but he regained the wheel, flipped a U-turn and accelerated down a one-way street.

Sirens wailed in every direction. He found the freeway entrance and merged onto it at full speed. He left the second county, lighting up switchboards along the way. The third county of police scrambled for updates. Dispatch radioed in for additional spike strips – and they hurried to lay them in Rick's path.

They beat him and managed to blow Rick's tires. Rick leapt from the car before it skidded to a halt. *Run for it, Rick.* He ran through a field, with cops drawing firearms - *Too far for a clean shot.* They set the dogs on him, instead. Rick lost the first canine when he scaled a tall fence and ran towards a housing development. *You've gotta hide, Rick.* He saw a yellow tool shed, behind a house, coming up on his left and barged in.

Think, Rick. He threw a rope over a rafter and tied it through the door handle. It was winter, and he wore a t-shirt, shaking from the cold, adrenaline and drugs in his system. Rick heard the dogs outside hunting for a scent. Cops from three counties stormed the neighborhood. He sent a text message to the girl, with his GPS coordinates; *Get here now!*

The girl's gave up Rick's position. Cops questioned her, and in a panic, she said too much. Within seconds, the shed got surrounded. *You're fucked, Rick.* He untied the rope from the door and exited, with his hands held high. At 9:30 pm, the three-hour pursuit concluded.

(That's my version, omitting a few hundred '*Dudes! Fucks!* And *Bro's!*')

Rick laid on his bunk, opposite mine, his mind still processing the event. He rolled his face to me, with a friendly expression.
"Hey Rick, can I ask you a question?" I said
"Sure. What's up?"
"What's your bail set at?"
"$250,000," he said, bewildered
I laughed, staring up at the ceiling.
"Why? What's yours?"
"$500,000."
Rick smiled with surprise. He didn't ask why. There'd be plenty of time for that.

"We're in the thick of it now, guys," Zach said

.

In the afternoon, the four of us were lively with conversation. Zeek chatted Rick's ear off, regaling him with stories Zach and I were sick to death of hearing.
"So I was banging this girl, right - *yeah baby!* - and she had these rings on all of her fingers, you know what I mean? I didn't know she was *married."*
"You didn't notice some dude's stuff in the house?" Zach inferred

"I thought she was a football fan! So we're doing it, and I think the front door opens, and I remember *I left my boots in the hallway.* Then this guy says *'Are these my boots?'* and he sounds like Ricky from *I Love Lucy*, you know? *'Lucy, are these my boots, Lucy?'* and she's like *'Oh shit, it's my husband!'* and I turn to see a guy standing in the doorway with this big hunting knife and I'm getting dressed fast, you know? I'm like *'Hey man! That's a nice knife!'* He tells me to get the fuck out, so I run for it. I get to the back door, and then I stop. I'm like, *'I wonder if they have any beer. No, I should run. No, I should check the fridge'.* So, I go in, and there's one tall boy left! I grab it and bolt. She was a cop, so I was too nervous to go back and get my own boots!"

"He adds something to that story every time, bro," Zach mentioned, to Rick

"I thought it was funny!" Rick laughed

"Thank you," Zeek bowed

"Seems like a comedy skit, to me," Zach said

"There's a comedy club downtown called Liquid," Zeek explained, "They do an open mic night, and you get sixty seconds to tell your joke."

"You should practice your speed, my friend," I suggested

"What's next, Zeek?" Zach asked, "The one with you drunk and lost on that country road when the bus flips and burst into flames, and you save everybody?"

"That's an excellent story!" Zeek argued

"Or how about that one with you drunk on private property, and if it hadn't been for you smelling that gas leak, all those people woulda died."

"That's an amazing story, too," Zeek said in his defense

"I don't know, bro. I think you look for ways to justify your alcoholism," Zach opined

So'd go the tales of Zeek. He'd vividly recount being chased by farmers with pitchforks, pregnant lesbians with dildos named Snuffleupagus, karaoke pipedreams, and his failed marriage proposals.

"How long have you been here, Zeek?" I asked

"Since, uh. I got arrested on -"

He checked the police report, and gave me the exact date - it was Elena's birthday.

"What?" I said, in disbelief, "What time? Does it say?"

"Yes. Yes, it does. 7:05 pm. That's the time of my arrest."

"Damn, I know exactly what I was doing."

I remembered checking my watch as I started mixing drinks for Elena and Mandy. *This jail has sixteen-hundred inmates in total, and I got locked up with this guy.* Zeek asked if I'd be willing to lie and say he'd been in my company that night. I politely declined.

.

Rick had a build like a UFC cage fighter - roughly six-foot-one, and two-hundred-twenty pounds. You'd do more damage riding a bicycle into a tank than you would to fight Rick.

He had remarkable black-and-gray tattoo work on his chest and legs. I learned that during his last stint in prison, his calves and shins were done by one of the institutions more renowned artists - in a single sitting, with the aid of prison yard painkillers. The art felt like a hybrid of H.R Giger and Adam Jones, with a dose of 1950's sci-fi in the mix. *Rick had good taste in art.*

Rick, twenty-nine years old, got insecure about his thinning hair. It didn't take long to see he had a boyish innocence to him. Rick liked to laugh; his voice naturally soft in tone. He wasn't the type to resort to violence unless he had no choice. *The man had heart.*

He knew several people in Cell Block 8, on our Walk, especially Trav. They'd apparently grown up together or at least known one another long enough to seem like it. It gave the impression the whole neighborhood was there, hanging out, and I don't understand why we failed to see that as more than a coincidence.

.

I saw Rick covering an intercom on our cell wall, by the panic button, with adhesive labels and asked him why. I assumed the speaker to be defunct.
"I was told they could listen in on our conversations, and we wouldn't know it. I mean, they *do* work. They're hooked up. Why take the chance, you know?"
"Huh! Good thinkin', Rick," Zach said, "I know a dude on Walk 1 who was going home in two weeks, bro. The FED's planted a snitch in the cell that got the dude talking, and they gave him ten years in prison for conspiracy."

.

Zach peeled his morning orange, and divide it into wedges. He put them in a small plastic bag and poured in red hot sauce, to marinate them. They were delicious.
"Hey dude, let me get your orange peels," Rick said, as he collected the pieces of rind
He tugged a stitching thread from his vinyl mat and ran it through the iron grate covering the air vent in the ceiling. It made a clothesline for hanging wet laundry. On this occasion, though, Rick hung the rinds, filling the cell with the scent of orange. It was surprisingly effective.

.

"Are you high? Dude, your pupils, are huge!" Rick asked me, "Zach, check it out, bro!"

"Huh!" said Zach, grinning

"I get that a lot. People ask me if I'm holding, but it's just the Zoloft."

"How much are they giving you?"

"A hundred milligrams."

"Does it help?"

"I suppose. I definitely feel it in the mornings, like a low-level high."

"What are you on, Zach?" Rick inquired

"Um, I'm on Geadon, for my schizoaffective disorder. If I go a day without it, my hallucinations come back, bro. I'm so glad I'm on the right medicine now."

"What do you see?"

"Ok, like, see that towel hanging? Without my medication that towel will look like it's melting downwards, you know?"

"Right on."

"Hey guys," I asked, pointing to the wall-mounted clothes hangers, "Why do they move like a joystick?"

"If they didn't, we could hang ourselves," Rick answered

"That makes sense."

.

I liked the weekends; the whole judicial machine ground to a stop. No one got paid to give a shit, for forty-eight hours. No developments, surprise visits or evaluations. To a large degree, I didn't think on my case.

One invents scenarios, speeches in court, and potential arguments. You rehearse them in your mind until you're vaguely proud of yourself. It's noise. Dead air. Static channels. A mind circling itself into shut down. When those events arise, you're standing there like an idiot, second-guessing yourself, relying on someone else to speak for you. *Did you think they'd sympathize with your pain?*

You're a blip falling off the radar. Life outside continues without you. Your job position gets filled. People come to terms with your absence. Justice becomes secondary to paperwork. Your attorney conducts a waiting game with an overworked prosecutor who barely recalls your name. *This is your fucking life, man.*

My only strategy upon release, however far away, was to push forward with extreme productivity. I knew the second I paused to reflect, I'd be finished in a bad way. I didn't have the mental tools to cope with this experience. I figured a cathartic emotional collapse to be the most I could hope for, painfully aware that I had no higher means of reconciliation or understanding.

Elena, in a second unannounced visit to my attorney's office, delivered – of all things – my mail. *Thanks, I was concerned about the internet bill.* What she said to him had far greater meaning.

"I'm leaving," Elena stated

"Where?" he asked

"I guess I'm getting back together with my ex-husband."

With that comment, Elena validated my entire defense. Our fight had not started over 'Jesus,' but Elena's lack of integrity.

"Where are the hard drives, Elena? You were instructed to bring them to my office," my attorney inquired

"I searched the apartment and didn't find anything like that," she claimed

A blatant lie, with video evidence to support it. It indicated to me that Elena lied for a reason.

I talked to Tony.

"Hey man, that was scary shit," he said of entering my apartment

I had a good laugh.

"I asked some of my friends to help me," he continued, "They wouldn't. They were afraid the crazy bitch had a gun. I tell ya, going in there, knowing she could show up at any second and don't take this the wrong way, but you have pretty weird style. I wasn't sure which clothes were yours."

"Well, I knew you'd handle it. I'm short on people I trust out there," I said, chuckling

Tony appreciated my sleepless nights, with losing my videography, and my gear. Besides, he got personally invested in my animated project, wanting to do the score.

"I know you're tearing yourself up in there. I can't imagine," Tony said, "Hang in there, man."

Elena paid the last month of rent, and Tony decided when to covertly enter the apartment, and get the rest of my things. Sadly, his dog passed from an illness. It tore him up bad. I couldn't ask him to put my troubles in front of his grief.

I grew less interested in retrieving my belongings. I accepted that when, and if, I got to Tony's house, there'd be a pile of objects in the corner of his studio. A fraction of what I owned when I arrived in Idaho, now without the truck I drove here in.

My mother tirelessly urged people to write letters on behalf, and mail them prior to the deadline. Hollace told my mother he'd help me if I forgave him, and that he still considered me his best friend. My heart, however, wasn't ready for forgiveness, and perhaps never would be. I couldn't afford it. He decided to assist regardless and collected letters from my old friends.

I thought the opportunity for payback might appeal to Will. His testimony would've supported my own. Unfortunately, he declined and sent his condolences. It was a disappointment, but I respected his decision.

I sat with my attorney as I read the photocopied letters, and they moved me. Friends and loved ones, some I hadn't spoken to in years, if not a decade, shared memories of me that I, with humility, had since forgotten. I couldn't believe that small acts of mine had left such a lasting impact.

.

Filing the police report against Elena boosted morale for my friends and family. After three weeks without word, though, I got a bitter taste in my mouth. The deputies were on a rotating four-day schedule, like us, and after the change-up, I'd approach the new officers on duty with my situation. *Have patience. Someone will talk to you,'* is all they'd say. Not until the fifth rotation did I get a straight answer.

"Wait, what do you mean a deputy on staff filed the report?" he asked, puzzled
"The officer on duty took what I wrote, and said he'd file it."
"And no one from Boise P.D spoke to you?"
"No."
"Well, that's not how a report gets filed. Who was this?"
"I can't remember his name. I have the date."
"We can't file reports for Boise P.D. All we can do is have them send an officer. That should've occurred that night, depending on how busy they were."
"So, you're telling me the report doesn't exist, and I've been getting screwed for three weeks? My entire life's work is on those drives."
"I'll get on the phone with them right now."
"That's fine. Thank you," I said in dismay

.

2:45 am - I got escorted to the lobby in booking to meet with an officer from the Boise Police Department. The man, surprised by my organization, glanced at my notes.
"Why did you wait three weeks to file this?" he asked

He raised his eyebrows at my response.

"It doesn't help your case with so much time having passed," he sighed with frustration

We spoke in depth. He supported my efforts to charge Elena and proposed multiple ways to approach the situation.

"I'm not going to lie to you," he said, closing the conversation, "It's going to be an uphill battle getting your property. These types of items aren't easy to reclaim."

"Understood. What crime did she officially commit?"

"Grand Theft. It carries a maximum sentence of five years in prison."

"Awesome. Let's do it."

I returned to my cell at 4 am, not feeling tired. *He listened.* Things were falling into motion.

.

A female caseworker visited me, during our lunch break, and asked me if I still had thought of suicide. I laughed out loud.

"You guys pick some stupid times to ask me that. Am I suicidal? I don't think so? I'm sitting here eating a peanut butter sandwich, watching 'The Social Network.' How are *you* feeling? Your day's busier than mine."

She directed me to a large medical office in a different location, for a routine exam and to check my weight. They couldn't figure why the Boost wasn't working. *'Beats me,'* I said. In the lobby, they had rows of empty seats. I took one and changed the television channel, to resume watching the movie. I heard an inmate sit behind me.

"Hey, Logan. How are the meds treating you?" said the familiar voice of Alex

"I'm doing alright," I said, adjusting myself to see him, "How are you holding up?"

"I have cancer," he said flatly

"...*Fuck, Alex.* I don't know what to say. What type?

"Non-Hodgkin's Lymphoma," he said, "It went in remission. Not anymore."

"What are the doctor's doing for you?"

"Not a damn thing. These fuckers don't care. I'll have to wait until I'm released to get any real treatment."

"And they sentenced you to a year?"

"Yep. I lost my temper in court. The Judge asked if I had anything to say after he sentenced me. I said, *'Yes. Fuck you. And fuck you, bitch,'* to the prosecutor.

"That probably didn't help."

"No, it didn't. Felt damn good, though."

"Well, you'll be in my thoughts, man. Fight for the best treatment you can."

.

Chris, Kyle's pal, had trouble integrating himself into our Walk. No one shared his sentiments. He approached me once, calling me Richard, then corrected himself and addressed me by my name.

"So, hey, I was wondering if you might hook me up with one of those Boost drinks?" he asked

I scoffed, "Maybe in a couple of days, Chris. Trav has dibs."

"Sweet. Thanks, man. Let me know what you want in trade."

"Nothing."

Chris drifted for roughly a week, attempting to make friends. His stay was short. I didn't grant him the favor. The last instance I saw Chris, he clung to the phone, talking with a girl, and crying his eyes out. Tears were *streaming* off his face. He faced the reality of going to prison for a substantial term, and he was scared. He could feel that void closing in.

I felt empathy for him.

.

"Hey, everybody! Gerald's is having a sale!" I announced to the floor, upon seeing a TV commercial

"What else is new!" a man hollered

It got followed by an ASPCA commercial, set to a Sarah McLachlan song. The lot of us sat there, enduring a slow-motion shot of a Shih Tzu in a cage, when Allen remarked, *'That kinda looks like Nichols up on his top bunk, sometimes.'*

We busted out laughing.

"Fuck you guys," said Nichols

You wouldn't have guessed that Nichols, with his upbeat personality, had been arrested for pistol-whipping a dude so bad his mom didn't recognize him. However, being his first offense, Nichols had a chance at the Rider Program.

Alex caught my attention, tapping on his cell window. He held up an empty coffee bag and pointed to the hot water dispenser. Every inmate on my Walk stared at me, wondering if I'd risk the mandatory three days in *The Hole* if I got busted by the deputy. *'You're in the thick of it now, Logan,'* Zach said

I'd seen the procedure; there was a thin crack between the wall and cell door. If you filled the coffee bag too full, it would burst as you tried to slip it through, and burn the poor bastards inside.

The deputies at the control desk were distracted. I snatched the bag from Alex
and quickly filled it to a level I hoped to be right and headed back to his cell. I heard
my cellmates muttering, *'Too full! Too full!'*, and I did a U-turn. *Dammit.* Now the
deputies focused on me. I motioned for a guy named Austin; I supplied him with
coffee since he missed commissary.

"I need a diversion. Can you help me out?" I asked

"Yeah, I'll get their fuckin' attention! Don't worry about it, bro," he said,
"Hey, officers! Where's my fuckin' mail!? Can you check the box for me?!"

I dumped the proper amount of water, ran to Cell 821, and fed the tip of the
bag through the crack. Alex carefully pulled it in. The cell cheered, and Alex extended
me a proud thumbs up.

.

11:30 pm – A deputy rapped on our door and opened the tray slot.

"Crannell! Delivery. Two books."

I hopped off my bunk and signed a form. He handed me a copy of Salman
Rushdie's *'The Satanic Verses,'* and a color photography book of Buddhist temples in
Thailand. My weekend lit up like a torch. I wanted a new form of expression, and the
written word was it. *No better place to learn,* I thought. I studied many authors.

"Is that book about satanism?" Zach asked of the Rushdie novel

I laughed, "No. Not at all. It's a satire on Indian mythology and the battle of
good versus evil. It's a comedy."

"Oh, ok. That's what's up."

I tore three color images from the Buddhist temple book and taped them to
the wall by my bunk. I kept my library at the foot of my bed, and a piece of paper with
the mantra *'This too shall pass'* written upon it. I organized my crate, storing my
finished notepads in manila envelopes. My earplugs, the best .49 cents I've ever spent,
were stored in their plastic wrapper, tucked under my makeshift pillow.

I used the pen The Reaper gifted me, securing it in my sock during out times.
The one day I forgot to do so, the deputies tossed our cell and confiscated it. That upset
me, but I made my own, wrapped with blue medical forms.

.

The Ramen noodle packets off commissary cost $.97. The noodles were
secondary to the flavor packets, which we used to season our meals. The order also
included the essential Styrofoam bowls - the only available to us.

The trick to making the jail food edible lay in mixing as many flavors as possible, such as adding honey peanuts to the steamed green beans, with salt and a Picante beef Ramen flavor packet. Pickle juice, from giant individually wrapped spicy pickles, served as a decent marinade for salads.

.

Zeek racked up six misdemeanors within the preceding four months, but the Judge ordered him released on probation. What's funny is that his court paperwork contained a typo that pushed his departure date by a week. The authorities knew it to be a typo; they *admitted* it was a typo – yet they refused to correct it. Zeek couldn't handle the frustration.

"I don't know, Zeek," Zach said with concern, "I see you getting outta here and heading straight for a gas station to grab a beer and hang out in the park with your buddies. I don't see you taking any responsibility for yourself."
Zeek listened to advice like a scolded child.
"I hope you don't buy a bus ticket and fuck off your probation. It's your choice. I want to see you do the right thing, you know?"

.

On Zeek's final night, he and Rick had a private conversation about faith, and guardian angels walking among us. I felt shitty and went to bed earlier than normal. Even with my earplugs in, the two seemed loud. I stopped myself from yelling at them.

As I fell in and out of sleep, I picked up muffled sections of their talk. I noticed Zeek spoke from the heart, in a tone I hadn't heard from him. He talked genuinely of the burden in following a higher calling in life, and the profound symbolism of a dream he recently had, the details of which I regretfully didn't hear.

Then, Zeek became a free man. In his emotional goodbye, he gave each of us a hug and shook our hands, in gratitude. He exited with tears in his eyes.

Felony Arraignment

On the evening before my court date, I met with my attorney in a visitor booth. I had written my conditions for a plea deal on a piece of paper, and slapped it to the glass, with the palm of my hand so he could read it:

Domestic Violence – Misdemeanor
Battery – Misdemeanor
Probation - 3 years

"I'll plead guilty to these charges right now."
"That sounds reasonable, Logan. I agree with you. That's fair."
He transcribed my terms onto his notepad.
"The key to this is Elena," he said, "If she keeps pushing, it's possible the prosecutor won't offer us the deal we're looking for. You know this woman. How far is she willing to go?"

I *didn't* know her. I could not answer the question posed to me. I didn't think *Elena herself* knew the lengths she'd go.
"She's influenced by this Mandy girl and her parents," he said
"Yes, she is."
"Then we need to prepare for the worst."

We ran through the charges, from every angle. Ultimately, it would be Elena's word against mine.

July 20th – Through the windshield of the transport bus, I witnessed sidewalks busy with people, wandering, arms full of shopping bags, wanting things. I saw Advertisements for phone plans, menu options at fast food restaurants, and bands wearing the latest fashion. I wasn't missing anything; Cell 846 was my comfort zone; I'd power through the day, and go to my bunk and rest.

My gaze shifted from the windshield to a black man seated in front of me, in the maximum security section. An iron gate divided us. He reminded me of Tupac Shakur - maybe it was the nose ring. *How did he get to keep his nose ring?* How strange, that you can sit next to a person on a bus, and say nothing to them - *and a month later, that person changes your life forever.*

My last courthouse experience left me psychically and emotionally drained, and I did not care to repeat it. Fortunately, this trip proved to be altogether different. Elena wasn't there, and I found laughter in the unlikeliest of places.

The holding tank got crowded. One by one, the inmates were called over the intercom for their court appearances, relieved to abandon that miserable cell. Perry and I remained. He was my neighbor, in the furthest cell on the row, who for whatever reason, hadn't made my acquaintance until now. We sat there like a couple of jerks.

"If anyone says you're thin," he said casually, "You correct them, and say that you're *Shfelt*."
"*Shfelt?*"
"Yes. It means 'graceful and slender in figure.' I, myself, am also *Shfelt*."
He was tall with a wiry physique. Short cropped curly brown hair, slightly gray. Although forty, he didn't look a day older than thirty-four. He had curious dark eyes and a voice designed for quick-witted mockery. Obviously well-read. In a past life, Perry would've been an aristocrat and aspiring scoundrel. In this one, he stole a motorbike with some drugs in his pocket.

He did hilarious running commentary on the inmates shuffling by. When he tired of that, he proposed an idea.
"Oh, I have a good one," he said, "Let's think of lines you'd *never* want to hear from your legal counsel."

He began.
'So, we may have made an egregious error. It's possible we've grossly underestimated the strength of the States case."

"Oh, I see. So, you've already taken out a second mortgage?"

"At this time we do have a variety of contingency plans available..."

"Are you familiar with the term Appellate Court?"

"We're as confused as you are, that the tests came back positive..."

"Our records show you have family in the Real Estate business?"

"Did you *really* have plans for your 401k?"

"Are you good at speeches?"

"So, did you feel like you were getting on well with your Probation Officer?"

"Well.... We had a good run...."

Since our hands were cuffed to our sides, we couldn't wipe the tears of laughter. We were ok with that problem.

Perry's name got announced. I had ten minutes to collect myself.
"They're gonna think I've been crying, man!" I laughed, as he got ready
"Tell them your allergic to bologna sandwiches," he suggested

.

The shackles gnawed at my ankles, and the pain adjusted my mood, as I traversed the hallway to the elevator, where the deputy issued warnings on my conduct in the courtroom. They had us in groups of eight, in a single file line; my name listed first on the docket.

The Judge was a very soft-spoken man. His microphone level was down too low. The man's barely audible words would determine the course of my future, and the rustling and scrapping of chains on the wooden pews were far more prevalent.
"Mr. Crannell," he began, "would you prefer to read your charges, or would you like me to do so?"
I completely misunderstood his question. I thought he implied that *one of us were required* to read them aloud, and my voice felt weak, so I asked him to. The Judge got perturbed by that. *Fuck, he meant to read it on my own, in my cell.* He must've viewed me as an idiot, and I was disgusted with my poor impression.
"In the future, don't jump the gun like that," my attorney said when the Judge finished
"I get it," I said curtly

The Judge explained the charges and discussed the maximum sentence of each if I were found guilty. Again, his words got muted, though my attorney wrote the information on his notepad as he spoke. I sat in disbelief, as the years mounted.

At the end, he circled the sum – fifty years.
Years fell like paper.

The prosecutor demanded a felony conviction, to be served in prison. No plea deal got offered. I could fight for the charges to run concurrent, but it chilled my blood that the Judge held the power to punish me for that duration if he deemed it necessary. My attorney requested a continuance for August 3rd. The situation was so unbelievable, the anger I felt over his microphone volume seemed more real.

.

Exiting the bus, in Ada County, Perry and I walked through the darkened parking garage. I hobbled in pain from the shackles.

"How are those cuffs treating you, Logan?" Perry inquired, with concern

"I can feel the blood in my shoes, man."

"I'll show you a trick. It'll help *immensely.*"

We entered a room, and the deputy instructed us to put our hands on a padded wall.

"Remain facing forward, gentleman, and raise your right foot," he said, beginning the process of unlocking our chains

"So what you do," Perry explained, "is you tuck your pant legs down into your socks, and then very tightly roll your sock up while continuing to tug down on your pant leg."

"Ok."

"That creates a cushioned ring roughly four inches above your ankle bone. Be sure you tell the deputy to put the cuffs *above* the ring. That prevents slippage, and you can hardly feel them."

We discussed the matter, not at all disrupted by the officer, carrying on the way people would over espresso, in a coffee shop.

The Three of Us

Rick was an artist. I watched him set up his workstation; I believed it to be as if a meditative practice for him. He started by creating his brushes. He'd take a paper, and tear it to specific dimensions. Then, he'd angle a piece in the palm of his hand, and with one rapid movement, roll it into a tight cone shape, its tip fine as a pencil. That brush he'd use for intricate details. He'd continue rolling the papers, with widening tips, to have brushes of varying sizes.

For the ink, Rick took three pens from commissary, removed the tip, and pulled the channel from the rubber tubing. He'd blow the ink onto a piece of cellophane, as a reserve to dip his brushes in. Then, he'd flip his crate and place it on his lap, holding it in position with his elbows.

Plain white paper was a rare commodity. Rick put a word out, and when an inmate received their Discovery which usually had at least one page with minimal text, he'd shave it off, for a blank canvas. I gladly donated mine. He'd peel the adhesive labels off the soap bottles and tape his paper to the surface of his crate. Rick Kellner then put his earplugs in and began drawing.

Inmates came to him with photographs of loved ones, and Rick did life-like portraits with ornamental backgrounds. In exchange, he accepted bags of coffee. Rick had exceptional shading techniques and avoided hard lines. Rather then freestyle, he implemented a grid system to increase the image size, using an overlay. He brought out a depth of field with the most rudimentary of tools.

For his own interests, Rick did cartoon figures, including a comic-style angry rooster, based on an image from a tattoo magazine. His version showed decidedly greater skill than the original. When the cell door opened, I went next door.
"Hey Trav," I said, "You should see Rick's cock! It's amazing!"
"What!?"
"Come check it out. Me and Zach have stared at it for awhile."
Trav inched to the doorway, expecting a prank. He peered around the corner, as Rick held the rooster drawing.
"Damn Rick! *That is an amazing cock!"* Trav declared

Nichols' creative skills were also in demand. He had a knack for writing lyrics and poetry, riffing on the color of a girl's eyes or some other attribute. I'd overhear him say to inmates requesting a poem, *'I'm like iTunes, the first one's free and then you gotta pay.'*

.

Rick appreciated my book of Buddhist temples. He marveled at their structural design, being a former contractor and builder himself. *'Nothing today compares to this, bro," he said, "When the shit we build falls to the ground, these temples will still be there.'*

Zach and I did our laps in the cell.
"Where are we walking to, Logan?" Zach asked
"The Santa Cruz Boardwalk."
"What time of day is it?"
"Nighttime."
"That's what's up. Let's go, bro."

Zach didn't waiver from his routine, and his daily yoga session piqued Rick's interest. By that point, I joined Zach a few times a week, and it improved my flexibility. The floor got cramped with three of us, so I let Rick take a lesson. Zach taught him the steps and proper breathing techniques.

Rick's body trembled, as he labored to maintain a stance.
"Zach, I can't hold it. I'm losing balance," Rick pleaded
"You gotta breath deep with the motion, bro. You can do it."
Rick's feet slid on the smooth concrete, "This is way harder than I thought."
"Yoga ain't no punk, Rick."

Rick stayed with it, each day growing confident, alongside Zach.

"Dude, I've never been able to kick that high!" Rick said
He'd kicked the wall and left a smudge with the cheap rubber sole of his shoe. They kept a competition going, with Zach consistently hitting a higher mark.

.

It's a mystery what Zeek said to Rick on his final night, in regards to that dream, and the burden of a noble path, but whatever he said, it had an impact. Rick began pondering his spirituality and religious beliefs.

Rick and Zach read passages aloud from the Bible and discussed their relevance. I was glad to see Rick searching for an intrinsic meaning to life, amidst this clusterfuck we lived in.

The two of them spent their early twenties in prison - in Montana and Idaho respectively. Rick, an Idaho native, grew up with founding members of the *Severely Violent Criminals* and had an older brother allied with the *Aryan Knights*. Rick didn't affiliate with either – *yet received protection from both,* with no pressure to join their ranks.

Zach knew nothing about the prison system in Idaho and understandably felt nervous. They had lengthy conversations about prison politics, and Rick was able to ease his apprehension.

On Cell Block 8, many inmates were federal cases, waiting for transport to prison. Also, Ada County housed convicts getting extradited to parts of the country, so we'd get inmates passing through, staying for a week or less. The rest of us either remained in county for up to a year or headed to Boise State Penitentiary *(The Yard)*.

.

In Montana, Zach's schizoaffective disorder escalated, and he self-medicated with hard drugs. He didn't recall driving to Boise, nor could he explain why his car was awkwardly parked on a grass median, with guns on the passenger seat. He simply wanted to die.

The staff of Ada County realized that they were in over their heads, when Zach built a telescope out of toilet paper rolls, to monitor the electric spiders on the tier landing.
"When they arrested me, bro, I thought I was still in Montana," Zach said, "That's how bad it was. The deputies told me I was in Idaho, but I didn't believe them. Then I got a letter from my grandma, and I saw the address for the jail on the envelope."

He got ushered out on transport and driven two-hundred-fifty miles east, to State Hospital South, in Blackfoot, Idaho. Zach had fond memories of the state hospital; a few of the girls there flirted with him. The sexes were mixed; thus he had the opportunity to hang out. The kitchen served good food, and they watched movies on a big screen TV.

Unfortunately, the medication the doctors prescribed made his condition far worse - like lighter fluid on fire.

Zach saw a show on television, about UFO sightings, and it planted a seed in his head. He became convinced the medical staff was trying to kill him - and with the meds, that wasn't entirely false. He lactated, for hell's sake.

On the morning of his escape, the weather must've seemed foreboding. He looked out the window, to a dense fog that had shrouded the fields, surrounding the penitentiary. *The aliens would come soon.* The doctors prepared him for his abduction. *This is a matter of life or death.*

During social time, he and the other inmates got chaperoned by a few nurses, who focused on texting their friends rather than doing their jobs. Zach broke from the group and entered a hallway. He pushed the front door open and started walking through the fields. His pace increased, as he sensed the aliens on the horizon.

The U.S Marshals issued a nationwide manhunt for one 'Zach Morris.' Authorities warned the public, stating the suspect had violent tendencies and may be headed to Boise or Montana. He was last seen wearing a gray hooded sweatshirt, pants, and gloves with white stripes.

Five days passed, and the calls kept ringing in. Zach seemed to be everywhere. The irony, however, is that he slept behind a Walmart, a few miles down the road. People fed him donuts. As the drugs wore off, he realized what he'd done. He walked back to the hospital. The police made a real show of it, to save face, and manhandled him at the front gate as if he were resisting.

Thus, the doctors tried him on a different medication, Geadon, *with positive results*. Zach's stabilized, and his physical maladies and hallucinations ceased. I'm guessing that's when he understood the deep shit he was in.

He got cleared for a return to Ada County Jail, to face his weapons charge for the Winco incident, and two months later, he and I ended up in a cell together.

> "Where are we walking to, Zach?"
> "I'm walking to the store, bro. Wanna come?"
> "Sure. Want a beer?"
> "Sounds good. Maybe a candy bar."

Zach and I paced *hundreds* of miles in that cell, side by side. It's hard to describe the bond you form with a person, under those circumstances, locked in such tight quarters, in a shared experience.

.

Zach was briefly housed in Maximum Security, next to an inmate named Ross. A nearby cell held an Iranian cab driver who'd been arrested with a trunk full of high powered assault rifles. Ross, a joker, enjoyed instigating a shouting match with the Iranian.
> "YOU TERRORIST! *YOU FUCKING TERRORIST!*" Ross taunted
> The Iranian eventually got pissed and screamed in his heavy accent.
> "God *DAMN* you, Ross! I VILL shit-*BOMB* you!"
> Ross and Zach burst into laughter. That catchphrase became widely used throughout Cell Block 8, thanks to Zach perpetuating it.

.

When Rick Kellner rolled into your house party and slammed a pound of dope on the table, wearing jeans and a gun holster - you knew you were in that shit for the duration. Rick loved it - the lifestyle, the risk, the money. He lived to fuel the party and take it to the next level, burning like a monster of energy. He loved his cell phone ringing night and day; he loved it because it filled his need for acceptance. The money was secondary to that. *'Bro, I'd jump out the window commando style, and run down the street, on to the next mission,'* Rick had said.

He picked up a drug trafficking charge in Canyon County. It went to trial – and he beat it. That got Rick a reputation. The downside is that it tarnished the police department's image, which they wouldn't allow a second time.

Rick told us the events leading up to the high-speed chase. He rode with a guy in the passenger seat whom he'd known for several months. Rick had an uneasy feeling that a white vehicle had tailed him. He did the deal, giving the man more than he paid for, who then invited Rick to his house. He made an excuse, and dropped the man off in a parking lot. As he drove, he again noticed the white vehicle and lost it on the side streets.

.

We each had our method for making PB&J sandwiches. Rick combined his two peanut butter and jelly packets into one big sandwich and topped it with both of his cookies. Zach put slices of banana, mixed with a little soy butter. Me, I went for the classic fold-over.

We rubbed the peanut butter packets in our hands, so the oil blended and chunks got kneaded. Tearing the right sized hole in the packaging gave us control of the spread.
"Hey, Rick. You've got jelly on your shirt," I said
He looked down and smiled.
"That's some fat kid shit, right there, Rick," Zach pointed out

I might be underplaying the value of peanut butter and coffee in Ada County Jail; they were the two great pacifiers. You can't be in a bad mood, with a PB&J sandwich in your mouth. It reminded us of childhood, sparking conversations about the cartoons and movies we watched as kids. Rick especially loved them. Whenever he got depressed, I'd cheer him up.
"Hey Rick, you want a peanut butter sandwich?"
"You got one, dude?" he'd ask, his eyes lighting up
"I do."
"Hell yeah!"

Coffee was our main currency, and generosity with our supply led to camaraderie. The ritual comforted us; we'd get excited for each cup. Spooning the instant coffee granules into your cellmates cup meant a sign of respect.

.

Zach, walking laps in the cell, hummed a song, *'It's just me, myself and I. Solo ridin' 'til I die, 'cuz I got me for life.'* He stopped and studied an area of the wall. He ashamedly rubbed it with his finger, as if to discount a mild hallucination. He observed it from different perspectives, still not convinced.

"What's up, Zach?" I asked

"I know I'm not crazy. There's a dark spot on the wall. Check it out, bro."

I examined where he pointed. There was indeed a faint dark spot, roughly the size of a silver dollar, from a paint job long ago.

"I don't see anything, Zach."

"You don't?"

"No, I don't."

"You don't like, see that, right there, that area?" he asked, rubbing it again

"Nope. It's solid white. Sure it's not a shadow?"

He raised his arms to see how the angle of the overhead light affected what he saw.

"Nah, bro. It ain't a shadow. Look. See? You don't see that?"

"No, I sure don't. Hey Rick, do you see a spot on the wall? Right here?"

He examined it from his bunk, "No, I don't see anything."

"You're not close enough, Rick," Zach protested, "You gotta get closer. It's right there."

Rick checked and discreetly winked at me.

"No, Zach. You're losing it, dude. The wall's solid white," Rick confirmed

Zach didn't give up. He got his face right up to it.

"Y'all are fuckin' crazy. I know there's a spot. You seriously don't see that?"

"Of course I see it, Zach!" I laughed, "It's right there!"

"HUH! Y'all tried to okie-doke me! You had me for a second! Now I'm gonna see that damn thing every time I walk by!"

"Me too. Crazy how we just noticed it. We stare at it all day long!"

During our extensive time in lockdown, Zach, Rick and I didn't have a single moment of bad energy or confrontation between us. When our situations got rough, we supported each other.

One afternoon, with a three-hour stretch before our dinner, the three of us played a wicked version of baseball. Since we didn't have a bat, the goal was to lash objects out of the air, using a shower towel that Rick folded with a specific method. It resulted in a reinforced whip that would've lacerated us, if it hit skin. *We made the biggest mess we possibly could.*

Rick was up to bat, and Zach threw rolls of toilet paper at him (we smuggled extra rolls from the control desk for this purpose). The lethal towel ripped through them, with a thundering clap, rendering small pieces like confetti, which fluttered about the cell. With a solid home-run strike, Rick cut a brand new roll nearly in half.

We laughed hysterically, like fools. When Zach informed us we ran out of toilet paper, we switched to apples (we'd each received one for breakfast, and pulled them from our crates). I pitched to Rick, and within a few minutes, applesauce had flown *everywhere*. It covered the walls, the mirror, the desk, our bunks. Zach and I had chunks of apple in our hair and smeared on our arms.

I picked up the remnants of a gouged toilet paper roll and tossed it to Zach, who high kicked it into the smoke sensor in the corner of the cell – setting off fire alarms in the entire building and shutting down the ventilation system. We stared wide-eyed at each other, *'Shit, brush the tissue out of sight. Hurry!'* We then laid on our bunks, pretending to read, *'Look natural, guys'* Zach said.

The deputy at the control desk determined which cell the alarm originated from, and arrived shortly.
"Is everything ok in there?" he asked through the window
"Yeah, deputy. Why?" Zach inquired
"The alarm started in your cell!"
"It's probably dusty!"
"We'll inspect it tonight at headcount!"
"Sounds good! Thank you, deputy!"

.

Whisper came back from *The Hole*, wearing orange and white stripes, assigned to a cell in the corner. I watched him saunter along the main floor. His feet naturally pointed outward, giving him an unusual gait. He had a gradual motion, a low center of gravity, causing him to shuffle as if he wore shackles. I thought to myself, *I need a shackle walk.*

I practiced as I lapped the cell. My muscle memory found a subtle rhythm. The right foot covered the length of the step, as the left foot followed by half step, aligning with the tip of the right shoe, rather than trying to pass it. That provided slack and combined with Perry's method of rolling my pant legs in my socks, *I might be able to get this done in style.*
"Whatcha doin', Logan?" Zach asked as we paced together
"Shackle walk, man."
"Huh! That's what's up! That's a good idea. Boy, you're in the thick of it now!"

.

The deputies brought in a man named Rook, to fill Billy's old bunk in Cell 845. Rick and Trav knew Rook from the streets, so he fit right in. His outward appearance, lanky and freckled, with thick glasses, may have given him the air of goofiness, but Rook was an educated man. He ordered books like I did, and shared his literature with the Walk. He loved ancient history and metaphysics.

His girl sent him envelopes with conspiracy theories she printed off the internet. He'd slip it to us after he and his cellies finished. We had fun debating - unlike the bullshit discussions Elena had.

We were big on theories of population control - weaponized viruses, chemtrails, toxins in water, and what we'd experience, as inmates, in the event of martial law. We read some Walmart stores closed throughout the southern states and got converted into prisons and FEMA camps. It *was* a fact that, behind the jail, a dozen railroad boxcars resided there. We speculated on their purpose. Being utterly helpless in these cells, stories like that intrigued us, or perhaps we liked to scare ourselves, striving to keep our imaginations alive.

Rook could be seen each night, going door-to-door as a beggar, extending his empty plastic cup for alms. We had no problem spooning him coffee, in gratitude for his reading material, and conversations he elicited. But that didn't exclude him from the good-natured civil war that erupted at medication time.

Half of the inmates on our Walk had prescriptions. When the med trolley appeared at 7:30, the deputies popped the doors on our row, two at a time, and we'd form a line at the top of the staircase. They positioned the trolley at the foot of the stairs, as a barricade. Once we approached, the nurse scanned our wristband and handed us our pills. We'd open our mouths for the deputy to inspect, verifying we'd swallowed the medication.

The whole affair gave us an opportunity to behave like idiots. Rick set a trap for Rook; we were locked up, and his cell got released for their meds. Rick placed a bottle of hand soap on the ground - it's opening aimed under our door. We scooted an important looking piece of paper onto the tier landing.
"Hey, Rook! Can you grab that paper? I dropped it," Rick pleaded
"Yeah, dude. Sure," he said, reaching down
Rick stomped the hand soap bottle, blasting it on Rook's hand, causing him to jump two feet straight up, like a cat, and yelp.

They got revenge – when we glanced in their window to make stupid faces, they were standing in a line, with their pants dropped to their ankles, mooning us.

I recall descended the stairs, and hearing Jimmy moaning through his door, *'She puts the lotion in the basket...'*
Jimmy did great impressions.

Rick, of course, threw out the classic - *'God-DAMN you!' I Vill shit-BOMB you!'*

The war carried on, nightly, for roughly forty-five seconds, until the deputies shut us down.

The Icarus Kid

Jeremy North, twenty-three-years-old, got assigned to our cell.
I couldn't help but see a version of my former self, at that age.

He had a thin build - thin as me - though slightly shorter. He tied back his long, auburn red hair, which revealed aspects of his freckled face, hidden under a beard, and prescription glasses. He moved fluidly. A brightly colored Egyptian tattoo adorned his right forearm. Jeremy exuded an inner calm - an awareness of the transient nature of all things. Rick, Zach and I saw that our new cellie was wise beyond his years, and fortunately for him, he got housed with three curious and welcoming inmates.

Jeremy was on transport, shipping east to answer for a probation violation, after his arrest in northern California, for trespassing or having a joint – some trivial matter. From the beginning of his current odyssey, Jeremy had the suspicion he ventured on a forbidden trail, seeing things that he not necessarily ought to be, or at the minimum, have the sense to ignore.

To say we had a conversation with Jeremy, on that first night at lights out, would be misleading; he *spoke*, and the three of us sat with rapt attention.
"I'd ended up in the hills of Mount Shasta, up in California," he began, "I meet a guy who lived in the woods, and he just did his own thing. He was an alchemist, man. He said he'd discovered the secret to making gold. I wasn't sure I believed him, but he offered to teach me. So, I hung around..."

"... One night we performed a healing ceremony, by a campfire. We each ate a handful of psilocybin mushrooms, and drank some peyote..."

Jeremy and his companion sat cross-legged, in front of each other. Their rhythmic breathing got deep. The drugs intensified. Jeremy's heart opened up, as he prepared to confront his demons.

Then, both of the travelers sensed a presence, circling the perimeter of the campsite. The natural fear of a wild animal dissipated, and they realized they were in the company of a far more intelligent entity – *perhaps more than one.* They remained seated, their eyes adjusting to the ever-changing light.

"...My nose filled with this terrible smell, it was almost putrid," Jeremy said, *"Then I heard these strange clicking sounds. I thought there might be several of them because it sounded like communication. They had this deep watery growl. I could make out the shape of a large figure, creeping slowly around us..."*

The entity felt as real to Jeremy as the man sitting beside the fire. But, as the experience progressed, Jeremy wondered if the creature was, in fact, a manifestation of his ego, an archetype, the projection of his own shadow form. If it *was* his dark half, then he perceived his goal as coming to terms with it, to achieve wholeness.

In the early hours, as their trip waned, he recalled his eyesight flashing green as if blanketed by an ethereal light, as he fell backward into the grass. He remembered there were flies and a lingering static in the air.

"I left my backpack with that guy," Jeremy lamented, "I'm sure he'll keep it safe, but shit man, I don't know when I'll be getting there."

Mount Shasta continued to draw him; it beckoned him, and he put thought into arranging his return.

.

In the early winter of 2003, I was twenty-three years old. At 3 am, I drove by the Bonneville Salt Flats, in Utah. Far up ahead I saw the distant lights of a city, and to my right lay the black void of the flats. I parked the car at a rest stop and slung a backpack over my shoulder. I headed straight into the darkness.

I walked for miles, my body numb from the cold. As I continued, *I chose to close my eyes and keep them shut.* I reached a point of ecstasy, a pure liberation, as my whole being accepted *that I could not run into anything.* I moved through an empty environment; with nothing there to touch me. I walked until that sensation exhausted me. I then sat on the barren surface and waited for the sunrise.

When it came, I opened my eyes to the vast expanse of salt surrounding me. It transformed from its nighttime shade to hot pink, and I felt the color radiate within me. Next came orange, then yellow and pale blue before it reached its zenith of blinding white.

The sun glared upon me like I was a foreign life form; I had to earn my passage. The salt was hard and sharp, and I had to urinate on a spot to soften it. I then jammed a stick from my backpack into the hole, and duct taped a microphone to it. I took two singing bowls from my bag, in different keys, and warmed them, with the little body heat I had.

Their resonance filled the crisp air, creating a union of sound and color. The cold dissipated as the sun warmed me, in aggressive acceptance.

All boundaries faded away from me that morning.

A U G U S T

7:30am

"Morning, gentlemen! Please stand for headcount! Bunk 1, feet on the floor! State your name, please!"
"North, man. *Geez...*"
"Kellner!"
"Crannell!"
"Morris!"
"Listen up, Gentlemen! You have ten minutes to get dressed and be in line at the main entrance! You're being taken to the outside rec area, while we do mandatory cell check."

We exchanged annoyed glances with each other. They always tossed our cells in the afternoon, during our regular out time, while we occupied the main floor.

Twenty convicts got woken prematurely that morning, given no chance to make coffee, and brought out to the chilly dawn.

The gate to Cell Block 8 opened, and they corralled us, half asleep and pissed off, into the small chamber leading to the hall. My gaze focused downward until a new deputy came nearer to me. I looked up, in disbelief - it was Marco, my security guard from the jewelry counter at *Gerald's.* He saw me and froze. We both had the expression of, *'What the hell are you doing here?'* In that painfully awkward moment, it was unspoken we should act like strangers.

He escorted us to the control hub, in uncomfortable silence.
Once outside, my cellmates and I went in separate directions. Jeremy, seated in a lotus position, meditated in private. Rick did light exercises with Trav, to get their blood circulating. Zach ambled with a neighbor.
"Hey, Logan!" I heard Clinton, a Redshirt, call out
"Yeah?"
"There's enough of us here to build a human pyramid! We're gonna send you over the wall! We've gotta get you out of here, man!"
The comment felt good. "Thanks for thinking of me," I said

An hour passed, and we were tired and thirsty. The sun radiated off the concrete. The towering wall cut a straight shadow, about three feet wide, running the length of the yard, and we sought refuge in its shade.

The twenty of us lined up, some sitting, others kneeling or standing, each in their own stance, lost in thought, eyes looking to imagined horizon lines. I stood at the end of the row, that image before me; I'd come to know these men by their first names. *Where would life take them?*

It would've been nice to have a camera.

.

I think Jeremy blew the minds of Rick and Zach, in the best of ways. They invested themselves in his nightly stories, absorbing exciting ideas and perspectives. For me, Jeremy incited my ambition to reclaim my spiritual path. For that, I am grateful.

Jeremy, keen on the Buddhist temple photographs I taped to the wall, also got intrigued by a copy of Whitley Streiber's memoir, *Communion,* that I found on the bookshelf. We talked at length on the book's implications. The last chapter we took turns reading, our imaginations ignited over life, not of this world.

The four of us had a conversation about aliens and visitations, to which Zach had an interesting account, based on a repressed memory from his childhood.

"When I was ten years old," he began, "I was riding my bike with a friend, in the summer. We went down a dirt footpath by this empty, abandoned lot in my neighborhood. I remember stopping because I saw this bright light up in the sky. I thought it was a plane at first since it was metallic, and the glare hurt my eyes, you know? It kept coming closer, and then I blacked out. When I woke up, I was laying on the ground next to my bike. It got dark, and I didn't see my friend anywhere, so I picked my bike up and walked home. After that, my friend acted cold to me, and his parents wouldn't let us hang out anymore. They moved to a different city a few weeks later."

I recalled an event that transpired in the field behind the house of Elena's parents, with the two towering trees in the center. It occurred late one evening, and although Elena and I weren't there, we talked on the phone with her parents, getting updates.

"Her mom heard a loud crash in the field, that she described 'as a huge pane of glass shattering, and an unusual metallic explosion.' There weren't any flames or smoke, so we had a massive sound, with no clear source. Within an hour, dozens of government officials were there with lights, forming lines, and scouring the field, for what we didn't know. When her parents went to their yard to investigate, a man with an assault rifle ordered them to get in the house and stay inside. The whole neighborhood was in disarray. Men were walking with guns, securing the area."

"Did you go out there?" Jeremy asked

"I read the newspapers for days, and there wasn't a single article on it. Nothing. I went to the field, to the spot where they searched, and it seemed normal. No scorched earth, freshly dug holes or debris."

"That's wild, man," Jeremy concluded, "Hey Zach, have you ever thought of getting hypnotized to try and recover the memory of what you saw?"

"No. Can you do that?"

"No, I can't. Can either of you?" he asked Rick and me

We shook our heads.

"I recorded a friend hypnotizing somebody," I mentioned, "like ten years ago."

We decided to take a vote – one of us needed to learn the art of hypnotism, and perform it on the rest of us. I got the vote. *Fuck it. Why not?* It's not like I had anything better to do on a Sunday afternoon than hypnotize a bunch of convicts. *Granted, I had no clue what I was doing.*

I called my brother and placed a book order.

"Hey, can you send me a well-regarded manual on hypnotism? I'm putting everyone under."

"Ok. Are you going to do the guards, too?"

"No, they don't sit still long enough."

"Alright, I'll shop around."

Prior to Mount Shasta, Jeremy temporarily resided at a compound, in Colorado. A group of people were building out there, living off the land. The older woman in charge took Jeremy in; she was in tune with finer energies and saw Jeremy had an old soul. He stayed long enough to make connections, and the woman treated him like her own.

One day, while Jeremy worked on the property, helping the others with job duties, the woman was in the house, preparing a meal. She heard an unexpected knock at the door; they didn't get visitors, being that remote. With hesitation, the woman stopped her task in the kitchen and went to see who was there. Through the screen door, she saw a man that put her in a state of unease; though not a person she recognized, he seemed so familiar, like a face from a dream. He stood tall and dark, wearing an old hat. His eyes weren't right - they detected too much.

"Yes?" the woman said, "Can I help you?"

"I'm looking for someone," the man said

"Who?"

"His name is Jeremy."

"What do you want with Jeremy?"

"I'd like him to come with me."

"No. You can't have him. Who are you?"

"I'm Thoth."

A chill crept through the woman, "No, sir. You need to leave. You need to go."

The man peered into the home. He nodded, and left the property, walking down the road.

Whatever it meant, Jeremy no longer felt comfortable at the ranch, and his journey carried him west, to California.

August 3rd – A deal was on the table, from my prosecutor.

I got presented with it during my fourth court appearance, and I asked for a continuance. The Judge gave me a week to consider it, and I must've read that piece of paper three hundred times.

The prosecution would drop the strangulation and kidnapping charges if I pled guilty to a felony for domestic violence. If I accepted the plea, I'd receive a series of evaluations to determine my likelihood of future violence. If I had a low to moderate ranking, the prosecutor would agree to probation, with a maximum of ten years, and a withheld judgment. *If they concluded me to be high risk, the prosecutor could argue for a ten-year prison term.*

At that point, it didn't matter to me if it were ten years or twenty; numbers could be debated, in the end. *This* was a battle of perception.

I entered my cell, to see Jeremy's bunk empty. He got cleared for transport, heading for the Utah border.

The Outlaw Spirit

A young man from Texoma, Oklahoma, rolled into our cell - lean and edgy. "Hey, Y'all. Name's Junior. What's up?" he said, giving us all a firm handshake. He had a flawless southern accent, black hair, blue eyes, and a thin mustache. Junior had tattoo work from the top of his neck, down to his knuckles. I could tell he'd done time, based on how quickly and precisely he set up his bunk. It was second nature to him.

Also on transport, Junior came from Oregon State Penitentiary, in extradition to his home state. The trip would take an entire thirty days, with layovers in at least eight counties. Understandably, he was pissed about it, wanting a bunk he could call his own.

Of all the crimes committed by the men on Cell Block 8, alleged or otherwise, Junior's may have been the ballsiest - *the crazy sonofabitch robbed an armored truck.* He told us his story.

Portland, Oregon - Junior rented an apartment for himself, his girlfriend, and his younger brother. Junior laid low, having dodged charges in Texoma. His ambition had grown, and the location of their temporary housing wasn't random. He spent the afternoons seated in front of his third-floor window, with a pair of binoculars.

Junior ran surveillance on a major department store across the street. With diligence, he documented the cash pickup schedules of the Armored Security Service. Junior felt confident he had their procedure dialed in, and discussed the strategy with his two accomplices.

It was a regular day at the store. The security guard inside prepared the deposit, filling the heavy canvas bag with cash. The driver waited patiently in the truck, out front. The guard exited the room and walked towards the automatic sliding glass door.
Junior came up behind him, with his brother
"Hey, Mister!" Junior said gruffly

The man turned sharply, as Junior sprayed his eyes with bear mace, dropping him like a rock, as he screamed in pain. Chaos ensued. The two of them pried the bag from his hands and ran from the store, and into the parking lot. His girl drove the getaway car, as the armored truck driver fumbled at his job.

They pulled behind a church down the street, as planned. It was a Wednesday, and the lot was vacant, except for a truck they intentionally parked there. They moved fast, lifting the satchel of money into the truck bed. They couldn't resist unzipping the bag. They must've paused, in awe of the tightly packaged block of cash; they had $250,000.

No time for dreaming - they filled the first getaway car with gasoline and set it on fire, started up the truck and sped off, seeing the smoke and towering flames in their rearview mirror. What they *didn't* know, is that there *was* a man in the church, possibly a janitor, or a minister working overtime. He saw enough to alert the responding police.

Junior and his crew were flying past lakes and marshland, when they heard the sirens approaching. They went off-road, taking the truck as far as they could into a wooded area, and accidentally plunged into a ravine. It rocked them badly. They got out and divided as much money as they could into three backpacks. They hadn't anticipated this and decided to flee on foot, unintentionally losing the girl, who later got caught.

The brothers waded into a lake, behind some tall grass, and sank, immersing themselves up to their mouths. They took deep breaths and submerged their bodies. When they came up for air, they heard bloodhounds in the distance, hunting their trail.

Junior held his brother tight against him, for warmth, forcing him repeatedly underwater. Their lungs ached, and those waters were cold. They were under for so long, waiting for the pursuit to end, hypothermia had to be setting in. From below the surface of the water, the howling of the dogs grew louder. The police were circling their location.

Junior reemerged, gasping for breath, and suddenly - *Chomp!*
The bloodhound, standing above him on the water's edge, had locked his jowls on Junior's face and was not about to let go. *Gotcha*, thought the dog.

The three armored truck robbers got booked into jail later that day, en route to Oregon State Penitentiary.

.

The officials at Oregon State Pen kindly put the brothers in a cell together. That must've made a huge difference, having the company of one another - but, those days were done. Although both convicted of the crime, the harsher sentence fell on Junior, who also faced the litany of charges he'd fled from in Oklahoma (I got the impression Junior liked to steal things with motors).

Junior's mom stood by her boys and did what she could to raise money for their defense. At this stage, the goal was to mitigate their losses and get as many charges to run concurrently as possible. They were shipping Junior to a rough southern prison for a minimum of ten years. He'd be thirty-five-years-old upon release.

Junior had a daughter with the girl involved in the robbery. She'd be turning three soon, in the care of the girl's mother. Junior thought a lot about his child, more so than he let on, and wondered what role he'd have in her life when all got said and done. She'd probably be in high school before he saw her outside of prison walls.

.

I overheard a conversation between Zach and Junior one afternoon as I laid in bed, covered with blankets. They assumed I slept, but I was resting my eyes.
"What's wrong with Logan, man? Junior asked, "I haven't heard him talk all day. Does he think he's goin' home, so he doesn't need to be social with us anymore?"
"Nah, it ain't like that, bro," Zach said
"I know. I was just playin'. Is he ok, though?"
"Yeah. He's going through it, because of what that dirtbag did to him."
"For real. What a bitch. Hasn't she ever heard of breaking it off with a dude?"
"I guess not."
"If a woman did that to me, I'd tie her to a tree and leave her ass there."

.

Zach busily plotted how to get a TV in prison. Having a personal television in your cell was a big deal, and the model issued by the jail cost $300, in color with about a dozen channels. For an extra $30 you got a pair of headphones. He had a laptop, stored at his uncle's house that he attempted to sell. I didn't make any promises, but I said if I got my finances settled, I'd try to get in touch. I needed a computer, anyway.

.

7:30am

"Morning gentlemen! Please stand for headcount!" the deputy announced
Rick, Zach and I were at attention, but Junior didn't stir. Rick grabbed his foot and shook it, rustling him awake.

"Weston!" the deputy shouted, "Feet on the floor! Morning headcount!"
"Gawd-damn, man! Fuck! I'm up!" Junior groaned, climbing from his bunk
"Are we gonna have a problem, Weston?" the deputy challenged
"Naw, man. We ain't gonna have no problem... *yet.*"
They had a brief standoff, staring coldly at one another. The situation diffused itself, and the deputy exited.
"Damn, man," Junior said, "How would he feel if I went up in his house at five-am and was like *'Get up. Get outta bed. You and your wife."*

He had a temper – that much we knew for sure. He didn't hide his contempt for authority. We talked sense to him on a few occasions, explaining it wasn't worth getting another charge in this county, *'If you want to hit a cop, do it in Oklahoma. If you slap around one of ours, they may bring your ass all the way back to answer for it.'*

.

Junior liked to joke. His immature brand of humor might have been the one thing about him not hardened by the prison system.
"Hey, Zach. Did they come for you?" Junior asked
"Who?"
"DEEZ NUTS!" he burst out with his goofy, uncontrolled laugh
"Huh! Hear that, guys? He just okey-doked me," Zach said

.

I preferred to eat my breakfast oatmeal in bed. I slinked up the stairs as Perry rambled down.
"Good morning, sir! You're looking very schfelt today!" he declared
"Why thank you! You as well!"
"I must say, you do look dashing in stripes!"
"I went for faded autumn tones this week!"
"Very wise!"

Perry was adept at many things, hair styling being one of them. Granted, only the Redshirts were permitted to touch the electric shaver, so Perry stood to the side, giving them step by step instructions on how to contour and fade. The Redshirts had no skill without Whisper, and we felt fortunate for Perry's supervision.

.

Rick sat for hours, combing his goatee, with a cheap black comb, lost in his thoughts.
"What are you writing about, Logan?" Rick asked
"Your beard."

"Really?"
"Yep."
"You like it, huh?"
"More impressive by the day, buddy. Hey, you want a PB&J sandwich?"
"You got one?" he grinned
"I do."
"Dude!"

.

Junior sang the country blues like no one's business. His voice had a raw sincerity. After final lockdown, we'd persuade him to sing us a few songs. Initially, he got shy and needed a minute to work up to it. Rick would ask him to close with the same Tim McGraw tune.

"Johnny's daddy was taking him fishin'. When he was eight years old.
A little girl came through the front door holdin' a fishing pole.
His dad looked down and smiled, said we can't leave her behind.
Son, I know you don't want her to go, but someday you'll change your mind.
And Johnny said "Take Jimmy Johnson, take Tommy Thompson,
take my best friend, Bo. Take anybody that you want as long as she don't go.
Take any boy in the world. Daddy, please don't take the girl.

By the time he reached the third verse, we'd feel it in our hearts.

"Same old boy. Same sweet girl. Five years down the road.
There's going to be a little one, and she says it's time to go.
Doctor says the baby's fine, but you'll have to leave 'cause his momma's
fading fast, and Johnny hit his knees, and there he prayed.
Take the very breath you gave me. Take the heart from my chest.
I'll gladly take her place if you'll let me. Make this my last request.
Take me out of this world... God, please don't take the girl

.

"Hey Junior, do you want to do yoga with us?" Zach invited
"Nah, that shit makes me nervous. I'll work out with Y'all, though," Junior

replied

"Cool. We do yoga for forty-five minutes. Then we work out," Rick said

.

Inmates on transport are forced to be indigent. They can't order from commissary since they'll be on the road before it gets delivered. That said, we didn't mind sharing our supplies with Junior. He got raised southern, and therefore was too respectful to ask for things, so we'd urge him to share our coffee or snacks. He liked Lemonhead candies if I recall correctly.

Maintaining a clean cell was important to us. We paired up, alternating the duties of taking out the trash, restocking soap and toilet paper, sweeping and mopping, scrubbing the toilet and sink. We had a few cellies that did little to help, and it said a lot for there character, though Junior dutifully lent a hand. I'd use the radiance of Trav's cell as an example, pointing it out to my cellies as we walked by, *'You see that? That's a proper cell, you bastards!'*

.

Junior liked the author, Iris Johansen. I saw a few of her novels on the shelf downstairs and went to find them. They were not there. Those pitiful library books had done more time than any of us; held together with the sticky labels from our hand soap bottles. I guess I had an Andy Dufresne moment because I decided to do something about it.

"Excuse me, deputy. I wonder what chance we had of getting new books in here. I'm starting to feel ignorant. I haven't learned anything in weeks."
"I've tried, but I keep getting denied," he said, surprisingly, "The problem is that inmates keep too many books in their cells that they aren't reading. There's supposed to be a two-book limit, per person. They won't let me bring in a new selection until all of these get checked in."
"Really? I didn't know that."
I imagined most of us were unaware of that rule. I went door to door on my Walk, encouraging the men to bring out their old reading material. I rounded up roughly sixty-five books, and the deputy saw my efforts. He got motivated to reinforce the two book policy in the entire cell block, and hundreds of books resurfaced.

A new cart arrived, most likely from Cell Block 7, and our shelf replenished with new work - including a few novels by Iris Johansen, which I tossed on Junior's bunk while he was at the rec yard.

.

My attorney received a phone call – from Mandy, speaking on Elena's behalf. She had the attitude of a teenager and defiantly stated that Elena was ready for me to take the case to trial.

Elena opened a new Facebook account, despite the problems it had previously caused. She bragged *'How nice it was to be free.'* She thanked her parents for rewarding her with a brand new car.

Elena wrote me a poem and posted it online

The sky has fallen deep into the ocean
and no one can save you now
You have made your bed now lie in it, LC.

Then, she publicly stated, on social media, that she was 'in a relationship,' with a new man. What happened to Scott? Elena had learned how to get the sympathy she craved, as the cycle repeated, under the watchful eye of Scott's lawyers.

Elena often spoke of having patience, while God destroyed her enemies. So, why such a vehement attack on me? Why the unrelenting anger? Didn't she believe God would do the job for her? I read a line in a book that said, *'The fanatic always harbors a secret doubt...'*

.

I concluded the past year of my life entailed one essential thing – language. At *United Bank,* my words and actions got recorded, then analyzed and assessed. I broke down speech patterns, writing and rewriting information in my mind until it had cadence and rhythm. I studied the tone and color of words, each counting as a measurement of my success. We were trained never to say 'I'm sorry,' or 'I understand,' when speaking to a person in crisis.

Likewise, in Ada County Jail, my words got documented, evaluated, and filed. In here, language is manipulated and used against me. The weight of certain words could potentially bury me. Here, they demanded to know how 'sorry' I was and the depth to which 'I understood' the pain I had caused. I had to speak with restraint and dignity, while I got dismantled by liars in public view.

With Elena, I learned through trial and error, what to say and how to say it in a calculated fashion. I walked on eggshells. I held my thoughts in, letting my few words carry over to try and calm the storm. I constantly underplayed emotion in exchange for logic, no matter how much opposition I faced. I knew if I said something that would later bite me, even if it was right and fair.

Now, I'm writing this book; so much information, condensed to a refined narrative. In my cell, I read manuals on style and grammar. I practiced cutting paragraphs and sentences in half, rearranging structures, and that act subconsciously affected the way I spoke in everyday dialogue.

I had a heated moment with my attorney.

"Do you want to know what I think?" he said, agitated

"What?"

"I think you have to plead guilty to a felony. There it is."

"Whoa, hang on. How the fuck did we jump to that? How did we go from misdemeanor probation to a felony in prison?"

"Look, they won't offer you a misdemeanor. The prosecution wants a felony, but we can beat it at trial."

"This is absurd!"

I faced the decision of taking the plea deal or going to trial. I thought about it nonstop, in the days before my court date. The system got so backlogged; my trial date would be pushed to February, *six months out.* I'd be incarcerated for almost a year, with every day that passed lessening my chances of getting my head above water when I rotated to society.

Exoneration was a pipe-dream. I'd admitted to the count of domestic violence from the beginning. I had taken accountability. I wasn't going to dodge that bullet. The best I could fight for at trial would be misdemeanor probation, a hard-won battle for little gain.

At trial, with the plea deal off the table, I'd be tried on all four charges. Things had the potential to go terribly wrong. In a case of her word against mine, if the jury bought into her pageantry, I could be found guilty on all counts. Or, I could end up with the deal I'd already been offered – felony probation – only at a personal and financial loss.

I didn't allow my anticipation of Scott's involvement to cloud my decision. I no longer believed he'd drag his name into this mess. Elena's new boyfriend hinted at his lack of support. I blocked him from my mind.

I thought about the Judge, to whom I had not given a good impression, then my jaded attorney, who wanted simplicity. My parents, who thought me incapable of bad deeds. The faceless, impartial jury. Those who might take the stand. The prosecutor to whom I represented a number, and the legal advice from scores of inmates.

A disjointed mass of voices trying to decide my place.

I wanted to write a letter to Carrie, but the words did not come. I had no mailing address, regardless. Her words had given me such comfort, and it was selfish of me to ask for them now. What right did I have to reenter her life, after disappearing for two years? Maybe I just wanted her to know I hadn't stopped caring, and that I felt happy people like her existed in this world.

.

August 9ᵗʰ – The night before my court appearance, I paced the cell, with Zach. He encouraged me. It's easy for others to sit back and say *'take it to trial, man,'* though Zach wasn't about that. He grounded me, and we talked risks and benefits.

"We're in the thick of it, bro. But, a year from now, this will all be a distant memory. You're gonna be alright, Logan. It's almost over," Zach said, as I laid to rest.

The Plea

On transport to the courthouse, I felt numb. I didn't look out the window, at the sunlight; I could feel a migraine coming on. My hands were shaking. My body knew how psychically draining this experience would be.

Upon arrival, rather than going to the holding tank, I got directed to a single man cell across the lobby. I was put in that cramped space with two other inmates – Whisper and a man named Mike, both of them *Aryan Knights,* on their sentencing day. Whisper wrote a letter to the court, and he wanted me to hear it. He took it from his shirt pocket, unfolded it and read aloud, in his raspy voice. He didn't dispute his charges and said little in the way of apologies. He stood ready to answer for his crimes, but asked the court for a simple request; to show him mercy at sentencing, for the sake of his newborn child. He asked them to please consider a reduced sentence so that he could be a part of her life.

Whisper received the mandatory ten years for his drug trafficking charge, and not a day longer.

.

I traversed the hallway to the elevator, practicing my shackle walk. The blood rushed in my ears as I entered the courtroom. I didn't bother to look at the audience – I knew Elena wasn't there. When my name got called, I brushed by the other inmates, to the aisle, and sat next to my attorney.

As the formalities ended, my guilty plea got discussed. The Judge asked for documents that were not prepared. My attorney wasn't given the proper forms for me to review and sign, and that irritated the Judge. They moved my case up the docket, giving me fifteen minutes to complete the forms.

A deputy led me to a private room with a pane of glass separating us. My attorney slipped the paperwork through the slat. It contained nearly sixty questions I had no chance to study. Every box I checked peeled at my liberty. My wrists were cuffed to my waist, and the height of the counter was too high. I could not finish in my hand, and sent the papers back to my attorney for completion, as he explained each stipulation.

"Most cases aren't worth taking to trial, but I think this one is, Logan. I wouldn't mind fighting this for you," my attorney said
Now you fucking tell me that, putting doubt in my mind at the last second. My thoughts were racing too fast for me to chase. A decision needed to be made *now. Right now.* I hadn't signed off on the document yet. I wanted to throw those papers across the courtroom, and expose Elena for the fraud she was, humiliating her in front of her family. I wanted to watch as she placed her hand on the Bible and lied to her God with every breath she could muster- as she tried in vain to use 'man's laws' to imprison me.
Breath, Logan.
What part of me so aggressively wanted justice?
Think.

It was my ego... My imagined self. The sick hunger in me that would never be satisfied. Ego is what Elena thrived on. People were urging me to fight – to carry on with the same behavior that got me arrested in the first place. *I had to be the one to let it go.* In doing that, I'd be able to sleep with a clear conscience – *and maybe therein lay the justice and grace.* However, letting go was merely a personal achievement.

I had to be missing something.
I knew in my bones there had to be another way to win this.

In one of the most vital decisions of my life – I chose to listen to my gut.

I entered the courtroom and stood before the Judge, who got upset that my papers weren't written in my hand. My attorney explained the restrictions of my shackles. The Judge asked if I was of sound mind, under the influence, or if I'd been bribed, threatened or persuaded to arrive at my answer.
"No, Your Honor."
"How do you plead?"
"I plead guilty, Your Honor."

In that moment, I signed my rights away and became a felon.

The Judge confirmed the gravity of my situation and set my sentencing date a full eight weeks out.

"To be clear," the Judge stated, "it will be an *open sentencing,* Mr. Crannell. I'm not bound to any recommendations of the prosecution. Do you understand?"

"Yes, I do, Your Honor."

.

When the door to my cell opened, I entered safety. A wave of relief and exhaustion hit me. Junior's bunk lay empty; he boarded the transport, heading south.

The three of us awaited our next cellmate.

Totem

I dreamt that I was laying on a dirt road; my body ached, my bones were bruised, and my throat felt dry. Gravel stuck to my scraped and bleeding skin. The sun shone partially through thinning gray clouds. It must've rained. I staggered to my feet, surrounded by rolling green hills as I imagined there to be in Ireland. Through my pain, I had a sense of awe, as a rainbow formed in the sky. It touched behind those magnificent hills and a curve in the path ahead.

I then saw a man, in the distance, walking casually towards me. He had a knapsack on his shoulder, and he carried a fishing pole. As he approached me, I recognized it was my friend Tom. He smiled and immediately engaged me in conversation. He said nothing of my injuries, and with that lack of acknowledgment, my pain faded, as I too stopped attributing power to them.

Tom pulled a freshly caught fish from his sack, and it glistened in the sunlight. He held it up, so I could see its face. *'It's a 'Snook' fish,'* he said. I hadn't heard of a 'Snook' fish and wondered if Tom, being from Georgia, used slang to describe a common fish I failed to identify. We agreed to cook it, as I knew how to prepare it.

I remember fading images of us eating at a camp, as smoke rose from a fire, and the dream dissipated.

.

Rick and Zach encouraged one another to rebuild the damaged relationships in their lives. People often mistake adrenaline and the instinct to survive as 'the human spirit,' when in reality, spirit is fragile and easy to destroy. I shared a cell with two men that understood that.

Zach fell out of favor with his parents, during his original prison term. He didn't blame them for being wary, *'I was a total shit-kid,'* he said, *'They have the right to be upset with me.'* His grandma had undying faith in him. Throughout his troubles, she wrote letters and motivated him to read the Bible, nurturing him, wanting him to accept that there's more to life than desires.

Zach got humbled by the unexpected support from his parents. His mom agreed to pay for half of his television in prison. They were catching on to what I witnessed firsthand; that Zach showed a genuine effort to better himself.
"You tired of being a knucklehead, yet?" his father asked lovingly, over the phone
"Yeah, pop."
"Well, good. I figured you get sick of prison eventually."

.

Rick had a junkie for a mother. At the age of twelve, Rick mainlined drugs in her company, while she got herself high. How shocking that Rick developed a serious drug problem and a need for acceptance. The saving grace of his childhood was meeting the girl he would one day marry.

At the age of fifteen, Rick became a father. They had a son. Prior to the prison term in his early twenties, they had a second child - a daughter.

In prison, Rick managed well. He got a job working in the sun, as a landscaper and groundskeeper. With his three-year stint almost finished, he got hemmed up with a ring of inmates importing chewing tobacco illegally. He got caught and refused to inform. For that, the warden added *three years* to Ricks sentence – and sent him to solitary confinement for nine months. It was a heavy price to pay for something as trivial as tobacco, and it strained his marriage and his willpower.

"I miss my grandfather," Rick said, "He died two weeks before I got out of prison. I didn't get the chance to tell him I loved him."
"I'm sure he knew."
"He told me once, that I was a good man. I've let people down and failed at so many things in my life. I don't think I deserved for him to say that."
I didn't respond to his comment. I didn't feel it was my place to do so, but I thought about his words.

Rick produced a work of art, while free, at a stable point in his life, on a canvas measuring roughly four-foot-by-six. He did the drawing in pencil; the image of an Elk, beside a river, on a cold morning.

He lost track of how long he spent perfecting it. Each blade of grass, drop of moisture and dew, the hair of the Elk's coat, its breath, all of it came through in vivid detail. He spoke of its majesty, considering it as his finest achievement, creatively. I believe Rick thought of that drawing often, in the darkest moments, pulling strength from it, when he felt at a loss. I think it helped him see the goodness of his capabilities.
"It's beautiful, bro. I wish I could show it to you."
"Where is it?"
"My sister's house. She has it framed, hanging on the living room wall."
"Nice. I'm glad it's safe."

It was during that period, of the Elk drawing, that Rick was doing well for himself. He had his own contracting company and spent his days with his wife and two children. For five years, he was clean and sober. *What the hell went so wrong?*

It was the smallest of events. While working on the construction of a house, Rick misfired with a nail gun and shot it through his finger. He couldn't manage without painkillers - relapsing into addiction.

"I wonder when they'll do my PSI interview," I inquired, walking laps with Zach, "They gave me the packet yesterday, but I haven't filled it out. It's intense."
"They'll wait till the last minute, bro. That's how they do it."
"So, I sit here for seven weeks for no reason?"
"Yep. They'll give you the results either the day of your sentencing or at the courthouse right as they call you. They might let you read it for ten minutes, and then they take it back. They don't want you having a chance to work on your defense, you know?"
"Unbelievable."
"Huh! You're in the thick of it now, bro!"
"Where are we walking to, anyway?"
"Oh, um. Let's see. How about Daytona Beach?"
"Works for me."

Rick, on the eve of his Preliminary Hearing, still had no idea of what he was dealing with. With several unanswered questions, he read his Discovery compulsively. It said his arresting officer stopped him for failure to use a turn signal – that alone, Rick knew to be false. The police searched his vehicle and found a bag of drugs in the driver seat of the car. Rick examined the photograph, *'That's not my bag,'* he said, and I believed him - Rick was a perfectionist. He got particular in regards to packaging. They also found a dirty scale on the backseat, and Rick had thrown his out the window.

Rick prayed, and the action brought him peace. He left in the morning, with high hopes.

Zach and I waited, with trepidation. The cell door finally rattled open in the late evening. Rick's face appeared ashen and drained. He sat in silence for an uncomfortable while, not wanting to hear himself voice the words.
"What's up, Rick?" Zach asked, softly
"The FED's have me on a controlled buy, for heroin."
The man in his car that night had been an informant.

The three of us were quiet. Zach put his hands to his mouth,*'Shit just got deep,'* he said in a hushed tone, *'Shit just got real...'*

We didn't know what to say.

.

Then, our vacant bunk got assigned to Jessie. A man in his mid-twenties, detoxing from bath salt addiction. At the peak of his delirium, convinced his amateur tattoo work sent secret signals to the government, he sat in front of a mirror and set a tattoo gun to his face, along with the rest of his body, covering his skin with nonsensical marks.

He took parsley and garlic baths, in his home, to kill the electrodes in his arm hairs – though that didn't help much with the entities who already knew his location. Jessie described them as malicious dwarves that dwelled in cupboards or on top of bookshelves. Jessie stalked around his home brandishing two machete's, for protection.

He had three children with the same woman, and Child Services thankfully got custody of them. However, in light of that tragedy, the addicted couple decided to have three *more* kids. To further complicate matters, Jessie learned while incarcerated with us that he had twins with another woman, leaving eight kids on this planet who had to call this dipshit their father.

He slept through the first four days in our cell, after getting laid low when a bag of harbored drugs burst in his large intestine.

I seated myself at a table under a skylight. In front of me, I had a cup of coffee, a book by Milan Kundera, and my PSI packet. It was thick, thirty pages in length, full of questions pertaining to my life, including a detailed account of the events leading up to my alleged crimes. *Did they know what they were asking?* I obviously couldn't write what you've read thus far in this book.

Perry gave me advice.

"There's one thing you need to understand," he began, "Whoever it is that evaluates you, they will act like they're your best friend. They're going to sympathize with you, so you open up to them. *Do not forget they are paid to demonize you and ruin your life.* That may sound extreme, but I assure you it's not. That's why they're on the payroll. It's a game.

The best advice I can give you is this, Logan. Whatever you write concerning your version of events – *don't ever ever ever change your story.* Stick to your guns, no matter what. Don't change even the smallest detail, because that's what they're looking for. They're trying to trap you, so internalize your answers. *Stick to your guns, Logan, and you'll get through it."*

Rick dug into his Discovery file. Now the pieces fit. That man in the car with him, the informant, had urged Rick to follow him to his house after they'd done the deal. He claimed to have more money there, but Rick wasn't interested. That's when the FED's lost control of the situation - they were waiting near the man's house. It was a trap, and when Rick didn't bite, he sent them scrambling to get organized. Rick wasn't paranoid about the vehicle following him; from there hell broke loose.

The man paid for the drugs with marked bills – and here's the kicker – Rick generously gave him extra. How apt that the informant only turned in two grams, pocketing the rest. I hope the prick enjoyed it because he now existed as a marked man.

That federal operation monitored Rick's crew and associates, and busted them one by one, with the aid of that the same informant. Rick had been in the company of that man for several months, and a hundred memories became paramount. *How much evidence did the FED's have?*

I had a disturbing talk with my attorney on the payphone.

"Logan, there's a new Discovery file."

"What do you mean?"

"Elena made a second testimony. A copy is being mailed to you by the prosecution. I don't know the details, but she spoke to a Victim Resource Coordinator."

I tightened my grip on the phone.

"She turned your hard drives in, to police evidence, so she had them all along. The prosecutor is claiming they have 'strangely violent material' on them."

"What?"

"I don't know, Logan. Let's wait and see what we're dealing with."

I felt speechless, both by the claim, and the fact my drives weren't lost. I couldn't allow myself to believe it. Equally overwhelming were the unknown details of Elena's testimony.

.

I stood at the cell window, visibly distressed, I'm sure.

"You should've seen it last December," Zach said from his bunk

"What's that?" I asked

"Those three huge skylights opened because of a mechanical problem, or a fire or something, and they couldn't get 'em to close again. It was snowing hard outside, and it drifted in. It snowed inside the cell block all night long. It was amazing, bro. It didn't even seem real, you know?"

"That does sound amazing," I said, "wish I could've seen that."

"It was..."

I meditated on that.

.

Once Jessie actively conversed with us, we learned he'd flopped the Rider Program, and waited to get the length of his prison term by the Judge.

"On the transport bus, I met a girl," Jessie said, "and by the time we got here, we were engaged."

"Bro, you got engaged to a girl on a prison transport bus?" Rick said, giving Zach and I a raised eyebrow

"Yeah, dude. She's my fiancee. But here's the cool part. She has forty acres of land she inherited from her family. We're gonna live on it when we get out of prison. She'll probably get out a few years before I do, but she promised to wait."

"She's gonna wait for you, huh?" Zach questioned, "That's the plan your banking on?"

.

"What are you in for?" Jessie asked me

"I ran over the mailman."

"Whoa. For real? Did he die?"

"No, but I heard he walks funny now."

"Damn. *That's crazy.* Hey, If I tell you something, promise me you won't let the other guys know," Jessie pleaded

"Alright."

"I got convicted of a felony domestic, but the prosecution offered me a plea deal for misdemeanor probation."

"What are you saying? You didn't take it?"

"No. I thought they'd drop the charges, so I refused it, and they gave me three years."

Jessie, being that gullible, made him easy fodder for prison gangs. It didn't help that he already had a brother in *The Yard* affiliated with the *Aryan Knights.* The pressure to join would be intense, if not insurmountable.

Zach and I stood at the front of the dinner line, while the deputy fumbled to get his papers in order on his clipboard.

"We're in the thick of it now, bro," Zach said

I saw Jessie towards the middle of the line, "Hey, Jessie! *There's a Koala Bear running up on you!*" I hollered, as he flinched and spun around.

"*We are in the thick of it.*"

.

Rick, out of kindness, tried to prep Jessie for prison, both mentally and physically. Each afternoon, Rick insisted he join in his workout, yet Jessie cited lousy excuses not to.

"Dude, if they recruit you in prison," Rick said, "They're going to push you so fucking hard, physically, you won't be able to handle it. They want you ready for war, bro."

Jessie failed to heed his advice, certain he could navigate *The Yard.* In reality, the Rider Program safeguards inmates from the majority of the actual prison environment; they get quarantined in a low-security section of the facility.

.

The hypnotism manual got delivered to my cell, and I instantly started reading it. Zach and Rick saw I had serious intentions, and looked forward to the experiment. I planned to do a memory regression, which I hoped to be beneficial. I knew Zach wanted to explore that moment he spoke of with Jeremy; the memory of that metallic ball in the sky, and subsequent confusion.

Rick urged me to hurry and master the craft, and I explained it wasn't an overnight process. I outlined a script that I could practice on myself while my cellies slept. I felt gratified by the results.

"A few more weeks, Rick," I assured him, "You don't want me to fuck your brain up."

"No, I don't."

"Is that another felony?"

"Good question."

Rick and I walked the yellow line, on the main floor.

"I'm concerned about putting Zach under, man," I said, "Hypnotizing someone with schizoaffective disorder, who has a documented fear of UFO's, might not end well."

"I think you're right, dude. We probably shouldn't."

"I don't want him to take it personally, though. Maybe we can stall. They have to take him to prison eventually, right?"

"Ok. Just keep studying your book. Tell him you're not ready."

"Alright."

"You're still going to hypnotize me though, right?"

"Oh, fuck yeah! I'm working on my script."

"Awesome!"

.

My mother informed me that Matt, taking care of Jack, planned a move to Eugene, Oregon, with his family. I panicked briefly when I heard the news, thinking either Jack couldn't stay with him, or that if Jack did go, I might not see him again. Matt's scheduled his departure date three days before my sentencing.

Although Matt was willing to hold off on his plans, I couldn't permit that. My day in court could change. We had no guarantee I'd be released, and I had nothing but a floor to sleep on, in Tony's apartment, which didn't allow pets. It pained me, though I knew Jack was in able hands.

.

I have to make a special mention of the wall dividing our cell from Trav and the guys in 845. We beat that wall without remorse. It served as our sounding board. Day and night, it suffered our aggression. Zach and Rick continued practicing their high kicks on it, the soles of their cheap shoes leaving streaks of rubber.

"Dude! My mark is one inch below yours! I'm almost there!" Rick exclaimed

"That's yoga, Rick," Zach replied

From a standing position, Zach could raise his foot directly above his head and touch the top of the door frame. If I'd seen him do that on the street, I would've assumed he did ballet.

After a month of competition, at least seven hundred black marks covered the wall. They made it a damn work of art; like a Zen landscape of a bamboo forest.

When we got riled up, the four of us formed a line and drummed the wall with both fists, until Trav and his crew retaliated by drumming their side, louder. The cell vibrated. On bad days, as we paced the cell, we'd punch the wall then turn to walk the other way. We even hit the wall in our sleep, stuck in bad dreams.

If we had to relay a verbal message next door, we'd beat on the wall to get their attention, and then cup our mouth to the crack in the door, while the recipient positioned his ear. Trav enjoyed shouting trivia questions at us, usually music or movie related, when he and his cellmates got stumped.

Through the wall, Trav and Rick did synchronized workouts.
"Alright, Rick! Do five burpees, and five push-ups then hit the wall!"
"Ok, dude! You start!"
As long as those knocks endured, the regiment continued.

The wall kept on, hammered and scarred. It had no choice but to accept its thankless job. We allowed it no rest.

.

Idaho is one of four states that doesn't distinguish a crime committed by a person with a mental illness. There is no insanity defense, which would've benefited Zach. I doubted he'd get the help required in prison.

Zach didn't take his case to trial. He and his public defender sought to minimize his sentence, fighting for Mental Health Court in a state with strict regulations. A Rider seemed unlikely, though also worth a try. Prison was the most probable outcome, and his defender would push for two years, plus three indeterminate.
"It'd be nice to get two years," Zach said, "But for the things I've done, I'd totally understand if they gave me more, you know?"

We each had a hard day; our cases beat us down. The same information kept repeating in our minds, and no amount of discussion clarified the situation. We agonized. My cellmates were facing prison terms; they only questioned for how long. *Was I?* I hesitated in preparing myself for the worst as if that act might somehow bring it to light.

We were mentally and physically exhausted. Then, Rick spoke to me.

"Logan, don't feel sorry for us," he said, a resolve in his voice

"Yeah," Zach said, "We did this to ourselves, bro. We knew what we were doing."

"Get out of here and live your life," Rick continued, "Don't blow it like we did. Don't come back here. Just forget about us."

And simply because they said that - I knew I never would.

.

Zach got withdrawn and talked to me in private.

"Hey bro, there's something I didn't tell you, about my arrest at Winco, that day."

"What's that?"

"While I was fighting those guys, one of 'em tried to wrestle the gun from my hand. It was aimed right at his face, and I didn't mean to, but I pulled the trigger. It was like for one second time stopped, *but the gun didn't go off, bro.* I've been thinking of that a lot. What if it wasn't an accident? What if I meant to pull the trigger? I keep asking myself that. I was so messed up in my mind, I just don't know.

"You can't let these thoughts drive you crazy. What's done is done."

"I thank God I didn't hurt or kill that man."

"Then there's your answer. You know what's in your heart."

"I believe that maybe it *was* God, giving me one last chance, you know? I think he's looking out for me, telling me I need to turn my life around. That's what I want to do, more than anything. I wanna do the right thing, and live a good life, and show God how grateful I am."

"That's the best way to view it, Zach. You *should* believe there is a higher order. You *should* believe it was God. Don't lose sight of that."

I paused, then said, "Besides, it's either that... or you left the gun safety on."

"Huh!" Zach grinned

.

Zach Morris finally had his sentencing day, and we sent him off with positive energy.

The Judge did not hide his disgust, and demeaned Zach strongly, *'Mr. Morris, who exactly do you think you are, coming to the state of Idaho and waving a gun around, threatening its citizens?'* Sadly, the proceedings did not go in Zach's favor, and he was given three years, plus five indeterminate.

"Thank you, Your Honor," Zach said, politely

Later, Zach said that he thought the ruling was fair. Nothing could be done about it now. It was over.

And, he still had to answer for his escape charge, in Blackfoot. The next bus would drive him there, before transporting him to Boise State Penitentiary.

August 15th – at 9:45 am, a deputy entered our cell.
"Morris! Roll it up. You're going on transport. You've got five minutes."
Rick and I made sure we had his contact info as we said our goodbyes.
"Thank you for taking care of me, Zach," I said, shaking his hand
"Absolutely," he said
Rick hugged him.
As Zach packed up his things, I could see his eyes glassing over.
Then, he was gone.

It's disarming, how the acoustics of a cell can change,
minus one friend and a mattress.

Kindness Befalls A Wicked Man

I've never been in the company of someone that chilled my blood, until David entered our cell. The air felt differently around him. My skin had a physical reaction to his presence. There is no lightness in sharing a confined space with a man suspected of being a serial killer.

There's an evil that can get beaten into a person by a sick society – and there's an evil inherent from birth. That's what I saw in David. I could see it in the corners of his eyes. It bothered me that he had Zach's bunk.

David, in his lazy Alabama accent, spoke of the night he came home covered in someone else's blood, with no memory of where he'd been. He recollected the story with a touch of pride and an otherwise unsettling lack of emotion. His current arrest, for a minor violation, brought him to booking carrying a backpack with men's and women's belongings. Why he had them, David could not surmise.

Could I prove my intuition? No, of course not. I had a resounding sense of what he seemed capable of afflicting if he hadn't already. I didn't give a shit about evidence. It wasn't my job to convict him - it was my duty to co-exist with him. I tried to hide my disdain, but I failed.

After his introduction, while my cellmates were distracted, my eyes locked with David's. He gave me a dispassionate stare, with a lackadaisical expression. A smile crept on his face, and he *winked* at me. David saw right through me, and I only saw as far into *him* as he'd let me, barely past his veneer of normalcy.

Rick, the outgoing, generous person that he was, freely conversed with David about his case and personal life and supplied him with coffee. Rick didn't have the hesitations I did, and that concerned me a bit.
"You know, Rick," David said with his southern drawl, "I don't think Logan likes me much."

With merely half a cup of coffee, David got violent. He talked incessantly about hurting Perry, working himself up for hours, certain that Perry conspired against him and spread gossip. I advised Rick to quit offering David coffee, and he agreed.
"I just don't know what happens to me, fellas," David said, of his outbursts, "My apologies. I'd best stay away from the caffeine."

David had problems sleeping, and I felt him shifting underneath my bunk.

At the height of police suspicion, David got arrested and profiled due to his proximity to unsolved slayings, and his time of place during the murders. Thus, he was housed with a notorious inmate in Ada County - a convicted serial killer I'll call Eric.

I think David admired Eric and spoke of him in a high regard. They discussed what could drive a man to kill a person, and perhaps the gratification of doing so.
"I've made a lot of ghosts, David..." Eric said to him.

David got impressed by the coldness of the remark - the ownership of it.

How fitting that on that evening, a dark entity manifested in their cell; a shadow figure that sent them reeling in panic. Eric pulled his knees to his chin, and wrapped his arms around his legs, screaming. David froze, as the entity passed between them and disappeared through a wall.

Over the years, many inmates reported paranormal activity in that section, and demanded to be transferred, traumatized by their experience. Eventually, the entire wing got torn to the ground and rebuilt as the new maximum security area.

Despite the efforts of police, they ceased their investigation on David. They had no evidence and released him from custody.

.

In contrast to the anger, David had moments of joviality. He mentioned a recent encounter with a stranger who'd shown him an act of kindness.
"I was penniless, at a Greyhound bus station in the rain," David began, "I didn't know what to do with myself. I was low. Then, I saw a man get out of a parked car. He came running towards me, wearing a rain jacket and said, *'Hey, do you need bus fare?'* I said yes, and he gave me fifty dollars, making me promise to buy a ticket with it. I asked him why he was doing this, and he said *'I help people out, bro. That's what I do. I used to be at rock bottom, myself,'* and then he ran to his car. I bought that ticket, but I had some money left, so I got some beer. Guess I broke my promise a little."

David would ask us if we wanted to 'wrestle,' to pass our time in lockdown. We declined. I shuddered at the thought of his hands touching me. It was unsettling to peer over the edge of my bunk and see him smiling up at me.

.

David had his day in court. The Judge, oddly forgiving, saw fit to drop the charges, advising David to make the most of the opportunity. He returned to our cell, rolled up his bunk, and waited impatiently for his release.

"Boys, I ain't free till that gate closes behind me," he said

He got concerned with retrieving his backpack and questioned the deputy about his property. David said he wanted his energy drinks and some other noise.

Within an hour, he stepped out the front door; having been in Ada County for five days.

I sincerely hoped it to be the end of him.

.

After his departure, a deputy granted my request for the bottom bunk.
"You finally got a bottom bunk after how many months?" Rick laughed
"I know, right?" I said as I sanitized the steel frame
I set up my personal items, and hung a towel off the top bunk, like Zach used to do, blocking the harsh fluorescent light.
"It's weird how this feels like a fresh start," I said
Rick agreed.

.

We also said goodbye to Jessie. Rick didn't miss the opportunity to make a fool of him. He stood at the window, pretending to be in conversation with a deputy.
"Jessie needs to pack it up? Yes, officer. Got it," Rick said, nodding his head, "Hey Jessie, you've got fifteen minutes to roll it up. They're taking you to the transport bus."
"Whatever, dude," Jessie said, in disbelief
What's funny is that there *actually was* an officer giving Rick those instructions. Rick warned him it wasn't a joke, though Jessie didn't buy it. We'd played too many tricks on him. Fifteen minutes elapsed, and Jessie decided to take a shit.
The cell door opened and the deputy entered.
"What the hell is this? Why are you not ready?" the officer demanded, observing Jessie's bunk.
"Oh! I, uh. Well, wait a minute. See I thought," Jessie stammered from the toilet
"You think I'm playing games with you?!" he snapped, "The transport is waiting! You have three minutes!"

With that, Jessie went off to prison - *Klaatu barada nikto, you stupid bastard.*

ISM

"How many mattresses are out there, Logan?" Rick asked
"Three."
"Do you see anybody yet?"
"Nope."

Rick and I were on our respective bottom bunks when the door opened. A confident black man named Daniel Weschler stepped inside.

"Alright listen," he said, setting his crate down, "Y'all get one nigger joke, and you better get it out of your system right now, *'cuz then I''m cuttin' that shit right off."*

He glanced at Rick, who knew plenty of racist jokes, considering the people he'd grown up with. He seemed oddly mute. Daniel then focused his gaze on me.

"The only niggers I've met have all been white," I said, shrugging my shoulders

Besides, Daniel Weschler was a black dude in an Idaho penitentiary. What greater punchline was there?

He looked familiar to me. I pondered it for a minute. *I sat next to him on the transport bus, a long month prior.* He had been in the maximum security division - the man who's elegant features reminded me of Tupac Shakur. He had lengthy, braided black hair, which he'd inherited from his mother, a Native American. In that culture, hair held a symbolic power; a belief to which Daniel subscribed.

In other words, *the man's hair was so impressive it had religious implications.*

.

Nighttime in the Nevada desert - Daniel Weschler drove his Lexus, with Nicki, a girl from his crew, in the passenger seat. He had developed feelings for her, though he'd deny that to the ends of the earth.

The headlights caught a herd of jackrabbits, jutting across the road. With no time to hit the brakes, half a dozen or so met their death. The grill of the car got covered with blood and fur, and as the two travelers crossed the Idaho border, into Boise to pick up a friend, he stopped at a car wash. Where he lived, in Portland, marijuana was legal. State legislation wasn't on his mind, nor did he expect the car wash attendant to call the damn police because his car smelled like weed.

When the cops arrived, a lot of bad noise ensued. They put Daniel against the hood of his car and searched him, finding a folded dollar bill in his waist lining, containing a fine white powder.

"What's this, Mr. Weschler?" the officer questioned

"Tylenol, asshole!" Daniel said, forcefully blowing the powder off the bill

The wind caught it and blew it into the officer's face. That's when the cop went for an Oscar, "OH GOD! IT'S IN MY EYES! I CAN TASTE IT! IT'S IN MY MOUTH!"

The cop got rushed to the emergency room for treatment, and Daniel was charged with possession and assault on a police officer. Nicki, briefly in custody, got released.

.

In the Maximum Security wing of Ada County Jail, Daniel had to stay sharp. He endured every racial slur the inmates threw at him, the brunt of it coming from one man, nearest his cell. It's easy to act hard, behind the protection of a concrete wall. When they got released for out time, Daniel challenged him to a fight. The white man naturally had his buddies with him, ready to jump in.

"Gimme the *one's* motherfucker! Just you and me!" Daniel said, bringing his fists close to his face, "Tell your ugly ass friends to take a walk. Gimme the *ones!*"

Without strength in numbers, the white man declined. The chemistry changed after that, as Daniel earned respect.

Nicki provided Daniel's lifeline; she put money on his books and promised not to abandon him. He spent his available time on the phone with her. *'It's you and me ok?'* she said, *'Tomorrow I'm finding you a lawyer. Call me whenever you can, Daniel. I'll be here'.*

Then, she disappeared. Her phone went silent. Daniel couldn't understand it, and it ate away at him. After that, he got transferred to Cell Block 8, with us.

.

Daniel, in the bunk above me, spilled a cup of coffee on his sheets, and it dripped onto mine. He asked the deputy if he could bring us new bedrolls, and he put in the request. In the interim, Daniel got called out for a visit from his public defender. When the linens arrived, I changed my sheets, and surprisingly, Rick made up Daniel's bunk, in his absence.

I knew Rick had a racist upbringing, but he carried those sensibilities out of habit, rather than any real personal conviction. You don't come across many black men in Idaho to test your bullshit theories on, and Rick had little experience to draw from.

Yet, there he was, prepping Daniel's bunk. When Rick finished, he leaned against the wall by the air conditioner and looked at me.

"I can't believe I just made a black man's bed," he said proudly
"You like him, eh?" I smiled
"Bro, he's fucking *awesome!*"
I laughed, "Yes, he is. He's a very cool guy. We're fortunate to have him."
"My wife is gonna love this."
"Hell, *I'm* proud of ya, Rick."

.

That night, the three of us played a game.
"Alright, guys. Let's guess the crimes of our next cellie," I directed
"DUI," said Rick
"Possession with intent," I voted, "How about you, Daniel?"
"Aggravated Assault."

The cell door cracked open, and the deputy entered, with a sympathetic look
on his face. *Oh god no. What's this?* He didn't have to speak – we knew the situation.
As he exited, our new cellie meekly scuffled in – Joseph Hamburg, older than dirt. The
dude looked like a tore-back alley cat, scraped off a train track, and he stunk to high
hell.

Assigned to the bunk above Rick, he labored to reach it, climbing first onto the
writing desk, and then weakly crawling over. He bundled up his sheets like a bird's
nest and collapsed, with no acknowledgment. We were not happy, least of all Rick,
who had to sleep underneath him.
"Hey, old guy," Daniel said, "You feel like telling us who you are, or what?"
He said nothing.
"Hey, old man! I'm talking to you!"
He blurted out a mess of syllables, *"Arkarkarkargarkarg!"*
"What the *hell* was that?" I asked, "Were those words, or did he seriously just
bark at us?"
"I think he barked at us, bro," Daniel confirmed
"What are you here for?" Rick asked, more aggressively
He muttered three letters - *DUI.*
'Well, I guessed it right," Rick shrugged, looking at us for credit

It's sad how fast the dynamic of a cell collapses, with one miserable addition.
Our minds recoiled a bit, *how long are we trapped with this guy?* When he sobered up, he
became marginally talkative.
"Police took my dog, Sally. I'm never gonna see her again," the old man
lamented
He was attached to the animal, and it disheartened us to hear the dog would
be put to sleep. We got disgusted at how little effort the man put forth to save her.

"So, you're going to let your dog die, and then what old man? What's your plan when you get out of here?" Rick inquired

"Figured I'd go to a bar and drink some beer. Then maybe I'll steal a truck from the parking lot."

"That's your plan?" Daniel said, dumbfounded, "Steal a dude's truck?"

"Are you fucking serious?" Rick said, "That's your fucking plan? You're pathetic, dude."

The discussion ended when the old man passed out, comatose, and slept through to the next day. That gave the three of us a chance to plan our strategy.

"At this rate, the dudes gonna be dead in less than a year," Daniel suggested

We asked ourselves if we had the patience and energy to aid the man, or if we should throw him out of the cell and face the consequences.

.

Rick sat on his bunk, plastic crate on his lap, working diligently on a portrait of Trav's three children, in a deep state of concentration. So deep, in fact, he hadn't noticed the old man shifting in his bed - his arm now hanging over the side, six inches away.

"Hey, Daniel," I said tapping on the bottom of his bunk

"What's good?" he said, poking his head down

"Watch this. Hey Rick. Rick! YO, RICK!"

Rick snapped to attention, "Yeah?"

"Don't look to your left."

He did anyway, and the proximity of the old man's claw made him jerk in reaction – like a spider descending towards him. After a good laugh, we marveled at the condition of the hand. The fingers were gnarled and swollen, his nails black, the skin, in general, was acrid and splitting.

"Holy fuck, dude!" Rick laughed, studying it

"That's Creature from the Black Lagoon shit," Daniel said, from a cautious distance

"Anybody have a bottle of lotion?" I asked

"Yeah," Daniel answered

"We're gonna need it," I said, stepping to examine the intake photo on his wristband, "Well, his name's Joseph Hamburg. What's left of him, anyway."

We would not refer to him as such for awhile - *he needed to earn his own goddamn name.* The verbal assaults of Rick and Daniel weren't designed to diminish Joseph. They were a plea for self-respect.

"Hey, fartbag! Why don't you climb off that bunk and brush the two or three teeth in your head? Your mouth smells like a garbage disposal."

"Old man! If you drop any more dead skin cells or pieces of bone or teeth on me while I'm drawing, I'm going to suffocate you with your pillow."

"Get your dusty ass off that bunk and do some jumping jacks you gangly old bum. We need to make sure your heart's still beating. We don't want another felony."

"Old Man River! Sing a song for us! *Jimmy crack corn, and I don't care! Jimmy crack corn, and I don't care!"*

"Don't look at me when I'm taking a shit, you goddamn barn yard sodomist!"

"Shut the hell up, you smelly old fuck! Were we talking to you? You speak when spoken to!"

"Hey, moon man! When's the last time you had tuberculosis? We're not about to catch a disease, you bag of piss. We'll throw your ass off the tier."

"Are you peeing with that dick?! Does it even work? Look how he has to stand completely over the toilet so it can dribble down."

"Yo, dumpster diver! Want some old bread or smelly pasta?"

"Hey, zombie dick! You gonna take a shower today or are you just giving up?"

And, resolutely *"...You really are an ugly smelly bastard..."*

.

Back in Portland, Daniel's friends saw his arrest report online and figured he was done for. *Not even Daniel can slide out of this one,* they thought. He had one pal, Benny, who also knew Nicki, so he became Daniel's primary contact. He wanted answers to her whereabouts.

His mixed feelings towards that woman drove him mad. He'd unburden himself upon me, playing out the conceivable scenarios of her vanishing act. I got personally invested in her disappearance – hell, I felt like I knew the girl. I waited for news along with him.

"I don't get it, bro," Daniel said of his attraction to Nicki, "She's not that cute, so why do I think she's so sexy?"
"Is she smart?"
"She's way smarter than the rest of the girl's I know."
"Does that intimidate you?"

"Nah, I like it."

Daniel tried so hard to fit her into a defined role, but she wouldn't conform. Had Daniel been in love? He didn't think so, or at least he didn't admit it.

The constant driving force in Daniel's life was his three-year-old daughter, Isabelle; wise beyond her years, very articulate, and what some folks refer to as an 'Indigo' child. Isabelle was disappointed in her father for not being at home. Daniel didn't know what to say to her, other than 'he had a job.'
"Daddy, why are you dressed like that?" she inquired, during a video chat
"Uh, it's a uniform baby."
"What's your job, exactly?"

Daniel knew the game had run its course; Isabelle got smarter by the minute. He had to make changes. Daniel grew up in the projects of Fresno, California, and he'd lost a lot of friends to guns, some of them in his arms.
"People don't just drop dead when they get shot, like the movies," he said, "One of my friends got shot in the head while we were walking down the street. He was standing up and talking, crying to me that he didn't want to die. I tried to stop the bleeding with my hands. He died while we waited for the ambulance."

He added, "The media says the reason black people get shot in the slums is because of drugs and gangs, but that's bullshit. The main reason is women. I *promise* you! *Dude's will blast homies from their own damn gang over women.*"

.

After Zach, Rick continued to practice yoga on a daily basis. I'd occasionally join him in a session. Then, I'd clear the floor so he and Daniel could do their exercise regiment. Rick found a solid workout partner in Daniel. They pushed each other to the limit, like those montage sequences in martial arts movies from the 70's. If making 'Kiai' karate sounds does, in fact, pull energy from another dimension, it should be well-timed, lest you laugh at the wrong moment and give yourself a hernia.

I chose to preserve my calories, preferring to sit on my bunk and yell at them, pretending to be a salty boxing coach.

Daniel had the physique of a street fighter, yet he managed to have considerable grace in his movements, floating in his steps. His fierce powerhouse kicks to our wall shook the cell; I couldn't imagine what they'd do to a man's rib cage.

'Hey, Logie, why don't we hear you giving the old guy a hard time?' Daniel asked, of Joseph Hamburg (He called us Ricky and Logie, as a term of endearment.)

"One of us needs to remain neutral. Otherwise, *who's he going to confide in, eh?"*

"Ah! Ok! I got it, I got it!"

I lapped the main floor when I felt Joseph hobbling up behind me.
"Hey Logie, wait up. Hey Logie, can I walk with you?"
"Don't ever fucking call me Logie. Only Daniel can get away with that."
"Oh, I'm sorry. Logan, can I walk with you?"
"Yes, you can."
"Those guys sure are tough on me, aren't they? I don't know if I can handle it."
"Yes, they are. They want you to try harder for yourself, Joe."
"They don't like me much."
"You need to earn their respect, Joe," I said, as he struggled to maintain my speed, "Why, are you going to hit the panic button on us?"
"No. I may do even worse in another cell."
"You probably would."
"Logan, do you always walk this fast?"
"Yes, I do."
"I don't know if I can keep up."
"Sure you can. Walk three laps with me, Joe."
"Boy, I'll try. I don't know how you do it."
"You in pain, Joe?"
"Yeah, I am."
"That's because you sleep on sidewalks."
"My legs hurt so bad. Logan, I have to sit down."
"That's fine, Hamburg. You did well."
"Oh hey, um, do you think I could have whatever food you don't eat tonight?"
"Yeah. Jimmy has dibs on the potato wedges, though."
"Oh, ok. Thank you. Thanks. I can give you some of my calcium packets."
"You keep your packets, Joe. I'm fine."

Joseph was a scavenger. At meals, we'd set our leftovers in front of him, rather than dump them in the bin. What he couldn't cram into his mouth, he'd stuff in Styrofoam bowls or empty bags. Soon the food would rot and stink up the cell. We'd have to steal his crate and clean it.

He loved those calcium supplement packets issued by the jail; he'd hoard them like a pack-rat, and treat them as currency when bartering for coffee and candy. Caffeine turned Joseph into a kitten. He'd lay on his bunk smiling, batting things around and wiggling his feet.

.

Jimmy migrated to our table for meal times. I wasn't sure who invited him, or if he maneuvered himself in subconsciously, though we were grateful for it (I'm sure the *Boost* was a factor). In his company, we consumed more energy laughing than we digested from our food. Whatever table manners we had, went straight to hell.

Jimmy seemingly had five or six personalities trapped in his psyche, each trying to claw their way to dominance. Fortunately, all of them were *funny*; being either shrewd old women or gay public defenders.
"*Interesting!*" Jimmy often said, in a shrill high pitched voice, curling and waving his upper lip.

He and I argued over the imaginary bill.
"Certainly not. I'm taking care of it. You bought dinner yesterday," I declared
"I insist. You've been wonderful to my family, inviting us for the holidays!"
"You know I'll find a way to pay it back."
"Well let's do lunch, then. My treat."
"That sounds delightful."
"Are you free tomorrow?"
"Yes, I sure am."
"Let's do Mexican! I know a great place!"
"Have a splendid lockdown. I'll be in touch."

Ah, Jimmy. With his good looks and perfect fucking hair; even the female deputies hit on him. In court, he'd catch them taking video clips of him with their phones, to show their friends.

Casey, an inmate in my old cell, was Jimmy's brother. He had a manic, nervous energy. Though roughly six feet tall at one-hundred-eighty pounds, he trembled like a chihuahua. Riddled with tattoos, he'd stand at his window, his unblinking eyes darting back and forth, trying to engage inmates as they walked by, as if he had something critical to say, or had a vital favor to ask of them.
Jimmy loved him to death.
"Look at that boy," Jimmy said, smiling and shaking his head, gesturing to Casey at his window, "He is *so* starved for attention."

.

Joe's public defender visited with regularity, which was rare. She saw the importance of saving his dog, Sally, before she got put down at animal control. She fought for Joe to be released on his own recognizance, or to at least get a bail reduction. She also asked permission to contact his family, whom he'd alienated years ago.

Joe had a meeting with a female bail bond agent - an attractive, middle-aged, black woman. Joe had a bit of a crush and bragged like he had a chance.

"Old man, give me her number," Daniel instructed, and Joe obliged him

Daniel phoned her and set up an appointment. When she came, a deputy escorted Daniel to the visiting area. Two *hours* later, Daniel reappeared with a smile. The woman offered to pay his bail, and give him a place to stay, on the condition he'd go to church with her.

"Damn dude. What's the secret?" Rick asked

"When you're talking you gotta flare up your nostrils now and then. It drives 'em crazy. They don't know what to do with themselves."

The arrangement, of course, didn't pan out. Perhaps Daniel enticed her to see if he could.

.

Daniel got his first plea deal – two years, plus five indeterminate.

As he exited the courthouse elevator, the deputy directed him past the women's holding cell. He removed his hair-tie and let his braided locks hang loose. He snarled his upper lip. The girls clamored for him, knocking on the glass.

In our cell, Rick advised him to ignore the deal.

"Don't take it," he said, "Be patient. They'll come at you with a better one."

"I can handle two years," Daniel opined

"Don't do it. They'll offer the Rider Program. Don't let 'em deceive you with a raw deal."

.

Rick and I had called each other's bluff for weeks, debating our transfer to *The Dorms*. I had my eligibility date on September 9th, and Rick's was September 16th.

"Are you excited to go to The Dorms, Rick?"

"No. I'm not going. I'm staying here."

"I don't believe you."

"Alright, dude. Guess you'll have to wait and see."

I watched Alex roll up his bunk and transfer to *The Dorms*, for the remainder of his sentence. Inmates shouted through their doors, saluting him. With Alex gone, Mendoza was as the last familiar face on that Walk.

I got mixed reviews about *The Dorms.* Clinton, the Redshirt, bunked there for three days, then demanded a transfer back to cell block. The deputies allowed his reentry, on the condition he perform the custodial duties of the red uniform. He agreed since he'd be headed to *The Yard,* shortly.

"God man, it is so fucking hot in there," he said, "It's a steady eighty-five degrees, and smells like sweat. On top of that, it's fucking *loud,* dude. There are so many people in there."

The politics of dealing with eighty inmates in a gymnasium-sized area didn't appeal to me. The dynamic of a four-man cell seemed easy, in comparison. However, a change of scene could be healthy, too. *Would I go when eligible, or decline? Did I have a choice?* The deputies wouldn't clarify, and I waited for my reclassification date.

"Hey Logan, I know you're going to the dorms when they call for you," Rick said

"I sure am."

"Wait, what? I was kidding. You *are* going?"

"Think I'm bluffing? I signed up for it on the computer, during lunch."

"No, you didn't."

"Yes, I did."

"You're lying, bro."

"Guess you'll find out."

.

11:00pm

The keys rattled, as the deputy opened our tray slot.

"Crannell! Mail!" he shouted

I climbed out of bed, and he handed me a thick, legal sized, manila envelope containing the new Discovery from the prosecution. I did not open it. I knew I wouldn't sleep if I read it, and decided to hold off until the afternoon.

As I read her words, It's hard for me to describe the sickness I felt in my stomach; I almost vomited. Elena claimed to have seen hundreds of disturbing images on my computer about torturing, molesting and killing women. She scoured my private journal, highlighting any passage that could be misconstrued as violent, and turned it in, with my messenger bag of weapons, to police evidence.

Elena said a voice told her to search our apartment for further proof and found a bag hidden in the closet, filled with satanic objects and a jar of ceremonial dirt. The material on my stolen hard drives got cited, by Elena, as containing terrible footage. Elena wept, saying she was so scared of the things she'd seen and the words she'd read in my journal, that it compelled her to bring it in, to the Crimes Against Children office, while the police filed for a search warrant.

None of the accusations hurt me more than her stating that I abused and tortured Jack. Elena said I continuously kicked and jabbed him, and yanked his legs. She said that I would 'hypnotize' him and perform cruel acts upon him.

This was coming from a woman who planned to have Jack euthanized at her convenience. *At no other point was it harder for me to remain dignified.*

My nausea gave way to abject fucking rage. How *the fuck* could any grown adult human being take this shit seriously? Was I expected to *address* this bullshit in *a court of law* and defend myself on charges of hypnotizing animals and worshiping Satan?

Why THE FUCK was that bitch not thrown in handcuffs for walking into fucking police headquarters with DOCUMENTED STOLEN PROPERTY, after disobeying a direct fucking court order!

On the contrary – she got congratulated for her bravery.

.

My neighbor Rook and I walked the rec yard, alone. It was a hot day, late in summer. I remember every detail of that moment; the stubble on his shaven head, the sweat on his brow, and the back of his freckled neck. The way the sun hit his eyes and reflected off his glasses. The tone of his voice. He and I were looking through the fence, at a group sex offenders from Cell Block 7. I didn't tell Rook that the courts were attempting to charge me with rape.
"Sick fucks," he said, gesturing to the men
"How many do you think are innocent?" I asked
The question caught him off guard.
"Fuck, man. I don't know. It's hard for me to think a woman could do that to a man."
I paused, "What would you do if you got accused of rape?"

The question pained him. He cringed. Having the words in his mouth bothered him. He hated to hear himself say it – *because he meant it.*

"I... *fuck*... I think I'd have to kill a bitch if she did that to me."

Did Elena understand the game she was playing?
Did she know what men of a different constitution would've done to her?

<h1 style="text-align:center; letter-spacing:0.5em;">SEPTEMBER</h1>

Rick and I walked the yellow line. It was an unspoken rule that two inmates in stride were discussing private business. Rick and I had a lot of those walks.

"I'm scared, Rick. Why did she wait two months to hand over the drives?"

"It is suspicious. There's nothing illegal on them, right?"

"No, not at all. Unless *she* put material on there herself."

"If she did, it'll have a timestamp on it. Whoever examines 'em will see that."

"Right, but if my arrest was premeditated on her part, which I believe it was, she could've put shit on there while I worked, and I wouldn't have known it."

"That is pretty scary, dude. Is she that computer savvy, though?"

"No. I'm paranoid, but it doesn't add up. She goes to police evidence with stolen property after telling my attorney she couldn't find them. It's lie after lie after lie.

"At least you got the drives back."

"Almost. I won't be happy until they're safely in my hands. How difficult will it be to get them from evidence?"

"I don't know. That's a good question. It might take awhile. It depends if they open another investigation. If so, they could keep them."

"My Discovery lists the iMac, a keyboard, and a green bag with my hard drives and journal. What gets me is that it doesn't say *how many* drives. But, you're right, Rick. It's progress."

.

Daniel returned from a court date in complete disgust. His last name had him at the end of the alphabet, so he heard other cases on the docket that included the sentencing of three rapists.

"I sat there listening to what these fucking rapists did. One of them raped a twelve-year-old girl with a *fucking broom handle,* and they got *three years* in prison?! *Motherfucking rapists?!* I watch these dudes only get *three,* and I'm facing *five years* for $20 worth of cocaine!? *Are you fucking kidding me?* What *the hell* is wrong with Idaho, bro?!"

When Daniel cooled off, he continued.

"I don't understand the courts here, man. You've got inmates walking around, and nobody knows if they're going home tomorrow or heading to prison for ten years. Look out the window. Is anybody reading their Discovery? No. Half of 'em don't even have one. They're watching TV. In Oregon, you get your charges, and you know where you stand. If you take it to trial, they set your court date a few weeks out, not *six months* like they do here. If you plead guilty, they sentence your ass *that day* and get the ball rolling."

.

I listened to a white man rapping a song he'd written, on the main floor. Inmates gathered together, impressed as I was, at his passionate delivery, as if he didn't need to breathe. His hands moved like weapons. He appeared sickly in health, which made his vocal attack disconcerting.

After a rapid-fire verse, his voice went from aggressive to high and melodic, shifting the whole genre of the song from hip-hop to a rock ballad, for the chorus. He received a round of applause.

Seconds later, he collapsed into a seizure and got taken to medical. *Was it epilepsy?* Four days elapsed when nurses brought him to my previous cell in a wheelchair. He gradually resumed walking.

.

Cell 862, on the upper tier, directly across from ours, had issues with fighting. Deputies would raid it, and drag each inmate out in handcuffs, isolating them from each other, to see if their stories added up. One man, in particular, got questioned four times, then relegated to *The Side Shoot*. He was middle-aged, and bald, with wild eyes from long-term methamphetamine abuse.

On the final outburst, he and two of his cellmates jumped the fourth man. Marco, my former security guard, bravely rushed up the stairs to confront them single-handedly, radioing for backup.

.

At some period, in Joseph Hamburg's blighted sojourn, he panned for gold in the mountains. He embodied the image of the western gold rusher; tattered, bearded, and scrappy.
"Old guy, did you ever find any gold?" Daniel asked, amused by the story
"I found a little bit... Sometimes," Joe replied

"Did ya? That's awesome. What did you do when you found it? Did you dance a little jig or what?"

"No, I stood up in the river and shouted *'HOOTENANNY!'*"

The cell exploded with laughter. We could envision Joe, haggard with three teeth in his head, bellowing out his lungs. He scored big with that joke, and whenever times were tough, Daniel beckoned him for a 'Hootenanny!' to cheer us up.

.

I walked past my original cell when Casey, Jimmy's brother, called to me through the door.

"Hey, man! You seem like a really smart, studious, thoughtful person!" he said, his eyes shifting constantly

I hadn't expected that comment, out of the blue. I'd forget that people may be observing *me,* as I did them.

"Thanks, Casey. I appreciate that!"

"Don't listen to any of the bullshit around here! I admire people like you, man!"

"Thanks for the advice. Hey, how's that top bunk treating you? It used to be mine."

"Really? Yeah, it sucks because the air blows on me nonstop."

"Right!?"

"Hey, you need some coffee?" he asked

"Oh, no I'm good! Thank you, though! Let me know if *you* need any coffee."

"I will! That's cool of you!"

Then, as Casey stepped aside, another inmate approached the window; the man that collapsed in a seizure. He knew my name and introduced himself as Ryan.

"Are you feeling better?" I asked

His unusually large eyes gazed at me.

"These people are waiting for me to die," he said

"What's wrong? You're sick?"

"I have pulmonary heart disease. It's terminal. I'm in a lawsuit against Ada County, for $400,000. They refuse me proper treatment, and they postpone my court dates, so they don't have to pay out the money. I have a wife and kid I may not see again. I fought in Afghanistan and caught shrapnel, so I already had to leave them once. And now this. I want them to have that money."

What could I say? I watched him fall into a second seizure later that week, and then a third. Rather than house him permanently in medical, they'd wheel him to cell block.

.

Alex rejected *The Dorms* and got sent to a cell on the ground floor. *'It didn't work out,'* he said dryly, *'I figured that going in. You might like it, though. You can buy Coke and use tablets for music.'*

My reclassification date came and went, and no officer discussed the matter with me. So, I went to the deputy on shift, to get a straight answer – and wouldn't you know it? I got one.

"You're not going to get classified for The Dorms," he said

"Why? I haven't caused any problems."

"With your violent charges, you're considered one of the more dangerous inmates. They won't put you in general population."

If I had a horse, I'd name it *Irony*.

Frankly, I didn't care. I had good company.

.

Rick hummed the Tim McGraw tune that Junior sang.

"Hey, Ricky, where'd you hear that song?" Daniel asked

"Why?" Rick said, shooting me a suspicious glance

"When I was in prison up in Oregon, the dude a few cells from mine sang that song every night, bro."

"Did you know his name? What did he look like?" Rick asked in disbelief

"Junior, I think. Had tattoos on his neck."

"Holy shit, dude!!" Rick and I laughed

"Why, what's up?" Daniel said, puzzled

"Junior was in this cell with us last month!" Rick exclaimed, slapping Joseph's bunk

"Hell no! For real! That shit's insane!"

.

My attorney and I had a fight, in an open room without glass walls. It started with the letter I'd written to the court; he called it rubbish and tossed it aside. I took offense, though in hindsight his criticism of it was right. In the heat of the moment I wasn't in the mood to be demeaned for not having experience with the legal system.

"I don't know how to defend you anymore!" he declared

"And why is that?"

"No one is being honest with me! I spend more time reviewing fucking emails from your parents than I do working on the case! Your dad isn't capable of writing a reference letter! He barely mentions you! It's all about him, and his opinion of how things should be. They treat you like you're a goddamn infallible child!"

"You don't think I'm aware of that? *None of this* is helping me! You want to be real, then let's be fucking real. Ask me anything!"

"Tell me about Elena's parents," he said, settling in

"Where should I start? How they kicked me out the house?"

"Why?"

"They accused me of working for Elena's ex-husband."

"This is fucking absurd. What kind of people are these?"

"What about your ex-wife, Logan? Was there any history of violence in your relationship? Were the police ever called?"

"No, of course not."

"Would she confirm that if I called her? Would she help you?"

"I don't see why not, but I don't want to drag her into this."

"We may not have a choice."

"Then do so as a last resort."

"Let's rehearse this. Stand up," my attorney instructed, "Pretend that door behind you is the front door of your house. Show me *exactly* what you did when she tried to leave."

"She picked up the keys from the counter," I began, as I choreographed our actions, "I grabbed her arm with my left hand and yanked the keys from her with my right, and I put them in my pocket."

"Right. Then what?"

"She started flailing, and I didn't feel like catching a fuckin' elbow to my face, so I whipper her towards the couch. If she hit her head, she made no physical reaction. Nothing. Not a flinch."

"Ok, that's what I needed to hear."

"This bullshit at the bar, Jim's Alibi, with Mandy. There's no surveillance footage of it. It happened off camera. They're using it to establish a pattern of violence."

"I wish there *was* footage. They'd see it didn't go down like that. I caused a scene in public, yes. I'm willing to plead guilty to it."

"I'm not worried. They'll probably drop it. Mandy isn't pressing charges."

"What a sweetheart."

"You're not honest with me about your drinking, Logan. You say you weren't drunk. I think you're in denial over your drinking problem," he said

"Fine. I'm an alcoholic, and sober three months. I get it. The courts want to get their guy. The drunken male aggressor."

"Well, in my opinion, it's better they see you as an alcoholic than something else. I say we push the alcohol. Let 'em write it off as booze. Take your classes. You don't want to complicate the issue."

"The accusation of rape disgusts me. Elena sounds more upset about you taking her fucking car keys," he said, "She can't pinpoint what month it occurred. January? February? In her testimony, she says she wakes up and there you are... That's it. No clawing at your eyes or screaming for help? No police? It's nonsense."

"In February, I was saving up for a wedding ring, and planning our vacation. Why would I perform a hate crime on her for no reason, and then propose to her? Why would she accept and talk about having a child?"

"The majority of false rape accusations are made by women with psychological and emotional problems. They do it for sympathy and attention. She claimed a family member molested her, so that's the start. She wants revenge."

"Yes, and the accusation of her ex-husband involving her in occult sexual practices. She even accused one of her bosses of sexual harassment."

"And you're footing the bill for all of them," he said

That comment hit home.

"Yes,' I paused, reflecting on his words, "That's very generous of me."

"Yes, it is."

"She pressured me for sex day and night," I sighed, "I did it so she'd leave me alone and go to sleep."

"You rejected her, and she can't accept that. I heard of a case, recently, where a young girl who didn't have legal citizenship, accused a natural citizen of rape," he said

"And?"

"He got convicted, and she got citizenship for it. There's a loophole in the system."

"That's fucked up."

"What you told me about Elena, paying $1500 to extend her Visa, it doesn't add up. There's something we don't know."

"I agree. How can you be married to a millionaire and not get the privilege to stay in the country? She told me repeatedly the government refused to grant her residence because she mouthed off to them."

We deliberated, hashing out the facts, and digging for information. We exceeded the length of our scheduled visit, and a deputy retrieved me.

When The Dead Come Calling

Lights out. I had my earplugs in, reading a book. Daniel and Rick were talking from their bunks. Joe slept. Suddenly, I felt Daniel jerk violently, above me. Rick turned his face to the center of the room.

"What was that, dude!" Rick said, his eyes wide with fear

I sat upright, yanking my earplugs

"You heard that, Ricky?" Daniel exclaimed

"Yeah! There!" he said, pointing near the writing desk

"Logan, did you hear that?" Daniel asked

He leapt from his bunk, his bare feet smacking on the concrete

"No, my earplugs were in. What's going on?"

Daniel went to the area where Rick pointed.

"There was a female voice," Daniel explained, visibly shaken "Clear as day. It said my name *Dan-IEL!*"

"It did, bro!" Rick said, "Holy shit."

"Describe the voice, Daniel."

"It was like," he paused, "You know when you whisper loudly? You know what I mean?"

"Yeah, hushed but firm."

"Exactly. But it said *my fucking name, bro!* It spoke loud. Ricky and I heard it over our conversation!"

Daniel replayed the event.

"Could you recognize the voice?" I asked

"What are you saying? Like maybe someone I know died, and they're trying to communicate with me?" he said, concerned

I regretted saying it; I didn't mean to put him in a panic. He did an inventory of his loved ones. Rick and I tried to change the subject, knowing Daniel had a court appearance in the morning and needed rest. He went to bed with lingering anxiety.

An hour later, and I was still awake. As I laid there, in the space between the cell wall and my right ear, I too heard the woman's voice – *Dan-IEL!* I shot up, stifling a shout, my heart racing. I didn't disturb the others. I paced the cell, deciding to tell Daniel after court.

.

"You're messing with me, right?" Daniel said, once I informed him

"I wish I was, man. It scared the hell out of me. I knew you'd freak."

"And you *seriously* heard it call my name?"

"An inch from my right ear, bro."

Daniel had hoped he'd imagined his own experience, and my confirmation dashed that theory. He went to the phones, contacting family and close friends, relieved they were fine.

We did an experiment. I verbally antagonized the spirit, if one was present, challenging them to move a Styrofoam bowl I'd positioned on the edge of the writing desk. We left it overnight, though it remained, and we detected no energy with our bodies.

.

7:30 pm – the following evening.

A tragedy occurred in *The Side Shoot*, and it had a lasting effect on us. Officers were rushing in and out of the corridor, and from our vantage point, we couldn't see fully down the hall. In single-man cells, murder was unlikely. We were witnessing a suicide in progress and did not know if they could save his life.

Seconds mattered, and the resident nurses weren't equipped to handle the situation. An ambulance arrived. Paramedics weaved their way to Cell Block 8; doors opened as they never would for us. They pushed a gurney loaded with gear. A woman medic took charge, heading to a cell barely out of view. The gurney couldn't fit in the hall, and they stationed it at the entrance. We watched her give any assistance she could, running back and forth, with each pass grabbing a new tool. She picked up so many I couldn't tell what the man had inflicted upon himself - a heart monitor, defibrillator, and instruments to clear air passages, and stop bleeding.
Our hope fell when she no longer hurried to the gurney. Her face held resignation, and her pace slowed.
"Why is she using all that equipment?" I asked
"They have to be able to tell the family they tried everything," Rick said over my shoulder.
A crowd of officials gathered around, conversing. We saw a few of them laugh. *They fucking laughed.* The coroner came in, with a young woman holding a camera. The flashbulb firing in the cell lit up the enclosed space. The medics packed up and exited, with disappointment, through a side door, to the outside. For five seconds we saw the night.

Then, a fight erupted in Cell 862, directly above *The Side Shoot*. Four of the deputies broke from the other staff members, ascending the stairs as the door flew open. They took the inmates to the ground, cuffing them. They got escorted down the stairs in single file, passing the entrance to the corridor, parting the group of officials. The man's body still laid in the cell.

An older officer did the rounds, performing the quarterly cell checks. As he came to our door, Daniel spoke to him through the window.

"Officer, what happened?"

"I can't tell you," he said coldly, "I've got better things to do than worry about that guy."

Daniel shrunk from the window. The four of us had a prolonged moment of silence; not so much for the departed, but because we'd never felt further away from human compassion. We knew, at that moment, that our lives were not worth anything within these walls. We said little, the rest of the night. I stood at the window until they lifted the man out in a body bag, and put him on the gurney.

As they wheeled him from cell block, there was an incredible event. It started in Cell 843. The solemn howl of a lone wolf could be heard through the door, and then an entire pack joined that call. Soon, the whole block reverberated, as we howled for the fallen, honoring his life.

To that farewell, his gurney passed through.

.

At 9:30 pm, they released us for medication. As I descended the stairs, I looked at the corridor of *The Side Shoot.* Sheets of paper had been taped up, covering the windows of each cell. The door to 851, slightly open, had the air of death, so close I could breathe it. We learned from a Redshirt the man tied a bag around his head and asphyxiated. The deputies made the Redshirts clean his bodily fluids off the floor.

A new inmate got assigned to that cell, and wasn't informed of the circumstances, and didn't stay long. He screamed in the middle of the night, claiming he saw a dark shadow in the corner of the cell. He transferred to Cell Block 7.

.

Even though we ignored the quarterly cell checks – every fifteen minutes, twenty-four hours a day – we still detected them on a subconscious level. The awareness of the timer sounding at the control desk, the rattling of keys, and the tap of footsteps, as the deputies came and went. We're aware of his shadow on the cell floor, his body at the window, illuminated from behind by the main floor lights. We adjusted to it, and that's the reason we were slow in catching on to an altogether different visitor at our door.

Beyond Cell 847, the one past ours, last on the row, you hit a brick wall - there weren't any stairs. The deputy had to turn and walk back *by* our cell to reach the staircase. That's the detail that clicked.

Rick and I talked, unable to sleep.

"Hey Logan," Rick said, nodding to the window

"What's up?"

"Didn't the guard check in on us a few minutes ago?"

"It seems like he did. Wait, yeah he did. His shadow caught my eye for a second. Why?"

"I swear he didn't head back our way."

"Maybe he's talking to 847?"

"No, we would've heard that door pop open," Rick said suspiciously, as he stepped up the window. He pressed his face against the glass, trying to see to the far right. No one was there, but Rick knew what he saw.

We resumed our conversation. Within ten minutes, the deputy paused at our window. We waved at him, noting the noise of his keys and boots. Daniel woke and joined us, and we lost track of time.

That's when I saw it. Before I could utter a word, Daniel interjected.

"What the *fuck* was that?!" he said

I flew to the window.

"You saw that! I saw it too!" I hollered

No deputy was on a return path. I looked at the control desk. Both officers were seated.

"What did you see, Daniel?" I asked

"Fuck, bro! It rushed by, in a hurry! It didn't stop. It was like a big dark mass!"

"Right! No definition at all! Just a blur!"

"Exactly!"

"You saw it, Rick?" I asked

"Hell yeah, I saw it!"

"How tall was it?" I pressed myself to the door for perspective

"At least six-and-a-half to feet, bro. *Way* taller than any of the guards."

"Did you hear *anything*?"

"No. Nothing. I glanced up as it went by. That's what you saw before, Rick?" Daniel asked

"Yeah, twenty minutes ago. I thought it was a guard, but it moved too fast. It didn't move like a person."

"No, it didn't," Daniel concluded

"Ok, look," I said, "If it appeared twice already, it might come again. Are you down to stay awake?"

"Fuck yeah," they both said

"Wake Hamburg's sorry ass. We need witnesses."

We held a vigil, though not until our attention wandered, did it reappear. I was reading my book, in the dim light through the window, when a semi-opaque shadow drifted across my page. It made the hair on my arm stand up, and we eagerly corroborated our experience.

The entity came *again* that night, and the activity increased over the next *seven days*. We heard reports from other cells on our Walk. Inmates in each cell kept a watchful eye, and beat on the walls, relaying warnings to the adjacent cells during sightings.

"Trav! Rook! Did you see it!" Rick screamed, hitting the wall
"Yeah! Holy *Shit!* We saw it!"

The black mass had a frantic, desperate energy to it.
Then, it got bolder.

"It's in the room!" Daniel yelled
You should've seen the look on Joseph's face – if it weren't for the concrete barricade, the old man would've run for the hills.
"I don't like this! Make it go away!" Joseph cried
The entity materialized inside our cell, and perhaps in seeing our alarm darted through the wall into 845. We heard a reaction from Rook, *'Fuck, guys! It's here!'*

Then, the activity abruptly stopped. We liked to believe it escaped.

.

A final unexplained event occurred in our cell, in the afternoon, as I stood by the writing desk, talking to my cellmates. I saw a bright white light, out of the corner of my eye, and it touched the side of my face, at my temple. I felt what I can only describe as an electrical current in my brain. I got confused and dizzy, stumbling backward. Rick got up, in case he needed to catch me. My cellmates were wide-eyed, staring at me.
"What happened?" I asked weakly

They all attested to an orb of light coming from the ceiling and disappearing into my head.

.

My attorney was notified of the suicide on cell block. He checked in on me, one evening. The sun must've been setting outside.

"How are you doing, Logan?" he asked through the glass, not picking up the phone receiver

"I'm holding up, I guess. They improved taco night."

He smiled.

"I heard someone killed themselves. I don't want you losing morale."

"I'm trying. How's the world out there?"

"It's the same."

"How are you?"

"I'm great. I took a vacation."

"Where did you go?"

"Burgdorf Hot Springs, in McCall."

"That's interesting. I planned to take my mother there when she visited me."

"It's beautiful. You should go. Have you been further north, to the quartz mountain?"

"I'm sorry?"

"Yes, there's a mountain made of quartz. It's amazing."

"That's.... *wow,*" I paused, "I'll have to make a pilgrimage to see that."

As the deputy escorted me, I visualized that mountain. I wished that I could dream of it on command.

.

"Kellner! You've got a court date," said the officer, in our doorway

"A court date? For what?" Rick asked, half asleep, "Nothing is scheduled."

"Sounds like they charged you with another misdemeanor. You've gotta make an appearance."

"I have to get up, and go on transport to the courthouse for a misdemeanor?"

"That's correct."

"Just tell 'em I fucking did it, alright? They can send me the paperwork."

"It doesn't work like that, Kellner. You know the drill. I'll give you ten minutes."

.

When Rick and his wife weren't arguing, they'd sent letters to one another, which Rick read aloud, at least in parts.

"She says she misses my Magic Mike routine."

"Say what Ricky!?" Daniel exclaimed, "Magic Mike, huh?!"

"I used to dance for her," Rick admitted, his cheeks blushing

"That's *scandalous,* Rick! You're a naughty boy! Old man!" Dee beckoned, "Gimme a hootenanny!"

"HOOTENANNY!" Joseph hollered

In response, Rick mailed her loving letters, filled with elaborate drawings, poetry, or Bible verses, accompanying his personal thoughts and wishes.

Those letters conveyed intense feelings; a lot of pain, hurt and frustration. They also showed an undeniable bond and love since childhood. They'd shared their whole lives, and now they had two children missing their father, that she labored to raise by herself.

.

By happenstance, I finally got a pillow. The deputies were doing cell inspection, tossing the bunks on our tier, and throwing extra bedding over their shoulders, onto the landing. As I walked by, a pillow flew by me, and I managed to catch it in midair. I headed straight to my cell and placed it on my bunk.

I ordered a biography of William Blake. I poured over the vibrant color plates, and sketches in the book; they transported me. I shared it with Rick, curious about spiritual art. *'I've been looking for an artist like this,'* he said, borrowing the book. I occasionally had to ask him if I could see it, myself.

Rick missed the resources of prison, where he had access to real art supplies. Inmates earned a living selling art and making crafts. Rick sold several pieces in his last term. There's a demand for it, and coalitions on the outside thrive on promoting their work. That was news to me.

I offered to help Rick, whenever I got released, by bringing his art to the collectives. He agreed, and I promised to do what I could.

.

To see the clock centered above the control desk, we had to press our cheeks to the window and squint one eye.
"What time is it?" Rick inquired
"Six-thirty."
I glanced at the floor. Surprisingly, Kyle Rory had returned, presumably from *The Hole.* I made it a point to talk with Kyle through his cell door.
"Morning, Kyle."
"What's up, dude!"
"How's your case going?" I asked
"I'm getting out in the morning! They dropped the charges! They didn't have any evidence to hold me on!

"Are you serious?!" I said, dumbfounded, "Well, congratulations!"
"Thanks! What about you?"
"I might be out on October fifth with felony probation!"
"That's awesome! You beat the Rider!
"Yeah. How's your wife doing?"
"She's a whore... But I love her."
"That's sweet, Kyle."

Sonofabitch. Kyle Rory had his charges dropped? Tomorrow he'd be a free man. Had Cleveland won three straight games? (Yes, they had.)

"Hey, do me a favor and go tell Stevie in 822 that I said he's a cocksucker!" Kyle requested
"Alright. Hang on" I waltzed to 822, and flagged the inmates inside. One of them came to the window.
"Hey, are you Stevie?" I asked
"Yeah, what's up?"
"Kyle says your a cocksucker!"
"Fuck him! Tell him I said he's a nigger loving faggot!"
"Alright. Hold up," I walked back across the floor
"What did he say?" Kyle asked in anticipation
"He says you're a nigger loving faggot. I didn't know you liked black dick, Kyle! You should've said something!"
"Funny! Tell him I have pictures of his mom sucking my dick!"
"Ok. Hang on," I walked to 822
"What did he say?" Stevie inquired
"He has pictures of your mom sucking his dick," I shrugged, "I haven't seen them, though."
"Tell Kyle I'm gonna whoop his sorry fuckin' ass when I see him!"
"Will do. Thank you."
"What did he say?" Kyle asked
"He didn't like that very much." (the cell busts out in laughter)
"Awesome! Thanks, dude!" Kyle says putting his fist to the glass, as I hit mine to his.
"No problem. Take care, Kyle."

Would I see Kyle Rory again? Not in person.

.

"I fought my last case and took it to trial, up in Portland" Daniel said, "In the Hatfield Courthouse, and that building's crazy tall. I think I was on the fourteenth floor."

"Damn."

"Anyway, I sat by a window, waiting for my name to get called, and outside I saw a hummingbird just hovering there, staring at me, an inch from the glass. I got mesmerized by it, bro. Then I started thinking, *why the fuck is a hummingbird flying this high? And downtown no less?* It wasn't the season. I wondered if it was an omen. It gave me peace, and an hour later I beat my charges."

In Ada County, if you had $100 on your books you were considered high society. Daniel had $3000. There was no competition in that. He traversed the moon, while we tied our shoelaces (err, Velcro). Granted, he wasted a third of it on the telephone with Nicki, before she vanished.

.

Thanks to Daniel, we assembled my first jailhouse *spread*. In retaliation against pasta night, we dumped our trays in the garbage and prepared our own meal. We planned it for a week, buying supplies off commissary.

We made *Piled-High Nachos;* a flat of Doritos, covered with spicy melted cheese, formed our base. We slathered it with diced sausage and jerky, jalapenos, seasoned Ramen noodles, steamed rice, and beans.

We carried half a dozen bags of boiling water to the cell to cook the ingredients. Then, we flipped a crate for the makeshift table, setting down a towel wrapped in plastic, and piled the meal on top of it. Joe's hands weren't allowed to touch the food, so we sectioned his share, and put it in a bowl for him.

It tasted amazing; the best meal I had in jail. We savored every bite, stuffing ourselves. Our stomachs felt gratified.

.

Daniel's crate contained a small grocery store. He ordered a dozen bags of instant cheesy rice and a dozen bags of dried spicy red beans. He'd lay newspaper on the floor, mix it all, then flake it with seasonings from the Ramen noodle packets. He'd siphon it into the bags, while I held them open. His special blend, for snacks, and late night spreads, was popular with the Walk.

When the Telmate machine went on the fritz, we made our commissary selections manually. The deputies handed us bubble sheets and menus. Each item had a four-digit number we'd circle in. I helped Daniel with the grocery shopping.

When he got concerned about his weight, I thumbed through his previous receipts, pointing out how many Honey Buns he'd eaten in August and September.

"We're not ordering any this week," I said

"Not one?"

"Nope."

To close the argument, I slipped the bubble sheet under the cell door for the guard to retrieve. When I fell asleep, Daniel, the fucker, somehow fished it back through the door and ordered a shortcake.

.

During extended out time, I liked to sit in the cell alone, reading and listening impartially to the noise on the floor. With the door open, I felt free, as if it were a choice for me to be there.

"Hey, Logan, what's up bro?" Trav said from the doorway, "Why don't you come watch TV with us?"

"I was trying to finish this chapter."

"You can do that during lockdown," he said, coaxingly

"Yeah, but this is when I can do it *quietly*."

"I hear ya. These knuckleheads make it hard to read, huh?"

"Occasionally. Besides, I don't follow sports."

"We'll give you the remote. You can watch whatever you want. If anybody has a problem, I'll take care of it," Trav said, with his impish grin

I laughed, "No, no. Let the boys have their football. Hey, are you going to the rec yard?"

"I was thinking about it. Why, are you?"

"Yeah, I could use some fresh air. Do you wanna head out with me?"

"Ok, cool."

"Sweet, I'll be right down."

"Sounds good."

Rick had spent weeks on the portrait of Trav's daughters, backlogging himself on other commissions. He messed up a single stroke on one of the faces and got discouraged with it. Trav, though eager to see it, didn't want to be pushy.

"Hey, Logan," Trav said, "I don't mean to pressure the artist or anything, but is Rick working on the portrait of my kids?"

"Yeah. Every day," I lied

"Ok, cool. Can you keep an eye on him and let me know how it's coming? Since we're going to prison soon I'd like to mail it out, you know?"

"For sure. I'll stay on him."

.

In a commissary delivery, the ten-count sugar packets shipped in different packaging. They normally came in a plastic Ziploc bag, but on this occasion, a wax paper pouch. The paper was delicate; the stuff of cafes and bakeries that you went to on vacations or with your grandmother. It didn't belong in here. Even the sound of the crinkling paper seemed out of place. I kept it.

.

When Joe lived on the street, looking for a safe place to rest on a chilly autumn evening, he found an old couch, behind a vacant house overlooking a field. He wrapped himself in a sleeping bag, atop the sofa. *What thoughts were in his haggard mind?*

He awoke in the early dawn and peered out across the property, seeing a herd of deer, enshrouded in fog, peacefully grazing around him. Speechless at the beauty of it, he lit a cigarette, careful not to disrupt the scene.

We got Joe over his pathological fear of fresh air and pressured him to venture the rec yard.
"Dude, you're a bum. You live outside," Rick said
"That's true, old guy. It's your natural habitat," Daniel added
With much haranguing, Joseph Hamburg exited the cell block and embraced the sun. He sat lazily against a wall with his pant legs rolled up. I dare say it brought color to his face.

Joe had all manner of excuses for avoiding showers.
"Hey, piss bag. You're coming down and taking a shower today," Daniel instructed
"I'll take one tomorrow, I promise. I have to use the phone."
"Actually, you're taking one today, or I'm gonna beat the fuck out of you. You're killing us in here."

.

Walking the yellow line, I interrupted Jimmy talking to Casey, through his cell door.
"Hey Jimmy, can I ask you a question?"
"Yes. What is it?" he replied
"Does your brother have eyelids? I've never seen him blink."
Jimmy stared blankly at me for a moment, then turned to look at Casey, as if observing him for the first time.
"Um... No. He doesn't."
"What did he say?" Casey asked anxiously, his eyes shifting back and forth

Benjamin also returned to cell block, on Walk 4. In Maximum Security, he briefly met Daniel and showed him the courtesy he'd given me on those opening nights. Ben was due to be released in thirty days, meaning he'd see his baby daughter.

Then, Ben snapped the metal handle off a mop and chased a white guy into a corner, by the staircase, ready to throttle him, when a deputy ran to stop it. Ben decided to swing on the officer instead, who ducked and shot Ben in the chest with his Taser; his muscles locked, and he hit the ground, half-screaming as cops removed the prongs, and dragged him to *The Hole. He may have added years to his sentence, for assaulting personnel.*

Daniel had success in court. His public defender, who was quite clever, mentioned the drug charge in a lighthearted tone.
"Your Honor, my client, had a small bag of *cocaine,"* as if it were old-fashioned
The Judge and members of the audience chuckled. It must've triggered a sentimental mood in the Judge, recalling the days of simple narcotic busts, long before cases of methylenedioxypyrovalerone filled his courtroom. Daniel followed his lead and kept the Judge smiling, who then ridiculed the prosecution for how the arrest had been handled. He berated the arresting officer as if he were a pansy for going to the emergency room, and wasting resources.
"Mr. Weschler," the Judge stated, *"IF* you stay in my good graces, and don't cause *any* problems or receive disciplinary action in Ada County, I'll consider putting you on a probationary period, regardless of what the prosecution recommends. I highly advise you to heed my words, Mr. Weschler. Do you understand?"

It was a gift.
"You better take that to heart, Daniel. You're fortunate," I said to him
"Yeah, I am?"
"Don't start a fight in here, or you're fucked. You're smarter than that."
"I know, bro. I've gotta hold it together."
"How do you do it?" I questioned
"Keep 'em laughing, bro," he said
"Well, that happens to be my life philosophy, too. If you can wrangle a joke from my charges, please let me know."

Joseph, once a church-going man, left the Lord behind and estranged himself from his wife and children. I don't know what brought Joe to his bitter and decrepit state. His son viewed him as a pariah, and Joe feared to contact him in his hour of need.

Rick helped Joe reconnect with a higher power. It was a commendable deed; Joseph Hamburg needed more than a bowl of oatmeal. Daniel supported the project, and thus began the old man's reformation. Joe got involved in Bible studies with Rick, and had exceptional reading abilities, though his vision was poor.

.

A ray of sunlight shone upon Joseph Hamburg. With commissary, Daniel and I presented him with gifts. Daniel bought him a pair of reading glasses, and I gave him earplugs. More importantly, his public defender exceeded her duties, and rescued his dog from the pound, providing shelter for the critter in her own home. *Kudos to that woman.*

Joseph sat in tears of joy. It filled him with vim and vigor. Grateful for these blessings, he sought to show his appreciation by cleaning himself and getting stable.

He took an active part in his self-care, doing things of his own accord, rather than us brow-beating him into submission. He'd come to us, saying *'Guys, look! I cut my fingernails today and put lotion on. My hands are better, don't you think?'*

"Hey guys, I'll clean the cell today, ok?" Joe said, "I wanna help."
"Joe, that's the first time I've walked by you, and you didn't smell," Rick said, proudly
"Thanks, man. Thank you, Rick. I'm trying."

.

"I'm worried about Ricky, man," Daniel said, as we paced the yellow line
"Me too," I replied
"He's putting on weight, and he doesn't work out anymore. It's like he's giving up."
"Yeah, he's eating a lot of cake. He used to be toned, man."
"Now he lays in his bunk, and stares at those damn photographs of his wife and kids."

Rick had several of them taped to the ceiling of his bunk.
"I hear ya. Personally, that would depress me to dwell on memories."
"It's like the FED's took his soul, bro."

Ricks case did weigh heavily on him. He grew quiet, meditating on those photos. He faced a minimum of fifteen years in prison, and couldn't bring himself to inform his wife. She expected him to be out in three years, and that alone pushed her to the breaking point. He feared she'd leave him, and he grasped at hope, praying for a change in his case.

"She deserves better than me. Better than a life like this," Rick said to me, while the others slept

He had tears in his eyes.

"She should be with a man that can always be there and provide for her. I wouldn't blame her if she left. I love her so much, bro. She's been with me through everything. All the stupid shit I've done. She's the most amazing woman I've ever met. I miss my kids so much. I failed them."

It hurt me, to see Rick in that state. If the courts wanted their fucking guilt, there it was. He had to communicate with his wife, painful as it may be. Both of them had to let go of their history of accusations, finger pointing, and lies, taking a tremendous effort. Without her, Rick needed to adapt to prison, either growing on his own or succumbing to the harsh environment.

.

I spent days rewriting my letter to the court. I laid in the dark, defeated. I figured Rick to be asleep, he seemed so peaceful. I got startled when he spoke to me.

"Logan, you know what you have to do, right?" he said, quietly

"What's that, Rick?"

"You have to forgive her."

I hid my reaction. Conflicting thoughts and emotions hit me. It hurt because part of me knew it to be true.

"I don't think I can, Rick."

I'm not sure if I voiced that response or merely said it in my head.

.

Walk 2 had their dinner break. An explosion of noise erupted from the main floor, and the four of us rushed to the window, cramming for space. Inmates were running into their cells - except Casey – who was throwing plastic chairs left and right, creating chaos, with deputies ordering him to stop. That's when we saw Ryan convulsing on the ground, by the payphones. *What's going on?*

Four officers tackled Casey, and used extreme force to restrain him - and did nothing to assist Ryan. Casey, being his friend, got enraged by their lack of concern, and threw every chair he could, yelling at the officers to help the man. By creating disorder, Casey hoped to crowd the cell block with staff, getting Ryan medical help faster.

"Please!" Casey begged, "I'm not resisting! Help my friend! I'm not resisting you!"

He struggled to get the words out, with two deputies driving their knees into his back. It got serious – Ryan's face went purple, and his seizing grew faint – he was dying – choking on his tongue. Still, all four deputies did nothing in his aid. Casey wasn't fighting, just pleading.

The cell block went on full lockdown. Inmates started beating on the doors and walls, screaming at the top of their lungs. Jimmy especially could be heard over the thunder, '*GET THE FUCK OFF MY BROTHER!*' The shouts echoed from everywhere.
"*YOU STUPID MOTHERFUCKERS! HELP THAT MAN!*"
"*GET MEDICAL IN HERE YOU FUCKING ASSHOLES! HE'S DYING!*"
"*YOU FUCKING PIGS! DO YOUR FUCKING JOBS AND SAVE THAT MANS LIFE!*"
"*GET OFF CASEY AND HELP THAT MAN OR WE'RE GONNA FUCKING KILL YOU, MOTHERFUCKERS!*"
Seconds felt unbearable. The four deputies shrank from the threats of violence encircling them, fearfully looking in all directions, aware they'd have a riot on their hands if the cells got unlocked. Finally, medics entered and rushed to Ryan's side, attempting to save his life. They injected him with something, and his breathing regulated. They urgently wheeled him to medical, to a collective wave of relief.

Two of the deputies lifted Casey off the ground, dragging him from the block. We cheered for Casey, and he wrestled one arm free from their grip to give us all a thumbs up, with a big smile. He did a selfless act – and he'd suffer consequences. I did not see him again.

Then, oddly, or perhaps not, a deputy went to each cell, and spoke to us *individually,* asking us how we *felt* about what we'd seen. I'm sorry since when did Ada County care for our *feelings?* How did I *feel?* He asked if I had questions, and it struck me that they were covering their asses, searching for liabilities. I said nothing.

.

Jimmy was livid. Watching those deputies manhandle his brother led him to punch the wall until his hands bled. He remained in his cell for a period, not wanting to take his anger out on us. I overheard him on the phone with his public defender, '*Look, I fucking did it! I enjoyed doing it, and I'm probably gonna do it again, okay! I want to go to prison! I'm done with this county jail shit! Get me the fuck out of here!*'

Roughly nine days elapsed when the deputies told Jimmy to roll his bunk, en route to *The Yard*. Inmates shouted farewells, as I did, while others remarked, '*See you at The Yard, Jimmy!*'

.

"Do you want to hear a wild story, bro?" Daniel asked

"I don't know. I'm awful busy."

"When I was little, I'd be sleeping, and I remember these blue angels coming into the room. That's what I called them. They glowed and had wings."

"I'm listening."

"They'd be standing in a circle around me, and I'd start to float off my bed. It was like they were raising me up, and I'd feel this amazing sense of protection. Then they'd set me on my bed and disappear."

"How often did it happen?"

"Quite a bit, bro. I always thought it was a dream. I shared that room with my sister, and we never mentioned it, you know? But the last time I talked to her, she asked me if I recalled anything weird from my childhood, and I said *'Yeah, the blue angels that lift me up at night. Why?'* She said *'I saw them too, Daniel.'*

.

I spoke to Rick.

"I'm ready to hypnotize you. I want you to focus on one memory, far into your past, that you wish you could see clearly," I said, "Let's make it a positive memory. I'll take you as deep as I can. We'll do it at lights out when things get quiet. Agreed?"

"Deal," Rick grinned

The four of us readied for the experiment. I instructed Daniel and Joseph to be calm and to not speak over me. Rick got comfortable, laying flat on his bunk. I flipped a crate and used it as a chair.

"Alright, Rick. What memory are we searching for?"

"My Aunt Laurie. I knew her when I was eight-years-old, and she died young. I don't remember her face. I don't have any photos of her. The last time I saw her, she fought with my mom, and she took her to the airport. I just want to see her again."

"That's good. I like that. Let's do our best."

As Rick relaxed, and noise from the block settled, we began.

"Ok now, close your eyes and start to relax
Right now there's nothing for you to do in this world but relax

I want you to concentrate on your breathing for me
Breath as deeply and as slowly as you can

Continue breathing, holding each breath for a moment, before breathing out
Just let go, as you slowly release your breath and relax

Now I want you to become fully aware of your body
I want you to notice any pleasant feelings

Your comfort is only increasing as you go into a trance
What part of your body feels the best right now?"
"My stomach."

"I want you to only focus on that area now
and let that great feeling slowly move throughout your entire body
Allow that feeling to get greater as you go deeper and deeper into relaxation

Now, imagine a color that makes you feel very calm and comfortable
Allow a wave of that color to spread across your entire body
Your whole body is relaxed now

Let go now
As you hear the sound of my voice going with you

Now, Rick. You're eight years old.
You're standing on the sidewalk, in front of your house

Describe your house to me."
"It's white. There's big windows. It's made of wood."

"What time of year is it?"
"It's spring. Maybe summer. It's warm."

"Can you feel the sun on your face?"
"Yes. It feels nice. It's bright out."

"I want you to walk now towards the front door
As you walk, can you look downward, at the shoes your wearing?
"Yes. I see them."

"Describe them to me."
"They're white and black sneakers."

"What does your front door look like?"
"It's white. Heavy. There's a window in the top half."

"Now, as you enter the house, what's the first thing you smell?"
"Cigarettes. Someone's cooking. Spaghetti."

"What do you see to your immediate left?"
"There's a closet. It's closed."

"What do you see to your immediate right?"
"The living room. I hang out in there. I see my stuff."

"Ok, I want you to go in there now and tell me about the room."
"It's pretty big. There's a couch and a stereo. A guitar. Clothes."

Is your Aunt Laurie in there now?
"Yes. She's by the window."

"What is she doing?"
"She's listening to music. She's kneeling by the stereo. Her back is to me."

"Is she nice to you?"
"Yes. She's always nice."

"How is she dressed?"
"She's wearing jeans. And boots. And a button up shirt."

"Is she wearing perfume?"
"Yes. It smells like flowers."

"Can you hear her voice? What is she saying to you?"
"She's asking me if I like country music. I tell her yes."

"Can you see her face?"
"Kind of. It's blurry.

"Concentrate. Take your time. Is she wearing makeup?"
"Yes. Lipstick. It's red."

"What color eyes does she have?"
"I think they're green. Maybe blue. I can't tell."

"What is she doing now?"
"She wants to take me somewhere. The park."

"Does she have a car?"
"Yes. It's in the driveway."

"Can you see it from the window? What does it look like?"
"It's cool. It's a classic car."

"Do you want to come back now, Rick?"
"Yes."

"Ok, I need you to concentrate on my voice

I'm going to count down from five to one, and when I reach one, you will awake, and feel relaxed and at peace. Five. Four. Three. Two. One."

Rick awoke, as if from a deep sleep, and a tear ran down his face. He rubbed his eyes and looked around disoriented.

"I feel, like a sensation, all through my body," Rick began, "I'm so relaxed. I feel high like I'm floating."

"Did you see anything you'd forgotten?" I asked

"Yeah... a lot. I never had a memory of her and I going anywhere together. I'd forgotten about her car and her perfume."

"What about her face?"

"It was soft... But I saw it. I remember her eyes now."

"I think we pulled it off, Rick," I whispered

What he said next meant a great deal.
"For that whole time, I completely forgot I was in jail, bro."

I'm glad I could give Rick that. We wouldn't get a second opportunity.

.

The Lighthouse Rescue Mission seemed a viable option for Joseph. They had the resources to get him reestablished, pending his release from Ada County. Rick got Joe the mailing address and told him to write a letter. He folded under the pressure and pleaded for help.

"I don't spell good, and it's hard to read my handwriting. Could you do it for me?"

"No, Joseph. It needs to be in your words," Rick said, "I'll tell you what's important, and I've seen your handwriting. It's not that bad. If you don't know how to spell something, ask Logan."

Joe stressed from long hours at the desk, and several rough drafts got discarded. Once a suitable letter had been written, we mailed it off. Joe waited anxiously for a response.

As the reformation of Joseph Hamburg commenced, Rick saw his efforts paying off. He noticed how helping others made him feel. Rick confided that he wanted to be a minister in the prison church.

"I think that would be perfect for you, Rick," I said, "I can see you doing that. It would keep you thinking positive instead of succumbing to that place."

"I'm going to do it, dude."

"You know you can't threaten people in the church, like you do Hamburg, right?" I joked

.

To be fair, Joe had maybe ten teeth, not three, though rotted, with accompanying gum disease. The Lighthouse Rescue Mission offered free dental work.

"They'll remove those suckers and give you dentures, Joe," Daniel said, "Think how it's gonna feel when you see your kids and grandkids, and you can give 'em a big smile that you're proud of, instead of scaring 'em and shit. You gotta *promise* us you're going to go through with it when you get to the mission."

"I will, guys. I promise," Joseph vowed

"Your health is going to improve too, Joe. You'll feel way better, and better about yourself," Rick added

"I hope so, guys. I'm looking forward to that."

.   .

With my sentencing day looming, my attorney received a bizarre phone call from Elena, with disturbing implications. He drove to the jail to speak with me.

"Elena is demanding to see you in person, for a face to face visit."

"What? No. I'm not ok with that," I said in disbelief

My attorney continued, "I told her she'd created a situation which makes that impossible. She can try coordinating it with Victim Resources, but I doubt that'll happen. She's losing it."

"Why the fuck would I agree to that?" I said, feeling chilled

"That's what I said. I asked her, 'What makes you think Logan would even want to see you or accept your request?' Then she said, 'Well if you're not going to let me see him, I'll write a letter and bring it to you."

"I don't want it."

"Good. That's smart. I said to her, 'Fine, but I won't give it to him. He's dealing with enough,' and she said, 'Well I hope you do, because he's going to prison for a very long time,' and I said, 'Wait, what are you talking about? What do you mean he's going to prison? What do you know?"

Then, Elena hung up the phone.

The thought of that letter grieved me; its existence put me ill at ease.

Elena's wasn't finished.

.

The jail-issued each cell a single ten-gallon trash bag, per day. They were too thin for Rick's plan, so the four of us asked the officers on duty at different intervals, hoping they wouldn't catch on. We did that for several days, stockpiling them. Rick then placed layers of bags within one another to reinforce their weight.

The sink, awkwardly designed like a drinking fountain, shot water straight up. So, we took the plastic straw taped to the side of my *Boost* drink, and wedged it into the sink faucet, thus diverting the water flow over the rim, and into the reinforced trash bags on the floor. The process resulted in a lifting weight, holding roughly eight gallons of water. Daniel tied it off and wrapped it in a towel, then inserted a rolled magazine through the knot, creating a handle.

One of us stood at the window, signaling the others as the deputies did their rounds. We'd put the weight on a bunk, concealed by the canopy of a hanging towel.

8:30 pm

We were in lockdown, and Walk 2 had the floor, for their late night extended out time. They were rowdier than usual. I felt a strange electricity in the air that I'd come to recognize; the sensation of things about to pop off. At the window, I saw a female deputy ascending the staircase, to approach our cell, *'Hide the bags, guys.'*

Rather than open the door, she unlocked the tray slot and lowered herself to look inside.
"Kellner, come talk to me," she said, summoning Rick
He crouched to hear her. I could faintly make out her words over the din and racket in the background.
"Kellner, I have to send you to The Dorms. You've got ten minutes to roll it up and say your goodbyes."
"Can't I refuse?"
"Well, you can, but you'd get written up for insubordination. The cell block is overcrowded, and you've been reclassified to go."
"I'd rather stay here."
"I know," she smiled, sweetly, "I'd appreciate it if you worked with me on this."

Rick relented and agreed to go.

"Logan, can you make sure Trav gets the drawing of his kids? I think Allen can finish the shading. It's pretty much finished," Rick said, passing it to me

"Yes, I can," I said, shaking his hand, "Your grandfather was right, by the way. You *are* a good man, Rick."

"Thanks, bro. That means a lot to me."

"Hang in there, Ricky," Daniel said, "Hold your head up, man. You're gonna get through this."

They hugged each other, and Rick turned to Joseph.

"I know you're glad I'm leaving, old man," Rick said, "But don't give up on yourself."

"I won't, Rick. Thanks for your help."

Inmates beat on their doors, saluting Rick Kellner with respect, as he walked by, and exited Cell Block 8.

Our voices echoed off the concrete; that emptiness, again. *'Fuck, man. They took Ricky,'* Daniel said. We got lost in thought, missing our friend. Daniel tried to clear his mind by lifting the water weight

It was quiet, except for the noise from the main floor.

Then – like a timed explosion – *the water bag burst.*

"GET TOWELS UNDER THE DOOR!" I yelled, too late. The floor wasn't level, and all those gallons of water flooded under the door, across the tier landing, and down onto the inmates below. The control desk immediately fired our door, and I ran onto the tier. The cascade of water had landed on a table of four men playing cards. One man, in particular, got drenched – Alex Ramirez.

I could not stop laughing.

Alex, furious, rose up and glared at me, *'That better not be toilet water, motherfucker!'* he shouted. I laughed even harder. The deputy ran up, with two Redshirts carrying mops and a bucket. Daniel hurriedly flushed the trash bags, and the deputy couldn't figure what had transpired. What could he do other than shake his head?

I mopped the small puddle on our cell floor. My eyes were concentrated on the task when an inmate stepped into the water and stood in front of me - an Italian man who'd gotten removed from Cell 862. He looked like Martin Sheen on steroids. He set his crate in a dry area and introduced himself.

"Hi. I'm Guy," he said, with a smug grin

Then, he said his last name, which I will not disclose, as I recognized him as a member of an infamous crime family. You could say he had notoriety.

You have got to be kidding me.

Counting Bricks

During the waterfall incident, Daniel used hand signals to communicate with Guy's cellmates, across the block. They gave him a thumbs up of approval, though Daniel and I had misgivings, opting to form our own opinions.

Guy rejected his bed sheets and pillow, lying on the bare vinyl mat. He slept with his arms flat to his side, his shirt tucked in and his Velcro shoes on.
"I want to be ready when they come for me," Guy said
"Bro, this isn't the fucking jungle. You need to ease it down," Daniel advised

It wasn't a healthy start; Guy dissolved into crying fits. *'I miss my family. I don't belong in here,'* he sobbed.

Guy shot and killed a man; being a bounty hunter, he thus got pardoned for the slight. He felt bad about it, and so began his brief, torrid descent into methamphetamine abuse, resulting in his arrest for assaulting his wife. A crime to which he claimed innocence.

I saw Guy staring at the wall.
"What are you doing?" I asked
"Counting the bricks. That's how I know what day it is."
"There's a *fucking calendar* taped to the wall, right in front of you."
"Is that what it is? What do all the numbers mean?"

It's common courtesy to inform your cellmates that you need the toilet, for a modicum of privacy, while they avert their eyes. Guy dropped his pants to his ankles, without warning. Within twenty-four hours, he violated the fundamental rules of the cell.

Daniel and I walked the yellow line.
"I don't think I can do thirty days in a cell with this asshole," I said
"Me neither. Dude's straight up pissing me off."
"What should we do?"
"We'll take it one step at a time."

With Rick's departure, Daniel and I became closer; we counted on one another.

.

"Crannell! You've got a visitor," the deputy said
"Alright. Hang on. Who is it?"

"The domestic violence assessor."

I met the man in a small room. He was older, in his late fifties, with a polite and professional demeanor.

"I want you to understand," he began, "that I don't work for the state so you can expect an unbiased opinion from me."

"That's great."

"Also, I asked Elena to take the same evaluation I'm giving you, *and she flat out refused.*"

"Oh, really?"

"Yes, she did. That works to your advantage, though."

"That's interesting."

"So, I'm guessing that if I read her testimony, there'd be pretty nasty stuff in there about you?"

"Yes, you could say that."

"Well, don't worry. I'm not going to bother reading it unless I feel it's necessary after you and I are finished."

"Thank you."

I got asked a series of questions over a two day period. On this occasion, he and I talked for roughly two hours, as he built a psychological profile of me. I didn't hide and answered him honestly. I appreciated his objective viewpoint, and I noticed he skipped a section of the test, concluding that it wasn't necessary.

"Well, thank you, Mr. Crannell," he said, as the inquiry ended, "My associate will be here this time tomorrow, to have you do a computer-based test, and then I'll give my assessment to the court."

"Your welcome. Thanks for listening."

The next day, I was presented with 1265 questions, on a laptop. Most were multiple choice or ranked by how often I think or feel in a certain way. Three minutes into the test, it was clear they were looking for patterns of consistency. I'd complete a question, and it cropped up again, albeit worded differently.

.

"Joseph Hamburg! Mail!" the deputy called

Joe anxiously signed for it.

"What is it, Joe? Your letter from The lighthouse?" Daniel asked

"Yes! It says The Lighthouse Rescue Mission on it! Hey, Logan, can you read it out loud for us?" he pleaded

"Sure, Joe."

He handed it to me and excitedly hopped on his bunk.

"Dear Mr. Hamburg," I began, in an orator's voice, saying the opening lines

As I scanned the first paragraph, my heart sank upon realizing that Joe got denied. *You bastards.* Daniel and I looked at each other. Joe was devastated.

"I'm sorry, Joe."

"There are other shelters, Joe. We can contact them, ok?" Daniel suggested

"Thanks, guys. I'm not gonna give up. I promise you."

"No, you're not. We're not gonna let you."

.

An officer finally brought out of my cell for the Pre-Sentence Investigation. My palms were sweating. *Breath, Logan. I'm on my own for this.* My performance would determine my risk level, and make all the difference for the prosecution.

The deputy at the control hub directed me to the impersonal visitor booths, where a woman awaited me. A middle-aged, blonde, with a southern accent. She seemed easy to startle. *Why the glass barrier? Was she hesitant to be in a room with me?* I knew that her opinion would *not* be an unbiased, unlike the gentleman before her, whose hand I shook in an open space. I picked up the phone, hearing the scratchy connection, and did a gentle wave.

She conveyed friendliness and sympathy, which I'd anticipated. Page by page, she went through my PSI packet, which I'd submitted roughly four weeks prior. I imagine they do that so I can't recall my written answers since she put each question to me once more. I tend to get animated with my hands when I speak, especially when it's a challenge to hear, and rather than look me in the eye she focused on my movements. She seemed intimidated, and I consciously refrained from it, sitting on my hand.

She said, sweetly, that I reminded her of someone in her family. With empathy, she took my side on matters, careful not to imply that any of my actions or feelings were wrong. A question as simple as, *'Where did you grow up?'* alluded to my environmental upbringing. That's not to say I lied – I just didn't *give* anything or engage in small talk, which she kept luring me to do when she thought I felt comfortable.

Thirty minutes passed, and she finished, giving the impression I shouldn't have a care in the world, and that I'd be fine. As cameras tracked me towards the security of my cell, my thoughts were racing. *Had I hurt my defense?* The gate to Cell Block 8 opened, and the cold blast of air snapped me to the present.

Unable to sleep that night, I stared at the wall, a few inches from my face. I ran the backs of my fingers across the concrete surface, feeling the texture. It was too stark a contrast from the caress of a warm shoulder; like a cold sidewalk at midnight. I imagined myself sitting on a street corner, as wind cut through the trees.

The jail's schedule prevented us from experiencing the night. I looked forward to a long walk under streetlights, more so than other lost privileges.

.

Through a scheduling anomaly, all four of us were taken out of the cell for either meetings or court dates. When I returned, I was alone. At first, it got disorienting. I could hear the echo of my voice. Was this privacy?

In case you're wondering if I jerked off, I didn't. Instead, I screamed. I screamed louder than I had in my entire life - over and over, viciously until my lungs burned, and deputies arrived, warning me to stop.

.

Daniel and I sat at a table, watching TV. I tapped him on the arm with my knuckle, *'Check it out,'* I said, pointing across the floor to Joseph Hamburg, who was seated, with his left leg draped over his right, reading a newspaper. He had a fresh shave, his hair slicked with pomade, wearing his reading glasses.
"He looks so suave and dignified," I chuckled
"Wow," Daniel remarked, "The only thing he's missing is a tobacco pipe and scotch!"
We marveled at Joseph, proud of his reformation, and of his heart.

.

"It was 'Kumbaya' wasn't it?" Guy asked me, biting his nails
"What?"
"I sang 'Kumbaya' the other day. Remember? That's why Daniel hates me, isn't it?"
I didn't respond. I figured if I let it fester, his head might explode, and we'd be rid of him.

"You should've seen it," Guy touted, "The last time I got arrested, they brought helicopters. The streets were lined with police cars."
During the courtroom charade for those charges, Guy's temper reigned.
"I threatened to cut the prosecutor's head off, as they dragged me out of the building. That bitch."
"That's a nice, touch. I'm sure the Judge liked that," Daniel said
"She had surveillance equipment installed all over her property," he boasted
"Hey Joe, you and Guy have cleaning duties tonight. Logie and I did it yesterday," Daniel instructed as he and I left to use the phones
It wasn't long before Joe came downstairs, trembling.

"He threatened me in the cell, you guys. While we was cleaning."
"Why?" I asked
"He was giving me a hard time, and I made a wise remark."
"Good!" Daniel said, "We got you, Joe."

We talked to Guy, and he dismissed his actions.

.

"You guys shoulda been at my wedding," Guy said
"Why the fuck would we be at your wedding, bro?" Daniel replied
"I'm tellin' ya. John Gotti was there," Guy continued," he gave my wife and I an envelope of money. A beautiful wedding. I miss my wife and kids."
Daniel and I were not impressed, and that flustered him.

Guy had a lack of regard for the no-contact order with his wife. *No one* told Guy he couldn't talk to his wife. *No one* was going to keep him from his family. He seemed so determined to violate the order that he devised a plan to get transferred to medical, to gain access to the all-hours phone.
"I need to call my wife. These people can't prevent me from talking to my family."
"Has it occurred to you that your family doesn't wanna talk to your sorry ass?" Daniel suggested
"No, it hasn't. Why wouldn't they?"
"They had you arrested, bro."
That's when Daniel and I saw the situation from a different angle; if this idiot schemed to bring himself additional charges, we should help him along.

Guy's inserted his spork utensil into his shoe, making it painful to walk. As he feigned a limp, Daniel, Joe, and I took a deputy aside and said, *'Look, you gotta get this dude to medical. All he does is complain about his damn leg, and he's too prideful and arrogant to request a transfer.'*

The fiasco went on for days, and the deputies denied him outright.
"Tell you what, Guy," I offered, "On our next out time, you head to the staircase, and I'll kick you so hard that you fall down them."
"You'd do that for me?" he said
"No, not really."

Guy wrote letters to his legal counsel with embedded messages to his wife. He claimed they said nothing incriminating.
"Read it, Guy," Daniel said
He obliged us, but by the end of the letter, he'd threaten lives, discuss murders, and slander the prosecution.

"Guy, how many times have you been hit in the fuckin' head?" Daniel asked
"Tens of thousands."

When he finally *did* receive mail from his family, he buried his face in the letter, melodramatically taking in deep breaths through his nose.
"It smells like my daughter," he sobbed, tears welling up in his eyes, "Smell it."
"Nah, I'm good," I said flatly, "I don't care what your daughter smells like."

.

Unknown to us, Joe applied for the worker dorms.

"Hamburg!" the deputy called
Joseph panicked at the sudden intrusion, *'Yessir?"*
"We found a job for you! You're going to the dorms. Someone will stop by to give you a uniform. What size are you?"
"Um, I'm not sure."
"Look at the letter on your pants," we gestured, supportively
"It's an M," Joseph said
"Medium. Ok, thanks. Be ready to go," the deputy instructed as he shut the door
"Oh, thank you, sir! Really? Ok."
"You sly dog, Joseph! That sounds like initiative to me, Daniel!" I said
"Damn, Hamburger! Good job! You know your actually gonna have to work, right? You can't sleep all day like you do around here," Daniel said, proudly
"What are they gonna make me do, guys?" Joe asked
"You're gonna to do whatever they tell you to, buddy," Daniel said

Time elapsed, and Joseph fidgeted on his bunk. The idea of change made him anxious. When a staff member came, he expected his clothes.
"Hamburg, I need you to step outside please, there's someone here to speak with you."
"What's going on?" Joe asked
"A new charge has been filed against you."

They raised the man up - and shot him down cold. He returned to the cell, sullen, accused of having stolen tools before his arrest, getting him another misdemeanor. His public defender could beat it, but we labored to reinstill Joe's confidence, *'A misdemeanor ain't shit. You'll be fine, bro,'* Daniel said.

Joseph Hamburg was then taken to his job, in *The Dorms*.

.

An hour past Joe's exit, the cell door opened.

"I have your cellmate, gentlemen," the officer said, "Let me know if he's a problem."

Giles Montgomery, forty-three years old. I identified him as the bald man with wild eyes, also removed from Cell 862, and relegated to *The Side Shoot.* Although he and Guy were both housed there, they hadn't lived together yet.

Giles, not in a good mood, aggressively set up his bunk, cursing under his breath. He'd done nineteen years in prison, and for the majority of that term, he served as a janitor on death row. He'd witnessed firsthand the pain others only read about, and I'm sure the experience taxed his psyche. In spite of that, he got pretty upbeat, with a goofy sense of humor and a *'What, me worry?'* attitude. An instigator, always hunting for a reaction, Giles became much needed comic relief.

I mentioned to Daniel, at lunch, "We're in that cell with two inmates from The Side Shoot."

"Damn, I didn't think of that. You're right. Why us, bro?" he asked

"I have no idea."

"We should stop talking altogether," he kidded, "Two fuckers from protective custody? Why us?"

.

Guy rambled, boasting of the cocaine deals he did in the 80's, scoring drugs for corrupt cops, and fueling their parties. He admitted to helping them set up closed buys on other dealers. *'It's motherfuckers like that, that get people like Ricky busted,'* Daniel said in private. *'Who the fuck brags they're a narc?'* I questioned.

The tension in our cell got oppressive. Suffocating. The inmates on our Walk heard us arguing through the walls, at all hours of the day and night. Each sentence that Daniel and I spoke, Guy interrupted, *'I'm tellin' ya, I'm tellin' ya,'* he'd interject.

Charles approached me.

"Hey, Logan. Are you holding up in that cell? You've got some tough customers."

"Honestly Charles, I'm going insane."

"How you do it, with Guy in there? He's a joke. What happened to his leg, anyway? Why is he limping?"

"He put his spork in his shoe."

"What?"

"He stuck his friggin' spork in his shoe so he can fake a limp, to get in medical."

"Oh my god," Charles said, rubbing his forehead

"So, uh, how's your new cellie?" Perry inquired, "We're a little worried for you."

"It's heading steadily downhill."

"You're writing a book, aren't you?"

"Yep."

"Well, you've got a wealth of material with that one! He is *the pinnacle* of ridiculousness."

"Aptly put, my friend."

"Does he always tuck his shirt in, or is it just during out times?" Perry asked

"Dude, he *sleeps* with it tucked in."

"No," he said, in amused disbelief

.

"FUCK YOU, BOBBY JO RILEY!" Giles shouted through the crack in the door, with a mock hillbilly accent. That was his ritual - goading people on their out time. He'd been in the system *for so long,* Giles now re-entered prison with *the kids* of the men he'd done time with *originally.* Giles knew everybody - and where they slept, like The Sandman.

"I don't know why people complain about getting hit in the face," Giles said, "I love it. It gives me a boner."

"Oh?" I replied

"Uh, huh. Yep. One time I was in prison and a dude beat me down with a padlock, and when I stood up, I had a big ol' boner."

Yes, Giles was missing a few ingredients, but at least he knew how to conduct himself in lockdown, unlike Guy. Giles had the strangest voice; like a deep throat frog from North Dakota. He could've accomplished voice-overs for cartoons.

.

"I'm thinking of getting a Masonic tattoo on my arm," Guy stated, "On my left shoulder. What do you say?"

"You're a Mason, Guy?" Daniel inquired

"Yes, I am."

"What degree?"

"First-Degree."

"Oh, so you're a tourist, then. You may wanna hold off on the ink. They don't dig that shit."

"FUCK YOU, NATHAN RICHARDS!" Giles hollered through the door

.

While half-watching TV, my eye got drawn to a Latino man sitting at the Telmate machine, waiting for a scheduled video visit. I could tell how important the call was to him; he'd cleaned up well. His mind searched for the right words to say. He kept readjusting, nervously, in the plastic chair.

The video screen stayed black, and the allotted time for the call to connect had passed. He continued to wait, slowly accepting that is wasn't coming. His gaze turned to the floor, crushed. His eyes glassed with tears, yet he remained seated, part of him hoping, or too disappointed to move.

I'm sure he felt alone, at that moment. Suddenly, the screen clicked on, and a dozen people filled the frame. Six kids crowded for attention. His friends and family got together to show him their love, as they tried to figure out who'd talk first. He wasn't expecting the turnout and wiped his tears. I walked by and patted him on the shoulder.
"I think you're loved," I muttered
"Thank you," he said, looking up at me

.

"Hey yo! Concentration Camp!" I heard Mendoza shout
I jogged to his cell
"What's up with your case, man?" he asked
"I'm looking at felony probation."
"No shit?! That's good!"
"How's it going with you?"
"I'm outta here tomorrow, bro! I posted bail!" he said, smiling wider than
usual
"That's great, man! Congratulations!"
"Thanks, man. Hey yo, if I don't see you again, good luck. Hang in there!" he said, touching his fist to the glass
I reciprocated.

Mendoza got released the next day.

.

I was filling a coffee bag with boiling water when the deputy issued a five-minute warning for final lockdown. The new inmates were brought in, to collect their mattresses from the table. One of the men got assigned to *The Side Shoot*, for protection. I turned and froze. *It was David.* He was back. *Why?*

I walked up. *"What the fuck are you doing here?"* I asked

He gave me a coy grin, and batted his eyes.

"Just some bullshit," he said, with his lazy Alabama accent

I stared at him, with contempt.

He turned his face and headed casually down the hall. I watched him until he disappeared from sight.

What did you do, David? I'd never know.

.

Ada County Jail distributed resource packets to inmates, which listed the businesses and institutions in Boise that supported discharged convicts. Daniel and I each grabbed one, and browsed it together. I had a floor to sleep on at Tony's, plus familiarity with the area, whereas Daniel had no connections in the city; restricted to living in a halfway house if the courts didn't allow him passage to Oregon.

While he contacted the houses, I circled the viable listings for food, clothing, jobs and financial aid, on both my paperwork and his.

"Listen, Daniel. If I get released, I'll be out twenty-five days before you," I said, "I'm gonna hit the streets and follow these leads, and see what's legit. I'll try to make your court date, but if I can't, I'll mail a letter to the cell. You have my word."

"Hell yeah, Logie. Thanks, bro."

"No problem. Managing in this town is hard enough."

"Do what you gotta do, bro. The first time a got outta jail, I lost my mind."

"I hope I don't. Who knows, maybe I can give you a tour of the city."

"That would be tight!"

I would've liked that; seeing one friend outside of this place, in the sun, in real clothes, happy and laughing. It would help me confirm that this experience had happened.

.

Guy had three kids with his wife. His eldest teenage daughter had a boyfriend, which Guy disliked beyond measure. She, however, loved the boy and disobeyed her father's orders to leave him. Guy had several run-ins with the law over domestic violence. Guy claimed this argument to be verbal, but he allegedly slapped her. He shared his Discovery with us, to get our opinions.

Daniel and I read it, both agreeing that his daughter's testimony damned him - the one who's boyfriend Guy threatened to kill. Was it an act of retaliation, for him controlling her life? If so, did this teach Guy anything on parenting? Not remotely. Rather than respect his child's wishes, he instead vowed to throw the boy's body in a river.

"Did anyone teach you how to solve problems with communication?" I asked
"No. I solve problems physically."
"Must be nice to be infallible."
"What's that mean? I don't know that word."
"It means your an asshole," Daniel chipped in
"I'm not an asshole. *I'm tellin' ya*, I'm not an asshole."

.

Perry and I sauntered around the rec yard, as he related the story of his own PSI interview, from earlier that morning.

He had relaxed in his chair, with a calm demeanor. The assessor, a woman, began the evaluation. Perry struck up a personable conversation, getting her to confide that she was hungry and looking forward to lunch. She admitted to being overweight and felt guilty for overeating.

"Well, here's what you do, ma'am," Perry began, "You take your favorite fruit, it can be anything, like peaches for example, and whenever you feel hungry, you eat a big ol' bowl of that fruit. Eat as much as you want."
"That's a great idea! I do love peaches," she said
"I could eat peaches all day long, ma'am," Perry said, with a debonair grin
It took her a second to catch the innuendo.
"Oh, you're dirty! I'm gonna take a shower after I'm finished with you!" she giggled

.

"Hey Logie, can I borrow your hypnotism book?" Daniel pleaded
"Why?"
"So I can learn how to put women in a trance."
"Absolutely not."
"Why, what's up?"
"You don't need *any* further advantage over women. It wouldn't be fair. You're managing fine in that department."
"C'mon, bro! Please?"
"Nope. Not a chance."
"I'll pay you."
"With what? Pastries?"

After dinner, we had a ritual of blacking the calendar day with a pen, *'It's that time y'all!'* I rallied, *'Time to say goodbye to this fucking day!'* The month of September was almost dark. As I paced the cell, my gaze drifted to those black squares; it got overwhelming. Instead, I focused on the shapes and forms on the stained concrete floor.

"FUCK YOU, GENE WILSON!" Giles hollered through the door

Giles's gleefully bred paranoia, for the sake of entertainment, along with cracking lewd sexual jokes. He had no shame.

"So I drove to my hometown to visit some family," Giles began, "But, I went to a bar first to have a few drinks, and I met this hot woman. So we get to talkin' and we end up in a motel room. We go at it, and I pipe her down, and we have a great time, you know, so I invite her to my families house. When we get there she's like *'Wait, your family lives in this house?'* I say *'Yeah, why?'* She says *'So does mine!'* It turns out she's my cousin! I'd never met her before!"

"What's for dinner tonight, Giles?" Daniel asked

"We're gettin' the Suppressed Chicken Sandwich, guys!" he said with mock enthusiasm, "We get the chickens that had broken tail lights!"

We called it 'Spaz TV.' Daniel and I pretended to have a remote control for Giles while he talked. He'd play along, jabbering insanely when we hit *'Fast forward!'*, or twist himself backward when we pushed *'Rewind!'* Other times we chose *'Slow motion.'*

It got stressful for Giles, maintaining a relationship with his wife and mistress. Especially since they were aware of each other. A bit awkward, I imagined. The thick letters he received weren't filled with loving sentiments.

.

Guy had run his finances, and his name, into the dirt. His family was in danger of eviction from their home, as he faltered in Ada County Jail. It put him into a state of despair.

"We're gonna lose everything," he sobbed

"Here's an idea," I suggested, "Instead of feeling sorry for yourself, why don't you think of ways to raise money?"

"Like what?"

"Do you own valuable things? You keep bragging about your gun collection. Why can't you sell that?"

"I'm never selling my guns. No one can take a man's guns away from him."

"You're such a douche-bag," I sighed, rubbing my eyes

"Excuse me? What did you call me?" he snapped

"You fucking heard him," Daniel stood in, "You've got the means to help your family and pay your bills, but you refuse to do it because you don't want to sacrifice anything. And you best back off Logan. I'm serious. And explain something to me, how is it that you have so many connections, and all these mentors, and famous friends and mafia affiliations and all these *fucking resources*, bro, yet *nobody* can post your bail?"

As usual, Guy deflected.

"FUCK YOU, DAVY THOMPSON!" Giles hollered through the door

.

Guy pushed for me to get a job at the car dealership where he used to work. He wrote an absurd letter of recommendation for me on a torn scrap of paper: 'Please hook up this guy. I was in jail with him. He was a debt collector, so he can close. With your training, he will be a hitter.' - Love, Guy. See you soon.

What more could I need?

Guy would get up at 4 am, when the fluorescent lights blared on, and pace the cell talking to himself.
"Cant..... do it..... gotta get out..... must be a way.... shoulder.... hurts..... can't take it anymore.... I don't belong here.....Miss my family... gotta get out."
This would go on for hours until it woke us in frustration. He'd apologize, sit to write another vengeful letter, and read it as he wrote.
"They..... don't...... know..... who..... they're...... fucking..... with.....Hey, Logan. Wake up. How do you spell revenge?"

His crying fits became more frequent - every fifteen minutes, rather than on the hour, *'My family. I miss my family. I don't belong in here.'*
Daniel and I prepared our weekly spread and invited him to join us. He laid on his bunk, defeated.
"Guy! Don't disrespect us by turning down our food," Daniel said, angrily, *"Be a fuckin' man and do your time!* We don't want to listen to you cry while we're trying to enjoy our meal."

He spurned showers; his arms covered in red sores. Daniel bought him a $5 bar of soap, which Guy met with refusal.
"It's the water," he said as if it were a conspiracy
"Guy, water doesn't give people skin conditions. You keep pickin' at that shit until it bleeds. You gotta keep it clean."
"I'm tellin' ya, it's the water."

At night, Daniel and I passed notes back and forth. We wondered if Guy's skin affliction might be contagious.
Daniel: 'Hey for the record those are definitely SCABIES spreading on that dude. Not a fuckin' doubt in my mind.'
Logan: 'Didn't he say he walked through swamps and shit in the jungle?'
Daniel: 'He ain't used soap in over a month on his body.'
Logan: 'Apparently not water either. IT"S THE WATER, BRO!'
Daniel: 'That shit's *highly* contagious. Just sayin'.

Logan: 'We may have to flamethrower his ass.'
Daniel: 'For real! We already trained one bum!' Hamburg was way cleaner
than this dude by far!'

.

Giles, sadly informed of his grandmother's passing, wanted to get a video visit
with his family. Guy reserved the Telmate machine to make a pointless chat with his
lawyer and would not relinquish his spot. He was a piece of shit, for not showing Giles
the courtesy, and he told him as much. *'What? I signed for it first,'* he responded.

Then, he had the nerve to take Dee and I aside.
"Hey, if Giles' is gonna get violent with me, we gotta get him out of the cell. If
he gets aggressive with either of you, let me know. We can work together on this."
The feud carried into lockdown, making the night unbearable with tension.

I rested on my bunk, with my eyes closed. Guy reached in and palmed my
face with his hand. I freaked. It genuinely scared me. Daniel, as livid as me, pushed
Guy away.
"What the fuck is wrong with you Guy?!" he yelled
"Don't ever touch a man like that!"
"What? I was joking."
"It isn't funny, asshole! You alright, Logan?"
"Yeah, I'm good. *Fuck, man.*"

.

I sat, with my patience at an end, writing notes for this book, trying to
concentrate. Guy continued to instruct me on how the plot of my manuscript should
read.
"I'm tellin' ya, it needs to be about you going through all of this terrible stuff,
then you get out of jail and get a job at the car dealership I recommended, and you do
great and find success! It could be an inspirational book! I know a lot of people in the
car industry that would love to read that. It's genius. I get the first copy, ok?
Autographed."
I stopped writing. I lifted my gaze from the paper – my eyes red with the
blood of a 1000 saints.
"What did you say to me?"
"What? It's genius, don't you think?" he said with his smug Italian grin
*Did this asshole just intimate that I should turn my memoir into a fucking
inspirational manual for car salesmen?*
"Logie! Hey, buddy! It's three minutes till lunch!" Daniel jumped in,
overhearing the conversation, "Best get your shoes on!"

I went outside to the rec yard, to clear my mind, on that cool Autumn afternoon. I breathed it in. I was surprised to hear music over the loudspeakers – the deputies hadn't done that for us, before.

The song playing on the radio was Survivor's *'Eye of The Tiger.'*

Daniel had taken his hustle to the online forums of eBay and penny auctions, making money reselling electronics. We discussed the topic for constantly.

Through Daniel, I felt my hustle coming back. He generously imparted his knowledge. We talked about maximizing profits, cyber laws, websites to research, and streamlining business with new technology, along with the benefits of getting a small business license. Most importantly, *we talked about the things people are hungry for.*

I wasn't scared of my financial situation anymore. I was regaining my goal of independence, that I had when I arrived in Boise. Only now, I had a legitimate plan. A realistic objective.

Daniel and I had our inspirational late night talks while our cellmates slept. Daniel sat on the stool, illuminated by the dim light through the window.

"Listen, I had a man tell me this once," Daniel began, "He said 'However you *met* the woman is how you're going to *lose* her."
It hit me - that I met Elena in a bar, with her in the midst of a legal battle with her ex. She ended our relationship in a bar, and here I am, in jail.
"That's classic! That's so real!" I exclaimed, laughing from my belly
"Right?"

"Daniel, you used a phrase, yesterday. I wondered what it meant."
"What did I say?"
"Fresh to Death."
"Fresh to Death! That's my *favorite,* bro! Ok, let me give you an example," he said, pausing to describe it in his mind, *"Fresh to Death* is like... A man that wakes up rested, at the same time every morning. Maybe his ritual is going to the barber for a shave or reading a paper while he gets his shoes shined. Then, the rest of his day, he's all about his *business. He's on top of it.* No distractions. He doesn't drink, smoke, or do drugs. A man that's Fresh to Death ends his night with class... That's Fresh to Death. That's what I want for myself, bro."

I may not have said it, *but I wanted that for myself as well.* Those words stayed with me.

In the beginning stages of my incarceration, I had the ambition to buy a bottle of whiskey at my release, that being my means of dealing with grief. Now, I didn't crave it. I didn't want to get high. I didn't need it.

We rehashed the theories of Nicki's whereabouts; *Was she in jail? With her mother? Did she go to school? Rehab? Did she find some other dude? Did her father, ironically a cop, plan to shoot Daniel in the street like a dog?* They were all valid theories.

"Daniel, has a woman that you cared for ever completely shafted you?"

"Nah, bro."

"*Ahhh.* I'm getting' it. It's not so much that she could've run off with someone else, but"

"No!" he said, interjecting, "She took my *Ism*, bro. It hurt!"

"Your what?"

"My *Ism*."

"Is that like your mojo?"

"Yes, your *Ism* is *who you are.* It's what defines *you* as a person."

Daniel got animated and passionate when he spoke. His hands moved in synchronized gestures as if his thoughts were in stereo. He continued talking, knowing that he reached me.

"People, especially women, will try and take your *Ism* from you, for your entire fucking life, bro. *But you can't let 'em have it.* If they do take your *Ism,* you gotta reclaim it. Nicki made promises to me, and she straight up disappeared without a word. I thought we *had* something, you know? Something real. Now, I gotta find her and take my fucking *Ism* back.

"Logan, that crazy woman that put you in this jail, she took your *Ism,* bro. She thinks she *beat* you! She's proud of herself, now. She's telling herself she *got* you! But look at me, Logan. Look at me, bro. Look me in my eyes."

I held eye contact with Daniel.

"You're gonna reclaim it, Logan. I *PROMISE* you! You'll get out, and that day will come. You'll *feel* that shit, and so will she, even if she's on the other side of the world, bro. She's gonna *feel* that shit leave her body. She'll be standing there like an idiot, not knowing what happened, saying, *'Oh my gosh! Oh my gosh! What?'* You're *going* to get your *Ism* back, bro. I *promise* you.

10 DAYS TO SENTENCING

Day 10: Barbwire at Sunrise

"ARE WE GOING TO HAVE A PROBLEM, DANIEL?!" Guy shouted
"Yeah, we are."

With those simple words, Cell 846 finally detonated. Just prior, Daniel was standing passively at the window, while Guy argued with Giles on a trivial issue.
"Don't bother, Giles," Daniel said, "He's not gonna listen."
Guy spun around and voiced his challenge.
Daniel, composed, almost peaceful, turned to look at his opponent.
Guy screamed, *"THEN COME ON MOTHERFUCKER! LET'S GO! LET'S GO!"*
The cell reverberated, as Guy charged up to Daniel's face. I saw Guy's closed fist shaking at his side.
"What's good?" Daniel said, unmoved
He locked eyes with Guy, and subtly, but firmly, planted his left foot forward. Daniel raised his fists, protecting his face.
"THEN COME ON YOU SON OF A BITCH! GO FOR IT!! GO FOR IT, YOU MOTHERFUCKER!" Guy bellowed, his body shuddering, the veins in his neck swelling.
"Lower your voice and fight like a man," Daniel said curtly, in a hushed tone, studying Guy's every movement.
"HIT ME, MOTHERFUCKER! COME ON! LET'S GO!"
"Lower your damn voice," Daniel said once more, holding his position.
In those terrible seconds, I knew if Daniel swung, he'd lose his chance of probation. And those precious years with his daughter, Isabelle, who missed him dearly. It rode on this painful moment.
And in those seconds, I know that Daniel thought of his daughter as well.
"FUCK YOU! FUCK YOU! FUCK YOU!" Guy belted out, disrupting the cell block
Guy was a dangerous man, yet Daniel showed no fear. The streets had done more than harden Daniel – they'd taught him loss, and what fights are worth winning.
"HIT ME YOU FU-" Guy's threats got cut off by the door flying open, as our cell flooded with officers. I couldn't believe what I saw - Not *one* of them touched Daniel. They parted like water, and engulfed Guy, taking him to the floor.

As deputies forcefully brought Guy down the staircase, we heard him yelling, *'It wasn't me! He started it! I'm a model inmate! I'm a model inmate! Why aren't you going after him!?*
Daniel, briefly questioned, did not get written up. After that, Daniel Weschler became a legend, congratulated by the inmates of our Walk, and Cell Block 8 as a whole; a story to tell his daughter, someday.

Day 9: Mud

Enter, Samuel Kesey, thirty-nine years old.

"Call me Mud," he instructed, giving us a proper handshake

Tall in stature, and pale skinned, Mud carried himself with purpose. A severely honest man, with grounded opinions.

"We're glad to have you," Giles said, "Because our old cellie was a first class A-Hole."

"Oh yeah?" Mud replied

"Yeah, bro," Daniel muttered, "I don't even wanna talk about that fuckin' dude."

"Good, then don't. If he's an idiot, I don't want to hear about him. I'd rather talk about ideas, then hear complaints."

Mud, keen on the law, motioned to represent himself in court. I found that admirable. *'They're a bunch of gerbil-headed finger pointers,'* he said of the prosecution, with his cut and dry humor. His actions were so calculated, that if a piece of information didn't aid him in getting from point A to point B, he viewed it as an insult.

Intent on staking his claim in this world, Mud prepared to head towards Alaska to build bridges. He sought to have his own operation, someday. Resolute, he'd spend his upcoming prison term studying his craft. He brought a small library with him and had people outside to send him further reading material. I noticed a copy of *'The Four Agreements,'* by Don Miguel Ruiz.

That was a *real* life, I thought; he'd have something fierce to show for his existence. Mud reflected on how it'd feel, to stamp the base of a bridge with his name and insignia – a bridge that would exist until nature itself tore it down.

I listened when Mud spoke of his relationships. It caught my attention how deftly he set boundary lines, not allowing them to be crossed. If my mindset had been comparable to his, I might've avoided this entire experience. Granted, he sat in jail, too.

He had a World Atlas, with satellite images of the major cities. I asked if I could thumb through it. *'You sure can.'* As I got absorbed in its pages, I noticed how the continents and countries had drifted in my mind; some had grown larger, others smaller, and displaced.

Each night, he wrote a letter to a loved one and mailed it, preferring to say comments that brightened the recipients day. Mud had a girl he cared for, who succumbed to drug addiction. He didn't want to leave her behind, yet couldn't be a part of that circle, anymore.

"I told her, look, you need to love *yourself* more *so that I* can love you more. I can't love a person who doesn't want to do anything for themselves."

"I like you, Logan," Mud said
"I like you, too, Mud."

Day 8: Paper

I had a dream about Elena.

Roughly ten years in the future, her and I were in court. My hair had grown long, and so had hers, with brown accents. We sat within range of one another, though she refrained from eye contact. The packed courtroom brimmed with tension. My council hadn't arrived, though I wasn't the least concerned. It felt so real I could detect the heat from a photographers flashbulb, near my head.

I went light on my commissary order, separating the bare minimums for myself, from the supplies I'd donate to my cellies. Daniel getting dibs.

I returned the books from the jail library and stacked my own at the foot of my bunk. I organized my legal paperwork and journals in manila envelopes and stored them in my crate.

Giles snapped. He leapt violently from his bunk and whipped a stack of letters through the air. The papers hit the wall, flying in every direction. He screamed, punching the wall, then spun in circles, throwing fists and stomping the ground. The three of us got in defensive positions, not knowing if his blind rage might swing on us next. Giles collapsed against the wall, hyperventilating. He pulled his knees up to his chest and put his hands on his head.

Mud quietly spoke to him. Initially, Giles told him to fuck off. Then he began to hear reason. Mud, exceptional at setting people on track, gave solidarity to Giles' thoughts.

It frustrated Giles; he didn't feel literate enough to express his feelings on paper. I could sympathize with that. The following day he concluded, *'To hell with both of those women. I told 'em to stop talking to me.'*
"That's probably a smart decision," I said
"Hey, at least I don't talk about Nicki all damn day like Daniel. Nicki this. Nicki that. I *try* to keep it light, you know?" Giles said, and we both chuckled

Day 7: Do *You*, First

The withdrawals from Zoloft were strong. As I peered out the window, a beautiful, mad rush of serotonin coursed through me; at least that's what I assume. I felt empathy and overwhelming emotions - a connection to all things. My breathing got labored, in an excited way.

"Are you alright, dude?" Mud asked

"Yeah... I'm just... *My god... It's all hitting me at once...* I just want to start crying, but I'm not *sad*," I laughed, bending over and placing my hands on my knees.

"That's a positive thing, then?" Daniel said

"Yeah... I mean, the wind is leaving me... *My god... I'm just....*"

On each new page of my notepad, I'd write a short list of my fears in the top right corner. As they ceased to have power over me, I cut them from the proceeding page.

How easy is it to find fault in the entirety of a man's life? Surely, the PSI assessment set me up for failure. Did the police examine my journals and hard drives? What could they misconstrue from hundreds of hours worth of video footage?

My final written fear lingered - *Elena's mouth.*

.

For dinner, we ate TVP hamburgers and watched 'Bloodsport,' with Jean Claude Van-Damme. We got into that shit and had fun.

The fire alarm triggered, shutting down the cooling system, on account of Mud's young son. He'd come to visit his father in person, and when the cops didn't permit him, he got pissed and yanked the chord as he exited the building. *Hell yeah, kid.* We can hack the heat for a cause like that. You made your dad proud.

I stared into the mirror; that piece of reflective metal bolted to the wall; sick of my image. I shaved my beard with a single blade razor, contouring my goatee and mustache. I asked the Redshirt, a new recruit, fairly adept at cutting hair, to buzz my sides and back with a #1 attachment, and a #3 on the top, with a fade.

Day 6: Laps

A member of the staff delivered a PSI packet to Daniel. I urged him to write rough drafts on scrap paper. He had a criminal record and needed to use caution, *'Keep it simple as possible,'* I advised.

I spent the duration of our extended out times walking laps along the yellow line. My cellies and neighbors would invite me to watch TV, but I couldn't stop; restless energy consumed me. They'd join me, one at a time, and we'd talk for awhile. Inmates in lockdown called to me through their doors, asking for favors. I ignored them, with one exception.

"Hey, man! Can you please get us hot water?" the man pleaded, sliding the empty coffee bag under the door. I didn't know him. I quickly picked it up and put it in the lining of my pants, checking the lone deputy at the control desk. He may have seen the transfer from the corner of his eye, but he wasn't sure. He didn't have a partner that shift, which rarely occurred. I became his sole focus, regardless. I feigned interest in a book from the library and headed to my cell.

I laid low for a bit. The timer signaled him to do quarterly cell check. When he entered *The Side Shoot*, I had a twenty-five-second window. I flew down the flight of stairs and ran to the hot water dispenser. I filled the bag to the exact level and tore across cell block, sealing it on the way. I skidded into their door, slipping the tip of the bag into the crack as the elated inmate yanked it through without a drop spilt.

"Enjoy your coffee, boys!" I hollered, knocking on the window

My Walk saw this transpire and applauded.

"That's some smooth action, right there! That's how you do it!" I said

The deputy emerged, puzzled by the commotion. He shrugged his shoulders.

Day 5: Don't Cross My Wings

I'd been incarcerated for 110 days - *yet my court appearances totaled 45 minutes.* It's hard for a lot of inmates to put that into perspective. To the court, I existed *only* in those 45 minutes. The rest of that duration, to them, was irrelevant. The problem is that the 'missing time' means everything to the person enduring it. It's far more real than the latter.

I had to let that go. I had to approach my sentencing without that momentum clouding my thoughts. I had to minimize the experience I'd endured, and carry on defending an old life that was no longer mine; a path, unrecognizable, to which I gave no credence.

.

The mystery behind the disappearance of Nicki finally got solved. She returned home to be with her mother. A huge weight lifted from Daniel's shoulders; the insecurities that plagued him dissipated. He relaxed, focusing on his case, and other matters
He was talking to her on the phone, with a smile on his face. He gestured for me to come over.
"Hey, bro! Nicki's on the phone!"
"Oh, yeah? Let me talk to her," I said, as he handed me the receiver
"Is this Nicki?"
"Yeah."
"Hi, Nicki."
"Hi."
"Fuck you, Nicki," I said, handing the phone to Daniel
"See!" he laughed, "I drove the dude crazy talking about you!"

O C T O B E R

Day 4: Run it Down

Perry and I were standing in line, waiting to be issued our weekly uniforms. We discussed dreamscaping, then got interrupted.

"What size pants, man?" the Redshirt asked me

"Small."

"Shirt size?"

"Medium. By chance, do you have anything without blood stains on it? I have court on Wednesday."

"Yeah, I've got a brand new one, I think," he said, rummaging through the linen stacks

"Wait, do you have one that's broken in?" I asked, changing my mind

I was deliberate about my appearance in court. In full body shackles and stripes, you're already guilty, but I contemplated methods to minimize that impact.

As a group, my Walk entered the communal shower to get dressed, tossing our dirty clothes in a bin. Imagine the acoustics of twenty men in a shower singing in unison, like a chain gang. Perry took the lead, belting out the lyrics to Edwin Starr's song 'War,' with the rest of us on backup vocals.

WAR! HUH! Yea,
What is it good for?
Absolutely nothing!
Uh huh Uh huh WAR! HUH!
Yea, What is it good for?
Absolutely nothing!
Say it again, Y'all!
WAR! HUH! GOOD GOD!

What is it good for?

Absolutely nothing, listen to me!

I exited the shower, and the Redshirt handed me a fresh bedroll, randomly from the pile. I unraveled it in my cell, to discover the top blanket covered with faded blood stains. It looked as though someone had their throat cut, or the material got used to wrap a stab wound. I did not ask for another one.

I wrapped that blanket around me at night to stay warm, telling myself it would be the last issued to me. I wore it tightly over my shoulders, as I paced the cell.

Day 3: Mantras

I'd repeat – *'This is your fucking life. Defend it. You're going home.'*

I'd revised my letter to the court with a dozen drafts. My attorney approved its honesty. I had my hesitations, though. The words were secondary to maintaining dignity. I couldn't count on a script if things fell apart. I had to go with my gut.

What troubled me was having to *apologize* to that woman. *How could I, with sincerity?* I had to internalize that an apology did not mean forgiveness - they are two different processes.

.

My body moved past the Zoloft and caffeine withdrawals. I wondered if cheap instant coffee and peanut butter sandwiches would continue to comfort me on the outside. I deep cleaned my Velcro shoes and dusted the insides with foot powder that vaguely smelled of mint. We'd puff it into the air, or on our bed sheets, for a deodorizer.

'When a person castes stones, it's because they have something to hide.'

.

That morning, Matt and his family drove through Boise, on their route to Oregon. Jack rode with them, and in all likelihood, passed by Ada County Jail, on the interstate.

That close, Jack.

Day 2: Freeway Way To Freedom

In the shower, the hot water soothed me. I'd cut the tip off a jail-issued toothpaste tube and fastened it to the nozzle, reducing the spray from a fine mist to a pressurized stream. Every muscle in my body ached. I let that water cleanse the jail from my skin.

I dried myself and wore my faded uniform. As I walked to the main floor, with my wet sandals leaving footprints, an inmate blasted Faith No More's song *'Epic'* from a music station. The deputy didn't care.

.

I had another dream about Elena, in a courtroom. Now, the realism had gone. The room looked like a pieced-together theatrical set. Elena, full of hate, refused to acknowledge me. I had headphones on, listening to music. It became an absurd game show. The legal representatives were given a short amount of time to answer each question. Their images got projected onto a large split screen monitor, for people in the audience to see.

.

I walked the rec yard, with Daniel. We had a casual conversation, while the others did exercises or sat in the shade of the wall.

After an hour, we agreed to return to cell block - except for Daniel. He wanted a solitary moment in the yard.
"Are you ok?" I asked
"Yeah. I just wanna be alone for a few.'

We rang the bell, buzzing the control hub to unlock the door. As I entered, I paused, looking over my shoulder to Daniel, in the distance. His movement appeared rhythmic; he heard music in his head.

As I lay in bed that night, I had a memory of Carrie; holding her in my arms, beside my truck, on Route 66, on that bright summer day. In an instant, I felt the shocking sensation that I'd forgotten *everything* I had learned in the last two years. It was *all* slipping away, and I was cycling to the beginning. I didn't *want* to forget - otherwise, none of this had a point.

I desperately regained my composure – then I got embarrassed. *Of course, I wouldn't forget how far I had come. I could not turn the clock.*

Day 1: Locked

My Attorney came to discuss the results of my PSI Investigation.

With no criminal record or history of violence, I still ranked as a moderate-to-high risk. I panicked when I heard him say, *'high risk,'* but he assured me of the plea deals validity. I was on the razor's edge.

The woman who'd assessed me stood behind him, the glass dividing us.

He and I prepared to the best of our abilities, confirming that Elena would be there.

.

Trav would also be sentenced in the morning. Of all the inmates I could've finished this with, I'm glad it was him. His impish smile put me at ease.
"Don't sweat it, bro. You're going to be alright,' he said to me

He received three years in federal prison, and boarded transport to Oregon.

SENTENCING DAY
(Broken Mass)

I entered the courtroom. Elena sat there, with her family huddled around, enabling her behavior. Caroline, Mandy's mother, whispered in her ear. Mandy, however, was absent. I had no one in the audience to support me, as per my request.

The sound of my chains disrupted the silence; even though Elena refused to look in my direction, they made my presence known. I walked with a rhythm and hardly noticed the shackles on my ankles.

The proceedings began. My list of charges got read aloud, and then the stipulations of the plea deal were discussed. The Judge received a copy which stated any rank *above* 'low risk' on the PSI exam rendered the deal invalid. That was not the agreement. My attorney had to clarify the terms and filled a form making the correction.

"Does the State feel there should be additional investigation or evaluation of the defendant?" the Judge asked

"No," said the prosecutor

"Is there any restitution claim?"

"No."

"Does the victim wish to make a statement?"

"Yes, she does."

"Alright. I'll hear that now," the Judge said

Elena rose from her seat and stormed towards the microphone, clutching a thick letter in her hand.

"Thank you, Your Honor, for giving me this opportunity to make my statement," Elena said, her voice shaking, emotionally, "While I stand in this court, in front of this Judge and these lawyers, and you're sitting there waiting for your sentencing, I'm still trying to understand my mind about you, Logan Crannell. You had it all. God was going to bless you with so much! You thought you could fool my family and friends? Well, there's one thing I want to tell you, Logan Crannell! *You can never fool God almighty!*

In those late hours where it seemed that peace was outside our door, there was hell inside. The argument started between eleven and twelve, and it didn't end until five in the morning. You didn't care how you treated my body. You threw me around like a rag doll! You choked me so many times I lost count! *Your hate towards me!* The destruction! Your eyes!

I remember you picked me up by my throat and my feet were hanging off the floor! You dropped me, and I fell. I didn't even get the chance to breathe! You grabbed my hair and pulled me across the floor like I was trash! Then you threw me on the bed, and you began choking me! *There's so much evil in you!* You grabbed me by the hair and threw me across the room! *You have no respect for human life! And you say you loved me and wanted to spend our lives together!?*

That's obsession, like an object you own! Again you threw me onto the bed and choked me! I gasped for air. I gathered my strength and said my ex-husband might be verbally abusive, but he'd never lay a hand on a woman! And you said 'Well I can do it better!' I lost control and urinated myself.

Then you threw me in the closet! Hitting and shaking me, and pushing my body into the wall. Then you locked me in the closet and wouldn't let me out! I begged you plenty of times to stop doing this to me, and you wouldn't! You only laughed at me and made fun of me and called me ugly names and profanities!

When you finally dragged me out of the closet, you said you were in control of the relationship! That I had no say in it at all! All I remember is I was walking backward, and you came at me and pushed me so hard I fell on the couch, and the left side of my head hit the metal studs! I saw stars and lost consciousness. You said it was my fault! *You have no remorse for life!* You took my keys, my phone, locked me in the closet and told me you fantasized *about killing me!*

You may think you can do those things to me, with no witnesses, but you forget! *You cannot hide from God almighty!* You cannot run from his wrath and his judgment! That's why he has authorities here on earth to work for him and declare his laws that he has given them. You're sitting there in judgment, and you are being sentenced today for what you have done to my best friend and me! Let me ask you – *What were you thinking!?* That night when you grabbed my best friend in front of thirty or forty people! You thought you would just walk away!? *You are so wrong!*

I feel like this kind of behavior has been practiced before and it's disgusting! You're sitting there with your mother looking for apartments and places for us to move into, like nothing happened! You have the nerve, the next day to get lunch and beer with your mother and go back home? And you have the nerve to call my mother!? *What were you going to say to my mother?!* I bet you were going on with your day thinking you got away with it! *You were wrong!*

You need to be stopped once and for all Logan Crannell! I also want to know what was in that satanic bag of yours! You hid it pretty well in the corner of the closet! You had piles of stuff on it so that it wouldn't get found! *Whose women's rings are those?! Three women's rings! Where are those women?! Are they alive!? What did you do to them?!"*

I started to lose my composure, and my attorney whispered to me, *'This is about dignity. Sit up straight. Maintain your dignity.*

"How do I apologize after this?" I asked

"You don't."

"You have those rings in a box, as possessions to remind yourself of what you've done, like a trophy!" Elena screamed, "That bag of yours is so disgusting! A bottle of dirt? A bell?! Strange bowls?! A camera? Tape? A small army knife? There are so many insane evil things in that bag! *Who are you?!* The computer also had evil images! Three-hundred-and-forty books about torturing women! Rape! Choking! Manipulation! How to pact yourself with the devil! I can go on, but it's just sick and mind-boggling!

You recorded yourself hypnotizing the dog! You are the abuser of that dog! *All you hold in your mind and heart is hate! There is nothing good in you!* You love evil instead of loving good! You deserve to be where you are! I know that me, and my best friend are not the only victims! I feel deep inside my heart that there have been more victims than us! *How could you even think about taking the life of a mother of two!?* Or my best friend, who also has two children that love her dearly! We are their mothers! We are their guardians! We are their protection!

My life has changed drastically. My throat hurts! It's hard to swallow! Sometimes, it's hard to speak! I'm constantly suffering from post-traumatic stress! I'm always looking over my shoulder. I get panic attacks and extreme anxiety. I can't live by myself! So many things trigger memories of you and me, horrible memories. I live in hell with you!

I had to submit myself to forty-eight-hour watch because of what you have done to me! Being in constant fear is not a way to live! *You did this to me, and you deserve to be locked up for years!* You don't deserve to walk the streets, or be in society! Especially near women!

You have no remorse for my life! That scar that you left on my upper right thigh, I will have that scar for the rest of my life! I remember waking up, and you raping me, and you wouldn't stop! *Sick! Sick! Sick! Sick!* I'm a human being! I don't know which is worse! The physical part fades, but the damage to my heart and mind is forever!

I will be strong because God saved me from the enemy! He has protected me from death! You choose to believe in a dead god, instead of the accepting the true living God! Look at where your dead God has put you! Now in chains and shackles! He's not here to save you from judgment! He's a coward that flees when he knows he's been discovered, and he uses idiots like you to commit crimes on others!

You sold your soul to commit evil things for your evil god! I remember one day you received a text from your brother, where he dreamt that you died and left behind a memorial that deeply confounded everyone, everywhere. I thought about it, and you are alive, but everybody knows what you've done. They know you're evil secrets! I fell in love with a fake person, my heart breaks and I'm grieving for someone who never existed!

I read a page from your diary! You wrote 'jealousy, greed, hurt, vengeance, slandering, lazy, psychopath, prideful, weak, hypocrite, self-serving, disgraceful, cowardly, child abuser!' God will cut you down from this life! *Who are you, Logan Crannell?!* I thank God almighty that he saved me from such a sick individual!

I know you never really loved me! You used my family and me to get what you wanted! If you asked for anything, it was given to you! You came from nothing! I took you into my life, I took care of you, and I never kept tabs on you!

I saw a file on your computer called 'stupidities,' and it had a list of responsibilities! Responsibilities are things we have in life. That's what makes us citizens of this world. I thought when you took me out on dates, it came from your heart! But I was wrong. It was just on your list. I never had a list! Because when you do it, you do it out of love. And it comes from your heart, and it's a joy to do it."

Elena's voice changed, and for that single moment, it conveyed real hurt, without anger. It pained me to hear it – our dates meant so much to me; the file referred to 'bill' dates. Her voice then quickly shifted to vengeance.

"But what hurts the most is that you betrayed God. There is no other God besides him! If you betray my God, you become my enemy! God gave me dreams, for you to change your life and put new shoes on, that he made for you! If you take off the old shoes and leave the old man behind, you become the new man! But you and your selfish pride thought you could get away! *You are so wrong, Logan Crannell!* With God, you don't play games! That's where you failed!"

Rather than focus on Elena, I studied the faces in the courtroom. Their eyes were cast downwards. The Judge leaned in, with a troubled expression on his face. The prosecutor appeared restless; did he know she'd read this? If so, he took advantage of her pain, by setting her up for ridicule. I watched the audience and their discomfort. *They didn't believe Elena.*

"The truck you owned, was it really stolen like you said?" Elena continued, "Or did you fake it so my parents would buy you a new car? I think you hired someone to steal that truck! I saw a video of you unlocking the back door of the truck from the inside because you didn't have keys for it. I think you made that video to show someone how to steal it! You are one sick individual! *You come from nothing, and you are leaving with nothing, you fool!* Everything you loved that meant dearly to you, God has ripped it from your heart and scattered it like the garbage you are!
I always wondered why you have scars on your body until I read from your notepad and it said, 'I'm tired of manipulating myself ten times a day.' *Who are you, Logan Crannell!?*
I would also like to know why you had my daughters homework in the trunk of your car!? *What were you planning to do with my daughter!?* Were you putting a curse on her?! *You are so sick! It's a nine-year-old little girl!* She was innocent! Questions after questions!
You joked about killing my ex-husband, and laughed about it? That's my daughter's and my son's father! Let me ask you this, you were going to leave my children without a father, and a mother!? Did you think of that!? It's a human life! It's not a piece of trash you throw away! It's a creation that God has made! Let God be the judge of my ex!
Now you sit in judgment in front of God, listening to the authorities of this world! Listen to their laws that God has created for them! Now you're going to learn to have respect for life! You have no choice! *May you rot in those four walls that you will call your home!* You're going to have time to think about the choices you've made! Think about the repercussions, when you finally hold yourself accountable for everything you have done, Logan Crannell!

May you be in a cage for the rest of your life! I hope you don't get out because I fear for my safety, the safety of my children, the safety of my family, and my best friends safety! If you get out, I know you will come after me, because all you hold is evil in that heart and evil in that mind of yours! May God guide the heart of this Judge today, and give you the sentence you deserve Logan Crannell!"

Elena cried, as she collected the pages of her letter and walked, weakly, to her family.

The prosecutor hung his head, and a brief silence fell across the courtroom. *It was shame.*

I again looked to the faces surrounding me.

This is how I win, I thought.
By sitting here in chains, not raising a finger or saying a word of retaliation.

This is how I win.

Elena *devoured* herself on the stand.
She was not ready to meet herself.

A surge of adrenaline hit me.

"I'll hear your argument," The Judge said to the prosecutor
"Your Honor, I'd like to ask the court to follow the plea agreement, as it has been indicated," he said, clearing his throat and stammering, "I would ask the court to impose a sentence, a ten-year sentence, withholding judgment. I also ask the court to impose three-hundred-and-sixty-five days in the Ada County Jail, as part of that sentence.

Again that wasn't the deal, and my attorney made note of it.

The prosecutor resumed, "There's a couple of things I'd like to touch on that I think might be relevant and important to the State's argument. From the State's view, the defendant doesn't seem to be taking full responsibility for what he's done. I thought it was significant in the domestic violence evaluation when asked who was to blame for this situation, his response was *'Her and I.'* That indicates he's taking *some* responsibility for himself, but I think it's significant that he puts *her* first.

I'd also like to add that the evaluation does present him as a moderate-to-high risk to re-offend. And I think that makes the fifty-two weeks of treatment necessary as well."

That was the only statement he made in Elena's defense – that I said *'Her and I.'* He showed her no emotional support, and I got faulted for using proper grammar.

"Thank you," The Judge said, and then instructed my attorney to take the floor

"Your Honor, our agreement in regards to the sentencing recommendation did not include three-hundred-and-sixty-five days in Ada County Jail. That's an inaccurate representation of the plea deal.

Paperwork rustled in the confusion.

"Judge, if I might, I'm re-looking at the agreement," the prosecutor said, "and it does suggest release at sentencing, so I would ask that be my recommendation to that."

"Noted," replied the Judge

"Your Honor," my attorney continued, "It's very hard for me to reconcile the Logan Crannell that is referred to in the victim's testimony, to the Logan Crannell described in the character letters, which show Mr. Crannell has a wealth of support available to him. He's portrayed as a man with docile demeanor, a kind soul, undisputed gentility, and love and kindness for animals. His evaluation also states he's a viable candidate for probation. The Logan Crannell described by Elena, aside from what is very dramatic, and not discounting Mr. Crannell's involvement in this matter, and the pain suffered by Elena, for which my client has expressed substantial remorse, is in complete contrast to these accounts.

I simply don't believe what the court has been told today. *I don't believe it.* I'm very cynical about these things. The truth is in there somewhere, but it's certainly not the demonic representations that have been given to the court.

They weren't arguing about Jesus that night, as the police officer reported, they were arguing about her ex-husband, who has custody of her children. He apparently demanded that she get rid of my client and her family also, insisting she come back to California.

I wish I had the opportunity to try some of these allegations, and cross-examine this complaining witness because there's so much ugliness there. *So much hatred.* I hadn't read the statement she made today. I heard it just now. Much of that I've never been confronted with in this case, nor has my client.

There is no rape charge. If it were true, then justice would demand it be brought before this court, and not used as some kind of ambush at sentencing. My client has no opportunity to respond to these histrionics and allegations that are now being made against him. Frankly, how *does* one respond to such things?

In terms of restitution for the victim, there is none. There was no serious injury and no medical records. There's a bump on the head, which her girlfriend claimed she felt the next day. Choking? There are no marks. No bruises.

In the police report, there's a reference to my client hitting her on a weekly basis. None of that exists in the record. There's no proof of any of that. *It didn't happen.* My client was married for five years. He has no criminal record. He has two traffic tickets. One for running a stop sign, and the other for speeding.

These allegations of satanic behavior? It's so difficult. And hurtful. I know it might sound like I'm minimizing – *I'm not minimizing.* This stuff's over the top. *The anger.* And the pain. The anger is from the pain. I can't discount that and nobody should.

For his punishment, my client has been humiliated and suffered substantial loss, and he'll have a felony record, even with a withheld judgment. He's been shamed, and he's here today to face the consequences of his conduct. Finally, Your Honor, he's done one-hundred-and-fifteen days in Ada County Jail, and I'm asking the court to follow the sentencing recommendation. Thank you, sir."

"Thank you," the Judge said, then turned to me, "Mr. Crannell, you get the last word. Is there anything you'd like to say before I decide what sentence to impose?"

I stood up. I calmed my shaking hands, by placing my fingers on the table.

"Yes, Your Honor. I originally came here today to apologize to Elena. I didn't expect there to be such an attack on me," I paused, my thoughts racing as I stabilized my voice and found strength, "But I'm going to apologize, anyway."

I instinctively glanced towards Elena, and the Judge ordered me to face forward.

"Elena and I started off as best friends, and we got lost along the way. We allowed alcoholism, stress, and depression to come between us, and we failed because of it. We failed our friends and family, and I am sorry for that.

I understand that it's my responsibility assure this doesn't happen again. I fully intend to stay sober. I thank God I have a strong support system that's willing to help me get through this and see me succeed.

I've reviewed the recommendations for treatment, and I think they're completely fair, and I'm just asking the court to please trust me with probation and a withheld judgment, so I can rebuild my life and do my best in society. I take absolute responsibility for any harm that I have caused. I truly apologize for what I've done. Thank you."

The Judge began, "Mr. Crannell, based on your plea, I'm going to find you guilty on the charge of domestic violence with traumatic injury," he paused for a breath, "Reviewing your pre-sentence investigation I was impressed by the number of people that were willing to step forward and vouch for your character.

I'm a little concerned over inconsistencies in your account, particularly as it relates to the victim's friend and the incident that took place at the bar. There's a disparity, but I don't think it's enough to deviate from the plea agreement that's been reached here.

I think that protection of society and rehabilitation are achieved by withholding judgment, and I will do so in this case. I'm going to put you on a period of probation for ten years, beginning today. I also require that you complete level-one outpatient treatment, and a fifty-two-week domestic violence course and any other class your officer thinks is appropriate. Do you have questions about the terms of your probation?"

"I do not, Your Honor."

"Are you willing to accept those terms?"

"Yes, I am."

"I will sign an order of release for you today, Mr. Crannell, giving credit for the time you've served."

"Thank you," I said

I remember awkwardly shaking my attorney's hand, with my wrist shackles on.

I descended in the elevator. In a blur, I floated down that long hall.

I had a meeting with my attorney, in private, and we said our farewells.

.

A deputy led me through the darkened parking garage.

The transport bus had already departed. I climbed into the back of a van, along with one other inmate. Two deputies sat in the front. The sound of the engine brought me to reality – to the acceptance I'd soon be free.

We merged onto the freeway, and an Eddie Money song came on the radio, *Take Me Home Tonight.'*

"Hey, deputy!" I hollered, "Turn the radio up!"

"Yeah, turn it up!" said the other inmate

The deputy in the passenger seat nodded his head and cranked the dial. The two of us in chains sang with all the heart we had.

"TAKE ME HOME TONIGHT! I DON'T WANT TO LET YOU GO TILL YOU SEE THE LIGHT! TAKE ME HOME TONIGHT! LISTEN, HONEY, JUST LIKE RONNIE SANG! TAKE ME HOME TONIGHT!

.

The cell door fired open, to my cellmates eager for news.

Daniel sprang from his bunk, "What happened, bro?"

"Logan, how did it go?" Mud asked

I raised my fists in the air, "I'm out!"

"For real!"
"Hell yeah!"
"Sweet!"
They exclaimed, congratulating me, with handshakes and high-fives.
"You got probation then? How long?" Daniel inquired
"Ten years," I said dryly, "I'll deal with that another day."
"Damn! But you're getting out of here, bro!"
"Yeah, you can appeal that," Mud added, "Stay on it."
"I will. Count on that."
"Well, you're in time for dinner!" Giles said, "We're out in ten minutes."

.

On the floor, my Walk enjoyed a celebratory evening. The food tasted bad again, and I donated my tray. Charles, also being released, did the rounds, giddy as a schoolboy, saying his goodbyes. Nichols had signed a plea deal for three years, though the judge over-ruled it and put him on a six-month Rider Program, instead. Nichols, ecstatic by the verdict, would be shipped off to *The Yard* at daybreak.

Perry took me aside.
"I'm so happy! You're a good guy, Logan. Hey, probation is rough at first. They don't want you to feel free, and they're going to try and catch you in a mistake. Don't let them do it, and don't spend your time worrying about it, either. Just do *YOU*. Stay out of trouble, and live your life. A year from now, you won't be able to reach your probation officer if you wanted to."

Giles, in a rare moment of seriousness, sat on a table and spoke to me.
"I'm sure you've got ideas of what you're gonna do on the outside, but I can guarantee you things won't turn out how you expect, and I don't mean that negatively. I'm sayin' keep an open mind. Plans don't go how ya think when you get released. Don't get frustrated by it. Ride it out, and appreciate it for what it is."

.

In lockdown, I sorted through my crate and placed my supplies on the writing desk for my cellmates. I wrapped my books and manila envelopes in a garbage bag.

"We chipped in and got you this," Mud said, handing me a gift
A book on social etiquette. They laughed.
"That's charming, guys," I said, "Thanks. I see there's a sticker on the cover for Ada County."
"Ignore that," Daniel suggested
"Isn't it a misdemeanor to steal jail property?" I asked

"Yep," Mud replied

"Ah, so y'all are trying to get me arrested before I get out the door?"

"We don't want you to go, Logie!" Daniel smiled

"Yeah, you should hang out with us," Giles said, "We don't want some shitbag to steal your bunk."

"Speaking of which," Mud pointed out, "They're sure taking their sweet time to let you out, aren't they?"

"Yeah, since you mention it," I frowned, in agreement

"Hey, I'm giving you the phone number for my babies mom," Daniel said, "That's how you can reach me until I get my cellphone activated."

"Good deal. Write it on my notepad."

"I'm three weeks behind you, bro," Daniel said, of his sentencing day

"Yes, you are. I'll be in touch."

.

7:30 pm.

"Evening Gentleman! Please stand for headcount," the deputy instructed, "State your name and bunk number."

We formed a line.

"Montgomery! 1!"

"Kesey! 2!"

"Weschler! 3!"

"Bunk 4! Nobody!"

The deputy glared at me, "I'm sorry?"

"The Judge said I could leave. Why am I still in custody?" I asked defiantly

"I didn't hear anything about that," he said flatly

"Then you best figure it out," Daniel replied, "This man doesn't belong in here."

The deputy shifted his gaze.

"That's right," Mud stood in, "He's a free man. You need to let him go."

The deputy, submissively, took a step back, "I'll check on it now."

I'll never forget that moment.

Thirty minutes later, I heard the cell door bang and rattle for the final time.

"Crannell! You're cleared," the deputy stated, "Roll up your bunk. You've got five minutes."

I said goodbye to my cellmates.

Daniel didn't notice, but I slipped the hypnotism manual under his pillow.

The clerk in booking handed me a bag containing my clothes; a pair of tailored jeans and a button-down shirt.

"I had a ring in my property," I said

"Should be in the bag," he gestured, "There's a stall around the corner."

I found the chain, with the ring attached, and secured it to my neck. I changed out of my uniform. My shirt had deep creases; it smelled old and faintly of chemicals. I didn't care.

I walked barefoot to the phone and called Tony.

"I'm getting processed. I don't know how long it'll take."

"Alright, man. I'll be waiting."

I paced anxiously.

"Am I able to get my things from evidence?" I asked the clerk

"No, that department closed at five."

"Ok.

Finally, an officer escorted me down the hall, and through a security door. I carried my bag of books and papers under my arm.

I entered the visitor area; the far wall, made of glass, revealed the outside. I saw Tony standing there, holding a pair of shoes by his side. The officer left our company. Tony and I hugged each other.

"Let's get out of this building," I requested

"No problem, man. Let's do it."

I put my shoes on and tied the laces.

I got overwhelmed by the sensation of stepping into the night. I heard crickets and felt a cool wind. It smelled like rain. I looked up at a streetlight, as it hummed and cast shadows. *God, I missed the night.*

During the drive, we talked about regular things and listened to the radio.

"How are you and your wife?" I inquired, "Is she ok with me sleeping on the floor?"

"She's fine with it. We're kinda going through a rough patch, bud."

"I'm sorry to hear that."

"Eh, we'll manage. We always do."

"I don't know if Elena and I are gonna make it," I said jokingly, "I think she's pissed at me."

We laughed, and I rolled the window.

"Mind if I have a cigarette?" I asked

"Sure. Help yourself. Let's stop at a store and get ya what you need."

"A soda sounds nice."

It was raining, when we reached Tony's apartment complex.

As I got out of the car, his headlights were on; illuminating each drop of rain.
The light shone on his neighbors, who were an African family.
Three young girls, in the grass, played and danced,
in their brightly colored kaftan robes.

I witnessed that brilliant image, in front of me. I felt it in my soul.

I was back.

4.

INNER STATES

'But I won't cry for yesterday
There's an ordinary world
Somehow I have to find
And as I try to make my way
To the ordinary world
I will learn to survive'

- Simon Le Bon, Duran Duran

I'm writing this chapter twelve months after my internment in Ada County Jail, from the home of a family friend, deep in the Everglades of Florida. I arrived with Jack, in my Oldsmobile '88, having gotten evacuated from Naples, where I lived with my mother and her partner, in anticipation of Hurricane Irma. Soon, the storm would hit the islands.

I packed half my wardrobe, a Mac I won in an auction, a laptop, a box of puppets, a synthesizer, and a cigar box with three external hard drives. A New Orleans postcard from 1908, a tiny dried and pressed flower arrangement from Japan, and ten of my most valuable books, including Shozo Sato's 1965 *'The Art of Arranging Flowers.'* I secured my Schwinn Varsity bicycle to a rack on my trunk.

I also had a box of legal documents, journals, and the rough manuscript of this book; printed so that I could hold it in my hand.

Jack held his face out the window as we neared the property, engulfed by cypress trees, at the end of a long dirt road. He and I felt a temporary peace there; in a few days, we'd be moving to a hotel, with a stronger foundation.

Jack and I sat on the old, moss-covered, concrete stoop. The winds of the distant hurricane were starting to rustle the leaves and branches, as scattered clouds rushed by.

.

I had stayed in Idaho for another nine months. As I expected, the period following my incarceration was frantic and manically productive. I had a stack of spiral-bound notebooks, full of notes. Each morning, I wrote a list of primary, secondary and tertiary goals. I'd tack one copy to my bedroom wall, and keep a second in my wallet. Notebook upon notebook of daily goals, accompanied by thoughts and observations. Eventually, my short list of goals got ingrained in my bones, and a written reminder wasn't necessary.

In hindsight, it's a bit unreal to sift through those notes. Many issues were relevant to me then, that I've since forgotten. I struggled for months to find a clothes iron for my shirts. And guess what? I still don't have one - *but at some point, I stopped attaching importance to it.*

At first, I slept on the floor of Tony's studio, nervous the cop's might come at any second. I found stable housing with the mother of Tony's wife. *Giles was right – things didn't turn out how I thought they would.* I pursued each lead in the resource packet I got in jail, just to have doors shut in my face. Most of them no longer offered assistance to people in my situation. When I exhausted the list, I typed a letter and mailed it to Daniel before his sentencing date.

I focused on selling things online, refining my approach, seeing what sold, and what gave me the highest profit ratio. In my second month, I made more money than I did at either of my jobs, and I earned it on my terms. Sales weren't consistent, though, and I knew the courts wouldn't accept it as valid employment.

I had to fulfill ten hours of weekly community service to get my food stamps. No one would hire me – not even on a volunteer basis. I felt defeated. Then, I stumbled across a thrift store that believed in giving people a second chance. I worked a shift for free, and they hired me outright. It was a small crew, and they treated me kindly. I got assigned the task of redoing the book department and organizing the four-thousand-plus books in the warehouse, piled at random in cardboard boxes. It was daunting, and I loved the challenge. I'd occasionally discover a book, which I'd covet for my collection.

.

When I retrieved my belongings from police evidence, they gave me two backpacks and a satchel, not mentioned in the paperwork. My messenger bag was not included. *Where are my hard drives?* I set the packs on the lobby floor and dug through them. The drives were missing. The clerk couldn't answer my questions. For a solid week, the department had no definitive explanation as to their whereabouts, if they even had them, or if they were handed to Elena, along with the computer.

Later, I sat on Tony's porch, and I emptied the contents of those three random bags, to clarify what Elena spoke of in her testimony. It was mostly junk and craft supplies. The jar of 'ceremonial' dirt that Elena implied I used in rituals, was a soil sample from the set of my animated video project, in the event I needed to color match footage while editing.

Among the objects deemed 'satanic' were a pair of Tibetan singing bowls; the same ones that I played in the Bonneville Salt Flats fifteen years ago, when I walked for miles with my eyes closed.

I opened a jewelry box of heirlooms from my grandmother. Inside I had a trio set of sterling silver rings, meant to be worn on one finger. They weren't special; I bought them for $15 as a fashion accessory. In Elena's mind, however, I had murdered three women and kept the rings as mementos. In the bottom, I found Elena's engagement ring and wedding ring. I immediately sold them.

In her letter to the court, she mentioned a page from my journal, full of hateful and violent words; I'd written a list of slanderous names she'd called Scott, while drunk. She had read *her own words* to the court and didn't know it.

Holding those items, so impartial in their meaning, yet the cause of such pathological despair, wore me ragged. It was sickening and sad.

.

My repeated attempts to get my hard drives, with no response or effort from the department, drove me mad. My attorney also contacted them. When they finally located the bag, it held only *three* of the five drives. Missing were the two storing the master footage of my animated movie. *Elena hadn't turned them into evidence.*

To have the most significant creative achievement in my life stolen, and presumably destroyed out of spite was a loss I've struggled in coming to terms with. The detective on the case contacted Elena and pressured her for information, yet she denied having any knowledge or involvement.

On one of the recovered drives, I had a backup of files from my computer; the 'demonic images' were screensavers of antique, hand-painted Japanese scrolls. The three-hundred-plus 'books about torturing women,' was, in fact, DVD cover art from the Criterion Collection film series.

.

My probation officer approved my drive to Oregon, to get Jack. My father and I took a road trip. He came from Utah in the Nissan, providing me with the title, and guided me on how to drive the stick shift. When we reached the lava fields of Willamette National Forest, we couldn't help but stop and experience the majesty of it; incredible rolling hills of lava rock, profound as walking on the moon. Solitary pine trees somehow jutted from the scorched terrain.

Jack and I were stunned to see one another. I thanked Matt, though words hardly seemed enough. Jack had been part of their family, and they'd miss him. Matt's young daughter got depressed to see her playmate go. *We honestly weren't sure if you'd be getting out, so we planned to keep him,'* Matt smiled. I laughed, *'Neither was I.'* We said our goodbyes. I hugged Matt and expressed my gratitude to his family; thanks to them, this story ends with happiness.

Jack's anxiety had faded, and he enjoyed being social. It didn't occur to me that Jack would develop in our time apart. I used to think that for him to be content and at peace, I had to create an ideal environment. But he overcame it on his own, by living in the company of those who loved him.

.

I contemplated sending Carrie a letter. I had her email address. *What should I say? Where would I begin?* I opted to try, considering I had nothing to lose. I cut the bullshit and told it straight. I closed the letter by saying, *'I wanted you to know that I thought of you often. Thank you. It helped me, during the worst of it, to know there are people like you in the world'.*

Carrie did not respond. I deserved that.

I sent emails, thanking everyone sent letters to the court, on my behalf. I couldn't handle the emotion of phone calls. The final person on my list was Hollace. My mother informed me that he did a stint in jail as well, for an alcohol-related charge.

I kept it simple, *'I've been released. Thank you for writing a letter to the court, and rallying others to do likewise. They were a deciding factor in keeping me out of prison. Hope all is well for you.'*

Hollace replied, *'I hope we are both through the worst of it! I wrote a bunch of music in my sobering up hermit faze and recording it... I hope we can keep to our regular schedule of art.'*

We haven't spoken since.

.

I had two options, regarding my court-mandated group classes. I could go into it with resistance, and waste a considerable amount of energy, or I could broach it with an open mind and gain insight.

The instructor for the co-dependency class, Rebecca, handed me a worksheet; on it was a triangle, each point representing either the role of 'Victim,' 'Rescuer,' or 'Persecutor.' It got quite humbled, to have the most complicated period of my life reduced to a simple shape. *How could I have been so blind?*

"I'm not going to lie, guys," Rebecca said to the group, "Lessons in this class can be painful. It's not easy to admit where we went wrong or to learn what we could've done differently. You're obviously in here because you were, or still are, in a co-dependent relationship, and I want to help you see what part you're playing in that drama.

She paused, then commented, "I'm guessing most of you connect with the role of the Rescuer?"

We nodded our heads. It took merely a second for me to acknowledge that, but *why* had I succumbed to it? Midway through the course, *I identified the cause as my need for acceptance,* and not just from others - I could not accept myself. It had plagued me throughout my life. Why did I not place value on my needs? I tried to support Elena until I ended up in the emergency room. I pushed even harder when I felt her slipping through my fingers. I *needed* Elena to be dependent on me, and fuck me for that. I enabled her, so I didn't have to fix my own issues. I used her as an excuse. It wasn't a selfless act, me working nonstop. It was a selfish one. I felt the more I sacrificed, the greater my eventual reward. Her affection fed my ego. The problems I fixed for her elevated my self-esteem. I needed her to see my accomplishments, or they meant nothing.

Even when I began to distance myself from her emotionally and rediscover my voice, I did so in secret, fearing consequences. In the mornings, I waited for Elena to tell me how I'd be feeling that day. I let Elena set the standard for acceptability. And what of that finish line we raced towards – the fancy house, with the children, in the city of Elena's choosing? If it were so real, why did we not take a single progressive step to attaining it? In futility I attempted to balance the negatives by adding positives; maybe that's why I bought the wedding ring.

Rebecca discussed the setting of boundaries. I got pissed at myself for failing so completely in that aspect

"You can't set a boundary with someone, *and* take care of their feelings. How they react is not your fault," Rebecca said

I suspected early on, that if I introduced boundaries with Elena, our relationship wouldn't survive. She'd reject them. That fear became my reason for not doing so. The trauma and stress Elena I endured, served to bond us, while we shut ourselves from the world. We had to sustain and fulfill each other's every need. I set myself up by having expectations that could not be delivered.

"How many of you have found yourselves drinking or getting high *for* your partner?"

She didn't have to elaborate; I raised my hand. So often, I'd swallow the remains of a bottle of wine while Elena slept. *I drank more so she'd drink less.*

"I won't ask you to raise your hands, but if you've ever gotten pressured for sex in your relationship, it is not ok. Not at all. It's a serious form of abuse. It's against the law. I know it's hard for guys to admit to an experience like that, but you need to understand that it is not acceptable behavior."

It felt vindicating, to hear that.

"I'm so excited!" Rebecca exclaimed one day, "I have to tell you guys what I did! I went to a museum for movie memorabilia, and I saw the dress that Ingrid Bergman wore in the 1944 film, '*Gaslight*.' Have any of you seen it? It's one of my favorite films."

"No," I said, with a curious frown

"Ok, are you familiar with the term gaslighting?" she asked

I had a gut reaction, as she explained.

"Gaslighting is when a person manipulates someone into questioning their sanity. It's an extreme form of psychological abuse."

I tried to hide my expression, but I'm sure Rebecca caught it. Her sideways glance paused on me as if to say, '*Shit, Logan... We're you in a relationship like that?*'

"What's the story about?" I asked, clearing my throat

"So, in the film, Charles Boyer drives his wife insane, by dimming the gaslights in their pre-electric London mansion, and then bringing them back up. When Ingrid Bergman questions what's wrong, he tells her it's figments of her imagination."

The reality hit me hard. I'd carried a bag of weapons with me, due to a perceived threat to my life. Elena intimated that a woman, paid to follow us, may have died as a result of seeking to come forward. Elena constantly raised the stakes and our sense of danger. *How many interpretations had I made without evidence?* I wasn't allowed to speak to her lawyers. Elena fed me hundreds of stories about Scott, accusing *him* of the violence she'd later pin on *me. Perhaps I resembled Scott more than I cared to admit.* I knew Scott to be an obsessive asshole, due to events I witnessed firsthand – *but they were few* – and as for the cars tracking us? I had to trust Elena on that as well. How many conclusions had I arrived at, based solely on the claims of Elena, whose words, in my opinion, had no integrity whatsoever?

Again, Rebecca gave me a concerned look, and said to the group, "*Please,* guys. I sincerely hope none of you have been involved in a gaslighting relationship, but if you have, *please* seek help. *Nobody* has the right to tell you what to think, feel or do. You have the right to your own thoughts, feelings, values, and beliefs. You deserve to be loved and respected. Don't be ashamed or afraid to stand up for yourself."

I'd convinced myself that Elena was the woman I'd searched for. If that were true, I wouldn't have had to be someone else to please her.

.

Greg taught my anger management class. It was similar to getting a two-hour pep-talk, once a week, from Robert Downey, Jr. - and I mean that in the nicest possible way. It refreshed me to hear a man speak unabashedly of his fuck-ups, addictions, and depravity. He had no qualms in discussing the shameless behavior of his past.

"We are in this life to lose everything," he began, "Think about that. You are here to lose. You are going to leave this world the way you came into it. With nothing. Now, I don't mean to dash your hopes and dreams, but you're gonna lose those too. You're going to lose it all. So, what defines a successful person? It's one who handles those losses with grace and dignity, rather than kicking and screaming and feeling sorry for themselves."

Greg commenced, "Life is pain. You cannot escape that. Sure, you can try, but you're going to fail. What do you do, then? You learn how to welcome the pain. That's right. Bring that bastard right into your center. Lean into the discomfort. Because it's trying to tell you something.

I have the utmost respect for each and every one of you. What you're doing, by coming here, and addressing these problems means you want to better yourselves, and that speaks of your bravery. Your struggle is part of your story. It's what makes you interesting. Don't be ashamed of it."

I went into his class misguided. Since I'd never outright gotten into a fist fight, I assured myself that anger wasn't my predominate issue. Then, I learned how it manifests itself in various ways; mine presented as chronic depression, which I internalized and negated.

"We rage when we don't have a sense of integrity in ourselves," Greg said, "We need to recognize those moments when they happen and get back to the original thought that crashed into that negative core belief, which then led to our aggressive action. If we want a different result, we have to get at those harmful beliefs."

"How many of you have road rage? I do," Greg confessed, "Man, if somebody cuts me off in traffic, I'm like *'People need to respect one another goddamit, and this motherfucker needs to learn that!'* Anger sure loves gratification, doesn't it?"

As I defined my core beliefs and their faults, I put them in perspective to Elena's.

"She'd ask me daily if I loved her, and wanted to be with her," I told Greg

"Right," he smiled, "She was testing you on a daily basis, to see if you were a safe place. Man, I tell ya, one sharp jab in the heart of someone like that, *and whoa. You're a goner.*"

"Yeah, I'm afraid I missed that boat, Greg."

.

In a state of contemplation, I imagined myself in an empty room, seated at a table; I welcomed Anger, in human shape, into the space, and he took a seat in front of me. Anger had rigid composure, and his eyes were blackened.

"What do you have to say, Anger?" I asked cautiously

"I'm fucking tired of people telling me 'Stand *here*, not *there*. Do *this*, not *that*. We need *you* to live according to *our* standards. We need *you* to be like *us* because you make us feel *nervous.* How do you *feel* about doing the things we force you to do? We need you to tell us how you *felt* so it can be documented and assessed to *our* satisfaction, and don't give us any lip. We're *busy,* you understand? We have *real* responsibilities. *Nothing* is more important than the work *we* do. *Our* needs will *always* come first. Don't you feel *sorry* for what you did to your victim? Don't you feel sorry for that poor woman, who loved you and trusted you? How could you do that to her? Don't you know it's wrong to control a person and tell them what to do? Don't you *know* you can't restrain people against their will? Listen, *we* can commit the crimes that *you* got arrested for whenever *we* feel like it. Don't think that you can undermine *us.* Now we hear you're claiming that poor victim wronged you? That's unacceptable. We don't have any evidence of that at all. Of course, *we* don't need any evidence to get rid of *you.* That poor woman's word is enough for us. We *tried* to put you in prison for fifty years. That would've made us feel *safer,* knowing *you* were gone. You don't feel like lashing out at *us,* do you? You're not upset that we set you up for failure, *are you?* Are you tired of being monitored? *You're a dangerous person.*"

Anger leaned in, closer.

"You want to know what else? *I don't think Elena truly wanted a spiritual center to her life.* I think she wanted to wage her own holy war, knowing that a god she read about in a book was on her side. *Make a pact with God?* As far as I could tell, *'Making God the center of our lives,'* meant that, aside from reading the Bible, we prayed over dinner, as a security measure, so God would favor us, and bless us with more expensive and faster things. I call that *'broom closet spirituality.'*

And Scott Bunk? He was *scared* of me, with all his power and money, he *feared* me."

Anger paused, breathing heavily through his nose.

"Fuck these sympathy-seeking victims, filing lawsuits and pressing charges because somebody *hurt their feelings.* Give me a fucking break!" Anger antagonized in a whiny voice, "That person over there hurt *my feelings,* so it's perfectly ok for me to *destroy* their existence, and sue them for everything they have, and ruin the lives of their family for generations. *That'll* show them they can't hurt *my feelings. Nothing* in the universe is more important than *my* feelings. If someone offends me, I will *decimate* their lives," Anger mocked, sarcastically, and then a smile crept across his face, "Yeah, well, I say *fuck you whiny malcontent people!* You miserable cowards.

Respect is something YOU EARN! You *ARE NOT* entitled to it simply because you're *a fucking self-important human being.* Those are the rules I abide by! *If you come up to bat, you better swing motherfucker!* I am *not* going to let you walk."

I listened carefully to what Anger had said, and then I spoke

"It hurts to have your intelligence insulted, yes. But, when I look unflinchingly at my life, I see that I've made bad decisions, which I regret. So, perhaps I wasn't as smart as I gave myself credit. Yes, it stings to have control stripped away, yet how well did I deal when I had it? My self-control was an illusion.

And you're right, Anger. Respect is a precious thing. To demand it, or expect it, from others cheapens its meaning. To give up my rights, my dignity and respect in the eyes of the court, doesn't bring me down. It motivates me. I have to *earn* it all back, and in doing so, I'll value it to a higher degree. I don't *want* respect through societal obligation. I want to *deserve* it through my successes, and even in my failures.

You're correct, Anger. You *should* commend those who offend you, for they have offered you a gift. They have revealed your insecurity. They have caused you to examine a piece of your identity that *you yourself* are not comfortable with, for why else would you react so aggressively? It only hurts if you secretly believe it. For that moment of realization, you should express unbounded gratitude."

"Those bastards sought to bury you for crimes you did not commit!" Anger exclaimed

"Yes, they did. However, the only *real* guilt is self-imposed. Others may try their hardest to impose it upon me, to point their fingers and slander my name, but I know what's in my heart, and without self-imposed guilt, the courts are powerless.

Getting incarcerated led me to a freedom I otherwise may not have known. In there I faced my shortcomings with humility and vulnerability. I know you tried to get involved, Anger, but I pushed you back. I couldn't deal with you, in that place. I couldn't let you govern my actions.

Over a million people have been locked in Ada County, in its history. That's batch processing. It's idiocy for one to think their case merits special attention. With that many names on the docket, why *would they* care about my story? I don't hold a grudge towards the police department. Regardless of their intentions, they supplied me with a clean break from a life spiraling into chaos.

"Logan, what they did to you isn't fair!"
"No. It isn't. It's not fair. Should I be mad?"
"Yes!" Anger protested
"Yeah? You want me to get upset?"
"Yes, I do! I want you to fight!"
"Is that really what you want?"
"Yes, it is!"
"I should get enraged, huh?"
"Logan, I want to be infuriated! I want you to be fucking pissed!"
"Yeah, well, I refuse."
"... Why?!"
"I don't need your instant gratification, Anger. It's weak. I want the permanence of this book in the reader's hands. I hope they share it. I instead choose to bring this negative experience into the light, and shape it positively, to help others."
Anger examined me in silence.
"There's another point you were wrong about, Anger," I said
"What's that?"
"Scott didn't tremble because of *you*, Anger. It was the awareness of things in this world worth more than money."

I checked the online roster of Ada County Jail and the Boise State Penitentiary, searching for my cellmates, to get an update on their cases.

I immediately saw the face of Kyle Rory. He'd been charged with murder.
Jesus, Kyle. Was it really worth it?
In his intake photo, he appeared thin; the fire in his eyes diminished. I read the news story – Kyle had gotten into an argument with a younger man, in the parking lot of a gas station. Kyle pulled his gun and shot the man in the chest, point blank. He died right there. He was arrested the next night, fleeing in a car packed with his things.

Months later, at my job, as I wrapped glassware with a newspaper; an article on Kyle caught my eye. I folded it and put it in my pocket. I'm not sure why.

Zeek was also in custody, for felony burglary. In the photo, his face looked red and bloated, either from alcoholism, a beating, or the winter weather. Or all three. He awaited sentencing and a prison term at *The Yard.*

Guy was serving a four-years in prison – though not for domestic violence. His charge read 'Major Contraband Within a Correctional Facility.' *Were you making weapons, Guy?*

But, how was Zach Morris? His parole eligibility date is in October of 2018, with his first hearing in April of that same year. If he stayed on track, he'd be out on parole, otherwise be locked up until 2023. I wrote Zach a letter, saying if he needed someone to communicate with, he could count on me. I didn't receive word from him.

The court, ruthless to Rick Kellner, sentenced him to fifteen years. I couldn't see information on the federal charges. I also wrote Rick a letter, saying I'd help him promote his artwork through a coalition. I asked how he was managing, and if his family held together. He did not write me back.

Daniel Weschler got released on probation, on November 1st. I called the girl, whose phone number he disclosed. She did not answer my voicemail or text messages. Either she fielded his contacts or Daniel wished for no reminder of his incarceration. I understood, regardless. His probation will end, pending his behavior, in October of 2021.

My sentencing satisfaction date was listed as October 6th, of 2026, in case I forgot.

.

I expected I'd often have dreams about Ada County Jail – though to date I've only had one, and it resonated with me.

I stood, by myself, on the stage of a darkened theater. The seating for the audience, in a crescent shape, climbed three tiers high. Rather than being lined with chairs, the tiers held rows of jail cells. Hundreds of them, curving to meet the stage. The windows to each cell were blackened, but occupied by inmates.

Then, a spotlight shone on me. I felt self-assurance. I bent over, comically pretending to be an old man with back problems, and hobbled about the stage, as the light followed me. I rubbed my thumb and index finger together as if I were dropping seed pellets on the ground, at the park. I called out, *'Here-chicky-chicky-chicky...Here-chicky-chicky-chicky.'*

Thunderous laughter emitted from the cells; male and deep in pitch. They enjoyed the routine, so I continued, *'Here-chicky-chicky-chicky...Here-chicky-chicky-chicky.'* As they cheered, I noticed the cell, in the top right corner of the theater, open with a light on. Two deputies escorted Alex out in a wheelchair, his leg in a cast. As he got pushed through an exit door, to my right, he gave me a rye grin and a wave.

Suddenly, I was in a large, bright study hall. Inmates were reading and taking tests. Sections of the world map got vividly transposed on the walls. Then, a loud voice over the intercom told me, *'It's time to go.'*

I found myself outside of the building, with the sun in my eyes, on a massive concrete ramp, sloping downwards into a vast wilderness. It air felt hot and humid, and my clothes stuck to my body. I made a step onto the ramp and realized I left my wallet inside, with my identification card. I hesitated, thinking I should retrieve it – and that's when my *own* voice said, *'You don't need it anymore.'* I turned to look at the wilderness. I removed my shirt, and I started *running.* I ran as hard as I could.

.

Orrin and Danielle assembled a care package, full of vegan snacks and toiletries, a purple blanket that Jack and I are fond of, and a gift card to *Gerald's* (inside joke?) which I exchanged it for a winter jacket. The gesture meant a great deal to me. Orrin, keen on getting me to quit smoking cigarettes, also gave me with a vaping device, and urged me to make the jump. I did, and we went to a vape shop for juice.

To see their apartment, you'd think the couple had kids, with all the toys scattered on the floor. In fact two rescue cats – Hobbes and Rooster Cogburn – ran the show.

Ironically, Orrin had established a successful eBay operation and converted the second bedroom into his office space. He'd found his niche, and the walls were lined with merchandise; Manga books, Legos, figurines, puzzles, comics, vintage board games, and all manner of toys. Orrin gifted me a box of things to sell, to build my inventory, along with packing and shipping supplies. Being a postal worker, he had tips on how to minimize shipping costs. *How could I repay the man?*

As we talked, my eye drifted to the view from his third-floor window. Across the street, I saw the Winco where Zach had gotten arrested, and the neighboring grocery store that Elena and I frequented. To the right of Orrin's apartment complex stood the courthouse itself. I walked in there once, emptying my pockets at the metal detector. I headed to the transcript office, for a copy of my court documents.

I had a realization in the elevator. The whole time, in that holding tank under the city, I thought it brought us to ground level when it actually lifted us several stories up. *I was that high in the air?*

Orrin knew which thrift stores to hit on any particular day of the week, for selection and prices
"I'm gonna hit three or four stores this afternoon," he'd text me, "There's a trifecta of 'em in that little area, down on Fairview. Did you want to come?"
"You know it."
"Let's meet at that one by your place, though. They have half priced books today. You might score!"
"Sweet!"

We had a healthy competition, he and I, seeing who stumbled upon the finest merchandise – and who yielded the biggest profits. A warehouse, owned by a local thrift store chain, packed dozens of huge crates with random donations. When our work schedules coincided, it was a ritual for us to check its stock. We'd spend hours digging through the piles, with gloves, loading our shopping carts. Rather than the items having a dollar value, the system charged by the pound.

My expensive Burberry sunglasses were, of course, missing in the fray. Orrin demanded I at least get cheap sunglasses for driving. I picked up a lousy pair for $9.
"Dude. It has a sticker on the side saying it's made with shit that causes cancer," I lamented
"Listen, when you have the money to buy a classy pair, I want you to shoot a video of you breaking those shitty sunglasses in half."
"Alright, I can do that."

.

I took my bicycle to a co-op and got it in working order. I exited the shop and pedaled around the corner to the library. I stopped beside a fountain, near the entrance of the building, and propped my bike with the kickstand. It was a hot day, and I held my face close to the fountain, feeling the cool mist. I put my hands in the cold water and ran them through my hair, and across my neck.

I got on my bicycle, and glanced to my right – and there I saw Mandy and her mother, Caroline, sitting on a park bench. They were laughing, so enamored by their ridiculous conversation, that they did not notice who was in front of them. I rested my elbow on my knee, still atop my bike; they carried on with themselves and did not look up. I rode off.

A month later, I went to the grocery store, rationing my food stamps for the week. As I picked up a basket by the check stand, I saw Chris – my cellmate from 821 – Kyle Rory's friend from the *Severely Violent Criminals*.

"Hey, Fuckboy!" he shouted, *"Richard! Fuckboy! Now what?!"*

The customers and employees looked at me, nervously. I paused. Chris had two people with him, maybe transients, based on their clothes.

"Fuckboy!" he said again

All eyes were on me. I chose to ignore him and resume shopping. I went to the back of the store to get soy milk, and Chris came running up to me, alone.

"Hey, Logan! Hold up. What happened with your case, man?" he asked as if we were buddies

"Felony probation. Ten years. I thought you were going to prison?"

"I beat it at trial, man. Hey, for real though, do you think you could hook me up with $20? I'm tryin' to get high. I'll share with you if you want."

"No, Chris. I'm not giving you any money."

I sat in my parked car, disturbed by what transpired. I breathed, trying to calm my nerves. *My fear had been irrational. He* was the one scared; living on the streets, unemployed, with a drug addiction. He couldn't cope on this side of the wall. He came to *me* for help, putting himself at a disadvantage. Where's the gang support now?

.

At my job, I had the duty of nighttime closer, counting the safe and locking the store. I used to transfer $10,000 payments for large business accounts or sell diamond rings. Now I handled a single cash register. I felt satisfied with that, working in a family-oriented business amongst friends. I was ok with comfortable feelings.

One evening, as I organized the warehouse, I heard two men rifling through our dumpster, stealing items we'd discarded as junk. I called the police, though the men vacated shortly after. I stood in the rear doorway, leaning against the frame, waiting for the patrol car to arrive. When it parked, I saw two officers inside.

The driver, a woman, approached, and we made our introductions. Out the corner of my eye, I watched her partner, another female, exit the vehicle and step toward me – *my arresting officer.* She held eye contact briefly, in recognition, before casting her stare downward, to the pavement. As I filed the police report, she didn't utter a single word. Her mind had to be racing.

I smiled at her; not with condescension or insincerity, but warmly, as I would greet a customer. I gazed at her, and saw no badge or authority; merely a scared girl in a big world, trying to do the right thing, though too encumbered by her fears and inexperience to make serious judgment calls.

As they departed, I asked why, *of all the people throughout my involvement in Ada County, did I re-encounter Chris, Mandy, and the cop who arrested me? Why not those for whom I had positive feelings?* Because to see them, the people I cared for, would be nothing more than an affirmation of what I already knew.

Then why those who caused me pain? *Because I needed to see them powerless.* For in seeing those three people, my response showed I was healing and overcoming. *I was getting better.*

.

Tony and his wife purchased a home, and I helped them move from their cramped apartment. They had a spare bedroom they wanted to rent out for extra income, so I took it. Jack loved the fenced backyard, and I looked forward to the grape vines in bloom. The room itself was spacious, with a window seat. A relative of Tony's wife donated a spare mattress. I valued the privacy.

Despite their new home, Tony's marriage had strife. From an outsiders perspective, I thought they'd piled on too many responsibilities at a young age, and then wondered who they were, and what they really wanted.

It pained me, to see the unceasing conflict affect them, especially their two kids, who got increasingly rebellious. I'd hear Tony argue with his wife, through the walls, saying things eerily similar to what Elena and I once had. It gave me anxiety, as I didn't want to get dragged into another domestic situation by proxy.

Unfortunately, Tony and I, both introverts in a troubled period, didn't reserve much time for fun activities. His marital problems consumed him, and I got obsessed with writing this book.

Tony, a modest guy, liked to play guitar and ride his Harley motorcycle. He found solace in either his Ibanez seven-string or customizing his bike in the garage, pausing in intervals, to get more cigarettes at the gas station. When he recorded a promising track, he'd beckon me out of my room, and pass me a headset, plugged into the computer I sold him when we worked for *United Bank* (he switched to a call center for cell phones).

Being a certified mechanic, Tony was itching to re-enter his field, thus avoiding the corporate politics of his job. With the drama of his marriage, and the kids getting belligerent, he seemed at his wit's end, frustrated that he couldn't pursue his interests.

I imagine Tony got tempted to hop on his motorcycle and disappear. Hell, I had to go, myself. I concluded there wasn't shit for me in Boise. My Nissan Sentra was in poor condition. The winter of 2016-17 had been the worst since the Great Winter of 1948-49, and it taxed my car badly.

Tony slaved under the hood of my car.

"I replaced the gasket. Gonna do the serpentine belt next," he said, "I think you may have a bad bearing, though. That sound doesn't come solely from a serpentine."

"How much is that to fix?" I asked, reluctantly

"Depends on where it is. If it's the water pump or alt, which are the most common, it's not too awful. I'll check it out. The alternator is pretty well fuckered, too. But my biggest worry is your valve cover and the part of the block it sits in. If we still have a leak after I replace the gasket, it may be warped. This is a pissed off little rig, bud."

"So you're saying it's a gamble to take it on a three-thousand-mile road trip?" He nodded his head, solemnly.

I had no choice but to sell the Sentra and buy a '96 Oldsmobile from an online ad. I instantly had a kinship with it. I inspected the car, taking it for a test drive; it ran surprisingly smooth. The tires were worn, so I set aside money for a new set. I bought the vehicle and drove her home, impressed by the girth and weight of it. *'This is a sweet ride, man,'* Tony said in approval, *'and much easier to maintain. This car'll get ya to Florida. I'm sure of it.'*

.

I had a day of paths converging; I received a phone call from my probation officer. He instructed me to come to his office, and fill out my paperwork for an interstate compact to Florida, which I applied for a month prior, not believing I'd get approved. Then, my phone pinged, signaling an email; *It was from Carrie.* Her letter began with, *'Holy crap! I'm sorry it took me so long to read this.'* My hand shook as I read it, *'Where are you now?'* she inquired *'And, I think about you too. Always good thoughts'*

I responded to her, *'Your timing couldn't be better. Last night, I finished a rough draft of the chapter in my book on Ada County Jail. Today, I'm signing off with my probation officer for a transfer to Florida. I'll leave the end of June. I can take a little time getting there. Jack and I could stop by if you wanted?*

Idaho released me. I got in the car, setting my GPS to the probation office, and the song playing on the radio was *'Sail,'* by Awolnation. Elena and I listened to it during our late night joyrides. It didn't remind me of her; it just sounded like freedom.

If there is a higher order in this universe, if these examples of synchronicity do have a meaning, it leads me to believe that, throughout this entire ordeal, I have remained on track, doing what I needed to, in the right moments.

Perhaps I was supposed to endure this.

.

I went to a thrift store, in a strip mall, scavenging for items to sell online. I found a rare DVD, literally on the floor, for $1, listed for $40-$60 on eBay. In my car, I sent a bragging text to Orrin, and curiously checked the storefronts. The strip mall had changed; the liquor store burnt to the ground, and modern restaurants filled the gap. One of them had persisted - *a tiny, well-reviewed Indian restaurant.*

I watched an older man click the open sign for the dinner crowd, and unlocked the front door. I decided to enter.

The air felt heavy; the man hosting the empty dining area seemed burdened. He had tired eyes and a strained voice.
"Good evening, sir. A table for yourself?" he asked, solemnly
"No, I'm sorry. Actually, I'm here for Sandeep. Is he in the kitchen?"
"Sandeep?" he frowned, "How do you know Sandeep?"
"I'm a friend. I told him I'd check in on him. How is he?"
"He is not here, now. He doesn't work that often," he said
I could tell I hit a sore spot. It made him uncomfortable to speak of the boy.
"You say you're a friend?" he questioned, "Who are you?"
"My name is Logan. Could you let him know I stopped by?"
"He isn't here that often," he repeated
"All the same, I'd appreciate it. Have a good day," I said, as I left

.

When business slowed at the thrift store, I got temporarily laid off. So, I had the gumption to apply for seasonal help at the neighboring floral shop. The second I opened the door, the aroma of flowers drifted over me.

The owner was a gracious and honest man; operating in the floral industry for thirty years, he had a wealth of knowledge. I said I wanted to be a designer, and he spoke candidly, hiring me on the spot.

Granted, I wasn't cutting flowers – I'd be arranging deliveries, and taking phone orders, during the peak hours of Mother's Day and Valentines. The designers, older women, pretty much came with the building. Their hospitality brought to mind the gals at the jewelry counter, and I assisted them in any way I could. It was chaos – like the stock market, with flowers instead of money. The owner rented a separate space in the strip mall, for the team of seasonal designers to work within, and I ran back and forth bringing them supplies.

During brief lulls in phone calls, the owner imparted me with wisdom, as to how the industry had evolved, for better or worse, and methods I could implement to stay ahead of the game. He gave me information no school ever would. *'Pick my brain whenever you want,'* he said.

In the late afternoon, on Valentine's day, a significant event occurred.

I had taken a phone order and proceeded to print the paperwork when the owner came to me.

"Logan, one of our delivery vans broke down, and the driver is stranded. The van is full of flowers for a funeral. We can't be late, and the flowers are going to wilt in this heat. I can't go myself. Can you fix this for me?"

"Absolutely," I said

"Thank you. Here, take the keys to my car."

I took a minute to get acquainted with his luxury vehicle, then barreled to my destination. I located the van, and the driver, in his late forties. We tried like hell to get it jump-started, to no avail. The battery was toast.

"We have to hurry," I told him, "We need to transfer the flowers and take his car. What's the address?"

"It's in the mountains."

We entered the foothills and climbed fast in elevation; my ears popped from the altitude. Our cell phones dropped service, and with no GPS, we resorted to the paperwork. Miles and miles went by, and he remarked we might be lost. We stuck to the directions, *'Damn, I can't believe it's this far,'* I said, *'Who was this guy?'*

The road abruptly ended at a large, impassable, iron gate. Far beyond it, we saw a residence.

"That has to be it. Do you have any cell service?" I asked

"None."

There was no sign of life; just a landscape, stretching to the horizon.

What were we supposed to do?

Then, a man on an ATV approached from a winding trail. I held my arms in the air, waving for his attention. He drove to the gate, kicking up dirt.

"What are you doing here?" he asked
"I'm here with the flowers. For the funeral."
He hung his head and unlocked the gate.
"Keep on this road. It's the house at the top," he said

We pulled into the driveway of an impressive estate; it had a sadness about it and appeared empty.
"Did we miss it?" I asked
"I don't think so. We're right on time."
"This place is deserted. There isn't a secondary address?"
"No. This is it."
We wandered the grounds, knocking on each door. As we did, I became strangely aware of my childhood. On the property where I grew up, the trees and flowers had a particular scent, and as I walked that man's estate, I smelled them flourishing there. I came to a series of ascending steps, made of stone, partially blocked by the limb of an ungroomed tree. I ducked underneath it, to an entryway, with a wooden door. I knocked, and then silence. *Should we set the flowers in the shade, and leave?* It didn't feel right.
"What do you want to do?" my partner asked
I knocked again, loudly, hitting the door with the side of my hand, foregoing courtesy.
"Wait," I said, raising my finger
I pressed my ear to the door. *I heard very faint singing.* I couldn't distinguish words.
"A woman is singing. To herself, I think."
She continued, despite our ringing the doorbell. We stood there, understanding we were intruding on a private moment. When the woman's voice ceased, I tapped once more. She opened the door, with a warm, yet confused, expression on her face; in shock, having lost her husband.
"Oh, please come in," she said, softly, as if inviting us for tea

The smallest actions, like pouring a drink, or deciding where to set up the flower easel overwhelmed her. She got concerned by how to water the wreath, and I showed her it was quite easy. *'They're beautiful, aren't they?'* she said, admiring the flowers. Having us there gave her comfort.
"May I show you pictures of my husband?" she asked
"Of course," I said
"This is a very nice home, ma'am," my partner mentioned
"Thank you," she replied, "My husband designed and built it himself, with only a few helpers."

She showed us photographs, and it dawned on my partner that he had known the man, years ago. A handful of people qualified as the modern pioneers of Boise; men who developed it from nothing, into the city it now was, through invention and dedication. I stood in the home of one of those men; a humanitarian and scientist.

"He was a great man. *So loving.* He took good care of me," the woman said, smiling

She told us about his life, and achievements. I felt honored.

"Will someone be staying with you?" I asked, worried for her to be solitary, in her grief

"Yes, my son will be here soon," she said, "Thank you for listening to me."
The woman hugged me.

On the walkway outside, my partner pointed to a secluded body of water, down in a valley, *'See that little lake, there? He told me he was gonna build that when I knew him, and I wondered if he'd get around to it. Guess he did, huh? He wanted a quiet place to take his family.'*

That encounter confirmed my choice to be a freelance floral designer.

.

Orrin's friendship returned me to a state of normalcy. I had no reason to go downtown, other than to visit him.
"Have you played Frisbee Golf?" he inquired
I hadn't, and he convinced me to join him in a game.
"Let's ride bicycles to the park. They have a great course. We'll get some fresh air," Orrin suggested, "You can borrow Danielle's. She won't mind."

We descended through the multi-level parking garage, on bikes, gaining speed, and then got washed in sunlight, as we passed cars stuck in traffic. *I remember this feeling of liberation.* We coasted along the green belt, and the Boise River, past the zoo, to Ann Morrison Park, with a hundred shades of green, yellow and blue rushing by.

We locked the bikes, and Orrin explained the rules of the game. He was practiced, with a good throwing arm, and trajectory. I found my groove towards the middle of the course. I enjoyed making a fool of myself, laughing at my failures, as my Frisbee veered into trees and ponds.

On the way back to Orrin's home, I requested a slight detour; past my former apartment. My tire stopped on the very spot where I'd been put in handcuffs. I felt a disparate energy there, by that stairwell, though it did not follow me as I pedaled onward.

Orrin cooked us lunch, always refining his fresh vegan recipes. He baked *delicious* cookies. He and Danielle would often invite me to dinner, to share a homemade meal.

The two of them were happy together, and I was glad for that. When they told me they were planning a move to Washington in the spring, I sensed a chapter ending. They'd venture to the west coast, and me to the east, putting the length of a country between us.

I went on a hike with Orrin and Danielle. Halfway up the trail, we came to the base of a deserted excavation site, with construction vehicles stationed about. The rock walls surrounding us were smooth and jutted sixty feet straight upwards. What captivated the three of us, were the dozens of tiny birds, nesting on the cliff face above. They flew fast as bats, and the cacophony of their voices ricocheted off the rock surfaces, doubling and tripling their calls. We were in awe of it.

We continued to the top of the trail, and overlooked the valley and city below. That image of Boise, from an aerial perspective, gave me closure.

.

On the morning of June 24th, 2017, I packed my car. I said goodbye to Tony, telling him I would've been screwed without his help. Jack and I hit the road, on a monumental trip. I debated writing about it, but I instead captured it with an iPod Touch camera. The footage may be in the fourth installment of my *Life Chronicles* series. I got curious to see the result, in me recording the world with a new pair of eyes.

Record heat waves caused a detour in my travel route. Without air conditioning in the Oldsmobile, I couldn't risk heat stroke for Jack and I, driving through the Arizona desert. I was not able to visit Carrie, and that saddened me. Life sent us in a different direction.

.

In the present, Jack and I now sit on this moss-covered, concrete stoop, in the Florida Everglades. The winds of the hurricane are growing stronger.
"We're in the thick of it now, Jack," I say, kissing his head
He sniffs at the intermittent rainfall.
'"I love you with all my heart, Jack. The whole thing."

Jack didn't leave my side, as I wrote this book. He'd paw at the keyboard, or my notepad, letting me know when I worked too hard, and that he and I should have an adventure.

Before I lost my internet signal due to the storm, I decided to check the prison roster in one final instance, for updates - *and I saw one.*

Rick Kellner was out on parole. *Bravo, Rick!* I don't know what you pulled off, but congratulations my friend! Embrace it.

In a thrift store, I came upon a vintage gray fedora. The partial remnants of a feather still clung inside the black ribbon. The hat, sized to 7 3/8, fits me fine.

The sweatband and liner tip got branded with the insignia of Scott Bunk's company, back when his father ran the business.

The price tag was secured to the brim with a needle. As I slipped it out, I accidentally pricked myself. I watched the blood collect on my fingertip.

I keep that hat with me as a reminder,
but there's no longer a knife in my pocket.

I've learned that my words are sharper, by far.

There may be a day, when Elena's driving her newest car, with Hetty and Aidan in the backseat, and the latest single from Bastille comes on the radio – *'Good Grief.'* It's Hetty's current favorite, and she insists her mother turn it up. Aidan doesn't much care.

"Mom, whatever happened to Loulou?" Hetty inquires
Elena stammers very subtly, and although she's wearing dark sunglasses, she averts her face to the left, pretending to check the side mirror. Elena manages to say something vague about God's will.

Hetty isn't satisfied by that answer, though she doubts it in silence.
Aidan processes it, in his own way.

At home, with her sunglasses on, Elena pours herself a glass of wine, and conceals it from the kids. She finds a show for them to watch.

Elena plays the song again and listens to the words, or perhaps it repeats in her head. She removes her sunglasses, but keeps her high heels on, and pours another glass of wine, as the kids get ready for bed.

Once they're asleep, Elena sends a text to the man she currently deems as 'safe.'
Elena pleads for his sympathy, and he surely gives it to her.

She pours herself another glass of wine.

As for me?

I still choose to see the good in people; I just do so from a further distance.
Sometimes *too* far, I know.

Although, at present, I have no interest in an intimate relationship,
I know that if I do find myself in one, I will not make the mistakes of my past,
nor will it be based on a craving for acceptance.

I used to believe that the way to achieve personal reinvention,
was to drive out of myself until nothing seemed familiar anymore.

I understand now that to change, one must move backward,
across one's entire life, and search out and diffuse those negative triggers

It'll take a little time, to establish myself in a new city,
and with excitement, I'll adapt, and thus carry on *fresh to death*.

Elena tried to take absolutely everything from me – and she failed.
What she did instead was set me up to receive it all.

Thank you, Elena.